INSTRUMENTS OF EMPIRE

INSTRUMENTS OF EMPIRE

Filipino Musicians, Black Soldiers, and Military Band Music during US Colonization of the Philippines

Mary Talusan

University Press of Mississippi / Jackson

The University Press of Mississippi is the scholarly publishing agency of
the Mississippi Institutions of Higher Learning: Alcorn State University,
Delta State University, Jackson State University, Mississippi State University,
Mississippi University for Women, Mississippi Valley State University,
University of Mississippi, and University of Southern Mississippi.

www.upress.state.ms.us

The University Press of Mississippi is a member
of the Association of University Presses.

Copyright © 2021 by University Press of Mississippi
All rights reserved

First printing 2021
∞

Library of Congress Cataloging-in-Publication Data

Names: Talusan, Mary, author.
Title: Instruments of empire: Filipino musicians, Black soldiers, and
military band music during US colonization of the Philippines / Mary
Talusan.
Description: Jackson: University Press of Mississippi, 2021. | Includes
bibliographical references and index.
Identifiers: LCCN 2021013932 (print) | LCCN 2021013933 (ebook) | ISBN
978-1-4968-3566-6 (hardback) | ISBN 978-1-4968-3567-3 (paperback) | ISBN
978-1-4968-3568-0 (epub) | ISBN 978-1-4968-3569-7 (epub) | ISBN 978-1-4968-3570-3
(pdf) | ISBN 978-1-4968-3571-0 (pdf)
Subjects: LCSH: Philippine Constabulary. Band—History. | Brass
bands—Philippines—History. | Loving, Walter Howard, 1872-1945. |
Soldiers, Black—Philippines—History. | United
States—Relations—Philippines. | Philippines—Relations—United States.
Classification: LCC ML27.P45 P434 2021 (print) | LCC ML27.P45 (ebook) |
DDC 784.909599—dc23
LC record available at https://lccn.loc.gov/2021013932
LC ebook record available at https://lccn.loc.gov/2021013933

British Library Cataloging-in-Publication Data available

In this book, some quoted material contains racial slurs
directed towards Black people. While those words have been retained
for the purpose of scholarly analysis, this is in no way
an endorsement of the use of such slurs.

CONTENTS

Acknowledgments

ix

Introduction: World's Fairs, Symphony Halls,
and America's Racial Others

3

— 1 —

Instruments of Empire: Brass Bands, Black Soldiers,
and American Imperialism in the Philippines

37

— 2 —

Marching to Racial Progress: Civilizing Filipinos
at the 1904 St. Louis World's Fair

67

— 3 —

Hearing with an Imperial Ear: Racializing the
PC Band on their Tour of America in 1909

119

— 4 —

Sounding Philippine Nationalism at the
Panama-Pacific International Exposition of 1915

173

— 5 —

Musical Resonances of Empire: The Golden Gate
International Exposition and the End of an Era

201

Notes

243

Bibliography

253

Index

265

For the next generation: Joli, Mia, Gavin, Jada, Evan, Kai, Norhanna, Zeke, and Otis

ACKNOWLEDGMENTS

I began research on this book during a yearlong stay in the Philippines made possible by the support of the Fulbright US Scholar Program (IIE). The National Commission for Culture and Arts, the Cultural Center of the Philippines, the National Library, the National Archives, and the Filipinas Heritage Library of the Ayala Museum and their staff were instrumental in helping me to find sources on the PC Band. The Moorland-Spingarn Research Center at Howard University and the St. Louis Archive assisted me with archival materials on Walter H. Loving and the St. Louis World's Fair. I benefited greatly from a Mellon postdoctoral fellowship at Tufts University with the support of the Music Department, especially Dr. Joseph Auner, and the Center for the Humanities with Dr. Jonathan Wilson. A course release provided by the Faculty Research, Scholarly and Creative Activity Intramural Grant at CSU Dominguez Hills assisted me in finishing revisions to the manuscript.

My history professor Michael Salman inspired me to write about the PC Band while in graduate school, and I am indebted to him for the ways that I developed a critical eye toward US and Philippine history. I am indebted to the following scholars, whose scholarship greatly contributed to my work on the PC Band: the late Dr. Claiborne T. Richardson, Robert Yoder, Ricardo Trimillos, Paul Kramer, Fritz Schenker, Richard and Iris Schwartz (who published crucial information about bands at the 1904 Fair), Roger D. Cunningham, and Cynthia Marasigan. I had meaningful conversations about Loving and African Americans in the Philippines with the late Adrian Gaskins. I want to thank Gladys Nubla for checking in with me during the writing of several chapters as she strove to successfully finish her own dissertation. I appreciate Natalie Masuoka for urging me to foreground the book's theoretical arguments, and Andrea Johnson, who helped me to clarify arguments about US history during a writing workshop at CSU Dominguez Hills. I am grateful to Lewis L. Gould for generously sending me a copy of his book *Helen Taft: Our Musical First Lady* so that I could understand the ways that she was instrumental in promoting the PC Band. Thank you to the anonymous reviewers with the University Press of Mississippi who advised me to focus my arguments and clarify aspects of the book. I am indebted to editor Vijay Shah, who never gave up on me even after my initial deadlines passed.

Over the years, I've given numerous presentations on the PC Band and received many helpful suggestions as well as encouragement. I am indebted to historian Paul Kramer, who has contributed invaluable work on the Philippines and the US, especially on the 1904 World's Fair. Thank you to Danielle Fosler-Lussier, with whom I presented at the Society for Historians of American Foreign Relations conference in 2009. At UC Riverside, I presented at the conference Tropical Renditions: Musics of Filipino America at the invitation of Christine Balance, who brought together scholars and artists in our community, including Oliver Wang, Tagumpay de León, Lakandiwa de León, Theo Gonzalves, and many more. Thank you to Deborah Wong, whose work has always been an inspiration to me. I am grateful to everyone at the UCLA Ethnomusicology Department and Archive who supported and nurtured me over the years, especially my dissertation advisor, Helen Rees. I was honored to share my work at the Nazir Ali Jairazbhoy Colloquium Series in 2011. I wish to thank assistant director (and dear friend) Barbara Gaerlan for inviting me to share my work at the UCLA Center for Southeast Asian Studies. Thank you to Timothy Chin and Carolina San Juan, who joined me on a panel entitled "Black/Asian Encounters in Asian Cultural Production" at CSU Dominguez Hills. I gave a joint lecture with Donna Nicol, chair of Africana Studies at CSU Dominguez Hills, entitled "Cousins of Color: Intersection of Filipino and African American Lives." I am grateful to her for helping me to understand the history of the community formation of African Americans and Filipinos in Southern California's South Bay in the aftermath of WWII through her own family's story. Thank you to Neal Matherne, who invited me to present at the Chicago Field Museum during Homeland

Memories, an event hosted by the Philippine co-curation group. In 2015, I participated in the International Symposium for the Fortieth Anniversary of the Center for Philippine Studies at the University of Hawaii and had many illuminating conversations with scholars and friends, including Vina Lanzona, Theo Gonzalves, Martin Manalansan, Patricio Abinales, Richard Chu, Kathy Nadeau, Lorenzo Perillo, Roderick Labrador, Allan Isaac, and so many more. My sincerest thanks to the Filipino American community of Carson, California for inviting me to give the keynote at address at the Filipino American History Month celebration in 2018. Through their hard work and the dedication to the Filipino American community, I was able to share with my *kababayan* the achievements of this little-known Filipino band and their African American leader who toured the United States over a century ago.

Thank you to Cherubim A. Quizon for including "Music, Race, and Imperialism: The Philippine Constabulary Band at the 1904 St. Louis World's Fair" in *Philippine Studies Quarterly* in 2004. My sincerest thanks to Hazel McFerson for including this article in *Mixed Blessing: The Impact of the American Colonial Experience on Politics and Society in the Philippines* in 2013. I am grateful to everyone in who worked on *Philippine Modernities, Commemorating 100 Years of UP College of Music* and the CD anthology *Saysay Himig: An Anthology of Transcultural Filipino Music (1880–1941)*, published in 2018.

The time I spent in the Philippines and the relationships that I made over the last three decades have been a dream come true. I am grateful for the support of the scholars and artists at UP College of Music for nurturing my work on Philippine music, especially Dr. Ramón P. Santos, Dr. José Buenconsejo, the late Dr. José Maceda, Prof. Josefino Chino Toledo, the late Lucrecia "Tita King" Kasilag, Dr. Felipe de León, Dr. Antonio C. Hila, Dr. Leticia DeValle, Dr. Verne C. Dela Peña, and Dr. Elena Mirano. I am encouraged by artists like Joey Ayala and Grace Nono for their contributions to music of the Philippines. Thank you to the Fulbright IIE office of the Philippines, especially Dr. Alex Colada, for their help and support. Gloria Agas and Deling Agas Weller of Tagudin, Ilocos Sur, and their family generously invited me into their home and brought me closer to the history of my great-grandfather's background in Ilocos Sur. Thank you to Mayor José V. Bunoan Jr. and Mrs. Bunoan of Tagudin, Ilocos Sur, who my relatives and I visited in 2013 and who in turn visited Los Angeles in 2014 to deliver to us the Outstanding Tagudinian Award, posthumously recognizing Navarro's achievements and contributions. Our family is so proud of this honor. Thank you to Arwin Tan for information on band music in the Philippines; Arnaldo "Bombie" Custodio, who digitized the score of many of Navarro's pieces and who performed Navarro's compositions with the Philippine Youth Symphonic Band; Prof. Rodney Ambat and the UP Symphonic Band for performing the works of Navarro; Major Gilbert Ramos; the Philippine National Police Band; and Marlon Taruc Agapito Jr. I appreciate the assistance of artist Bren Bataclan for information on his uncle Lt. Col. Augusto C. Bataclan; the descendants of Col. Walter and Edith Loving especially grandchildren Edith Loving Lucas and Walter Loving III, and great-grandson Robert E. Loving Lucas for sharing their insight into Col. Loving; Joseph Suarez for information about medals won by the PC Band; Gilbert Ramos for Navarro's scores; and other participants on the Facebook page "Philippine Constabulary Band 1904" for several leads. Thank you to Robert Schroder, conductor of the Filipino American Symphony Orchestra and a descendent of a Philippine Army bandsman Lt. Augusto R. Samaniego Sr.; Jilly Canizares; Mr. Virgilio Fresnido, son of Capt. Alfonso Fresnido, and his daughters Luvia Hernandez and Mia Miralu-Fresnido Gildernew and their families; and Grace Talusan and Alonso Nichols for the countless ways they gave me their expertise.

Since I began research on this book decades ago, I have incurred *utang na loób*, a debt of gratitude, to many relatives, scholars, and friends. I am grateful to Navarro's children, who have all passed away, especially my grandmother, Irene, his daughter Leonora ("Lola Orang"), his eldest son Pedro ("Lolo Pepe"), and youngest son and musician Bienvenido ("Lolo Bien"). *Maraming salamat po* for the time we spent together, for your stories, and for the connection you provided me to this history. I extend my deepest love and gratitude to my late uncle, Emilio N. Navarro, grandson of Capt. Navarro and son of Irene, who was a young boy when he accompanied his grandfather to band rehearsals and concerts, often carrying a bottle of his favorite drink hidden in a bag. He often remembered Col. Loving and his wife in the Philippines, and even visited Mrs. Loving in Oakland sometime in the 1970s when he was in the merchant marines. In 2013, we stood together onstage when Tito Emil was honored at a concert of Navarro's music by the UP Symphonic Band under the direction of Rodney D. S. Ambat. I miss him very much. My heartfelt appreciation goes to his children, who encouraged me over the years, especially the late Manong Ronnie, Manong Gene, Manong Jojo, Ate Gaie, Ate Xenia, Kuya Dennis, and Kuya Glen, and their beloved families. Tito Emil and his siblings answered my endless questions over the years about what they remember of their grandfather, including my mother Araceli G. Talusan, Aleli G. Kliatchko, Aida G. Kasman, Edgardo N. Gamalinda, Lydia G. Silvestre, and their first cousins, Tita Victoria, Tita Geia, Tita Sally, Tita Cynthia, Tita Moren, Tita Nanette, and the late Uncle Al Peter, who gave me the mysterious *baul* (trunk) of compositions that was hidden away for sixty years. My cousins and their families hosted my visits to the Philippines and generously gave their time to shuttle me to universities, libraries, archives, and interviews over many years, especially Manong Joel and Ate Beth Silvestre; the entire Silvestre family; Angela Kliatchko, who wrote the first paper on Navarro; the Kliatchko clan, especially Mariel and Jacobson; the Gayanelo family; and the Kasman family, especially my late uncle Tito Ed; and Lawrence and Kuya Nico, who helped with photographs. To all my relatives, *maraming salamat po sa inyong lahat.*

I have benefited from the friendship and support of fellow students at UCLA, especially Eleanor Lipat-Chesler, Gladys Nubla, JoAnna Poblete, Bernard Ellorin, Peter Paul de Guzman, and so many more. At Tufts, David Locke and Richard Jankowsky were supportive colleagues during my postdoc. Thank you to the faculty and staff of the College of Arts and Humanities at CSUDH, especially Dean Mitch Avila and Jung-Sun Park. I am grateful for the encouragement and support of my wonderful colleagues, including Anne Choi, Annemarie Perez, Sheela Pawar, Marisela Chavez, Corina Benavides Lopez, Tim Caron, Laura Talamante, Vivian Price, Katherine Chu, and many more.

I am forever grateful to my parents, Ed and Arcel, for always nurturing my passion in music, and to my siblings, Grace, Liza, Paul, and Jon, and their spouses and children, for their love and encouragement. My dearest husband, John Patrick, and my children, Gavin and Norhanna, gave me the time and space to complete my work. I deeply appreciate the support of the Lacanlale family. To everyone who touched my life in small and big ways, please know that you have my sincerest gratitude and appreciation.

INSTRUMENTS OF EMPIRE

INTRODUCTION

World's Fairs, Symphony Halls, and America's Racial Others

> The Philippine Constabulary band of eighty native musicians has furnished the musical sensation of the World's fair, being pronounced by John Philip Sousa [as] the most wonderful military band he ever listened to.
> (*Milwaukee Journal*, August 22, 1904)

> Never before perhaps did wealth, society and rank turn out as they did to the concerts given by the world-famous Philippine Constabulary Band.
> (*New York Age*, March 18, 1909, p. 3, col. 4)

Early in the twentieth century, the world-famous Philippine Constabulary Band of more than eighty Filipino musicians, and their leader, an African American officer named Lt. Walter H. Loving, toured the concert halls of the United States and participated in three of the century's grandest world's fairs. At the St. Louis World's Fair in 1904, the band played Sousa's marches with such gusto that crowds rushed to cheer them on at parades and hear their signature piece, "The Stars and Stripes Forever." In addition to their role as a popular marching band, they impressed concert audiences with "highbrow" European opera overtures and symphonic excerpts. The Philippine

Constabulary Band (henceforth PC Band) was compared to and put on par with the world's finest military bands, including the John Philip Sousa Band, the British Band of the Grenadier Guards, and the Garde Républicaine Band of Paris. This was remarkable, newspapers claimed, because the PC Band was founded just a few years after the United States "liberated" the Philippines from Spain in 1898 and began its project of colonial tutelage in order to civilize Filipinos in preparation for self-rule.[1] Reference to the colonization of the Philippines wasn't just a fact—it was a representational strategy that positioned US intervention as the condition for "civilized" Filipino music-making to emerge. The PC Band's popularity with American audiences, therefore, was much more than an appreciation for musical artistry; the band's achievements validated the political aims of US imperialism and provided aural and visual proof of the success of "benevolent assimilation," a concept rooted in a proclamation by President McKinley that the United States intervened in the Philippines "not as invaders or conquerors, but as friends," in order to "win the confidence, respect, and affection of the inhabitants of the Philippines" (quoted in Kramer 2006, 110). To demonstrate Filipinos' consent to the "friendship" and rule of the United States, over a thousand Filipinos were sent to the St. Louis World's Fair in 1904, and the PC Band played a crucial role. The orderly, disciplined bandsmen performing familiar American patriotic marches were juxtaposed with unassimilated tribal people of the Philippines playing "primitive" music in order to impress upon fairgoers the magnificent progress achieved by US colonization. To make this simple narrative plausible, newspapers had to erase complexities by highlighting specific details and remaining silent on others. Loving's role as a Black American officer in charge of the prominent PC Band proved difficult to reconcile with the racial logic of sociocultural evolutionary paradigms promoted at the fair, and his race was often left unidentified, while the diverse "tribal" backgrounds of the band musicians themselves were regularly listed. On the rare occasions that Loving was identified as a "negro," according to conventions of the time, newspapers underscored his educational achievement as racial explanation for his position of leadership, while demeaning his race: "Lieutenant W. H. Loving, the chief bandmaster and the man responsible for his musicians' wonderful execution, is a crinkle-haired negro just brimming over with martial melody. He is a graduate of the Boston Conservatory of Music [sic]"[2] (*San Francisco Call*, April 14, 1904, p. 4, col. 6).

Pvt. Walter H. Loving went to the Philippines as a soldier with the 48th US Volunteer Infantry (48th USVI) in 1900.[3] He organized concerts with his regiment and became an instant hit with weary American soldiers and Filipinos, who appreciated a break from the tense atmosphere of war. William H. Taft, then governor-general of the Philippines, was impressed by Loving's musical leadership and asked him to establish a military brass band for the colonial government, to perform in official ceremonies, much like the US Marine Band. A band was approved in 1902 as part of the Philippine Constabulary, the insular police force of the US colonial government in the Philippines. Each unit of the Philippine Constabulary, charged with keeping peace and order among the populace, was staffed by enlisted Filipino men under the direction of white American officers, with the exception of Loving. Loving's racial identity and social positioning as a Black American soldier and musician in the emerging formation of Philippine colonial society was significant in cultivating goodwill among Black soldiers, who had to confront their ambivalence about their own racist treatment in the US military and their role as subjugators of other nonwhite peoples (see Marasigan 2010, Cunningham 2007, Powell 1998, and Gatewood 1972, 1975, and 1987). The PC Band, with Loving as its leader, symbolized visually and aurally the successful collaboration between Americans and Filipinos, as well as among Americans themselves. Thus, in the spirit of benevolent assimilation, the PC Band was fostered by Taft's civilian regime in order to win the hearts and minds of Filipinos and to encourage their cooperation with the new rulers. In this way, the band became an instrument of empire during US colonization of the Philippines. For Filipinos, however, the meaning of brass bands was entirely different from the ways that Americans deployed them. Brass bands had already been a vital part of life in town *fiestas* and in the Catholic Church for three hundred years under Spanish rule, and bandsmen came from generations of musicians who found recognition of their talents and a place of belonging in colonial society. When the United States colonized the Philippines, military band music became an effective instrument of empire to form a cultural bridge, a *lingua franca*, and a mutually valued endeavor for colonizer and colonized, subjugator and subjugated alike.

Capitalizing on the PC Band's popularity as a world-class musical organization after the 1904 Fair, president-elect Taft summoned the eighty-plus-member organization back to the United States in 1909 to march at his presidential inauguration. Taft literally paraded the PC Band in front of thousands of American spectators to demonstrate that the controversial colonization of the Philippines was an achievement rather than a failure, and that ongoing rebellions throughout the archipelago were little more than isolated incidents of banditry. Because they were such a hit with audiences in Washington, DC, the PC Band toured the US for months after the inauguration, playing to tens of thousands of music lovers from Boston to Chicago to Seattle. Newspapers hailed the PC Band as one of the best military band organizations of the day, citing their "exact precision, ... harmonious blending of instruments, and ... fine appreciation" for European and American concert repertoire (*Washington Herald*, April 26, 1909), and thus demonstrating the success of benevolent assimilation. While audiences enjoyed their fine musical performances, in other ways, the PC Band's popularity seems unexpected if not perplexing. How did American audiences manage to understand the PC Band's exceptional performances of "civilized" European music, given the pervasive circulation of images of Filipinos as "half-naked savages" and widespread racial evolutionary theories presenting nonwhites as uncivilized?

To investigate these paradoxes, I theorize about the ways in which predominantly white audiences developed an "imperial ear" when listening to the PC Band's performances of Euro-American band repertoire. Emerging out of the conditions of the Philippines' forcible incorporation into the US body politic, the imperial ear was a discourse that reduced the musicality of the PC Band members, and by extension, all Filipinos, to a "natural" state of being, capitalizing on prevalent ideas about race. Since Americans had arrived in the islands to civilize the natives just a few years prior, the PC Band's apparently sudden, highly developed mastery of Euro-American music must be explained by Filipinos' natural, biological, and thus racial talent for music and mimicry. Filipinos' excessively natural—and thus rather *unnatural*—musicality was a myth that developed and sustained Americans' imperial ear, which heard Filipino accomplishment in European and American music as an outcome of US intervention and tutelage. Filipino natural musicality became an object "open to appropriation by society" (Barthes 1972, 109), a signifier of American benevolence and discipline (Rafael 2000, 23). What emerges here is a fantasy that US colonization and benevolent measures to assimilate Filipinos were beneficial for both parties—a fantasy made possible by novel ways of representing Filipinos that circulated through the mainstream media of newspapers and international expositions.

In this book, I investigate the entwined myths of natural Filipino musicality and American superiority by tracing the development of an imperial way of hearing the PC Band. By scrutinizing hundreds of newspaper accounts, I analyze complicated imperial and racial interactions between the US and the Philippines in what Mary Louise Pratt calls a "contact zone." A contact zone is a "space of colonial encounters ... in which peoples geographically and historically separated come into contact with each other and establish ongoing relations, usually involving conditions of coercion, radical inequality, and intractable conflict" (Pratt 1992, 6). The term *contact* highlights the "interactive, improvisational dimensions of colonial encounters so easily ignored or suppressed by diffusionist accounts of conquest and domination" (7). For American audiences at the PC Band's concerts, this interaction did not take place on a distant shore but rather in the tightly circumscribed spaces of world's fairs, framed by contending colonial objectives, evolutionary ideologies, and the entrepreneurial aims of concessionaires (see Kramer 1999 and Kramer 2006, ch. 4). The social, cultural, and political cacophony of the world's fairs proliferated mixed messages, with disorderly results. For example, one spectator at the 1904 Fair exclaimed, "No one could listen to the playing of 'The Star-Spangled Banner' by that band of Filipinos ... and doubt that they are loyally American" (*The Bourbon News*, Paris, Kentucky, August 30, 1904, p. 3, col. 1). While the listener was willing to embrace Filipinos as loyal Americans, he also made assumptions about the musicians' patriotic intent and willful submission to US colonial rule. Rather than deem Filipinos to be skilled musicians in their own right, an imperial ear heard their musicianship in a way that legitimated American authority over Filipinos and the Philippines. Filipinos' musical labor, artistry, and ownership of Western musical traditions were imperceptible to the imperial ears of the American public, who heard and felt validated by the sound of their own achievement in assimilating Filipinos through the enjoyable and thus "benevolent" genre of band music. These dense contact spaces of face-to-face interaction with American audiences created novel ways of understanding Filipinos that coincided but also conflicted with the colonial and racial propaganda that was embedded into and promoted by world's fairs.

Concert halls also provided a contact zone of face-to-face interaction between American audiences and the band musicians—one that troubled the simplistic racial categorizing of savage and civilized. While seemingly benign or even complimentary, the stereotype that all Filipinos possess natural musical talent racializes musical skill as a biological state of being. Furthermore, this view supports an imperial claim based on notions of Manifest Destiny that considered Filipinos' "raw" talent as another natural resource to be harnessed and exploited by US rule. For example, a *New York Times* caption marveled that "Men Who Seven Years Ago Had Never Seen An Instrument Now Play Wagner and Beethoven" (March 8, 1909, p. 4). To make this miraculous assertion plausible, a centuries-old brass band tradition in the Philippines was effectively erased from view. Contrary to the American public's naïve belief, members of the PC Band came from generations of regimental and town band musicians or studied music in Spanish monasteries from an early age. Politically, this bizarre characterization—that Filipinos were childlike but musically talented savages before American rule—was an attempt to negate accusations by some anti-imperialists that the US was colonizing a people who were already capable of self-rule (Kramer 2006, 116), thus preserving notions of US exceptionalism and the country's commitment to the ideals of freedom, democracy, and self-determination.

By critiquing an imperial ear that was developed within the context of early twentieth-century racism and US imperialism, I argue that the musical accolades bestowed on the PC Band by American audiences were neither neutral nor simply about music. My intention is neither to diminish the triumphs of the PC Band nor to reduce their legacy to a mere consequence of American intervention. By bringing into focus how Americans' imperial ear praised the Filipino musicians in a way that ultimately served the purposes of colonization and a belief in white superiority, I hope to break a "circle of interpretation" engendered by a racial stereotype about Filipinos that continues to posit Filipino music-making as competent and at times exceptional but ultimately imitative of the West. Homi Bhabha explains,

> Racist stereotypical discourse, in its colonial moment, inscribes a form of governmentality that is informed by productive splitting in its constitution of knowledge and exercise of power. Some of its practices recognize the difference of race, culture and history as elaborated by stereotypical knowledges, racial theories, and administrative colonial experience, and on that basis institutionalize a range of political and cultural ideologies that are prejudicial, discriminatory, vestigial, archaic, "mythical", and crucially, are recognized as being so. By "knowing" the native population in these terms, discriminatory and authoritarian forms of political control are considered appropriate. The

colonized population is then deemed to be both the cause and effect of the system, imprisoned in the circle of interpretation. (Bhabha 1994, 83)

A "circle of interpretation" positioned Filipinos in a double-bind that produced a harmful paradox. A double-bind is complicated form of communication because there is "never 'a message' singly, but in actual communication always two or more related messages of different levels and often conveyed by different channels—voice, tone, movement, context, and so on. These messages may be widely incongruent and thus exert very different and conflicting influences" (Bateson et al. 1962, 155). Filipino musicians could play civilized music but were not as such considered *civilized*; in attempting to prove that they were civilized by mastering Euro-American musical forms, Filipinos only demonstrated to the imperial ear that they benefited from colonial rule. In this paradoxical cycle, Filipinos were "caught up in an ongoing system which produces conflicting definitions of the relationship and consequent subjective distress" (257). Repeated utterances of the stereotype of Filipinos as "natural musicians," in combination with the moniker "little brown brothers,"[4] shaped Americans' imperial ear, creating a circle of interpretation of the band's fine musical skills as an affirmation of the United States' benevolent assimilation project rather than as a product of the band's own history, without the necessary intervention of the US. In this way, Filipino musicians were contextualized in a web of contradictory meanings made to preserve the otherwise unstable and permeable category of "civilized" as being for whites only.[5]

Far from simply embodying the colonial project, the PC Band's fine performances actively circulated an audible and tangible means for American audiences to hear and see benevolence in action, while at the same time falling deaf to interpretations of Filipinos as creative musicians in their own right and as "individuals in full possession of themselves" (Rafael 1995, 128). Heard this way by the imperial ear, the PC Band's performances allowed for colonization to be, according to Vicente Rafael, "envisioned as a project for forging sentimental bonds between colonizer and colonized: a 'special relation' that would mimic that between a parent and child rather than between master and slave" (128). This way of hearing and interpreting Filipinos emerged out of the specific context of race and empire in the early twentieth century, but in many ways continues to this day. This idea is disseminated by countless musical performances, structuring the perception of future performances of

Filipino musicians as talented yet imitative of Western musical forms and styles, while disregarding the authenticity and creativity of Filipino music-making and artistic expression. Listening with an imperial ear, American audiences' enjoyment of the PC Band's music-making was an exercise of imperial and racial power to sustain and perpetuate cultural hegemony, in the face of the racial fears of the early twentieth century brought on by overseas expansion and increased immigration in the US.

Racial Anxiety in the Early Twentieth Century

The entangled histories of the US and the Philippines began on May 1, 1898, when the US Asiatic Squadron under the command of Commodore George Dewey defeated the Spanish fleet in a mock battle in Manila Bay. Expecting Dewey to aid their cause to expel the Spanish, Filipino[6] revolutionaries led by Emilio Aguinaldo returned to the Philippines from exile in Hong Kong on May 19, 1898, and declared independence from Spain on June 12, 1898. Refusing to surrender to their colonial subjects, Spanish officials signed the Treaty of Paris on December 10, 1898, which in part ceded the Philippines, Guam, and Puerto Rico to the United States. President McKinley declared that the US wanted to protect Filipinos, not as conquerors but as their friends, and that it was the duty of Americans to uplift Filipinos and prepare them for self-rule. Urging the US to go home, Aguinaldo sent diplomatic emissaries to the US and to Europe to rally support and recognition of Philippine sovereignty by arguing that Filipinos were already civilized and capable of self-government (Kramer 2006, 100–101). Filipinos vigorously continued their resistance to foreign rule, resulting in the Philippine-American War in February 1899. Rather than being represented as the continuation of a revolution to oust foreign rule, Filipino resistance was characterized as an "insurrection" against US authority perpetuated by *"ladrones"* (thieves) and "bandits." Despite the resistance and violence that continued for another decade, President Roosevelt declared the Philippine-American War over in 1902. Enticed with promises of protection, equal rights, and eventual transition to Filipino rule, Filipino elites worked within the confines of the new colonial society as the US tightened its control over the Philippines (see Ileto 1998, Go 2008, and Kramer 2006). Meanwhile, American anti-imperialists vociferously expressed their doubts about the merits of administering the Philippines, Puerto Rico, and Guam. These opposing voices were soon drowned out by the imperialists' agenda of maintaining control over the islands in order to expand US territory overseas and capitalize on new economic opportunities.[7]

While the US was expanding into overseas territories, within its borders it was dealing with an influx of nonwhites and foreign others, intensifying Americans' racial anxieties over the direction of the nation. Though the US benefited tremendously from their cheap labor, Asian immigrants were subjected to segregation, violence, and exclusion by immigration and nationality policies (see Jacobson 2000 and Aarim-Heriot 2003). While the Chinese Exclusion Act of 1882 barred Chinese laborers, it did not stop American and European plantation owners in Hawaii from seeking cheap labor from Japan, Korea, and the Philippines. As conditions on the plantations worsened, these laborers headed for the US mainland, causing nativist and xenophobic reactions, culminating in the Immigration Acts of 1917 ("Asiatic Barred Zone") and 1924 ("Asian Exclusion Act"). Within the US, African Americans migrating out of the South after the Civil War and Emancipation were met with violence and disenfranchisement across the nation (see Schneider 2006), and their cultural visibility became more pronounced as ragtime music gained popularity with America's masses. Thus, the movement of people into and within the US, as well as the expansion of the US overseas, brought increased racial tensions and fears to many Americans, and the presence of nonwhites in American culture was not only visually apparent but also aurally perceptible. Lawrence Levine describes these audible cultural threats in his groundbreaking work *Highbrow/Lowbrow* (1988):

> Afro-Americans dancing their strange ritual dances to exotic rhythms within their own churches; Irish women "keening" [wailing] weird melodies over their dead at their own wakes; Germans entertaining family and friend in their own beer gardens. But these worlds of strangers did not remain contained; they spilled over into the public spaces that characterized nineteenth-century America and that included theaters, musical halls, opera houses, museums, parks, fairs, and the rich public cultural life that took place daily on the streets of Americans cities. (Levine 1988, 177)

It was in this racial cacophony of the early twentieth century that the Philippine Constabulary Band emerged as a unique organization among the

US empire's "racial others." They appealed to middle-class and elite Americans by mitigating racial and cultural anxieties through the beloved genre of military band music, with a pleasing repertoire of European "high-class" music and American patriotic marches.

European Musical Hegemony and the Rise of American Popular Music

Euro-American band repertoire brought a certain audible order to the racial cacophony of the early twentieth century—a cacophony that threatened white cultural hegemony and that was brought about by US expansion to overseas territories, waves of immigration, and African American migration out of the South. The interplay of these imperial, racial, and cultural anxieties becomes apparent in the ways that audiences responded to the PC Band's repertoire of Euro-American music. To mitigate cultural and racial chaos, American elites invested in "maintaining and disseminating pure art, music, literature, and drama [to] create a force for moral order and help to halt the chaos threatening to envelop the nation" (Levine 1988, 200). During the 1800s, Levine explains, Americans of all classes consumed and engaged with a variety of European art, music, and literature, but by late 1800s and early 1900s, elite control of cultural institutions redirected the meaning of European arts to represent the "highest" form of civilization, in order to uphold America's Anglo-Saxon heritage as superior during a period of great social transformation. European culture became "one of the mechanisms that made it possible to identify, distinguish, and order this new universe of strangers" (177). Concerts of "classical" European music in symphony halls represented a way of holding on to the past and projecting it into the future—"the response of the elites was a tripartite one: to retreat into their own private spaces whenever possible; to transform public spaces by rules, systems of taste, and canons of behavior of their own choosing; and, finally, to convert the strangers so that their modes of behavior and cultural predilections emulated those of the elites" (177). The PC Band's performances of Euro-American concert music suitably fit these aims, appealing to both elite and general audiences while simultaneously epitomizing the triumph of the United States' colonial enterprise.

Military band music was immensely popular among the masses of Americans for most of the nineteenth century and during the early twentieth century. While band music was not the "pure" music of the symphony hall, it was an appropriate middlebrow musical genre that could package elite music for consumption by the masses by arranging the most popular movements of operas and symphonies. Conservative elites often considered brass band music as plundering the art of great composers, and often it came "under attack . . . because [these arrangements] represented impure art, pseudoculture, and disorder" (Levine 1988, 165). John Philip Sousa, America's premiere musical figure, was famous for his spirited marches written specifically for concert and brass bands.[8] Sousa's band concerts represented safe middlebrow music for those upholding nineteenth-century white American values. As a product of military training in the Marine Corps and as director of the US Marine Band, Sousa imposed a strict sense of discipline on his band that "touched a chord that ran deep at the turn of the century," when there was yearning for a sense of cultural order (178). But, despite his respectability, Sousa often came under fire for programming both "serious" works and popular selections like "Turkey in the Straw" and ragtime music in the same concert (237). These musical tensions and debates had overt as well as subtle racial implications.

Ragtime (and later blues and jazz), rooted in the Black American experience, was co-opted by the commercial music industry and consumed enthusiastically by the masses during the late nineteenth and early twentieth centuries. Tin Pan Alley, the thriving center of American popular music, disseminated sheet music for ragtime, "coon songs," and minstrel songs. The word *ragtime* originally referred to a style of lively rhythmic syncopation attributed to Black musicians who "ragged" marches and other types of songs that accompanied dances. By the late 1800s, the music industry applied the term *ragtime* to any upbeat song, such as "coon songs" and minstrel songs, or dance music such as the cakewalk, even though rhythmic syncopation was actually minimal (Berlin 2002, 12). Sousa had to justify his inclusion of so-called ragtime pieces in his band concerts because cultural elites were concerned that ragtime's "primitive" syncopations would cause listeners to engage in immoral behavior and lead them to spiritual degeneracy (43). Ragtime posed a threat to Victorian values embraced by "respectable" Americans because it originated not from European civilization but from its "very antithesis—the sensual depravity of African savagery, embodied in the despised American Negro" (32). Sousa's choices of concert repertoire aimed to uphold elite and middle-class white American values while simultaneously catering to the tastes of the masses. He called "Turkey in the Straw" a "magic melody," even though "musical high-brows" looked down on it because it came "not from a European composer but from an unknown negro minstrel" (Sousa 1941, 341). Despite his acknowledgement of "negro" cultural contributions to American music, Sousa nevertheless made racist comments about ragtime: "most of it made you want to bite your grandmother" (quoted in Bierley 1986, 142). In this statement, he implied that ragtime inspired a most savage and depraved act, and by extension, was created by a culture of similar merit. But rather than exclude ragtime from his repertoire altogether and disappoint mass audiences, he drew on his musical and social capital to legitimize it:[9] "I have washed its face (and) put a clean dress on it. . . . It is now an attractive thing, entirely different from the *frowzly-headed* thing of the gutter" (quoted in Bierley 1986, 142; emphasis mine). This is a racial insinuation, for clearly Sousa meant that though "it" was Black, he could nevertheless rescue and reform ragtime through his intervention to make it suitable for his concerts. Notwithstanding his hostility, Sousa acknowledged ragtime as a music with Black origins cultivated in America, but he continued to uphold European classical music as the highest form of art, in order to escape criticism. Even when criticized by "highbrow" cultural elites about including popular pieces such as "Molly and I and the Baby" or "Has Anybody Here Seen Kelly?" in the same concert as serious compositions of European composers, Sousa would "react aggressively to these charges" to defend his choices (Levine 1988, 166). He insisted that if he mixed popular tunes with works like Wagner's *Tannhäuser* Overture, he would be able to reach a larger audience and thus educate them and elevate their taste (166). Many reviewers praised Sousa's ability to emulate the sounds of a concert orchestra (by his increasing the proportion of reed instruments in the concert band), and words "like 'dignity,' 'refinement,' and 'quality,' were often used to describe the tone he and his musicians set" (165–66). Thus, Sousa came to "symbolize good taste and order and was perceived as muting some of the most grating features of bands" (165–66). Sousa's commitment to American music, despite his general animosity toward Black culture, had both positive and negative results toward recognizing Black music as *American* music, while simultaneously preserving the myth of European "classical" music as the highest form of art.

A veneration of European classics was "part of a development that saw the very word 'culture' as becoming synonymous with the Eurocentric products of the symphony hall, the opera house, the museum, and the library, all of which, the American people were taught, must be approached with a disciplined, knowledgeable seriousness of purpose, and—most important of all—with a feeling of reverence" (Levine 1988, 146). By maintaining a deference to all things European and rejecting Black music, elite society reinforced a notion that any American artistic endeavor paled in comparison to "real" European art: "in 1884, [when] the critic Richard Grant White was invited to write a history of American music, he refused for lack of an American music to write about" (143). Such reverence, however, masked a glaring contradiction in the convoluted logics of imperialism and white superiority—if Americans had no uniquely *American* music, how could Americans themselves be civilized? Were they not simply mimicking European music in the same way that they accused racial others like Filipinos of doing? With the power to appropriate and to invisibilize its origins, American music would nevertheless be defined by the very culture that America sought to reject.

Black music, like Black people, was excluded from elites' definition of a uniquely *American* music because, "though there were some who began to see in American and, especially, Afro-American folk music evidence of an indigenous American musical tradition, that notion flew too directly in the face of the comfortable evolutionary predispositions of the day" (Levine 1988, 144). Despite elites' disapproval, "American music" would soon be defined by an origin in, or at least association with, Black culture. For example, the famous Czech composer Antonín Dvořák, who immigrated to the US and served as director of the National Conservatory of Music in New York, incorporated African American spirituals into his Symphony No. 9 in E Minor ("From the New World") (1893). James Reese Europe and his regimental band in WWI started an international craze for ragtime in France, and thus ragtime came to be known to the world as *American* music.[10]

Hearing Racial Others

These two opposing forces—casting European music as civilized, and racially coded ragtime and popular music as lower class—provide the framework for understanding how American audiences made sense of the PC Band's musical performances in the context of the prevalent colonial and racial ideologies of the day. While John Philip Sousa mitigated criticism through his social capital as a popular American composer and respected band master, the strategy of the PC Band and Loving was to avoid ragtime pieces altogether, opting instead to play symphonic excerpts, opera overtures, and patriotic marches. As I will discuss further in chapter 2, I do not believe that they were making a statement against Black culture or Black music per se; rather, in most cases they deliberately chose to align themselves with music that American audiences held in high regard, compelling their predominantly white audiences to recognize their high level of musicianship by expressing themselves in the accepted language of civilization. By doing so, the PC Band induced Americans to invent novel ways of representing Filipino musical labor, in order to resolve contradictions within prevailing beliefs about Filipino racial inferiority and white superiority, developing an imperial ear to contain their breach of racial hierarchy. Recognizing Loving's leadership as a Black American, as I will analyze, was even more difficult to manage within the sociocultural, evolutionary, and racial logic of the time, and he was often left unidentified by mainstream newspapers.

Peculiar representations of the PC Band musicians in American newspapers provided a cultural mechanism that corresponded to "an ingenious array of legal and political mechanisms by which the uplifted savages themselves might be held at bay" (Jacobson 2000, 262). The development of an imperial ear toward the Filipino band's outstanding musicality is but one of the baffling ways by which "United States imperialism at the turn of the century ... was predicated on the disavowal of imperial motives" (Rafael 1995, 127). This was akin to McKinley's twisted notion of benevolent assimilation itself: "We came not as invaders or conquerors but as friends, to protect the natives ... to win their confidence, respect and affection" (*United States*, Correspondence 2:859, quoted in Rafael 1995, 127). The responses of audiences toward the PC Band stemmed from the deliberate ways that an imperial agenda was concealed to protect American exceptionalism and white cultural hegemony. An imperial ear heard the PC Band as "little brown men" whose "natural" musical heredity was civilized by American tutelage and US rule, providing a comfortable myth and a convenient framework from which to make sense of glaring contradictions circulating in the discourses of race and empire-making.

Before developing an imperial ear toward Filipinos, Americans already listened to and heard Black music-making in some comparable ways after the end of the Civil War. Jon Cruz's insightful discussion of what he calls "ethnosympathy" informs my analysis by tracing the ways that abolitionists' "humanitarian pursuit of the inner world of distinctive and collectively classifiable subjects" (Cruz 1999, 3) came to interpret slave spirituals not as "alien noise" (Baraka 2002 [1963], 29–30) but as culturally expressive music that revealed "black subjectivity and authenticity" (Cruz 1999, 3–4). Represented in this way, Black spirituals became "fathomable, accessible, and decipherable, and could be drawn into new circuits of familiarity" to which white listeners could comfortably relate (6). Hearing spirituals as authentic expressions of Black subjectivity was radical at the time, but in another way, these spirituals represented the most acceptable genre to those whites who were "championing the new mode of benevolent cultural reception" (6). Therefore, while hearing the Black spiritual as resonant with familiar Christian values, thus allowing whites to hear Black people as humans, whites' interest nevertheless silenced "the argumentative, critical, and elaborate black voices that had already emerged in the slave narratives. These voices had preceded the discovery of the Negro spiritual, but were overshadowed by the larger, newer, aesthetic appreciation of the preferred black culture" (7). Listening aesthetically, then, was neither neutral nor simply about musical evaluation; it was a selective and preferred way of hearing fulfilled by a desire to mitigate racial and moral anxieties among sympathetic whites: "Yet what self-flattery it was for abolitionists to think (after Douglass's contribution) that the souls of black folk could be had for the simple price of reading a transcribed song or witnessing a black religious assembly. Every pathos-oriented listener who understood that the spirituals were slavery-induced cries of anguish to God could be a full-fledged cultural interpreter, a reader of what had hitherto been the slave's secrets" (119). In order to take pleasure in listening to spirituals, sympathetic whites had to pursue a "disengaged engagement," a cultural logic that allowed them to appreciate the "authenticity" of Negro spirituals while ignoring the realities of anti-Black racism and violence (22 and 30). "Disengaged engagement provided a safe distance from the immediacy of flesh-and-blood social trauma; it dislocated one from personal implication, from the pressures of reflecting on one's responsibility to a raging crisis" (31). By immersing themselves in the aesthetic appreciation of Black music, whites were able to diminish their culpability in the production of the conditions that enslaved people bewailed. Similarly, a "disengaged engagement" allowed the imperial ear to ignore forcible takeover of the Philippines and colonial violence in order to relish the PC Band's playing of familiar European musical repertoire and American patriotic marches. While hearing the Filipinos as competent musicians, sympathetic whites were nevertheless deaf to their utterances of self-determination and autonomy in projecting their own centuries-old band tradition over the perception that Americans civilized them through cultural tutelage and benevolent assimilation.

Inspired by Simon Frith's work (1998), I examine how audiences imbue musical performance with value judgments, infusing ways of listening with social meaning to gratify listeners' particular needs. In order to understand cultural value judgments, "we must look at the social context in which they are made, at the social reasons why some aspects of a sound or spectacle are valued over others" (Frith 1998, 22). American audiences' imperial ears heard the PC Band as an aural embodiment of the colonial process—natural musicians guided by US tutelage who not only willingly conformed to Euro-American values, but also obeyed an American leader as subjugated "little brown brothers." Music-hungry audiences sought out the PC Band's performances of fine Euro-American band music with a "disengaged engagement" to feel gratified by the erasure of colonial violence and coercion, the success of benevolent assimilation, and the preservation of American exceptionalism. Racial others competently and successfully rendering Euro-American concert pieces, devoid of suggestions of Black music, quelled racial anxieties threatening to erode Euro-American cultural forms in a way that promised to uphold white supremacy domestically and internationally. With their "racial imagination" (Radano and Bohlman 2000, 5), American audiences heard the PC Band's music-making as an expression that affirmed their own investment in white superiority. In this way, musical accolades bestowed on the PC Band by white audiences were neither neutral nor entirely about musical performance, but rather the product of an imperial ear.

The PC Band embodied a nonthreatening vision of the successful incorporation of Filipinos, and to some extent Blacks, into modern American society as represented in part by an aesthetics of music performance that promised assimilation to middle-class American values and elite objectives. The imperial ear was deaf to Loving's contribution as a Black person, and his racial identity was rarely mentioned in newspapers, because it would have complicated a simple narrative of white authority over Filipinos and challenged the supposed inferiority of Black people. This representation of the PC Band became a "comfortable alternative" or narrative substitute (Lott 2013 [1993], 61) for the violent realities of colonial domination and the ongoing resistance of Filipinos to US rule, made possible by listening with a disengaged engagement. Despite Americans' imperial ears, the Filipino musicians, led by Loving, played with conviction, intention, and enthusiasm for quite different reasons than those assumed by white audiences. The Filipino bandsmen regarded themselves as highly skilled musicians engaging in a centuries-old *banda* (Philippine brass band) tradition, striving for the utmost level of mastery in their own musical language, which, due to the history of European colonization, overlapped with Americans' own musical language. To disavow an interpretation of Filipino capabilities and capacity for cultural autonomy, the myth of Filipinos' natural musicality emerged so that the US could take credit for civilizing Filipinos. Loving's success and excellence in music was also deeply personal—he prided himself on his musical education and artistry, which included performance, conducting, arranging, and composing. For Black elites who aimed to demonstrate that African Americans deserved equality by adhering to white middle-class and elite values, Loving served as an example of the possibilities and success of racial uplift. Reaching its height during the Harlem Renaissance, racial uplift ideology involved the performance of Euro-American concert music as an indicator of class and education.[11] I argue that, placed within the context of US racial politics, Filipinos' struggle for recognition as worthy American subjects connected to the Black racial uplift ideology of the early twentieth century. My exploration of the history of this long-forgotten Filipino military brass band and their African American conductor plays directly into lesser-known themes of the racial intersections of Filipino and Black experiences outside of the Philippines.[12]

Unlike the abolitionists and other whites in Cruz's work who appreciated the "authenticity" of Black spirituals, the musical performances of Euro-American music by Filipinos did not include recognition of Filipino cultural authenticity. Authenticity in music was, and in many ways still is, measured by distinct differences in musical sound, language, timbre, instruments, vocal aesthetics, genre, form, and other elements that, in their totality, identify unique music cultures. In order to be considered unique and thus authentic by this definition, music cultures must be distinct from, rather than derivative or imitative of, Western music. Indexing and measuring musical distinctions between cultures structures a "racial imagination" around and about music, because "music contributes substantially to the vocabularies used to construct race" (Radano and Bohlman 2000, 7). Only by discovering and identifying the "metaphysical essence" of a culture's music, thus verifying its *authenticity*, can the term *hybridity* be deployed to describe the interaction engendered by cultural contact between the West and "the Other" (7). The writings of the early ethnologists, anthropologists, and comparative musicologists who formed the foundation of ethnomusicology laid the groundwork for the racialization of music and culture, which contributed to this way of defining authenticity and indicating hybridity. Facilitated by imperialism, early researchers engaged in a project of discovering, charting, and categorizing musical essences in the cultures of racial others and constructing a music-evolutionary timeline that organized musical cultures on a scale from primitive to civilized. Before the movement toward cultural relativism became the norm among later ethnomusicologists, researchers like Frances Densmore sought to discover, in the origins and evolutionary stages of the musical development of "primitives," what would eventually culminate in civilized Western music (see Moon 2010). In her study of the music of Filipinos at the 1904 Fair, Densmore completely dismissed Filipino band music performances—because they did not fit into the schema of music evolution—and instead focused on the "primitive" music of tribal people. She does not mention the incredibly popular Philippine Constabulary Band until the last paragraph of her article "The Music of Filipinos," when she laments that native (read *authentic*) music in the Philippines "shall be merged at last in The Star-spangled Banner" (Densmore 1906, 632) and disappear into extinction.[13]

Filipino music-making in Western genres exceeds simple binaries of Western vs. non-Western and indigenous vs. hybrid, so that Filipino authenticity is effectively obfuscated from definition. When researchers were guided by a method of hearing that formulated differences from Western music as confirmation of a race's distinct music culture (and therefore recognizable music-making), Filipinos' authenticity in European music was obscured and silenced because they shared a musical language and repertoire with the colonizers of the West. European music in general, and brass music in particular, which had been rooted in the Philippines as long as it had in the US, was only authentic in the hands of Europeans and white Americans—"racial others" could not "own or occupy the music that the Self purports to own" (Radano and Bohlman 2000, 6). The PC Band's American enthusiasts neither engaged in what Houston A. Baker Jr. called a "tasteful, raceless listening" (Radano and Bohlman 2000, xi), nor did they recognize Filipino authenticity in Western music, thus reinforcing the construction of race in the interpretation and definition of Filipino music and music-making (4). Despite the fact that Filipinos were engaging in their own musical tradition, the band musicians were heard as racial others who were "natural imitators" that "perforce depend[ed] on external stimuli to shape their internal disposition. Merely reactive rather than reflective, they existed in immediate and sensuous relationship to their surroundings rather than as self-conscious agents of their own transformation" (Rafael 2000, 34). To the imperial ear, distinctive elements of Filipino music-making were imperceptible, and thus Filipinos were deemed imitative, culturally inauthentic, and invalid.

In these ways, American audiences were able to remain deaf to alternate readings that did not corroborate racial stereotypes of Filipinos as natural musicians shaped by US tutelage—an example of confirmation bias, a way of interpreting information that validates one's presumptions. The PC Band's superb musicianship, cultivated in the *banda* tradition, was "evidence" of and substantiated observations that music was a natural and racial condition of people in the Philippines. To confirm this bias, one only had, if one had the power, to erase Filipinos' long history of European music and brass band performance from narratives about the PC Band. The appropriation of the Filipino *banda* tradition into the United States' colonial vision was facilitated by the fact that colonizers did not have to invest labor and resources into teaching European or American music to Filipinos (or imposing it upon them); they only had to redirect the meaning of this already well-entrenched type of music-making in the minds of American audiences by emphasizing the benefits of colonial tutelage and benevolent assimilation. Since Filipinos did not have control over the representation of their musical labor in American newspapers, their capability in Euro-American band repertoire was regarded by the imperial ear as assimilation devoid of resistance and authenticity. The power of the US to reshape and disseminate its representation of Filipino music-making served to uphold and legitimize white American supremacy over its colonial subjects.

American audiences were overwhelmingly encouraged to hear the PC Band's performances with an imperial ear, allowing racialization and its effect, racial domination, to be carried forth and sustained. Once created, the imperial ear became what Bourdieu called a *habitus* (a "structuring structure, which organises practices and the perception of practices" [1984, 170]), one that naturalized racial domination of Filipinos, shaped future thought about Filipino musicality, and influenced the ways that audiences heard their music-making. Music, race, and imperialism aligned with audiences' prevalent response to the PC Band, and over time, became deeply embedded in the ways that Filipinos are heard in American culture. This relegated Filipino musicians, and by extension Filipinos in general, to the status of contingent participants[14] in American culture, in a way that resonates with the sort of "inclusionary racism" identified by Kramer as a novel racial formation invented by American imperialists to both encourage the collaboration of Filipino elites and to delimit their actual power (2006, 191). Infantilized as "little brown brothers," the Filipino bandsmen could be included and praised in musical performance while also being subordinated racially, culturally, and politically.

Listening to Filipinos

Rafael poses a crucial question: "What was at stake in the compulsive theorizing of Filipinos as 'imitative', unoriginal, and therefore childlike?" (1995, 129). In the context of US colonization of the Philippines, the necessity of employing the trope of Filipinos as natural musicians rendered their music-making as imitative rather than authentic, in order to contain their breach of colonial and racial hierarchies and make invisible Filipinos' qualifications for civilization and thus self-rule. Naturalization of musicality was racialized to sustain a myth of white supremacy, and repetitions of the stereotype were convincing because such observations appear as "disembodied and disinterested" statements of fact (130). In colonial travel writings, the European or white observer "has no place in the description" (Pratt 1992, 32), and her/his "authority and legitimacy are uncontested" (Rafael 1995, 52) because one assumes that she/he is making an observation of objective reality, not an interpretation loaded with meaning. Memoirs of American women living in the Philippines in the early twentieth century, for example, described the "brownness" of Filipinos to emphasize the women's own whiteness as a symbol of power: "native bodies appear as accessories reinforcing the link between whiteness and mastery" (130). Descriptions of the PC bandsmen as "natural" musicians and "little brown brothers," seemingly neutral statements of fact, were deployed to contain and prevent hearing Filipinos as authentic, imaginative, and self-determined creators with the capacity to govern themselves. In this way, intellect, individuality, creativity, and ownership were reserved and preserved only for whites. By erasing the Filipino *banda* tradition in descriptions of the PC Band, newspapers enabled audiences to be deaf to their ingenuity. To listen attentively to Filipinos' authenticity in musical expression, I turn to a number of innovate scholarly works on Filipino and Filipino American cultural production and creativity. I sketch out some of their main contributions and will continue to draw on them throughout this work as I elucidate the ways by which the PC Band engaged their creativity in a form and genre that was regarded as belonging only to the purview of Europeans and white Americans.

Analyzing the colonial military band's role in facilitating the construction, circulation, and reinforcement of stereotypes about the Philippines and Filipinos offers insight into US imperialism's cultural project. Without investigating the cultural aspects, it can seem that imperialism imposes itself by violent force, while in reality there are myriad ways that colonial influence spreads beyond centers of colonial rule into the daily activities of the wider populace. Writing on the first decade of US rule in the Philippines, Julian Go examines how the political elite played an important role as both collaborators and "students" of tutelary colonialism, as the colonial regime reoriented their political conduct toward American-style democracy and ideals (2008, 3). As analyzed by the important works of Warwick Anderson (1995) and Vicente Rafael (2000), even "seemingly neutral state technologies (such as the colonial census) and ostensibly benign projects like sanitation and colonial medicine were important cultural dimensions of American colonial power in the Philippines" (Go 2008, 6). Brass band music in the Philippines shared the musical language of the colonizer and as such represented a familiar, pleasurable, and congenial exchange between Filipinos and Americans, momentarily relieving social tensions during the Philippine-American War and highlighting the benefits of benevolent assimilation in the early years of US rule. For Filipinos, military bands established by the US in the Philippines provided the space for band musicians to see themselves as valued, indispensable participants in the new colonial context, as they had been for centuries under Spanish rule. Unlike other state technologies implemented by the colonial government, military band music did not significantly transform "local ways of life, restructur[e] habits and values, and impos[e] new classificatory schemes" (5); it merely offered another avenue for Filipinos to continue to participate in colonial society as they had done before. Coming from generations of musicians, Filipino bandsmen were already experts at European music and saw themselves as equal if not superior to Americans in this realm; they did not conceive of band music as assimilation to American culture, but rather a continuation of their own native *banda* tradition.

To gain insight into and listen to a native point of view, I take inspiration from Reynaldo Ileto's inquiry into how the masses in the Philippines "actually perceive, in terms of their own experience, the ideas of nationalism and revolution brought from the West" (1998, 4). In *Pasyon and Revolution*, Ileto delves deeply into ways that ordinary people engaged their "own categories of meaning that shaped their perceptions of events and their participation" in mass action. Attending to the ways that ordinary people interpreted the *pasyon* (an epic that narrates the life of Jesus Christ), Ileto highlights how "folk religious traditions and such cultural values as utang na loób and hiya, which usually promote passivity and reconciliation rather than conflict, have latent meanings that can be revolutionary" (1998, 10).[15] The meanings of *pasyon* plays, whether written down or passed on orally, were never fixed, but "rather dependent on social context" and always open to interpretation or argument (18). Using a similar approach, we can begin to bring into focus the ways that the Filipino musicians of the PC Band understood their own performance of Euro-American band repertoire in radically different ways than did American audiences who heard them with an imperial ear.

To listen to and for Filipino authenticity, then, we must turn to scholars who argue for the numerous ways by which Filipinos and Filipino Americans actively resisted, localized, indigenized, and appropriated the signs, symbols, and ideas of colonizers into their own meanings and actions. The meaning of authenticity must be redefined because it has been deployed for far too long in the racial imagination of whites as a way to obscure and disguise Filipino autonomy, self-determination, and identity. In order for the US to deny its imperial history,[16] Filipino authenticity must be rendered invisible, thereby protecting American exceptionalism and disavowing continued cultural hegemony in the Philippines as well as discrimination of Filipinos in the US. Represented as "mimics," lacking a culture, culturally inauthentic, and internalizing "colonial mentality,"[17] Filipino and Filipino American performers bear the burden of over a hundred years of misrepresentation and prejudice. Scholars like Cannell (1999), Manalansan (2003), Ng (2005), See (2009), Gonzalves (2010), Burns (2013), and Balance (2016), among others, inspired me with innovative and compelling theoretical work to address the ways that Filipino and Filipino American creative labor demands to be heard, seen, acknowledged, and celebrated.

Several scholars challenge a definition of imitation that has been deployed to substantiate the idea that Filipino performers are simply mimicking or simulating American culture, proof of a "colonial mentality" that regards American culture as superior. Writing about nationalist dramas, Rafael argues that "mimicry acquires a value different from that assigned to it by colonial sources in relation to native 'characteristics'" (1993, 209). Mimicry in what colonizers called "seditious" plays becomes "a sign of acute, even ironic, self-consciousness geared toward acting out historical narratives that ran counter to official versions" (1993, 209). Lucy Mae San Pablo Burns criticizes the logic of how imitation is identified and analyzed through a concept of *puro arte* that "interrupts the original/copy dichotomy and proffers a more supplementary form of analyzing acts of, and at times those read as, imitation" (2013, 13). In her treatment of adept Filipino dancers in taxi dance halls of the 1920s and '30s, Burns argues that the "splendid dancing" and "dazzling performance" of waltzes and foxtrots by Filipino men in America served as a "profound spectacle of colonial mimicry" (58) to Americans. In the dance hall, Filipinos empowered themselves through dance, making their bodies "splendid" and smooth, in contrast to the "mute Filipino worker's body that is contained, exhausted, and made to perform monotonous physical labor" (64). Rendering their kinesthetic abilities as colonial mimicry, therefore, was a strategy of ideological disciplining that served to delimit their masculinity and sexual prowess:[18] "The Filipino body's smooth gliding across the dance floor was inseparable from the growing threats of miscegenation and contagion" (65). Filipinos were characterized as mimics of American dance rather than skilled dancers because their "mastery of 'Occidental ways' equally enacted the worst nightmare of those who had foreseen the effects of the conquest of the Philippines" (58). The immigrant laborers' success in American dance forms did not inspire social or cultural acceptance, nor did it provide a sense of belonging in American culture. It became instead "troublesome, overly visible, exceeding, as it were, the assigned script of Filipinos as docile US colonial subjects" (7), which further "enhanced Filipino difference and contributed to the hostility toward Filipinos" (58). A mimicking body, an imitative performance, or a derivative form are never what the "authentic" original is, nor original by themselves. Rendering the dancers as skilled mimics caused them to appear in excess of the white American original and norm; made hyper-visible and spectacle, Filipinos became worthy of ridicule. In this way, "the very markers that make Filipinos visible are also the very signs that make impossible their acceptability in and belonging to American political, social and cultural fabric" (58). The PC Band's remarkable performances of civilized music exceeded comfortable narratives about Filipino savages in need of colonial rule, and thus their representations as "little brown brothers" and "natural musicians" served to contain this breach and allowed audiences to enjoy their music-making with a disengaged engagement.

Fenella Cannell's work on gay beauty pageants in the Philippines provides a powerful analysis of the ways that performers engage mimicry to critique social and cultural domination. She emphasizes the creativity of transvestite beauty contestants as more than just imitation in the ways they appeared as, or "even better" than, women (1995, 245). They transform not only their appearance, but also their lives when, for the moment on stage, "the *bakla* [gay] are beautiful and elated, and the audience is elated with them and caught in their triumphant beauty" (247). On the surface, while beauty contestants may seem to approximate or imitate Western aesthetics of feminized beauty filtered through Manila's mainstream media, this process resonates deeply with older Southeast Asian modes of appropriation that capture the outside or the foreign and domesticate it into local meanings (249). Furthermore, Cannell argues that the standards of American glamor are not always valued as superior and are often critiqued and kept at a "distance by constantly pointing at its incongruity in the lives of 'those who have nothing'" (251). Martin F. Manalansan's work on Filipino *bakla* who cross-dress in New York's Santacruzan festival analyzes how mimicry "fully exposes the ambivalence on which it is founded" (2003, 140). Rather than serve as an act of assimilation indicative of "colonial mentality," mimicry is transformed "from mere simulacrum to a strategy that questions colonial and postcolonial power" by confiscating the "feminine ideal as object of scrutiny and spectacle into a vital medium in negotiating the interplay of difference, borders, and hierarchies" (140). By creatively engaging in imitation and transforming images of feminine beauty in America, Filipino *bakla* who cross-dress actively problematize American cultural hegemony and open other avenues of identification. Mimicry "articulated an aesthetics that engaged other forms of 'distance' with the white hegemonic world and realigned their relationships to other groups such as the home country and Latino and black gay men" (140). Transformation of self-identity and critique of negative stereotypes and images here are important for performers, because offstage, *bakla* are "not always treated as persons of equal dignity," but onstage, they become objects of beauty (Cannell 1999, 214). In these ways, the value and meaning of mimicry is transformed into empowerment and authenticity by challenging the domination of social, cultural, gender, and racial norms.

Similarly, Stephanie Ng (2005) argues that imitation by Filipino cover band musicians is creative labor, not passive replication, as heard by an imperial ear. Filipino cover bands profit from their abilities to perfectly imitate Western singers, and they enjoy some privilege by being identified as *Filipino* in five-star hotels throughout Asia. Rather than be regarded as inauthentic, Filipino cover band musicians are advertised as providing *authentic* representations of the voice quality and singing styles of great singers like Whitney Houston (Ng 2005, 275). While Filipinos must be "'unoriginal' in their singing in order to sound like the 'original'" (275), they put many hours of practice and creativity into perfecting not only the lyrics, harmonies, and rhythms of the songs themselves, but also a particular artist's vocal quality and timbre, inflections, accents and annunciations, breathing techniques, and even facial and bodily movements (123–24). Imitation is purposeful and takes much creative labor and skill. Ng urges us to look beyond their repertoire of Western pop music and the conventions of cover band performance to hear Filipino creativity in the performance process. Indexing only the elements of the music itself as the primary way to perceive and mark cultural difference, and thus define a cohesive cultural identity, misses the authenticity and creative labor of these expert performers. When analyzed in these ways, the PC Band's mastery of Euro-American repertoire critiqued the representation of both Filipinos and Blacks as incapable of achieving the hallmarks of civilization in music. For example, when Sousa conducted the PC Band playing his famous march "Stars and Stripes Forever," he declared, "When I closed my eyes, I thought it was the U.S. Marine Band playing" (quoted in Flores 1976, 75). The PC Band's work to prove that they were civilized by flawlessly capturing the playing style of US Marine Band, however, was heard as imitation and co-opted by an imperial ear to indicate the success of benevolent assimilation and colonial tutelage.

In her compelling approach to abstract art, Sarita See states that "Filipino American artists have forestalled critics' raced tendency to evaluate their work purely on the basis of content, i.e., the figural representation of brown bodies" (2009, xxv). She intimately links political matters with performance practice by stating that, because the "American empire constitutively forgets that it is an empire, it offers neither space nor speech for the exploration of its post/colonial cultures" (xvii). In this way, it is "nearly impossible for Filipino America to articulate its history of multiple colonialisms and racial subjugation" (xvii), which often leads to misunderstanding Filipinos' engagement of and with mimicry. For example, See brings to light the genius of comedian Rex Navarrete's use of Pilipino accents in English to create translingual puns, wordplay, and bicultural jokes that critique American double standards and the "illogical irregularity of English-language spelling" in words such as *manslaughter*, which enigmatically contains the word *laughter* (76–78). In this way, the colonized "exploit gaps and flaws in colonial rule opened by this foundational lawlessness. Encoded in the jokes and laughter of the colonized and in other socially acceptable forms of aggression is the threat of anticolonial insurrection leading to the death of the colonizer" (78). Navarrete creates community among Filipinos in the diaspora through laughter, using a Pilipino accent to articulate their experiences and thus creating a "language for and of Filipino America" (79). Innovative analyses by these scholars bring to light the inventive ways that Filipino and Filipino American performances evade and circumvent rigid definitions of authenticity and creativity that routinely undervalue and misrecognize their artistic contributions.

To decode, uncover, and reveal authentic Filipino artistic expression in the PC Band's performances, I engage with critical ways that scholars approach Filipino and Filipino American performance and suggest my own analytical approaches. I am intrigued by what Christine Balance calls a "method of disobedient listening," through which "we are able to move through and beyond preoccupations with authenticity by listening against and beyond the dominant discourses that continuously constrain and narrow our understanding of the sonic and musical in Filipino America" (2016, 4). Rather than define, delimit, and catalog the elements of a cohesive—and thus elusive—"Filipino music," I am more interested in the crucial ways that Deborah Wong "shifts the focus from categories to processes" (2004, 11). Since the trope of natural musical ability and the moniker "little brown men" endlessly coded the PC Band musicians' music-making as subordinate to whites', thus "enact[ing] historical memories of subjectivation and injury," like Wong, I choose to "rescue those memories by refashioning their labor as cultural work" (170). Throughout this book, I delve deeply into the political and cultural representation of Filipinos and, in related ways, Black Americans, at the intersection of music, racialization, and imperialism through close readings of reviews of the PC Band's performances in the US and the Philippines in a variety of concert venues and contexts. I interpret the perspectives of Loving and the Filipino bandsmen whenever possible, guided by Loving's letters, interviews with the bandsmen's family members,[19] the work of musicians and scholars, and my own experience as a descendent of one of the band members, a trained classical musician, and an ethnomusicologist.

From Stories to History

I first heard about the PC Band and Loving through the personal stories of my maternal grandmother, Irene Navarro Gamalinda. When I was a child, she visited us in Boston from the Philippines and often reminded me that her father was a famous band conductor who toured the concert halls of the United States and garnered praise from the likes of President Taft and John Philip Sousa. I heard the stories so frequently, and recited in exactly the same way, that I often braced myself in anticipation of the climactic moment when my grandmother's emphatic voice crescendoed to full force, her words punctuated by a crooked finger waving in the air as if she was conducting a grand opera. "My *father*, Captain Pedro B. Navarro," she proclaimed, "became the first Filipino conductor of the world-famous Philippine Constabulary Band!" Then, she launched into a legend about the PC Band that is well-known among musicians, scholars, and descendants: "When they were playing at the St. Louis World's Fair, someone tried to sabotage the Filipinos by putting off the lights; it was so dark that they could not even see, but they kept playing from memory. Oh, how the Americans cheered for the Filipinos! They were so impressed that they gave my father a bronze medal for his piccolo solo in the *William Tell* Overture." (I will discuss this legend further in chapters 2 and 5.) She added that "the great John Philip Sousa said that the PC Band was the best band he ever heard." Her face beamed with pride, and my disbelief transformed into admiration for the musicians' determination and triumph in the face of adversity.

As incredible as it was, this was not the end of her fantastic story. She added, "The conductor, Colonel Loving, was a Black American. He was a very good leader to the musicians. When he retired, they had a farewell concert for him at the Luneta [Park] in front of all the Americans and Filipinos. In the middle of 'Auld Lang Syne,' Colonel Loving handed the baton to my father, who finished conducting the piece. It was then that my father took over as the first Filipino conductor of the PC Band." As a skeptical teenager during the 1980s, I thought this story sounded impossible, because I had never learned anything about the United States' involvement in the Philippines in school. What were Americans doing there in the first place? How did a Black American become the leader of a famous Philippine band so *long ago*? How could the histories of the Philippines and the United States be so intertwined, yet my American friends knew nothing of the Philippines? How was it that my great-grandfather came to the United States so many times when it was expensive and difficult for Filipinos to travel here? How could John Philip Sousa, someone I read about in history books, have complimented my great-grandfather personally? In my experience, American society had so few positive things to say about either Filipinos or Blacks, that to me, my grandmother's story seemed implausible. Two decades would pass before I entered graduate school to pursue ethnomusicology and learn about the historical context and theoretical frameworks that would provide me with tools to interrogate my grandmother's stories further.

Having immigrated to the United States before kindergarten, I did not know very much about the land in which I was born, nor did I learn much about the Philippines in school, except for the fact that some "hostile natives" killed the great explorer Ferdinand Magellan. Occasionally, I saw news about the Philippines on television, filled with images of impoverished children digging for food on an enormous garbage heap called Smokey Mountain. These clips and sound bites depicting the Philippines as poor and backward were familiar to some Americans, but the role of the United States in the condition of the Philippines was not. I wanted to understand this entangled history and, in a larger sense, my place in it as an American of Filipino heritage, but I had no resources to pursue my questions. I was fortunate that my Tita Aida and her husband, the late Edward S. Kasman,[20] who taught at University of Santo Tomas, came to live with us in Boston when I was in high school. He explained to me that the Philippines was a colony of the United States from 1898 to 1946, and that the reason I was growing up in a place so far away from "home" was the historically asymmetrical relationship between the two nations. Facing a shortage of medical professionals in the late 1960s and early 1970s, the United States encouraged doctors like my parents from English-speaking countries to immigrate to the United States. Yet, these immigrants scattered around the US often felt unwelcome and faced prejudice.

Talk of the Philippines in the US news suddenly became more frequent. In 1983, Benigno S. Aquino Jr. was assassinated after returning to Manila from a brief exile in America. He had been living in Boston among our community since 1980, when he underwent heart bypass surgery and received research grants from Harvard University and the Massachusetts Institute of Technology.[21] My family and I met him briefly at a picnic held for Filipino Americans living scattered across New England. As a young person, however, I did not understand his role in Philippine politics. When he was assassinated at the hand of President Marcos's military dictatorship, our small community felt outraged and quickly mobilized to protest his killing. I want to acknowledge their stories and input into my queries about the Philippines and how their politicization shaped the way that I viewed this history and developed my own ideas about what it meant to be a Filipino in America. Thus, my journey began into studying Philippine history, investigating the relationship between the United States and the Philippines, and trying to understand how Filipino Americans fit into American society. By doing so, I began to uncover my own family history in this mix.

What started from my grandmother's narrations about her famous father has become a fascinating personal journey for me as an ethnomusicologist and a scholar. As a musician myself, I chose musical performance as the main site to examine the intersection of racialization and imperialism, and to understand domination, resistance, and transformation in relation to Philippine and US history and culture. I was compelled to do this work because I wanted to understand how these early formations shaped Filipinos' identities and representations in the larger context of American culture and how they continue to inform the ongoing interaction between the two, especially in the realm of music. I feel that these early formations still profoundly structure the dynamics between the Philippines and the US in the time period in which I find myself living. In these ways, my book contributes to the literature, history, and knowledge about the Philippines and Filipinos, and along with many scholars of the Philippines, challenges prevailing notions of Filipinos' lack of authenticity to provide a deeper understanding of their artistic and historic contributions.

Overview of Chapters

In the first chapter, I discuss the significance of colonial military bands in European colonies and argue that the Philippine context was unique. European music in the Philippines under Spanish colonialism evolved within a colonial structure but developed into its own tradition under colonial rule; in many ways, *banda* (the Filipino band tradition) continued under the United States and did not disappear. The military band, as an instrument of empire, was an avenue that was open to Filipino musicians, who capitalized on its economic benefits and social prestige because of their already existing experience and expertise in band music. Even while they were integrated into the US colonial apparatus, the Filipino bandsmen, like Black soldiers, strategized within the colonial contact zone in order to thrive, albeit with limited agency in a tightly controlled and highly policed setting. When Loving and other segregated Black soldiers arrived, they struggled to uphold their positions as combatants fighting other "colored people" while confronting racism in the military. Loving's talents in music provided him with a unique opportunity to rise to fame, because military band music formed a welcome bridge to ease tensions between Filipinos and Americans, and possibly Blacks and whites, in the contact zone of US-occupied Manila.

In the second chapter, I analyze and interpret newspaper accounts of the PC Band's participation in the 1904 St. Louis World's Fair to understand how the PC Band was contextualized within the Philippine Exhibit as proof of the benefits of colonial rule. Filipino military men in the Philippine Constabulary and Philippine Scouts and their respective bands were purposefully juxtaposed geographically, temporally, symbolically, and in the case of music, aurally, with the "savages" from the Philippines to justify continued US involvement in the Philippines. The influential work of Robert Rydell on world's fairs (1984) helped me to understand how ideologies, imperialism, American identity, and racialization were expressed in and through these turn-of-the century popular spectacles in which the PC Band was a prominent feature. Paul Kramer's work (1999) elucidated the varying agendas of fair organizers, colonial agents, anti-imperialists, scientists, and the Philippine Exposition board. Fairs were not monolithic undertakings, and neither fair organizers nor US government officials were always in control of the messages they wanted audiences to absorb. American colonialists' framing of Filipino military men and the PC Band as assimilated but subordinate subjects was not always successful in binding them to their proper place in the racial hierarchy. The band members and Loving traversed some of these racial-social boundaries, but their successful performances never emancipated them from domination, nor were they regarded as socially equal with whites, even though there were moments that they came dangerously close. The St. Louis World's Fair profoundly influenced the ways that Filipinos were racialized in the media, and in subsequent performances this shaped the way American audiences heard Filipino music-making with an imperial ear. American showmen continued to exhibit and exploit the "Igorrotes," tribal people of Cordillera region, for profit for almost two decades after the fair (see Prentice 2014), sustaining malicious stereotypes of Filipinos as headhunters and dog-eaters. This book argues that, in addition to these negative representations, seemingly positive characterizations about Filipinos' natural musicality, introduced in the US by the tours of the PC Band during the same time period, also served the purpose of denigrating Filipinos.

In the third chapter, I investigate the PC Band's participation in Taft's 1909 presidential inauguration, their tour of major American cities, and finally the Alaska-Yukon-Pacific Exposition in Seattle, Washington. Representations of the PC Band in the press contended with images created at the 1904 St. Louis Fair, and newspapers proclaimed that the band would change the public's erroneous view of Filipinos as "savages." Newspapers explained that the Filipino bandsmen were natural musicians made into superb band musicians by "benevolent" assimilation, but safely subordinated, at least socially and racially, as "little brown men." During his inauguration, President Taft literally paraded the PC Band as evidence of his success in the Philippines and his worthiness as the United States' leader. By contrast, elite African Americans in Washington, DC, chose to highlight Loving's position as the leader of the band and as a military officer as confirmation of the possibilities and successes of racial uplift. On the band's tour of symphony halls in major cities such as Boston, New York, Chicago, and San Francisco, newspapers made sense of the Filipino musicians and Loving in novel ways to ensure that racialized others were contained and subordinated, allowing audiences to enjoy and praise their performances of Euro-American band repertoire. Most often, newspapers erased or obscured Loving's identity as a Black person and cast the bandsmen as "little brown men," while expressing great enthusiasm for the band's superb performances with a "disengaged engagement." Nevertheless, doubts about the PC Band's musical skills persisted, and in

Boston, audiences subjected the PC Band to a series of test compositions to prove that they could sight-read music and were not simply mimicking music by ear (*Boston Globe*, March 21, 1909, p. 39). Knowledge of reading music, especially at first sight and without practice, was proof of the highest level of musical education, knowledge, and ability. When the musicians proved themselves capable, newspapers explained the band's success as the outcome of American tutelage of Filipinos' natural musical talent, attempting to reconcile the breach of racial hierarchy with stark evidence to the contrary.

The PC Band's participation at the Panama-Pacific International Exposition in 1915, the focus of chapter 4, provides a critical glimpse into the Filipino bandsmen's agency. At first, they refused to make trip because of insufficient pay, showing that their main concern was not to glorify the flag of the United States or the colonial Philippines. Filipino nationalists pointed to the PC Band's performances to argue that Filipinos were indeed civilized enough for self-rule and must be awarded their independence. The ways that both American colonialists and Filipino nationalists represented the PC Band's performances were not accidental or incidental; they were intimately connected to changes in politics over time and the agenda of politicians.

The last chapter extends beyond the time period on which the bulk of the book is focused. The PC Band, now renamed the Philippine Army Band, returned to the United States twenty-four years after the last tour, with only Loving as one of the original members since its founding in 1902 and its first trip in 1904. Loving spent years in retirement in the US before returning to the Philippines in 1938, at insistence of then president of the Philippine Commission Manuel L. Quezon, to revive and prepare the PC Band for the 1939 Golden Gate International Exposition. Loving was promoted to lieutenant colonel in the Philippine Army and was already a legend in the Philippines. By this time, the US no longer needed to legitimize the colonization of the Philippines, and Taft, the PC Band's strongest American supporter, was long dead. Filipino nationalists like Quezon deployed the band to demonstrate Filipino achievement and capacity for self-rule as the Philippines headed toward independence, and Filipino communities in California sought out the band as a way to transform negative attention toward Filipino male laborers and Filipinos in general. To Filipino bandsmen who made the final trip with Loving to the US, the Golden Gate International Exposition in San Francisco, near Loving's town of residence in Oakland, was incredibly meaningful and personal. Interviews with PC

Band (PA Band) members who went to San Francisco with Loving in 1939, the only existing firsthand accounts by the bandsmen themselves, reveal that they characterized their performances much differently than the way that American audiences heard them.[22] Their excellence in Euro-American music was not an expression of American patriotism, but proof of their own personal and professional mastery and musical skill in a *banda* tradition that Filipinos sustained and supported for several generations without American influence. To me, this demonstrates that a Philippine brass band tradition did not cease to exist under US colonization, but rather continued to develop, grow, and flourish beyond the Philippines.[23]

In addition to scholarly and archival sources, my personal connection as the great-granddaughter of Capt. Navarro, assistant conductor to Loving from 1905 to 1915, allowed me to access first-person accounts about Loving and Navarro. Sadly, neither man kept written diaries or written accounts of their personal experiences on their tours, but nevertheless, I found a few rich sources of ethnographic accounts that I interpret in creative and critical ways. Much like the approach of William Henry Scott who, in *Cracks in the Parchment Curtain* (1982), read extant Spanish colonial documents against the grain of colonial domination, I uncover moments of native transgression, agency, and triumph in a musical form that was heard by most Americans with an imperial ear as an acquiescence to colonial rule and the inevitable assimilation of Filipino culture by American cultural hegemony.

1

Instruments of Empire: Brass Bands, Black Soldiers, and American Imperialism in the Philippines

Military brass bands are musical ensembles that communicate ideas and sentiments about the nation they represent. The nation's military character is conveyed visually though the size of the ensemble, the glint of powerful, modern brass instruments, the strict code of dress, and the precise, coordinated movements of band members under the direction of an officer. Military music compositions, like many national anthems, including "The Star-Spangled Banner,"[1] typically contain elegant, stately melodies supported by conventional Western harmonic progressions that are enhanced by the swell of sound to a loud but controlled expression of patriotism's emotional force, driven by heroic rhythmic gestures and punctuated by the crash of cymbals. Outdoors, sound waves from the powerful brass and drums can be felt viscerally by those in the crowd, enhancing the emotional force of self-affirming pride in the nation. For example, the US Marine Band playing for presidential inaugurations and Independence Day is an iconic part of American patriotic celebrations. Patriotic marches like "The Stars and Stripes Forever," "God Bless America," and "My Country, 'Tis of Thee" enculturate Americans to connect music and musical sound to expressions and feelings of patriotism. Military brass bands like the US Marine Band are rooted in European aesthetics of military band performance, an influence that made its way to the United States by the nineteenth century.

Centuries earlier, however, the earliest military bands appeared in India and the Middle East. During the twelfth century, Ottoman Turks deployed *mehter* (military) bands with loud horns, drums, and cymbals in battle to spread fear among their enemies (Suppan and Suppan 2001, 684). By the seventeenth century, European armies employed ensembles of drum, fife, and pipe in the field, as well as larger ensembles with additional wind and brass instruments for social and ceremonial functions (685). A worldwide brass band movement burst forth during the nineteenth century, and the ensemble became an iconic feature of the modern nation (see Herbert 2000 and Smith 2004). In the colonies, European-style military bands played a central role by constructing "an image of empire" that served to "authenticate ideas of authority through military power" (Herbert and Sarkissian 1997, 169). By the late nineteenth century, when Americans arrived in the Philippines, the military band was already a well-established instrument of empire.

In the Philippines, following three centuries of Spanish colonial rule and religious influence, the brass band underwent pronounced localization and existed as a distinct tradition called *banda* by the 1800s. Each regimental unit of the Spanish colonial army included a brass band manned by natives who the Spanish called *indios*, and some of these men were promoted to the prestigious position of Spanish regimental bandmaster (Tan 2014, 62). Respected musicians went on to found numerous civilian town bands that developed rich musical and cultural traditions in their respective communities (Rubio 1977, 4). In the early twentieth century, American imperialists neither introduced the brass band tradition to Filipinos nor radically altered it after colonization in 1898; they simply redirected the *meaning* of the performance of brass bands in the Philippines to portray their uniquely elaborate logic of benevolent rule, tutelage, and assimilation.

Drawing on texts that trace the history of colonial brass bands in the British Empire, I analyze how colonial military bands in the Philippines were deployed to symbolize the benefits and benevolence of American rule. Then, I provide an account of European music in the Philippines to establish that it was a language and tradition with which Filipinos already had a long history before US rule. Hence, Filipino band musicians easily fit into the culture of US military bands and excelled in the repertoire and performance style, offering a way for them to envision their role as valued members of colonial society. After connecting the history of brass bands in the Philippines and Americans' hegemonic redirection of the meaning of military bands, I bring into this dialogue the specific context of Black American soldier-musicians in the Philippines. Doing so elucidates how Walter H. Loving attained recognition in the context of segregation and racism in the US military to become the perfect public figure to lead America's premiere colonial military band. While this specific context makes the PC Band unique, the band's performances were meant to purvey and indoctrinate "civilized" Western values among native populations, similar to other colonial military bands in European empires. Given that Filipino musicians brought with them exceptional skills in European music, this message was even more effective in the US colonial Philippines in circulating the perception that the PC Band's playing of the patriotic tunes of the colonizer could be equated with Filipinos' enthusiasm and patriotic intent toward the United States, a key feature of the concept of benevolent assimilation. Despite this strong message, I highlight some of the ways that the bandsmen and Loving exercised agency to express their own identities as excellent musicians in their performances.

Military Bands and the Colonial Context

In British India, the military brass band was "a crucial part of the apparatus through which Indian subjects could be impressed by, and British rulers reassured of, the strength and purpose of the imperial enterprise" (Herbert and Barlow 2013, 254). By the mid-1800s, native musicians in India were paid from public funds, evidence that the "provision of military music was important, and that it was accommodated on substantial scale" (265). A booming commercial business in the production of brass instruments produced surpluses of secondhand army instruments in Britain that were sent overseas (Herbert and Sarkissian 1997, 170). In the tropical climates of many colonies, brass instruments were the perfect instruments of empire because they were durable and unaffected by extremes of weather or humidity and symbolized the invincibility and endurance of European culture in the colonies. The sonic strength of the brass instruments supported by percussion was most powerful at outdoor public events, especially before the invention of electric sound amplification, and brass band music created a potent soundscape to draw in listeners. Indeed, "the very adoption of the brass band for public, collective affairs has been frequently attributed to its volume and attention-grabbing capabilities" (Reily and Brucher 2013, 18).

For the colonized, the colonial military band heralded not the independence of their nation, but an imperial power's superiority and authority. The colonial band was a "small-scale metaphor for the colonial process itself—a single foreign bandmaster exerting authority over numerous native bandsmen who were expected to abandon their traditional ways of making music in favour of more 'civilised' European ways" (Herbert and Sarkissian 1997, 172). The superiority and domination of European culture seemed to be accepted by the natives themselves when they adopted the colonizer's musical language, their uniforms, and the bodily comportment of the European military band aesthetic. This symbolized not only subjugation, but also assimilation to European values, projecting a future directed by Western modernity and progress. Colonial military bands were most visible in official ceremonies of the colonial state, where music was used "as a means of demonstrating and disseminating their values, particularly European notions of order and discipline" (170). In this way, the colonial military band was not only a political expression, but a cultural one that had a formidable impact among the populace through its sound, repertoire, and appearance.

But this is only a partial account of the story. Despite the tradition's veneer of European superiority, skilled native musicians found brass instruments and military march music relatively easy to play, and they learned the repertoire quickly (Herbert and Sarkissian 1997, 167). Rather than being mastered by Western music, native musicians mastered it quite easily, and by playing along with this arrangement, native men seemed to give their consent to foreign rule and demonstrate a high degree of assimilation to the colonizing power. If we look closely, however, we might see that the white bandmaster and the native musicians were not segregated completely but rather required to work together toward a common goal. If we listen critically, we might hear a successful musical performance that depended on the effort and skill of the native musicians working in collaboration with the white bandmaster. Musically, each individual had to "play his part" in the collective, whether he was a soloist or one of several instrumentalists in a section, to follow a leader that kept the group together. As an ensemble of skilled musicians, "much of their sonic impact is predicated upon the mobilization of a group of people for collective musicking" (Reily and Brucher 2013, 17). "Musicking," according to Christopher Small, is an "activity in which all those present are involved and for whose nature and quality, success or failure, everyone present bears some responsibility" (1998, 10). Native musicians and European bandmasters had to collaborate seamlessly and equally to achieve musical unity and to convey a sense of enthusiasm and excitement to the crowd, presenting the possibilities of successful colonial partnership.

At public concerts and parades, music could be enjoyed communally across otherwise segregated sectors of society, albeit in socially complicated ways. For colonized audiences, bands provided an "uplifting element when it was sorely needed and unlikely to transpire from any other source" (Herbert and Barlow 2013, 243). For colonialists, military bands "enliven[ed] the social life of officers and maintain[ed] the morale of the rank and file" (241). For both colonizer and colonized, band performances broke up the monotony of daily life and released tensions between social groups. The exciting sound and the creation of collective effervescence was not necessarily an indication of the enthusiasm of colonized people for colonial domination, but represented the possibilities of affable collaboration and the natives' own success at mastering European music.

Colonial bands represented a newly configured social order taking shape under colonial rule, including the possibility of modernization, especially to those who were marginalized in their precolonial societies. In many cases, though certainly not all, native musicians came not from a single ethnic group or "tribe," but rather were brought together as multiethnic participants (Herbert and Sarkissian 1997, 173). This unifying of diverse people into a single organization was in and of itself an expression of modernity, because it radically diverged from traditional ethnic, social, and political divisions. European brass band music became the lingua franca of diverse cultural and linguistic groups to communicate and express colonial modernity breaking away from customary, restrictive social norms. As modern expressions, brass bands became highly esteemed in the colony, and local rulers "quickly adopted both the military band and the notion of it as a symbol of royal status" (171). Soon enough, brass band ensembles were localized into native cultures, long before the independence of colonized nations. The agency of musicians and audiences resulted in the "huge diversity of hybrid forms to be found within the global brass band complex" (Reily and Brucher 2013, 16), and many of these localized forms of brass band music, repertoire, and cultural context continue to thrive today (see Boonzajer Flaes 2000). For the native musician, joining a colonial military band was a way to gain employment and recognition in ways that were restricted before colonization.

For audiences, music enlivened daily life, enhanced festivities and celebrations, and modeled collaboration between colonizer and colonized as well as between local groups. Following de Certeau's (1984) assessment of how space is transformed by how people utilize it, Reily and Brucher assert that "bands can transform places into spaces and spaces into places, continuously actualizing spaces during their performances and identifying places through their presence" (2013, 18). Unlike the Ottoman *mehter* band, whose purpose was to scare and threaten enemies with its volume of sound, brass band performances in European colonies created spaces for collaboration between disparate groups. Small argues that the "act of musicking establishes in the place where it is happening a set of relationships, and it is in those relationships that the meaning of the act lies" (1998, 13). The "meaning of the act," however, is contingent on the context of time and place, is subject to change, and is often shaped by the perspectives of the powers that be. The agency of native musicians and local audiences must be analyzed in what James C. Scott refers to as "hidden transcripts" embedded in the "manifold strategies by which subordinate groups manage to insinuate their resistance, in disguised forms, into the public transcript" (1990, 136), since the official voices of "many historically important subordinate groups [are] irrecoverable for all practical purposes" and their acts of agency are "muted and veiled" (138). I will return to this theme of hidden transcripts within representations of the PC Band's performances by newspapers and international expositions throughout this work.

In the Philippines, the appearance of collaboration and assimilation between colonizer and colonized was much easier to achieve since the natives were already experts at band music and thus could be presented as exceedingly adaptable to American ways. The language of European music through the Catholic Church was already the norm among the populace of lowland Christian Luzon, and few sonic traces of indigenous music endured in these cultures.[2] The already entrenched tradition of *banda* (brass band) music in the Philippines made a superficial transition to American military band style, itself heavily drawing on and defined by European models. In this milieu, it only appeared as if Filipinos wholly adopted Euro-American brass band music because obvious sonic markers of indigenous Filipino culture were invisible or at least inaudible to the imperial ear. Evidence of distinct local practices in *banda*, Philippine brass band performance, is inaudible when regarding musical sound as the only manifestation of cultural distinctiveness. As I discuss below and throughout this book, Filipino distinctiveness existed not in the musical composition itself, but rather in performance style, as well as conceptualization of and meaning-making within, the language of military band music.

European Music in the Philippines

Hundreds of years before the arrival of the United States, starting in the sixteenth century, Spanish religious institutions taught and disseminated European music in the Philippines. D. R. M. Irving's book *Colonial Counterpoint: Music in Early Modern Manila* examines in rich detail the imposition of European music by the Spanish and its integration into local traditions by indigenous musicians. While European religious music was compulsory and enforced by the Catholic Church, Irving's central argument was that Spanish colonialism did not simply wipe out indigenous music among Christianized populations in Luzon, but that a flourishing native musical tradition emerged out of Manila's cosmopolitan, global milieu. Irving insists, "If we are to begin to understand the globalization of musics, we need to examine its history, and return to where it all started in 1571: Manila" (2010, 8). Manila, as the Spanish Philippines' colonial capital, was "the missing link in the concatenation of mercantile, political, and intellectual enterprises that characterized the emergence of a global consciousness and global networks in the early modern period" (8). Piecing together extant archival material from the late sixteenth century to the end of the eighteenth century, Irving explains that there was a gradual assimilation of European musical forms into indigenous music-making as well as an accommodation of indigenous practices by Spanish authorities. While Spaniards banned most indigenous practices, they had to allow some elements to continue: "European missionaries censored and modified [indigenous musicians'] song-texts and composed many new works, actively encouraging [them] to 'forget' precolonial non-Christian practices. European dances and dance music were introduced, and indigenous dances were retained but performed to European music" (235). In addition to allowing some indigenous forms of dance to continue, the Spanish used the melody, harmony, and form of European music to accompany indigenous musicopoetic genres called *auit*, *loa*, and *pasyon*. Irving argues that these poetic forms with European musical accompaniment "enabled the assertion of an indigenous musical identity within the cultural framework of Roman Catholicism" (235). These dispensations resulted in hybridized practices, not, as many believe, the complete eradication of indigenous expression or creativity. If there had been a complete eradication of content and form, practice and performance, and ritual and social meaning, native musicians would not have been able to adapt, thrive, and engage creatively in a new musical language and culture.

The willing participation of indigenous musicians and the hybridizing of indigenous musicopoetic forms with European-style music encouraged the Filipino population to accept, practice, and make their own new musical sounds. This was not blind acceptance, nor always by choice, since "violence played a part in pedagogic methods" in forcibly putting to a "stop music- and merry-making" lest it become "too much of a diversion among some Filipino communities" (Irving 2010, 111). Nevertheless, indigenous expression by native musicians and music-makers survived in and around new hybridized forms: the "collaboration of indigenous musicians themselves played an important part in the extent of Western music's diffusion, given that there was a relatively small number of missionaries and a large number of indigenous parochial musicians" (235). European music was not just an imposition—it was localized by the creativity and resilience of Filipinos themselves.

The infusion of European music into the everyday lives of the masses and the transformation of indigenous elements and practices to Hispanicized and European forms developed into distinct Filipino practices in religious rituals, ceremonies, and celebrations. For example, the religious procession is still a vital part of Filipino life and has deep religious and cultural meaning that syncretizes Spanish and indigenous practices from centuries ago. An early account of a religious celebration by Murillo Velarde describes a procession of Our Lady of Peace and of Good Voyage (the Virgin of Antipolo) when it arrived in Manila on a galleon in 1748.[3] Nearly all of Spanish society greeted the statue at the beach, along with masses of Filipinos, bringing together an otherwise segregated society for a mutual celebration in which music was a vital component. Activities lasting for several days included many types of musical performances, from choirs to orchestras and band ensembles. During the eighteen-kilometer procession of the statue, a band of "drums, horns, and clarions"[4] emitted "joyful warlike harmonies" punctuated by the "continuous shots of the fireworks" (Velarde, quoted in Irving 2010, 220). Bands were adept at marching in musical processions, but Filipino musicians were also capable of performing concert programs in more intimate settings. Inside the church, "arias, recitatives, fugues, graves, and all other variety of genres [were performed in] good taste.... Many wind and string instruments were played with delicacy.... And without difficulty the two serenatas could have earned applause in any large European city" (Velarde, quoted in Irving 2010, 221). Considered in these ways, musicians and native participants were crucial actors in the transplanting and growth of European music in the Philippines, not simply the victims of extensive and absolute assimilation. Reading and listening against the grain for "hidden transcripts" allows us to dismantle the orientation of our imperial ears and hear the contributions and voices of these musicians. Musical processions and concerts were part of the centuries-old musical life of Filipinos, and these traditions contribute to understanding the extraordinary musical heritage of PC Band musicians.

By the nineteenth century, European classical music was not only taught in the Catholic Church, but also in boys' colleges, normal schools for boys, Ateneo de Manila University, the University of Santo Tomas, the Beaterio colleges for girls, and also privately (Irving 2010, 119). Conservatory-style training was available through the Colegio de Niños Tiples at the Manila Cathedral, which has been "cited by a number of histories of Manila and the Philippines as being of seminal importance in the growth of music schools in the country" (168). Founded in 1742, the cathedral had been operating in Manila for 150 years before the arrival of American rule (169). It adopted a "curriculum similar to that followed by the Conservatory of Music and Declamation in Madrid" and taught "vocalization, harmony, piano, violin, and organ" (Bañas 1975, 111). Music historian Raymundo C. Bañas points out that this predecessor of music conservatories in Manila was established well before other famous conservatories, such as the Conservatorium at Leipzig, Germany, the Royal Academy of Music in London, and the New England Conservatory of Music in Boston (113). Music in the Philippines was regularly infused with the newest trends from Europe: "A plentiful and regular supply of missionaries arriving from Spain and Latin America represented new musical entries to the contrapuntal texture of colonial Philippines" (Irving 2010, 193). *Ilustrados* (educated Filipino elite who studied in Europe) brought back to the Philippines the latest news about the musical scene in Europe.

Many of the musicians who formed the PC Band would have been quite familiar with European opera, which included the numerous overtures that the band regularly performed in its repertoire. Opera was so popular in nineteenth-century Manila that opera companies from Europe frequently toured the Philippines. An English operetta company presented *Lucia di Lammermoor* on November 26, 1886, at the Tondo Theater; an Italian opera company presented the same opera in 1888; and another visiting troupe performed Verdi's *Aida* in the same year. A French opera company came to Manila in 1893 and returned in 1897, and a Spanish zarzuela company performed in 1899. While these performances employed opera singers from Europe, Filipino musicians accompanied them and furnished the instrumental music (Bañas 1975, 201). Opera overtures were an important part of the repertoire of many professional concert brass bands during the nineteenth and early twentieth centuries, and learning this music was central to the musical training of Filipino band musicians.

Besides visiting opera companies, local orchestras were an active part of Manila's musical scene. These included the all-women's orchestra called Orquestra Femenina de Pandacan (founded in 1800), the Gruet Orchestra, the Rizal Orchestra (founded in 1898), the Marikina Orchestra, and many more informal groups (Bañas 1975, 92). Orchestras performed for a popular indigenized form of opera called *sarsuela*, a version of the Spanish zarzuela (Maceda 1973, 224). The four most important genres considered as emblematic of Philippine national music today—*banda, rondalla, sarsuela*, and *kundiman*—evolved not from American times, but from the Spanish colonial period (Trimillos 1973, 19), establishing that Filipinos had a strong tradition in European music and a developed native musical tradition before US colonization.

Several musical and artistic societies flourished in cosmopolitan Manila, such as the Unión Artístico Musical (Artistic-Musical Union) and the Sociedad Musical Filipina de Santa Cecilia (Philippine Musical Association of Saint Cecilia), which played the works of Mendelssohn and Beethoven at Malacañang Palace on March 11, 1892 (Bañas 1975, 151). Filipino elites and intellectuals actively supported operas and concerts by visiting foreign organizations in addition to local ensembles, and local art and literary societies had musical components as part of their activities (see Maceda 1973 and Bañas 1924). Irving writes that the "patronage of church music by Spaniard and Filipino alike allowed for a certain degree of egalitarianism within the otherwise intractably stratified society of Manila" (2010, 193). Not only did European music performance allow for a semblance of social egalitarianism between Spaniards and Filipinos, it also provided upward mobility and interaction between elite mestizos and the non-elite *indios* who were often the musicians.

Native musicians received material and social benefits from the Spanish colonial state and "also unwittingly acted as agents for the reinforcement of the hegemonic authority of Church and Crown over indigenous society" (Irving 2010, 194). Under Spanish rule, an "appointment as a cantor provided the means by which a Filipino musician could become socially mobile and enjoy a greater degree of enfranchisement within colonial society" (189). There were relatively large numbers of paid and privileged musicians in the Philippines, "for [in] no other territory of early modern Asia could there be found such a substantial corpus of professional ecclesiastical musicians literate in European musical practices" (191). Outside the church, town bands provided jobs and opportunities, individual mobility, and elevated social status for non-elite *indios*. It was this milieu of European music and musicians in the Catholic Church, institutions of music education, societies of music, and civilian town bands that provided the foundation for the formation of the Philippine Constabulary Band.

"Banda": Brass Band Tradition in the Philippines

European-style brass bands were introduced to the Philippines in the early eighteenth century by the Spanish army (Rubio 1977, 4). Some native musicians achieved a high status in Spanish regimental bands as bandmasters, positions from which they accumulated social, cultural, and economic capital that extended, even after retirement, to their families (Tan 2014, 65). As early as 1810, native musicians trained in these regimental bands and in church ensembles paved the way for civilian brass bands in towns and provinces (Rubio 1977, 4). Friars identified children, usually boys, with exceptional talent early on and provided them with rigorous formal musical training in places like the Colegio de Niños Tiples (Tan 2014, 68). Young men could join a regimental band at the age of fifteen, and only after an examination could they become apprentices to master musicians. With rigorous training, native musicians developed skills in band music, including orchestration and composition, encompassing a broad range of styles, through the study of works by European composers (69). Strict rules of service and rank existed; for example, one had to serve for at least four years before being approved to continue on, and this process had to be initiated by formal request and was subject to meticulous evaluation (70). The role of bandmaster was highly coveted and very competitive, and thus became highly respected among legions of rank-and-file musicians. This context contrasts sharply with later claims by American newspapers that any Filipino, because of innate, racial musical ability, could be trained by the US to miraculously become an expert in band music performance.

Band musicians passed on their knowledge and sometimes their positions to their sons, and these families became prominent as "musical dynasties that commonly provided the successors" to their posts (Irving 2010, 189). In the nineteenth century, several famous bands founded and directed entirely by Filipinos were renowned, including the Banda Peñaranda from Nueva Ecija founded by Pedro Mercado in 1876 and directed by celebrated composer Apolonio Bernabe in 1888 (Bañas 1975, 107). Other bands famous before the US arrived were the Banda Arevalo of Quiapo and the Banda Pasig of Morong province (now Rizal province). Bands founded by musical families participated in "every rite of a town's existence from birth to baptism, to marriage and death" (de León 1977, 1). During *fiestas* and other celebrations, town bands would play all night in a *banggaan* (Tagalog for "collision") that would frequently expand into the "so-called '*tambakan*,' a duel of bands lasting for several . . . days and nights" (Rubio 1977, 4). Musicians would seat themselves in a circle "where everybody could follow the signs of the '*bombista*' in the center" (4). European-style bands would often be arranged in a semicircle, so these innovations make clear that while European-style music began as an imposition of Spanish rule, it developed into distinctive a Filipino cultural form and practice. Physical and musical prowess were the goals of this masculine competition that lasted well into the twentieth century. Reporting on an incident in which authorities had to put an end to one of these *tambakan* competitions that had been going on for days, an American newspaper explained that "there were no judges of the affair, it being the custom in these contests for the bands to play until one admits defeat, frequently from exhaustion" (*Poughkeepsie Eagle News*, December 16, 1924, p. 8, col. 2). The musicians were required to play hundreds of pieces without the use of scores, even though they could read music, because "playing from memory has been an acquisition of Filipino musicians from Spanish times" (ibid.). This form of native band competition, as I discuss further in chapters 2 and 5, played a crucial role in the legend-making of the PC Band when, during one of their concerts at the 1904 Fair, the lights suddenly went off and the band kept playing in the dark, to the amazement of the audience. While their uninterrupted playing was possible because of their skill and prowess, to the imperial ear, playing pieces from memory seemed to be a magical feat rather than a Filipino localization of band performance in the tradition of the *tambakan*. The ability to read music was considered more civilized than playing by ear, and on several occasions, the Filipino bandsmen were asked to prove if they could read music at all. For example, in 1909, Boston audiences at Symphony Hall demanded that the PC Band sight-read "test compositions" to prove that they were not simply mimicking the playing of music (*Boston Globe*, March 21, 1909, p. 39).

While it is difficult to uncover or recover indigenous responses to impositions of European music from centuries-old Spanish archival material, there are ways to read into hidden transcripts, in the words of James C. Scott, to interpret native perspectives as historian William Henry Scott accomplished in *Cracks in the Parchment Curtain and Other Essays in Philippine History* (1982). He refers to the "parchment curtain" as "the official documents of the Spanish colonial regime which prevent the modern Filipino from forming a clear picture of his ancestors' conditions." This parchment curtain contained cracks, "through which fleeting glimpses of Filipinos and their reactions to Spanish domination may be seen" in the "unintentional and merely incidental" descriptions (1982, 1). The seemingly superficial descriptions of town bands reveal by hidden transcript that their styles, behavior, practices, worldview, and social relations are indeed uniquely Filipino creations, innovations, and practices that show an independent *banda* tradition. European music—its structures of melody, rhythm, harmony, form, and conventional modes of articulation—was rooted in the Philippines for centuries and was not only practiced but also developed and localized by indigenous musicians and ordinary folk well before the arrival of the United States on the country's shores. I will continue to interpret cracks in the reports of American newspapers that reveal hidden transcripts of the PC Band's self-expression and resistance to racial domination.

When the Philippine Scouts and Philippine Constabulary were established by the US, military bands were included within their regiments. As Filipino musicians joined these regimental bands, the aesthetics of Euro-American band performance redirected some stylistic qualities of Filipino *banda*. Filipino music scholar Hilarion F. Rubio describes the renovations in performance style, instrumentation, costume, and repertoire that came about as civilian town bands began to pattern themselves after American military bands. For example, silver and gold-plated American instruments replaced European-brand instruments; wooden piccolos and flutes were discontinued for metal ones; and new Zildjian-brand cymbals replaced Chinese cymbals. Regarding style and practices, Rubio writes,

> Since the advent of the Americans, the Filipino bands had undergone transformations in their uniforms, instrumentation, discipline, performance and music interpretation. The more ornate and clownish uniforms of the Spanish period were changed into simple, elegant ones....
>
> Too much elaborated and ornamented articulation in the playing of yester years are tabooed today. Over-expressive interprobation [sic] and sluggishness in tempo of by-gone days are now substituted by more elegant execution and high-spirited movement. (Rubio 1977, 4)

Rubio's portrayal of how bands transformed after the change of colonial powers captures the perceived benefits of American rule over seemingly idiosyncratic and antiquated Spanish ways. He positions Spanish-style Filipino bands as archaic in dress, playing styles, behavior, instrumentation, and musical aesthetic. Spanish costumes were "clownish" and "ornate," while American ones were "simple" and "elegant." Native developments in playing styles were deemed excessively elaborate, ornamented, and dramatic when juxtaposed with the "modern" style of American of band performance. To Rubio, American tutelage transformed Filipino bands into orderly, disciplined entities embracing the traits of modernity and moving toward the "progress" that America itself idealized and promoted. Adopting American styles was symbolic of twentieth-century modernity, a move away from the outmoded Spanish-influenced past. However, these shifts and changes were only on the surface and did not fundamentally alter the existing Philippine brass band tradition. Read against the grain of Rubio's description, these replacements and renovations reveal a hidden transcript that a distinct brass band tradition existed before Americans' arrival.

The adoption of a "modern" American style and sensibility (an aesthetic that at first seems to be a close mimicking of European performance norms) was not necessarily a rejection of a Hispanicized Filipino tradition; it was partly a necessity. Band musicians, who did not have much artistic or cultural agency under US colonial rule, adapted to the demands of new opportunities. They were likely attracted to the modern approach, which took their tradition in a new direction. For the Filipino musicians of the PC Band, this conflation of modernization and Americanization, I think, was the "buy-in" for adopting the new style, repertoire, instruments, and behavior of American military brass bands. Considered this way, American impositions of their own musical, performance, and cultural conventions resulted in the continuation of the Filipino *banda* in a new stylistic mode, not the tradition's extinction. Filipino collaboration included the agency of Filipino band musicians, because they continued their tradition hand in hand with—and simultaneously limited by—colonial imposition, just as they had under the Spanish. The existence of the *tambakan* (demonstrating musical prowess by playing from memory) into the twentieth century is but a one example of this continuity.[5]

The Philippine-American War, Black Soldiers, and Walter H. Loving

The United States declared war on Spain on April 21, 1898. Under the command of Commodore George Dewey, the US Asiatic Squadron landed in the Philippines on May 1 to defeat the Spanish fleet in Manila Bay. Dewey convinced Aguinaldo and other Filipino revolutionaries that he considered "insurgents as friends, being opposed to a common enemy" (dispatch to US secretary of the Navy John D. Long on June 27, 1898, quoted in Kramer 2006, 94). With an assurance from Dewey that Americans would assist Filipinos to free the Philippines from the Spanish empire, Emilio Aguinaldo returned from exile in Hong Kong and landed in Cavite on May 19 (Kramer 2006, 94). On June 12, 1898, Aguinaldo and revolutionaries declared Philippine independence and issued the Act of the Proclamation of Independence of the Filipino People (95), the culmination of a revolution against Spain that began in 1896.[6] The Philippine flag was unfurled and the national anthem played for the first time (Ignacio et al. 2002, 15). Unwilling to submit to their former colonial subjects, Spain devised a plan to surrender Intramuros, former seat of the Spanish colonial government, to US troops in a mock battle in mid-August. Aguinaldo was warned by the US, "Do not let your troops enter Manila. On this side of the Pasig River, you will be under fire" (quoted in Kramer 2006, 97). Hoping to rally support and recognition for Philippine sovereignty, Aguinaldo sent Felipe Agoncillo to Washington,

DC, and diplomatic emissaries to Paris, seeking Filipino participation in the crafting of the Treaty of Paris (Ignacio et al. 2002, 15). Using a legal-sovereignty argument, Agoncillo claimed that when the United States declared war on Spain, Filipino revolutionaries had already "advanced sufficiently against Spanish forces" and that Spain "had no legal title or right to cede the islands to the United States" (Kramer 2006, 100). During a constitutional convention in Malolos, capital of the new republic, a Philippine Constitution was drafted on September 15, 1898, and approved in January 1899 (Ignacio et al. 2002, 15–16). Like Agoncillo, editors of *La Independencia* waged a campaign for recognition of Philippine sovereignty in the "language of civilization," arguing that Filipinos were already civilized and capable of self-government, "ground[ed] . . . in the capacity of our race" (Kramer 2006, 100–101). Elites in Manila courted American officials to support their cause with acts of hospitality, including concerts, dances, and dinners (105). In turn, American officials attempted to cultivate support for US rule among elites, hosting a Thanksgiving dinner on November 24, 1898. American soldiers, on the other hand, grew restless and disappointed at the "loss of genuine combat opportunity" and "strict orders not to engage Filipino troops" (103). They had been unable to fulfill Theodore Roosevelt's belief that "martial endeavors were good for the nation because they vitalized American men" and "made overseas colonies appear desirable not only for their economic and strategic benefits but also for their character-building potential" (Hoganson 1998, 143). In his diary, Irving Speer of the Colorado Infantry complained that "people in the city call us cowards and the spaniard [sic] women spit on you as you pass beneath her [sic] window" (quoted in Kramer 2006, 103).

On December 10, 1898, the US signed the Treaty of Paris, officially ending the Spanish-American War. Despite Aguinaldo and Agoncillo's efforts, no Filipinos were present at the drafting or signing of a treaty that claimed US sovereignty over the entire archipelago (Kramer 2006, 109). While Cuba was granted independence, McKinley decided to hold on to the Philippines, instructing US military commanders to announce that Americans had stayed "not as invaders or conquerors, but as friends, to protect the natives in their homes, in their employments, and in their personal and religious rights" (quoted in Kramer 2006, 110). Passionate public debate ensued in the US Senate in December and January, and hoping to convince the nation of his decision, McKinley traveled to the South to spread the word about US sovereignty and "duty" in the Philippines, emphasizing that the goal was to prepare Filipinos for self-rule (Kramer 2006, 110). Anti-imperialists, mainly Democrats, called imperialism a threat to "racial integrity" and US domestic freedom. Those who wanted to annex the Philippines, including many Republicans, argued for commercial opportunities in Asia, "extension or nonretraction of the flag," and a duty to "uplift" Filipinos (110). To convince the public, the US deemed resistance to its rule in the Philippines an insurrection against the United States rather than a continuation of a revolution against colonizers (Ileto 2002, 4). Fighting officially broke out on February 4, 1899, when US sentries fired on Filipino troops, blaming Filipino aggression as the catalyst (Kramer 2006, 111). In this act, Filipinos "failed" to recognize Americans as liberators and rulers, while Americans refused to recognize Filipinos' self-determination and autonomy. It was, as Kramer states, a "war for recognition" (111), and US and Filipino forces engaged in battle with high casualties. This war for recognition and the refusal to acknowledge Filipino capability extended into the cultural sphere in the case of the PC Band.

Before Black regiments arrived in the Philippines to fight against "insurgents" in August 1899, Black newspapers expressed sympathy for Filipinos and their independence movement. On November 11, 1898, an article in the *Colored American* called Filipinos "our colored brothers" and "our kinsmen" (quoted in Gatewood 1987, 13). Despite their sympathies, however, Black soldiers felt a strong sense of loyalty to the US Army and endeavored to demonstrate their patriotic duty: "We are now arrayed to meet what we consider a common foe, men of our own hue and color. Whether it is right to reduce these people to submission is not a question for the soldier to decide. Our oath of allegiance knows neither race, color nor nation, and if such a question should arise, it would be disposed of as one of a political nature by a soldier" (M. W. Saddler, 25th Infantry, Manila, Philippines, November 18, 1899, quoted in Gatewood 1987, 248). Soon, many soldiers' points of view shifted, as they fought Filipinos at close range and experienced racism, frequently witnessing how some whites deployed similar tactics toward them as toward Filipinos: "I feel sorry for these people and all that have come under the control of the United States. I don't believe they will be justly dealt by. The first thing in the morning is the 'Nigger' and the last thing at night is the 'Nigger.' You have no idea the way these people are treated by the Americans here" (Patrick Mason, 24th Infantry, November 19, 1899, quoted in Gatewood 1987, 257). Insults hurled at Black soldiers employed "coon song" lyrics: "White troops not only refused to salute black officers but also delighted in taunting Negro soldiers by singing, 'All coons look alike to me'[7] and 'I don't like a nigger nohow'" (Gatewood 1987, 244). Cynthia Marasigan writes, "Recognizing racism transported from the United States, Calloway [a Black soldier] observed how whites perpetuated racist fears toward blacks among Spaniards and Filipinos at each stage of the colonial project. Whites tried to control knowledge about African Americans to secure racialized hierarchies in military and civil rule, and Calloway envisioned such race hatred as part of a larger structure facilitating colonial processes of knowledge production over time" (2010, 60).

The ways racist white soldiers lumped Blacks and Filipinos together allowed the two to see themselves as similar: "Tell my friends that I am just the same as a Filipino" (Edward Brown, 24th Infantry, April 14, 1900, quoted in Gatewood 1987, 277). Some soldiers forged bonds with Filipinos by sharing their experiences: "I have mingled freely with the natives and have had talks with American colored men here in business and who have lived here for years, in order to learn of them the cause of [Filipino] dissatisfaction and the reason for this insurrection, and I must confess they have a just grievance. All this never would have occurred if the army of occupation would have treated them as people" (Unidentified Black soldier, May 17, 1900, quoted in Gatewood 1987, 279). John W. Galloway, sergeant major in the 24th Infantry, interviewed a Filipino medical doctor, who told him, "I unreservedly believe that all my people would look very kindly upon your people as neighbors.... The colored people, being of like complexion to our own, ... they would become good Filipinos" (Señor Todorica Santos, November 16, 1899, quoted in Gatewood 1987, 254).

Playing on the divisiveness within the US military, Emilio Aguinaldo reached out to Black soldiers by circulating placards. These missives "advised black soldiers to reassess their position in the war, urging them to realize that their self-sacrifice only furthered white Americans' imperialist motivations. They pointed to the stakes of endangering the existence of the black race, reminding them of recent lynching and the enduring brutality of racism by whites in the United States. Black soldiers saw such placards in Pampanga, and some would respond to them via letters to the black press or to their families later on during their service" (Marasigan 2010, 67). One such placard, printed in *The Richmond Planet*, was addressed "to the colored American soldier," stating, "It is without honour that you are spilling your costly blood. Your masters have thrown you in the most iniquitous fight with double purposes. In order to be you the instrument of their ambition. And also your hard work will make soon the extinction of your race. Your friends the Filipinos give you this good warning. You must consider your situation and your history. And take charge that the blood of your brothers Sam Hose and Gray proclaim vengeance" (November 11, 1899, p. 8, col. 5). The most infamous of the few Black soldiers that joined the revolution was David Fagen, who defected from the Colored 24th US Infantry in San Isidro, Nueva Ecija, in November 1899 (Marasigan 2010, 1).[8] Fagen was a twenty-four-year-old laborer from Florida who enlisted in 1895 and served in all but one of the six Black US military regiments stationed in the islands between 1899 and 1902. He served as a lieutenant in the Philippine revolutionary army under General Urbano Lacuna and rose to the rank of captain. David Fagen fought with the revolutionaries for two years before purportedly being captured and beheaded by the US military; the 24th Infantry, the very regiment from which he deserted, played a little-known role in his capture (312–13).

Black soldiers made a positive impression on many among the native populace: "The colored soldiers are making for themselves a fine reputation among the Filipinos, and no one has a disrespectful word to say of them except some renegade American" (Theophilus G. Steward, 25th Infantry, April 21, 1900, quoted in Gatewood 1987, 263). Their shared experience of racist treatment by whites allowed Blacks and Filipinos to cultivate friendships and alliances. Evidence of their congruence was expressed as recognition of a similar skin tone, although in reality they represented a range of skin tones; more meaningfully, they recognized in each other a shared denigration by whites based on race and a shared demand for equal treatment. Kind acts of Black soldiers who empathized with and saw themselves as the same as Filipinos demonstrated qualities consistent with cultural values appreciated by Filipinos, including getting along with others, mutual trust, and rapport (see David 2013, 110–11 and 215). The context for understanding the Black soldiers' unique racial and social position in the Philippines helps us to contextualize the exceptional rise to fame of Walter Howard Loving, his rapport with Filipinos, and the role of military bands in alleviating some of the racial tension between whites and Blacks and also between Americans and Filipinos.

Loving was born in rural Lovingston, Virginia, in 1872, the son of formerly enslaved persons Emily and Alex. His mother passed away when he was a toddler, and his father struggled to raise seven children (Richardson 1982,

5). At the age of ten, Walter went to live in Saint Paul, Minnesota, with his older sister Julia, who was a domestic worker in the household of Charles E. Flandrau, a successful lawyer and former associate justice of the state Supreme Court (Cunningham 2007, 5). When Flandrau's daughter "Patty" married Tilden R. Selmes, both Julia and young Walter moved with the family to a ranch in North Dakota. There, they befriended the young Theodore Roosevelt, and Walter met him on several occasions. After their daughter Isabella was born, the Selmes family moved back to Saint Paul before relocating to Washington, DC, in 1891. As a high school student at the prestigious M Street High School, the only Black secondary school in the District of Columbia,[9] Loving demonstrated exceptional musical talent by playing the cornet and also directing the Second Baptist Church choir (5). The high school's Cadet Corps, in which Loving participated, aimed to instill "a sense of pride, self-respect, and self-assurance" among its students (Robinson 1984, 143). After graduating, he enlisted in the army in June 1893, "hoping to emulate the black soldiers who had been stationed at nearby Fort Snelling when he was a boy" (Cunningham 2007, 5). The military provided opportunities for Loving and other African American musicians to use their talents in a field that had more prospects than most. When Loving entered the army, there were about eight hundred other African Americans enlisted in four segregated regiments—the 9th and 10th Cavalry ("Buffalo Soldiers"), and the 24th and 25th Infantry regiments, comprising 8.4 percent of the Army's 25,361 enlisted men (Cunningham 2007, 5).

Loving was assigned to the 24th Infantry, stationed at Fort Bayard in New Mexico, an isolated Western post that "reduced the chances for racial conflicts with white settlers" (Cunningham 2007, 6). When the 24th Infantry transferred to Fort Douglas, outside of Salt Lake City, Utah, in October of 1896, locals did not welcome them with open arms, and the *Salt Lake Tribune* called their arrival "An Unfortunate Change" in the demographics of Utah. By 1897, however, the *Tribune* apologized for its earlier apprehensions due to the soldiers' commendable conduct and lively parades: "on many occasions the splendid band has supplied music, and it has always been with a hearty and cheerful spirit" (quoted in Cunningham 2007, 6). The soldier-musicians of the regiment's band changed the minds of the community because they held the special attention of the public by providing a means to recognize and express a shared value—patriotism. Loving was likely at the forefront of the direction of the 24th Infantry Band, and he participated in the community by helping to orchestrate music for a local high school's performance (Cunningham 2007, 6). Forging relationships between disparate communities through music became an effective strategy throughout Loving's career.

In June of 1898, Loving's five-year enlistment ended. He secured a letter of recommendation from the 24th Infantry's Black chaplain, Allen Allensworth, stating that he would be "successful as a Chief Musician of a regimental band" (Cunningham 2007, 7). Loving did not get the appointment he sought and was discharged before the 24th Infantry deployed to Cuba in 1898.[10] Loving reenlisted, was appointed the chief musician in the 8th US Volunteer Infantry (USVI), and traveled as far as Louisville, Kentucky, to find the best musicians for his band (7). Searching far and wide for the best musicians was something that Loving would do in the Philippines, evidence that contradicts claims that any Filipino could be trained to become a fine band musician. The *Colored American* reported that he had "succeeded in building up for the 8th Immunes one of the finest regimental bands in the service" (quoted in Cunningham 2007, 7). Soon, however, the 8th USVI was sent home, and Loving returned to Washington, DC (see Cunningham 2007, 8). In the spring of 1899, Loving enrolled in classes at the prestigious New England Conservatory of Music in Boston. He excelled in music theory, composition, and cornet performance, and was praised by his professor J. Wallace Goodrich, who urged him to finish his diploma. Musicologist Robert Yoder speculates that Loving chose to reenlist in the army because Judge Flandrau, who was underwriting Loving's expenses, may have decided to discontinue financial support (2013, 24).

Loving joined the 48th US Volunteer Infantry on September 23, 1899, as the chief musician. Before leaving for the Philippines, his unit was sent to Angel Island in San Francisco Bay due to an outbreak of smallpox. While they were quarantined, Loving organized a chorus of four hundred voices that would perform in Japan. Sergeant W. H. Cox Jr. of the 48th wrote that they were the "first regiment of a foreign country that has ever paraded the streets of Yokohama, Japan, under arms and the first chorus of Negro singers which has ever appeared in that city" (*Richmond Planet*, April 14, 1900, p. 1, col. 6; see also Richardson 1982, 7; and Cunningham 2007, 9). When the 48th and 49th USVI arrived in Manila on February 4, 1900, conditions were much different than those that were faced by the 24th and 25th just a year or so earlier: "There, the 48th U.S.V. saw little signs of war on the north line surrounding Manila, prompting some soldiers to

Lt. Col. Walter H. Loving, Philippine Constabulary, 1936. National Archives.

recognize Filipinos' friendliness, to profess their loyalty to America despite appeals by revolutionaries, or to focus on Filipinos' unusual customs. On the south line, the 49th U.S.V. captured key revolutionaries in Manila and witnessed amigo warfare at work, while some endorsed America's mission in the Philippines and acknowledged cordial relations between blacks and Filipinos" (Marasigan 2010, 100). With this huge chorus, Loving performed at the Orient Hotel, and it was described as a "scene of pleasure that will long be remembered in Manila" (*Richmond Planet*, April 14, 1900, p. 1, col. 6). The *Manila Times* expressed its gratitude: "The night was drawing up to twelve when the concert came to a close, and the public felt that they owed this gratitude to Col. Duvall for granting the permission that made it possible for his men to give Manila an entertainment that she has never witnessed in the history of the past" (quoted in ibid.). While "Prof. Walter H. Lovings [*sic*]" is credited with training "this enormous chorus of male voices," ultimately Col. Duvall, who was part of the colonial government, was thanked. Certainly, the performance brought attention to Loving's skill as a musical leader and

Company I, 24th Infantry regiment officers, ca. 1900. Library of Congress Prints and Photographs Division. https://www.loc.gov/item/2010651628

the men's talents as musicians. The *Army and Navy Journal* proclaimed, "If music hath the effect on the savage breast declared by the poet, it would seem that the 48th would be just the men to send against the wild tribes in the mountains" (quoted in Cunningham 2007, 9).[11] By March, Loving's regiment was sent north—not directly to the mountain region of the "wild tribes," but to the coastal city of San Fernando, capital of La Union province (Cunningham 2007, 9). Concerts given by Black soldier-musicians proved to be a hit with locals and Americans alike, providing a temporary release from the tensions of war and a space for disparate groups to enjoy a shared activity. Early in 1901, Governor-General Taft attended one such concert by Loving and the 48th Regiment Chorus and Band.[12] He was so impressed by the performance that he proposed that Loving form a brass band for the Philippine Constabulary once it was established (Richardson 1982, 8). Before this materialized, the 48th US Volunteer Infantry's service ended in June 1901. Loving returned to Washington, DC, and applied as a second lieutenant in the Philippine Scouts, but was turned down despite high recommendations from his superiors. His sister's employer, Mrs. Tilden Selmes, wrote to her old friend Theodore Roosevelt, who was then vice president, to help Loving secure an appointment as a messenger in the US Senate. Roosevelt replied that he already had a "colored messenger" and could not ask other senators to appoint Loving. Loving would have to wait to return to the Philippines.

The Founding of the Philippine Constabulary Band and Filipino Musician Pedro B. Navarro

In addition to increasing the number of white and Black troops used to contain the rebellions throughout the archipelago, American officials employed the strategy of enlisting native support to aid in combating these uprisings. In 1901, the first of these to be established was the Philippine Scouts, under the command of the regular US Army officers (Laurie 1994, 48). Then, on July 4, 1901, a civil government was established by President McKinley under the leadership of Taft and the Second Philippine Commission, whose members would head various departments throughout the islands. For this civil government, the Philippine Constabulary, an insular police force, was established in 1902 (Hurley 1938 and McCoy 2009). These shifts of military labor, Paul Kramer explains, would allow US soldiers to return home, leading the American public to believe, erroneously, that the insurrection and armed resistance against US control had ended completely (2006, 155). By representing continuing armed conflict as "banditry" rather than "insurrection," the US suppressed Filipino resistance to colonial rule in the eyes of the American public. This control of information, invisibilizing continued rebellions against foreign rule, would profoundly shape American audiences' imperial ear, which heard the Philippine Constabulary Band's musical performances as willing cooperation, assimilation, and even enthusiasm.

The Philippine civil government, and within it, the Philippine Constabulary, strategized to quell revolutionary movements by integrating Filipinos in a subordinated way. "During the first decade of U.S. rule, the colonial security services, particularly the multifaceted Philippine Constabulary, succeeded in demobilizing a deeply rooted national revolution and advancing a conservative elite to fill the political void.... The creation of sophisticated modern policing was crucial to the U.S. pacification of the Philippines" (McCoy 2009, 16). The Philippine Constabulary incorporated former Filipino insurgents into its ranks but was led by white officers. McCoy states, "To an extent not fully grasped by many historians, the U.S. occupation of the Philippines succeeded because it co-opted this revolutionary nationalism, making an American presence seem a vehicle for the realization of Filipino aspirations. Moderate Filipino collaborators were rewarded with a degree of access to colonial offices unparalleled in an imperial age when colonial office was a white man's privilege" (7). The civil government, the Philippine Constabulary, and the PC

Band all held the promise of limited mobility and inclusion for Filipinos, and for some Black Americans, including Walter H. Loving.

In 1902, Loving returned to the Philippines with the rank of subinspector in the Philippine Constabulary. He was the only African American that Taft appointed to a leadership position in the Philippine Constabulary, and it seems to be intentional that this musical organization would not be in active battle: "Taft demonstrated his unwillingness to appoint African Americans as commanders over native policeman on the ground, strategically positioning his sole black Constabulary officer in a role with much less, if any policing responsibilities and with more significance in symbolically displaying American benevolence" (Marasigan 2010, 344). This strategic placement of Loving as a bandmaster, juxtaposed with Taft's denial of positions of command to other Blacks, was effective in appeasing some racial tension while allowing Taft to remain in control. Nevertheless, many in the Black community perceived Taft to be a champion of their concerns: "Here in his years of Philippine service, as more generally across his career, [Taft] demonstrated his own commitment to racial justice, African-American causes, and equal opportunity, a position familiar to and acknowledged by the black press" (Lefferts 2013, 156). Taft was able to circulate an impression of benevolence and inclusion while upholding white power. Upon Loving's appointment to the Constabulary, an enthusiastic letter written by the Provincial Board of La Union was sent directly to the chief of the Philippine Constabulary, stating that they had just heard of Loving's appointment and "should be very much please [sic] if you can see your way clear to assign Mr. Loving to this Province for duty. Mr. Loving was very popular here, both among the Ilocanos and the Americans and we believe his service would be valuable here."[13] The love of music and Loving's popularity formed a bridge between disparate groups and held the possibility of easing tensions. Loving's relationship and rapport with Filipino audiences and band musicians were an important component of his success.

The men who formed the original PC Band were some of the most promising musicians of their time. Some of them were descended from a long line of town band musicians or were former members of regimental bands under Spanish rule. Others were already enlisted in infantry bands under US control, and a few were "trumpeters who had served under Aguinaldo" (Richardson 1982, 9). Most men came from or lived in the Manila area, while a few came from Ilocos, the Visayas, or other provinces. One musician, my

Capt. Pedro B. Navarro, First Filipino Conductor of the Philippine Constabulary Band. Courtesy of Mary Talusan.

great-grandfather Pvt. Pedro B. Navarro, an Ilocano, would become Loving's right-hand man and his first successor in 1916. Born with the name Pedro Navarro Bravo on September 17, 1879, he came from humble beginnings as the only child of a fisherman, Pedro Bravo, and his wife, Bartola Navarro, in the rural town of Tagudin, Ilocos Sur. Before he reached the age of nine, tragedy struck, and young Pedro lost his father to the sea. Fearing that she could not properly educate him on her meager earnings, his mother brought him to the local convent, where he studied music and served as the angel brought down at the *salubong* (Easter dawn) celebration. It was not long before a Spanish priest, Father Mariano Ortiz, recognized Pedro's exceptional musical talent and took him from his small *barrio* to the bustling urban capital of Manila to study at the San Agustin Convent.[14] From ages eleven to nineteen, Pedro sang in the choir and excelled in both piccolo and violin. He studied solfeggio and harmony with the famous composer and teacher *Maestro di Cappella* Marcelo Adonay from 1894 to 1898 (Bañas 1924, 98). Adonay himself was a product of a thriving musical school in Manila, founded in 1742 by Spanish priests trained in methods used in the Conservatory of Madrid (Maceda 1973, 219–20).

At the end of the Spanish-American War in 1898, Pedro left the convent and joined several American military bands in Manila. He changed his last name from Bravo to Navarro, his mother's maiden name, because Navarro was less common.[15] Between 1899 and 1903, Navarro joined several bands, including the Philippine Band of Manila (directed by American conductor Charles Mindt), the 29th US Volunteer Band, the 6th US Artillery Band, and the 30th US Infantry Band (Bañas 1924, 99). He was already making a name for himself when Lt. Loving heard him playing and was impressed by his talent and skill. Sometime in 1902, Loving convinced him to join the newly forming Philippine Constabulary Band, "even though the pay and privileges were less in the Constabulary than in the U.S. Army," because the Philippine Constabulary "could offer him better opportunities for promotion" (Richardson 1982, 9). Loving believed this because the US was willing to give him a higher rank in the Philippine Constabulary than in the Philippine Scouts or the regular US Army. Accepting Loving's offer, Navarro enlisted in the Philippine Constabulary on July 15, 1903. Navarro's career before meeting Loving shows that even before the official establishment of the civil government and the Philippine Constabulary Band, native musicians were already playing for US army musical organizations, just as they had done under the Spanish in regimental bands. This refutes the claims by American newspapers in 1909 that members of the PC Band were introduced to Euro-American music only when the US took over the Philippines (see chapter 4).

As was the case for Filipino musicians, there were limited avenues for Black musicians in the US to make a decent living, even though there was a vibrant classical music scene among elite northern Black communities (see Schenbeck 2012). Black musicians like Loving, whose background was in European music, could find stable work in military bands, which became "an important training ground and a source of steady employment for African-American musicians outside the entertainment industry" (Lefferts 2013, 153). In the Philippines, Black soldier-musicians and Filipino band musicians found pathways for employment during the early American colonial regime. The *Colored American* reported that, capitalizing on the popularity of minstrel show performances, members of the 24th Infantry, who were "experienced in stage craft, have organized a minstrel company, and are giving performances at the theaters. It is reported that they are making $500 a day" ("Doings of

Stage People," January 13, 1900, p. 6, quoted in Lefferts 2013, 152). By the time Loving established the PC Band, this minstrel company was earning "several thousand dollars for extra-military engagements in the Philippines" ("The Twenty-Fourth Infantry and Its Famous Band 1903," quoted in Lefferts 2013, 153). Vaudeville was already popular in the Philippines, by the late 1880s and early 1890s, well before US colonization (2016, 59). While there are no accounts of the content of these shows or the social events at which they performed, it is clear that Black soldier-musicians who started off in military brass bands profited from the Filipino public's desire for entertainment and garnered recognition for their talents among Americans in Manila. When the 24th Infantry left the Philippines after it gave its farewell concert at Luneta Park on June 24, 1902, the *Manila American* reported that "the artistic advantages enjoyed through the presence in the city of the regiment's incomparable band, have all combined to make its presence in Manila a thing to be remembered" (quoted in *Iowa State Bystander*, Special Holiday Number, December 18, 1903, p. 3). The 24th Infantry Band's final program in Manila demonstrates that they were classically trained musicians, because they played not popular music of the minstrel show but light classical Euro-American compositions for concert band, including the overture "Morning, Noon, and Night in Vienna" by Suppe, "Runaway Girl" by Caryll, "Grand Selection" from *Faust* by Gounod, "Manila Waltz" by Chofre, "Home Again" arranged by their chief musician Wilfred O. Thompson, "Auld Lang Sine," and "The Star-Spangled Banner" (quoted in ibid.). The PC Band was organized just in time to fill the void of band concerts left by the 24th Infantry Band's departure.[16]

There were a number of factors that made Loving uniquely suited to lead the Filipino bandsmen in a successful way. Loving spoke Spanish, a great asset in interacting with Filipinos, especially his bandsmen.[17] Part of Loving's success was that he was a bridge between different groups—white and Black Americans, Americans and Filipinos, and elite and middle-class audiences. Loving created rapport with audiences by taking requests, a practice common in nineteenth-century America, when conductors agreed to "request programs" by the audience. By the early twentieth century, this practice was unpopular with most conductors, who privileged the musical composition over the desire of the audience. "The thrust of the conductors' efforts was to render audiences docile, willing to accept what the experts deemed appropriate rather than play a role themselves in determining either the repertory or the manner of presentation" (Levine 1998, 189). Loving's continued willingness to take requests in his concerts helped him and the band to develop rapport with audiences in an otherwise hostile environment, enhancing Loving's social capital among Filipinos and Americans, and bringing visibility to the PC Band. The earliest recorded example of Loving's practice appears in June 1903 at Luneta Park, near the former Spanish fort of Intramuros (Hila 2004, 76). The most requested piece by the music-loving public in Manila was not a European or American composition, but one by Filipino composer Ladislao Bonus: the overture to the opera *Sandugong Panaginip* (Dreamed Alliance), with 263 requests. The second most-requested piece was "Aires Filipinas" by Ruiz, with 131 requests. The rest were Briccialdi's "Carnival of Venice," with 89 requests; Rossini's *Semiramide* Overture, with 81 requests; and lastly, Sousa's "Hands Across the Sea" and "Stars and Stripes Forever," each with 13 requests (*Manila Times*, June 22, 1903, quoted in Hila 2004, 76). The number of requests correlates to the small minority of Americans in Manila compared to the larger population of Filipinos, but also reveals subtle expressions of nationalism by Filipinos. Two decades later, Filipinos expressed nationalism more conspicuously by keeping their hats on during the playing of the US national anthem before concerts in the Philippines, and American military men attempted to enforce their dominance by knocking the hats off Filipinos, including Filipino officials. I will further discuss how this development was part of the changing attitudes toward US rule in chapter 5.

 First and foremost, Loving was an exceptionally talented musician, arranger, and composer who brought an orchestral quality to the military band of the early twentieth century. Like John Philip Sousa, he elevated middlebrow brass band music, bringing it closer to the level of the "high-class" European orchestras that were less accessible to most Americans. He accommodated audiences' requests for certain pieces that sometimes exceeded the length of the concert itself. This demonstrates that, far from simply fulfilling expectations of his role as representing the US and the Philippine colonial military, Loving went above and beyond to transform the standard band concert to one of his own making, allowing audiences to take an active role in choosing pieces. His life experiences, background, and the people he knew aided in his rise to a high rank in the army over the course of his career. Army historian Roger Cunningham argues that it was Loving's talent and reputation that encouraged US Army officials eventually to appoint Black chief musicians to Black regiments, transforming the structure of having only white chief musicians leading them (2007, 5). In stories about Loving handed down from the people who knew him, and their descendants, he is described as strict but true to his word. He demanded hard work and rigorous training from the Filipino musicians but rewarded their dedication by treating them well (see interview with band members in chapter 5). The musicians in turn were extremely loyal to Loving as their leader, as well as dedicated to his vision of musical performance, as shown by their willingness to play the most highly regarded pieces in Euro-American concert repertoire, which demanded highly skilled musicians.

The PC Band's seeming display of consent to colonial rule and assimilation to Anglo-American values was a major objective in organizing, promoting, and supporting them, but there were other ways that the band was important socially. Americans needed the collaboration of Filipino musicians in band concerts that allowed Filipino masses, Filipino elites, and Americans in Manila and in the US to experience an idealized vision of collaboration between colonizers and colonized. Filipino band musicians as colonial subjects were drawn into a context in which they had to "play along" in order to survive, thrive, and express themselves, but they also found ways to resist domination, and to covertly and subversively advocate for their own sense of ethnic pride. In this way, Filipino subalterns were speaking (Spivak 1994) or, rather, musicking (Small 1998); however, American audiences, listening with an imperial ear, were unable to hear their sentiments, despite (or perhaps because of) the fact that they shared the same musical language as the colonizer. The confluence of several factors—American colonization, a rich band tradition in the Philippines, the popularity of brass bands around the world, Black soldiers-musicians in the Philippines, the racialization of music (juxtaposing "civilized" Euro-American music with Black-influenced music of ragtime), and the need to prove to the American public and the world America's success in the Philippines—created the context for the PC Band's significance. Their first introduction to the US public was at the 1904 St. Louis World's Fair, when the myth of Filipinos as natural musicians was exploited, with deep political and cultural implications.

2

Marching to Racial Progress: Civilizing Filipinos at the 1904 St. Louis World's Fair

There are some people who still assert that the United States obtained nothing through the annexation of the Philippines, but a lot of naked savages.... That a great many of the natives of the islands could already be cultured and refined would be set down as utterly preposterous by this class.... They should only be enticed to listen for an hour to the playing of the Constabulary band. No man with an ounce of appreciation in his soul could hear that band without being convinced that the 81 men who compose its membership are far above the ordinary in both intelligence and sentiment. A nation or a race may be judged by its music.

    No one could listen to the playing of "The Star-Spangled Banner" by that band of Filipinos, the pavilion surrounded by other Filipinos, their hats over their hearts and their heads bowed, and doubt that they are loyally American. ("Filipinos at the St. Louis World's Fair, Wonderful Music Rendered Daily by Islanders on Plaza of Philippine Building," *Bourbon News*, Paris, Kentucky, August 30, 1904, p. 3, col. 1 and 2)

The writer of this letter to the editor, a witness to the spectacle of the 1904 St. Louis World's Fair, seemed to arrive at an epiphany that did not wholly conform to the popular vision of racial hierarchy prevalent in the early twentieth century. In this view, the darker and thus more savage races lacked the markers of civilization, including a mastery of Euro-American music. But, using music as proof, the writer instead posits that Filipinos like the band musicians were *already* cultured and refined before the intervention of the US. He recognized that, while derogatory depictions of Filipinos created pernicious stereotypes in minds of most Americans, his personal encounters with Filipinos differed drastically from images promoted by sensationalist press coverage of the World's Fair. Therefore, he challenged his fellow Americans to "listen for an hour to the playing of the Constabulary band" as evidence that they were above the "ordinary in both intelligence and sentiment." Musical performances by the PC Band opened the writer's eyes, and indeed his ears, to other possibilities that deviated from the incendiary representations fostered by newspapers and some World's Fair organizers. However, while uncoupling the linkage between race and savagery, the writer still employed race to make sense of musicality by linking musical ability to racial heritage; he did this to support his argument about extraordinary Filipino intelligence and their "loyally American" sentiment. He dismissed the perception that Filipinos were uncivilizable savages, but he continued to employ an imperial ear to make sense of a glaring contradiction in sociocultural evolutionary theory by arguing that, because they possessed *natural* musical talent, a biological-racial condition of being musically endowed, Filipinos could be made into proper colonial subjects and civilized by American tutelage. He noted that "even the savage headhunters, in their peculiar tribal dances ... possess the musical instinct that, with time and training, may be developed into just what the members of the two Philippine bands already possess."[1] The performances of the Philippine bands gave substance to the merit and success of "benevolent assimilation," a message that American colonizers intended to disseminate, and one that was overwhelmingly what most audience members heard.

The PC Band's representation as successfully colonized subjects, clad in military uniforms and enthusiastically playing American patriotic songs, allowed the writer to reposition Filipinos in a complex web of symbols that was taken as evidence of their patriotic intent and cultural worthiness, despite their racial position on the evolutionary ladder. But if it was possible for some Americans like this man to "hear" the Filipinos' cultural capacity in ways that challenged the logic of racial hierarchy, how did the subjugation of Filipinos continue to be rationalized by ordinary Americans? It seems that

Philippine Constabulary Band at the St. Louis World's Fair, 1904. Courtesy of the Missouri Historical Society, St. Louis. http://collections.mohistory.org/resource/146090

while the observer praised Filipinos' musical abilities and their suitability as loyal subjects, he nevertheless absorbed the message about America's central role in assimilating and educating Filipinos. Their singing of the US national anthem and recitation of the Pledge of Allegiance were taken as an indicator of actual patriotism and proved that they were "loyally American," willing to assimilate to American values. As explained in the previous chapter, many people of early twentieth-century America were encouraged to use music to gauge a culture's level of civilization—the closer to European music, the more civilized the culture that produced it. European music represented a higher cultural achievement than folk music or American popular inventions, such as the ragtime music or Tin Pan Alley songs that were the entertainment of the masses (Levine 1988). This way of thinking is certainly flawed, but nevertheless, categorizing a culture's music on a spectrum from primitive to modern, based on its distance from or proximity to Western music, is an idea that persists today in many cases.[2] While the writer saw beyond notions of Filipinos as entirely savage when observing and hearing the PC Band's patriotic performance, he nevertheless internalized the message intended by the Philippine Commission and the US government: Filipinos needed the guidance and discipline of the United States to succeed in the modern world. American audiences, listening with an imperial ear, heard Filipinos as expressing patriotism and, in this way, confirmed their own beliefs about

Manifest Destiny, white superiority, and benevolent assimilation. Because of his unusual role as leader of the PC Band, the inconsistent and strange ways that Loving was contextualized in American newspapers also reveal the novel strategies used to pursue this agenda.

The ways that Loving was represented in this complex colonial context varied depending on the situation and viewpoint. Loving, both because of and despite his identity as a Black leader in the early twentieth century, represented to Americans the guiding hand of their country abroad. To Filipinos he was an ally, to African Americans, a symbol of achievement; and he was seen by all as an educated and accomplished musician. Many American newspapers presented Loving's leadership of the naturally talented but otherwise childlike Filipinos as the reason for the PC Band's development into a successful organization. Loving's representation as a symbol of US tutelage and leadership, I argue, explains both the curious omission and, at other times, careful contextualization of his race in American newspapers. The above passage is an example of omission when it states that music can indicate a nation or race's value and potential, yet makes no mention that Loving is a Black American. If the writer's argument was that music and race are inextricably linked, why didn't the writer apply this logic to Loving in particular and to Black Americans in general? How did Loving's race, in the tense and heated domestic racial atmosphere of the US (as well as St. Louis), just disappear into thin air? Like all audiences for music, the writer projected meaning onto the PC Band's performance that reflected his own desires and values.[3] His emphasis on Filipino achievement through American tutelage allowed him to be selective in his racial gaze and imperial hearing, strategically ignoring and hence obscuring Loving's race, while making a racial argument about Filipinos. The writer omitted, whether opportunistically or subconsciously, Loving's racial difference in order to maintain white superiority over both racial others, Filipinos and Blacks. The omission subtly erased an alliance between Filipinos and Black Americans, as well as Loving's military success and prestige. Loving's identity, whether acknowledged or ignored, was deployed in ways that were politically and racially strategic.

These racial omissions and commendations tell us much about how Americans reconciled contradictions between popular "scientific" racial theories and their personal encounters with "racial subjects." Americans compared Filipinos, as foreign racial others, to domestic racial others, especially Black Americans and sometimes Native Americans.[4] Since white Americans could not fit Filipinos neatly into their existing racial schema of exclusion, they had to create new ways of understanding them, especially in the face of contradictory messages by World's Fair officials, American colonialists, and anti-imperialists who questioned the rationale behind the acquisition of the Philippines. As Kramer analyzed, these "novel racial formations" were necessary to court the collaboration of elite Filipinos in the US colonial enterprise but were also at work in the positioning of Filipinos in the minds of Americans in the US (2006, 283). Though the writer neither completely embraced the proposal of Filipinos' unalienable rights to independence and freedom nor categorically excluded them from becoming "loyal Americans," he advocated for their contingent inclusion as colonial subjects and trained musicians, but without social or political equality. His perception of the PC Band's patriotic intent is similar to ethnosympathetic listeners who ignored with a "disengaged engagement" the trauma of slavery to revel in the authenticity of Black spirituals (Cruz 1999, 31). This ambiguous and ambivalent racial positioning to which Filipinos were subjugated had mixed outcomes. Even while being admired, Filipinos could make little progress forward to break through social, political, and cultural barriers beyond the stereotype of "little brown brother." I make this argument by focusing on the Philippine military men at the 1904 Fair and how their performances of Euro-American concert music played a special role in the ways that Americans granted them admiration without equality.

The Philippine Constabulary Band in particular and the Filipino military men in general, who represented assimilable and civilizable American subjects, have not been the focus of academic work on the 1904 St. Louis World's Fair. Several excellent scholarly works on the fair analyzed the context of the Philippines and Filipino participation, but none have analyzed thoroughly the generally favorable reception of the Filipino military men and their bands. Most writers concentrate, and rightly so, on the egregious ways in which the US government, the colonial government in the Philippines, and the fair organizers exploited Americans' perception of the "savageness" of the "Igorrotes"[5] in particular (see Rydell 1984, Vergara 1995, Kramer 1999 and 2006, Afable 2004, Buangan 2004, Brownell 2008, and Parezo and Fowler 2009). Of 1,100 Filipinos, 280 were Scouts and 420 were Constables; together, they made up 70 percent of Filipinos at the fair and received as much attention as the "Igorrotes" in newspapers. The context of the Scouts and

Constabulary men provides a rich source of analysis, because their generally positive reception by American fairgoers exposes the glaring imperfections in the hegemonic fabric of racial superiority and the lapses of control and power over racialized others.

Since it is impossible to assess exactly what 1904 Fair visitors thought or how they understood the multiple and often contradictory messages about Filipinos, I interpret accounts of their interactions with Filipino military men published in newspapers and other sources. The variety of ways that fair visitors evaluated, responded to, and interacted with Filipino Constabulary men and Scouts complicate our current understanding of cultural and political oppression at the St. Louis World's Fair by including acts of agency by Filipinos. Newspaper articles and letters by the public uncover a surprising and curious fascination with the Filipino military men, revealing a range of sentiments, including admiration, desire, voyeurism, fear, jealousy, and friendship. I interpret these written accounts by treating the newspaper reporter as observer, witness, and recorder of public perception. Newspaper reports are part of the "dominant means of *ideological* production" that produce "representations of the social world," including "images, descriptions, explanations and frames" to shape understanding about the world (Hall 1997, 82; emphasis in original). In a larger study on newspapers and journalism, John Richardson employs critical discourse analysis to examine how newspapers communicate messages, how arguments are made and supported, and how their texts may be "implicated in the production and reproduction of social inequalities" (2007, 8). Newspaper representations of the PC Band not only shaped knowledge of band itself but also developed a body of knowledge about the Philippines, Filipinos, and Filipino music-making in ways that supported and were supported by colonial, imperial, and racial ideologies. While newspaper reports were a powerful tool for dominant society's ideological dissemination and production, they also offered some firsthand accounts, with ethnographic descriptions of these events that are otherwise unavailable today.[6] Inspired by William Henry Scott (1982) and James C. Scott (1990), I search for cracks and hidden transcripts to interpret ways that audiences did not always absorb dominant messages about Filipinos, ways that they did, and responses by the band members and Loving. Whatever racial formations white Americans were encouraged to develop about Filipinos through the 1904 Fair, their actions and words often revealed a greater complexity in the way they conformed to, and other times, transgressed dominant views and social norms, especially in the Jim Crow South. Oftentimes, these less socially oppressive ways of interacting with Filipinos were temporary and fleeting, but nevertheless they occurred and opened up new possibilities for analyzing Filipinos' participation at the 1904 Fair.[7]

Exhibiting the Philippines and Filipinos for American Consumption

The Louisiana Purchase Exposition of 1904,[8] also known as the St. Louis World's Fair, was a defining moment in the cultural representation of the Philippines. The fair allowed the American public, for the first time, to meet people from the Philippines face-to-face, with the aim of fostering support for continued US investment in the islands. The Philippine Exhibition, also called the Philippine Reservation, was an "exposition within an exposition" encompassing forty-seven acres on the grounds of Forest Park in St. Louis, Missouri. It was the largest exhibit at the fair and cost more than a million dollars. Eleven hundred Filipinos, representing diverse "tribes" and levels of civilization, were brought to St. Louis alongside thousands of objects and materials from the Philippines. In every way, people, objects, and ideas from and about the Philippines were exhibited to justify and promote US intervention and investment to the American people, to collaborating Filipinos, and to the world at large (see also Rydell 1984 and Kramer 1999 and 2005).

The visual layout of the exhibits at the Philippine Exposition was designed by American colonial officials and organizers, who wanted visitors to understand their vision of the Philippines' place within America's vision of progress. Visitors accessed the exhibit by passing through a "time warp" into the Philippines' recent past, crossing the Bridge of Spain and entering through Manila's Walled City of moss and stone. Inside, they encountered an exhibit of the Philippines' "primitive" weapons, designed to impress upon visitors the "futility of continued rebellion" against the United States (Parezo and Fowler 2007, 167). At the main entrance of the exposition grounds, a tall column stood as tribute to Ferdinand Magellan, the Spaniard who "discovered" the islands, echoing the statues found elsewhere on the grounds of Lewis and Clark, who completed the first transcontinental expedition a hundred years earlier. In this way, the acquisition of America's overseas territories, like its westward expansion, was woven into a history of the US that cast imperialism as the natural progression of Manifest Destiny (167). Entering the main grounds of the Philippine Exposition, visitors faced the Manila Plaza, which was surrounded by Spanish-style structures, including the "civilized" government, education, and fine arts buildings, which housed displays devoted to agriculture, forestry, photography, and mining, as well as thousands of artifacts "chosen to appeal to American men" (167). Surrounding the central plaza were recreated villages of native peoples, displayed so that American observers could study the natives in their natural habitats. Nearby stood the encampment of the Scouts and the Constabulary, as well as the Visayan Village, representing Hispanicized Filipino culture. The enormous diversity of peoples, cultures, languages, histories, and "levels of civilization" did not make for easy understanding in the crowded, chaotic atmosphere of a world's fair. The layout of the exhibit provided a simple model imposed on Philippine history and cultures that took visitors from past to present, from antiquity to modern day, from before American rule to after, in a way that supported and legitimized the benefits of US colonization.

These simplistic messages about the Philippine Exposition were complicated, however, by several contending agendas, formed at the intersection of empire and exposition. Kramer explains that empire and exposition were not "automatically congruent," because "colonial officials sought to make use of the exposition for purposes tailored to specific struggles against U.S. anti-imperialism and local Filipino opposition, while the leadership of the St. Louis Fair had its own priorities, among them sheer profit, municipal competition and historic and aesthetic grandeur" (1999, 79). Colonial officials and exposition planners were forced to concede to each other's needs, creating mixed messages for audiences to make sense of and interpret (Kramer 2006, 229–84), often with varied results. Representations of "native peoples," both in the educational exhibits and the Pike's entertainment zone, were at best inaccurate and misleading, and all of them sustained the idea of white American superiority. It was this guiding principle that allowed most fairgoers to resolve the conflicting information in a novel way, especially by developing an imperial ear to understand the PC Band's superb performances of Euro-American music.

Fair directors in charge of various departments had their own specific personal and political agendas, which both aligned and conflicted with the overall goals of the LPE. William J. McGee, director of the LPE Anthropology Department, sought to promote anthropology as an academic field (while also boosting his profile in the field) by providing an easily applicable framework for grasping the world's complexity and hierarchical diversity. In general, his placement of the world's peoples was simplistically color-coded: "The darker a specific group, the lower the stage number he assigned to it" (Parezo and Fowler 2007, 48). A geologist by training and head of the Bureau of American Ethnology from 1893 to 1903, McGee "ranked living tribes, nations, and races on their supposed degree of advancement in activities. Which activities he emphasized in each case reflected his determination to fit individual groups into his predetermined, universal model" (48). Despite criticism by Franz Boas and other anthropologists who advocated for cultural relativism, McGee's racial schema was supported by the scientific and educational design of the fair; it was crudely straightforward, but also powerful and enduring. This notion of fixed hierarchy, however, ran counter to the Philippine Exposition Board's aims to emphasize Filipinos' capacity to assimilate to American culture, because it threatened to prove that Filipinos, especially tribal people, could never be assimilated. The Philippine military men and bands were crucial for American imperialists and elite Filipinos promoting a positive image of Filipino assimilation and allaying the controversy over continued US investment in the islands. The fair, as an amalgam of these contending agendas, ultimately sent mixed messages for the public to sort out, making it a "difficult charge both to persuade American audiences that Filipinos were racially and culturally inferior—properly subject to the scorns of Jim Crow—and to persuade Filipinos that they were respected, if junior, partners in the colonial enterprise—lucky recipients of little brown brotherhood" (Kramer 1999, 80). While McGee's "monistic paradigm with its convoluted terminology" did not ultimately shape the established canon of anthropology (Parezo and Fowler 2007, 48), the model of equating skin color with level of civilization was easily understood, visually convincing, and tenacious. Mixed messages driven by contending agendas and a color-coded model of civilization led to an imperial way of hearing, a convoluted rationalization that made sense of the musical performances of the PC Band in a way that preserved white superiority.

The Philippine Exposition Board, directed by Dr. W. P. Wilson and including Dr. Gustavo Niederlein, also incorporated two Filipino members, Mr. Pedro A. Paterno and Dr. Leon Ma. Guerrero (*Report of the Philippine Exposition Board* 1904), because collaboration with Filipino elites was deemed necessary to the successful implementation of US rule in the Philippines

(Kramer 2006, 232). By inviting Filipino elites, the US attempted to encourage their continued participation by "providing them an intimidating vision of its benevolent might and reconciling them to its colonial rule" (238). However, Filipino elites were not convinced of the merits of including native people in the Philippine Exhibition and had every reason to be wary. Citing the Exposition of 1887 in Madrid, Filipino nationalists lamented that the inclusion of tribal people would impart the belief that the Philippines was filled with "savages" in need of colonial rule and derail their goals of promoting Filipino participation in the colonial government (243, 248–49). To encourage cooperation by the resistant Filipino critics, the colonial government released funds to provincial governors and collectors, though with reservation and mistrust, exposing its "reliance on local collaborators" while giving them the impression that they were included in the process of creating the exhibit (245). Despite the concerns of Filipino elites and politicians, promotional materials from the fair and the St. Louis press emphasized the "savages" in order to capitalize on visitors' desires to see the new, exciting, and bizarre. Colonial officials insisted that the display of "non-Christian" peoples was for scientific purposes and assumed that the American public would give equal attention to the educated, Christianized Filipinos. This approach failed, however, because American fairgoers generally ignored the "representative" group of educated, Hispanicized Filipinos—members of the honorary commission and *pensionado* students studying in America—in favor of the exotic and attractive tribal peoples (246–47). Despite their misgivings, the Philippine Board's aims (to promote civilian rather than military rule of the islands, quell the objections of anti-imperialist critics, and persuade Congress to reduce tariffs on products from the colony) aligned with those of Governor-General Taft, President Roosevelt, and Secretary of War Root (237). The board's overall goals of increasing industrial and commercial production in the Philippines for export to the US and developing markets in the Philippines for the consumption of American products trumped other cultural concerns (241). In an effort to legitimize the success of US colonization with the consent of Filipinos, the American media underplayed the ongoing armed resistance to US rule, and the participation of Scouts and Constabulary at the fair contributed to this image of pacification and collaboration to encourage trade and business with the Philippines.

To promote the possibilities of assimilating Filipino natives into proper colonial subjects, tribal people were deliberately juxtaposed with Filipino military men, allowing fairgoers to marvel at the progress of the US in civilizing the savages. With much fascination, fairgoers scrutinized the "savage Igorrotes," who went about their daily activities and reenacted rituals such as marriage, warfare, and funerals on an hourly schedule, while nearby the Scouts and Constabulary performed their disciplined, orderly military drills. While newspapers were filled with comparisons that detailed the differences between the two extreme ends of the evolutionary hierarchy, in the minds of most fairgoers, these distinctions collapsed, and Filipinos from every social and cultural background often were simply lumped together as savages rather than assimilable subjects. While the "non-Christian" tribal groups represented only a third of the Filipinos at the fair, American newspapers and fair promotional materials ensured that they made the most impact on fair visitors and on Americans who read about the event from afar.[9] Americans' confirmation biases equated the indigenous people with caricatures already familiar to them (from their exposure to political cartoons used to represent Filipinos in the recent war) and with other racial others such as Black Americans, Native Americans, and people from Hawaii and Puerto Rico (see Ignacio et al. 2004).

While the "savages" received much attention from the media, newspapers were also fascinated with Scouts and Constabulary men. Next to the fair's official band, the Philippine bands played more frequently than other visiting bands, and the drills of the Scouts and Constabulary were immensely popular among the American public. In the book *Indescribably Grand*, Clevenger argues that the Philippine military men and bands were mentioned more often in the diaries and letters of fairgoers than were the "savages": "That there are precious few references to the ethnological exhibits is in and of itself significant, especially when one also notes a similar absence of overt commentary on the phenomenon of imperialism or Western expansion, race theory, or Social Darwinism" (1996, 22). Of five eyewitness accounts of the fair in the book, only one commented on the "Igorrotes"; however, I think more accounts are needed to make a strong argument about whether or not the ethnological exhibits were "significant" in the minds of fairgoers. Also, equating the absence of these references with fairgoers' dismissal of imperialist and racist messages is not that simple, because they did not need to comment overtly on beliefs that they had already internalized, thus speaking to the power of hegemonic messages confirming and legitimizing white superiority. I do agree, however, that the generally positive encounters between the fairgoers and Filipino military men need more attention.

The first Filipinos to arrive in St. Louis were the "savages," accompanied by the Philippine Scouts. A news article described the diverse groups disembarking from the train as Negritos, Igorrotes, Moros, and Tagalogs ("Filipinos from Four Savage Tribes Leave Train for Quarters at Fair," *St. Louis Republic*, March 27, 1904, p. 6, col. 3–4). Most Americans had few points of reference to understand the foreign tribal names, so associating the diverse Filipinos under the umbrella of "savage" was probably the easiest way to regard and describe them. Images of Filipinos as savages abounded in newspapers and political cartoons throughout the Spanish-American War (see Ignacio et al. 2004 and Kramer 2006, 87–158) and were already familiar to the vast majority of Americans, providing a framework for understanding the arriving Filipinos. These participants traveled on the tourist cars of the Northern Pacific Railway (Buangan 2004, 491) and encountered Black porters, with whom they connected and communicated through music. A porter taught the Moros[10] the American popular tune "Hiawatha,"[11] which they played on their indigenous musical instruments:

> Then came the Moros, each lugging some kind of musical instrument. They can play modern and ancient airs, and the strains of "Hiawatha," were heard emanating from their car before they were told to prepare to leave the train, inquiry developed that they had learned the tune on the train from one of the porters, who had not, however, taught them "Bedelia," . . . as he had not heard it on the Pacific Coast as yet. ("Filipinos from Four Savage Tribes Leave Train for Quarters at Fair," *St. Louis Republic*, March 27, 1904, p. 6, col. 3–4)

This is probably the earliest known example of musical and social exchange between Black Americans and Filipinos, more specifically Muslim Filipinos, on America's shores. While there is no evidence of continued musical interaction between Black porters and Muslim Filipinos, I am fascinated with this example because it demonstrates how people from the Philippines interacted socially and culturally with Black Americans in ways that circumvented white presence and authority.

In contrast to this example, newspapers depicted all tribal people as potentially violent to each other and in need of policing by colonial authorities. One newspaper warned, "how to keep the Irrogotes [sic] from going on hunting expeditions after the skulls of the other natives is a question that has not yet been settled" ("Dog Feast to Be Reward of Igorrotes' Work," *St. Louis Republic*, May 8, 1904, p. 1, col. 4). The Scouts were seen as the mediators between these tribes and thus had tensions with them:

> The Igorrotes are very much afraid of the Filipino scouts. All one of the soldiers has to do is to step toward an Igorrote, and the latter will run. Three Igorrotes came up to the barracks of the scouts yesterday to work, and they ran the gauntlet of the scouts—actually ran, too. The Filipinos laughed heartily and seemed to enjoy the fact that their brethren of the islands were afraid of them. ("Dog Feast to Be Reward of Igorrotes' Work," *St. Louis Republic*, May 8, 1904, p. 1, col. 4)

Indeed, this is what the US colonial government wanted to emphasize about Filipinos: that they were not one people and could not yet be one nation without the guidance of the US. The men of the Philippine Constabulary and the Philippine Scouts, who were part of the US army, represented the US vision of assimilating Filipinos into American culture. Other interactions, such as the example of the Moros and the Black porters, were less publicized.

Many news reports were complimentary of the Scouts as soon as they arrived in St. Louis. They were "none of your dog-eating, head-hunting, half-naked Igorrote," but rather "well-built ... with a countenance as intelligent as a Japanese or any other civilized person of the Orient, and in manner and bearing he is considered a credit to his race" ("Philippine Scouts Arouse Admiration," *St. Louis Republic*, April 18, 1904, p. 3). Americans projected and perceived assimilationist values through descriptions of the Scouts' physical appearance, which seemed to exemplify their discipline and level of civilization; the Scouts had "square shoulders, stand perfectly erect, look the soldier from head to foot, and work with vim and determination" (ibid.). The article pointed out that the Scouts were "regular members of the United States Army," and because they had an "appreciation of their rights and privileges, no one can molest them without subjecting himself to the dangers of the bayonet." It boasts that "the Philippine scout is an American citizen and he knows it" (ibid.). As part of their privilege as US army men, they were allowed to stay in the country after their tour of duty if they chose to do so.[12] Scouts commander Major W. H. Johnston stated favorably that these Scouts were the same men against whom the US Army first fought in the Philippines: "An army that can defeat these fellows is deserving of some credit. There are no cowards in this crowd and every man in the battalion would die fighting for the Stars and Stripes. They are intelligent and educated, and they are fond of Americans" ("Philippine Scouts Arouse Admiration," *St. Louis Republic*, April 18, 1904, p. 3). As I discuss below, it was the American public's and government's recognition of Scouts as regular members of the army that afforded the Scouts a privileged if ambiguous social position in the context of the World's Fair—and in the social climate of St. Louis in the Jim Crow South—that would cause debate and confusion over where the color line was drawn.

Unlike the other Filipinos, the Scouts were allowed off the fair site to tour the city. They were granted a leave of absence so that they could "improve their knowledge of American customs and saloon facilities" and, taking full advantage of the opportunity, the "fighting natives from Luzon were conspicuous figures on the downtown streets" ("Filipino Scouts Tour of Inspection," *St. Louis Republic*, May 2, 1904, p. 8, col. 2). Patrons accepted them warmly and were "not only willing, but eager, to buy them all the drinks their physical system would cope with" (ibid.). Locals must have had some fun with them, because "scouts were stood up on the bars in some saloons" (ibid.). Expressing themselves in Spanish, the Scouts marveled at the wonders of St. Louis. Americans, in turn, were enchanted by the Filipinos. A picture of identical-looking Scouts in uniform standing in orderly rows appears with this description:

> The scouts are neatly attired in the regulation blue of the army, and they look like good soldiers. They are models of politeness, and accept readily the cordial advances of Americans.
>
> The scout has sacred respect for women, and when he meets one, whether he knows her or not, he removes his cap and holds it in his hand until the lady has passed.
>
> As a return for this mask of respect, the scouts have been generously complimented by the women employes [sic] of the World's Fair, and some of the women, in fact, have even pronounced the Filipinos the "cutest fellows on the Exposition grounds." ("Filipino Scouts Tour of Inspection," *St. Louis Republic*, May 2, 1904, p. 8, col. 2)

The favorable reception of and response to the Scouts, made possible by their ambiguous social position as members of the US military (and complicating

Philippine Scouts on Parade at the St. Louis World's Fair, 1904. Courtesy of the Missouri Historical Society, St. Louis. http://collections.mohistory.org/resource/141295

their racial identities), would soon upset the balance of Jim Crow race relations in St. Louis and culminate in violence by the end of the summer.

While the Philippine Constabulary and the Philippine Scouts represented the assimilation of Filipinos, there were marked differences between the two. The Constabulary was funded and controlled by the insular government of the Philippines, while the Scouts were part of the regular army of the United Sates. This distinction would have important social implications in St. Louis that I will attend to momentarily. Four hundred twenty Scouts attended the fair, compared to 280 Constables, but together they accounted for more than two-thirds of Filipinos who went to St. Louis. Men in the Scout units came from diverse linguistic groups who had antagonistic relationships with each other. At first, Maj. Gen. George W. Davis of the United States Army, who commanded the Philippine Division, was hesitant to send the Scouts to the fair and pointed out the serious risks engendered by the "hostility that existed between the different native units at home, hostility that often resulted in open conflict and bloodshed" that could rupture abroad (Laurie 1995, 49). The Tagalogs and Macabebes, having fought each other under the Spanish, had a particularly antagonistic relationship. Nevertheless, Taft was in favor of sending the Scouts because it put the financial burden on the federal government, costing the Philippine treasury nothing (50). In order to bolster his position, Taft pointed out that the number of Scout desertions was well below the number of desertions by Americans in the Philippines (50). Scout troops were carefully screened and selected from four companies organized by "tribe"—Ilocanos, Tagalogs, Visayans, and Macabebes—to form one unit. This temporary organization, created solely for the purpose of sending the Scouts to the fair, was officially designated as the First Provisional Battalion, Philippine Scouts, US Army. The Scouts were given new uniforms and new weapons, intended only for display, because in the field, they had never actually used the new and more effective Krag-Jørgensen rifles (51). This demonstrates that Scouts were included without equality, and that their equal status and participation in the US Army was little more than theater directed at fairgoers, meant to represent America's assimilation of its colonial subjects. Theatrical performances (like the mock battle in Manila Bay, ending with Spain's surrender to the United States) and the Philippine Exposition itself contributed to the development of Americans' imperial ear, which heard the PC Band's music-making as the success of US empire.

To accentuate fairgoers' perceptions of the dichotomy between savagery and civilization, units of other tribal groups that could have bridged the two extremes were excluded from participation in the fair. For example, units of "Igorrote" Scouts and Constables who wore military-style jackets with their *bahag* (loincloth) and traditional headdress, as well as Muslim Constables who were given modified headgear that allowed them to touch their heads to the ground in prayer, were excluded from the Philippine Exposition. American adaptations to Filipino elements of dress were also omitted; for example, white officers in some units had adopted the traditional "Igorrote" headdress as part of their uniforms (see Cojuangco et al. 1991, 26). To incorporate representations such as these would have conceded the notion that it was possible to have an indigenous Philippine identity—one that did not erase local distinctiveness—and also be civilized. This would have gone against the claims that civilization could be attained only through assimilation to American culture, without exposing how Americans assimilated to Philippine culture. A similar fear of racial contamination was expressed in Rebecca Taylor's 1903 essay "Disposition of the Philippine Islands." She warned, "We will find ourselves Malayed Americans, even as they shall have become Americanized Malays" (quoted in Kramer 2006, 208). As much as possible, neat and impenetrable divisions between cultures in the Philippines were emphasized, and American adaptations to and assimilations of Filipino cultures were hidden—and remain almost entirely unknown today.

The Philippine Constabulary, along with the PC Band, arrived a month after the Scouts and the indigenous groups. Even before they landed on America's shores, the PC Band had already impressed audiences in Manila, Nagasaki, and Honolulu. They left Manila Bay on March 15, 1904, on the long journey for San Francisco on the transport *Sherman*, along with the rest of their battalion of two hundred enlisted men and ten officers ("Brings Famous Filipino Band," *San Francisco Call*, April 16, 1904, p. 4, col. 6). When the *Sherman* docked in Honolulu, the PC bandsmen played on the deck, alternating with the United States 11th Cavalry Band, seemingly without any enforcement of racial segregation: "With the Filipino Constabulary band and the band of the Eleventh Cavalry times were anything but dull on the *Sheridan* [sic] from Manila up" ("Sheridan from Manila," *Honolulu Evening Bulletin*, April 6, 1904, p. 1, col. 2).[13] Brass band music as a shared musical language provided a way for the Filipino and white bandsmen to interact amicably with each other and their audiences.

Reporting from Hawaii, a journalist wrote glowingly about the Filipino bandsmen:

> The constabulary band ... is composed of seventy [sic] of the finest Filipino musicians, who are said to have been drilled to a wonderful degree of perfection. Besides their own selections they play the highest class German, French, Italian and American music. Those who have heard them play in Manila accord the native musicians the highest praise and state that they render Sousa's marches with a snap and brilliancy that will make that composer look to his laurels when they play his music at the St. Louis Exposition. ("Splendid Band, Organized by Philippine Constabulary, Will Soon Be Heard Here," *San Francisco Call*, March 18, 1904, p. 7, col. 1)

The PC Band's repertoire of Euro-American band music, in addition to their excellent musicianship, is key to understanding why they were so popular with audiences. They played the "highest class" of European and American music, music that was already familiar to them before colonization, but which to the imperial ear seemed to conform to Euro-American values not to be found in the more controversial, popular ragtime songs. The reporter warns

John Philip Sousa, the most highly regarded conductor and composer of American band music, that he will "look to his laurels" when he hears the PC Band play his marches. The implication that the Filipinos might challenge America's most acclaimed band conductor was not "racially" threatening to the above writer; it also demonstrates that musical performance in a highly respected genre allowed American audiences to evaluate the PC Band in a manner different than the strict order of racial domination represented ideologically at the fair. There is nothing diminutive or insulting in this description of the Filipino bandsmen (though such ways of describing and racially marking would become prevalent in the context of the 1904 Fair). But still, there was a tacit acknowledgement of why they were so accomplished—they had been disciplined by American hands and "drilled to perfection."

Reports from Hawaiian newspapers applauded Lt. Loving without any mention of his race:

> At the close of every piece the applause was spontaneous from end to end of the garden, and cheers were called for the bandmaster and for the musicians whose fame and reputation had attracted to the roof garden a packed throng on scarcely more than an hour's notice. . . . Lieutenant Loving, the band master, was congratulated by scores at the close of the concert for the masterly exhibition and treat given by himself and his organization. The leader was admired on every hand and praised for his unquestioned genius as a director. ("Far Eastern Music," *Honolulu Evening Bulletin*, April 7, 1904, p. 5, col. 3)

The writer was well informed of Loving's military history; he mentioned that Loving visited Honolulu in 1899 as part of the 48th US Volunteer Infantry. But he did not find it important or remarkable to mention Loving's race—or to mention race at all, even when relevant, since the regiment was reserved for African Americans. No one who met Loving in person would have mistaken him for white, yet the perception and representation of Loving as an excellent conductor exceeded the need to identify him as a Black person in this case. While racial prejudice did exist between European and American whites, Hawaiian natives, and Asian immigrants in 1904 Hawaii, Loving's success in Euro-American band music and his military privilege seemed to supersede the need to emphasize his racial identity. At the St. Louis World's Fair, however, avoiding mention of Loving's race served an entirely different purpose. Rather than acknowledging Loving's achievement as an African

American, the newspapers minimized his race, which was strategic to the maintenance of his—and by extension, other Blacks'—racial marginalization. His racial identity, leadership role, and mastery of Euro-American music did not fit easily into the narrative of white domination over Filipinos and thus remained undisclosed. Identifying Loving as a Black person in this context would have highlighted African American achievement, thereby contradicting racial paradigms and threatening belief in white superiority.

When Loving and the PC Band landed in San Francisco, an entirely different scenario emerged when a reporter unleashed racist malice upon them. The reporter targeted Loving's physical appearance for the purpose of racial ridicule: "Lieutenant W. H. Loving, the chief bandmaster and the man responsible for his musicians' wonderful execution, is a crinkle-haired negro just brimming over with martial melody" ("Brings Famous Filipino Band," *San Francisco Call*, April 16, 1904, p. 4, col. 6). Loving's race was not just a matter of fact, but rather was rendered hyper-visible by employing caricatures common to one of America's favorite forms of entertainment: blackface minstrelsy. Blackface minstrelsy, writes Eric Lott, was a performance in which "white men caricatured blacks for sport and profit" (2013, 3) through speech, dress, song, dance, and theater. While white actors' distortion of Black culture "depended on the material relations of slavery, the minstrel show obscured these relations by pretending that slavery was amusing, right, and natural" (4). Racial denigration in blackface minstrelsy deployed stereotypes to control the identities of Black people through social constructions of the body, and thus Loving's achievement as a graduate of a prestigious conservatory of music could not erase, in the mind of the reporter, that he was a "crinkle-haired negro." The reporter turns next on the Filipinos and minimizes their musical success by denigrating them as animals:

> Although good musicians, the bandsmen were bad sailors. Seasickness played no favorites with the natives. They all succumbed and nearly all the time the transport was at sea 280 dusky constables suffered the dismal tortures of marine biliousness and in groaning heaps lay about the trooper's decks like a bunch of sick monkeys. ("Brings Famous Filipino Band," *San Francisco Call*, April 16, p. 4, col. 6)

The reporter represents the bandsmen as less than human, tacitly contrasting them to what one might expect from "real" (white) military men. Drawing on ideas of Filipinos as identical nonindividuals, he casts *all* of the 280 "dusky" Constables as "sick monkeys" who lay in "groaning heaps" about the deck. He renders their skin tone as other by applying the term *dusky*, meaning not necessarily black or brown, but "dark." This "dark" hue excludes them from whiteness and also prevents them from aligning with Blacks. This way of describing Filipinos' skin color would appear many times in descriptions of the bandsmen and served to emphasize their racial otherness and racial inferiority to whites, as well as differentiating them from Black Americans.

Filipinos' ambiguous position in Americans' binary conception of race as black or white posed many problems, because they were not recognizable as either.[14] In one case in 1904, four Filipino male students were barred from a Kentucky public school due to racial confusion. One member of the school board asked if they "were not negroes" ("Filipino Students Barred," *The Bee*, Kentucky, July 14, 1904, p. 1, col. 4), and the decision was made to apply the term *colored* to everyone who was not white, but also not Black. Questions over racial status as white or nonwhite had to be determined in the case of new immigrants in order for them to be eligible for US citizenship (see Lopez 2006). Filipinos span a wide range of skin tones and thus "break the rules of race" (Ocampo 2016) in the US context. The arrival of Filipinos in the US forced constructs of race to be reexamined and revised to accommodate and exclude them from the white category. However, while judgement based on their skin color was a literal or direct application of racialization, Filipinos were also subjected to orientalization, representations that denigrated them as foreign others from Asia, integrating domestic racism and anti-imperialism.[15]

The following description of the PC bandsmen's arrival in America projected the desire of Americans to be admired by Filipinos. When they embarked, the Constables

> landed by the cars at the corner of Third and Market streets. They gazed around in great amazement at the whirl and buzz of the city, and were especially interested in the electric light display. They looked at the towering Call building with admiration and delight." ("Brings Famous Filipino Band," *San Francisco Call*, April 16, 1904, p. 4, col. 6)

While the Filipino men were staring in awe at the lights and tall buildings, American eyes were staring at them. The reporter read into their reaction and interpreted it for the reader—the bandsmen "admired" American architecture and the modernity of electricity, and by extension, (white) Americans themselves. Emphasizing Filipinos' lack of modern advancements legitimized US rule over the Philippines. This way of viewing Filipinos resonated with the aims of colonial officials hoping that Filipino admiration for the US would develop into loyalty and engender their cooperation (Kramer 2006, 247). However, the bandsmen surely felt other emotions that were not recognized by the reporter, including apprehension and perhaps homesickness.

Newspapers often treated the arriving bandsmen with voyeuristic admiration while simultaneously belittling them, and this influenced the interpretation of American readers. The same article described the men as "small, but smart looking and soldierly, each little constable looks like a duplicate of the others" ("Brings Famous Filipino Band," *San Francisco Call*, April 16, 1904, p. 4, col. 6). They looked identical, according to the report, yet they were identified as being from a variety of different tribes: "Tagalogs, Visayans, Ilocanos, Moros, Bisols [*sic*], Cagayans, Macabebes, Gadons and Ibanags, in the neat uniform of the constabulary service, all look alike" (ibid.). The contradiction of identical-looking but nevertheless diverse men seems like a conundrum at first, given that racial diversity in the American context was usually glossed over or simplistically taken to mean differences in skin tone; yet readers must have been comforted by a sense of control at the meticulous listing of the unpronounceable "tribal" groups. To name, categorize, systematize, and fix the strange and incomprehensible is to divide "things Oriental into manageable parts" and quell what Said calls "a form of paranoia" about the Orient (1979, 72). Filipinos may be overwhelmingly diverse by "tribe," but rest assured that they "all look alike" and are "identifiable" visually by Americans as nonwhite, identical, and diminutive. Utilizing the categories created by the colonial census,[16] this meticulous list of tribes fulfilled a "desire to consolidate the relay between knowledge and power" (Rafael 2000, 24). Engaging a peculiar representational practice that "recast Filipino appearances" to reinforce the "link between benevolence and discipline" (23), officers reassure the reporter (and readers) that the men "are all imbued with the same spirit of loyalty to the flag and devotion to duty" ("Brings Famous Filipino Band," *San Francisco Call*, April 16, 1904, p. 4, col. 6). Finally, the report is clear about the intention of bringing Filipinos to participate in the fair: "People of the United States will have first-hand opportunity of learning a good deal about the people that inhabit Uncle Sam's Far Eastern possessions" (ibid.). The ability and power to categorize and name the different tribal groups demonstrates that Uncle Sam is indeed in charge of his possessions.

The Scouts and Constabulary, made up of Filipinos from lowland Christian groups and excluding those units that were "tribal" or Muslim, represented the possibilities of and necessity for US tutelage. Christianized Filipinos were said to respond favorably to the tutelage of the United States: once assimilated, in some years' time, they would be able to rule over the non-Christian tribes. Colonial officials hoped that Americans would understand this "bifurcated" process of assimilation, "with its parallel tracks of progress" (Kramer 2006, 260). While this may have been the intention of colonial officials and the Philippine Exposition board, Kramer argues that the average American spectator ultimately failed to make these distinctions: "American audiences would, [exposition officials] believed, take in the display proportionately, absorb its parallel narratives of Christian/non-Christian evolutionary progress, and not mistake non-Christians for the Philippine population as a whole" (265). As many scholars would agree, Americans collapsed the representations of Filipinos together onto one evolutionary track that equated civilized Filipinos with savage Filipinos, believing that Americans alone were responsible for Filipino achievement. While there were various tribes among the Cordilleran ethnolinguistic groups—Bontoc, Suyoc, Tinguian—they were all lumped together into the category of "Igorrotes" and sensationalized as "dog-eaters." Efforts to describe, distinguish, or inform ordinary people about differences between the Christians and "non-Christians"[17] were futile. For example, when Filipino students studying in the US (called *pensionados*) arrived at the fair in August, they were asked if they "liked wearing clothes" (*St. Louis Post-Dispatch*, August 10, 1904, p. 1, col. 2, quoted in Kramer 2006, 274).

Trying to understand the differences that the colonial government was emphasizing between Christian Filipinos and "non-Christian tribal people" was confusing for American observers. Contradictory ways of describing Filipinos reveal that reporters and observers saw Filipino characteristics through the lens of their own biases. For example, in a long article entitled "Features of the World's Fair: Filipinos Contrasted" (*St. Louis Republic*, May 9, 1904, p. 1, col. 1–2), Filipino military men at the fair were described as civilized and hardworking, but other articles characterized them as barbaric and lazy. Accounts of the "Igorrotes" also reveal conflicting perceptions by newspapers: for example, one article states that "women do all the hard work"

("Dog Feast to be Reward of Igorrotes' Work," *St. Louis Republic*, May 8, 1904, p. 1, col. 4), while another says, "The men work: the women do nothing" ("Features of the World's Fair: Filipinos Contrasted," *St. Louis Republic*, May 9, 1904, p. 1, col. 1–2). Comparing savage and civilized Filipinos, Lieutenant-Governor Hunt of Bontoc Province, who was in charge of the Igorrotes, stated that "it is only his uncivilized crew which displays eagerness for work, while the civilized Filipinos discover an unexampled laziness" (ibid.). The article continues to describe the Scouts: "The civilized fellows, mostly of the Filipino Scouts, are assigned upon afternoons to the completion of thatching upon houses in the main Philippines reservation. And the way that they abandon the task to lie down to bask and snooze in the sunlight is marvelous to behold" (ibid.). In this case, civilization is equated with a desire to enjoy life rather than toil in the sun—an idea projected onto American slaves in the not-too-distant past. This could be read as an expression of regret in freeing the slaves who, once no longer oppressed, were not eager to do the labor that whites demanded.

The same reporter then embarks on a richly detailed and revealing description of the Scouts' bodies:

> Fair-goers are beginning to realize the pleasure there is in watching the Filipinos drill. . . . We can well afford to take pride in them. Their small, lithe bodies, as erect as pine saplings and carrying their highly polished instruments as if they genuinely cherish them, the band members march to their station. The companies then form and go through the evolutions of drill to orders given in English. The fine appearance of the Scouts and their intelligent compliance with the minute detail of military regulations evoke a burst of applause each day from the assembled on-lookers.
>
> The only danger of the thing is that they may become so very well pleased with themselves in this particular that mere work without show will be more distasteful to them than ever.
>
> The Filipino First Lieutenant is taller than the others, and as gracefully slender as any Apollo ever modeled. The truth of it is that he is remarkably handsome. He carries himself with an easy air of command which, though knowing nothing more of him, convinces you that he is thoroughly "an officer and a gentleman."
>
> Of a similar type, though smaller of figure, is the Sergeant Major, also full-blood Filipino. When he stands attention at parade rest the perfect poise of

his body, his truly statuesque pose which knows not even the twitching of a muscle, provokes you into frantic hand-clapping of approval.

The most impressive moment of all is when the Filipino Band strikes up "The Star-Spangled Banner." Every civilian who has sufficient sense of the dignity of the moment—not all have—bares his head in respect. The swords of the officers are lowered; the Scouts are rigid in the attitude of honor to the flag and the United States. Such a picture, seen thus in the glow of a declining sun—soldiers from a land new to the Union, 10,000 miles away, joining with our own citizenship in reverence to the nation—is not soon to be forgotten. ("Features of the World's Fair: Filipinos Contrasted," *St. Louis Republic*, May 9, 1904, p. 1, col. 1–2)

I include this description of the Scouts in its entirety because it demonstrates how people at this time conflated different aspects of what they were experiencing visually and aurally, correlating their observations with ideas about Filipinos already in circulation in American media. The writer of the article engages a voyeuristic white gaze, one that, as Rafael argues, "surveys and catalogs other races while remaining unmarked and unseen itself" (1993, 200). The reporter is constructing, consuming, and making sense of these images and behaviors by drawing them into his ideas of savagery and civilization. Watching the Filipinos drill was a "pleasure" and filled the admirer with "pride" at the marvelous assimilation of the US colonial subjects. He writes about the men's bodies in an almost erotic way: "Their small, lithe bodies, as erect as pine saplings." He projects his own sentiment onto their comportment: "carrying their highly polished instruments as if they genuinely cherish them." The reporter is impressed that they are given drills in English—proof of their assimilation and adherence to American culture and values. Others take pleasure in watching them as well: "The fine appearance of the Scouts and their intelligent compliance with the minute detail of military regulations evoke a burst of applause each day from the assembled on-lookers." The first lieutenant is "naturally" the tallest in the group, as if the men's rank followed their height: "The Filipino First Lieutenant is taller than the others.... He carries himself with an easy air of command which, though knowing nothing more of him, convinces you that he is thoroughly 'an officer and a gentleman.'" Even the sergeant major, the lowest-ranking and most diminutive solider, has been made into a proper colonial subject: "When he stands attention at parade rest the perfect poise of his body, his truly statuesque pose which knows not even the twitching of a muscle, provokes you into frantic hand-clapping of approval." The most impressive moment for the writer was "when the Filipino Band strikes up 'The Star-Spangled Banner.' Every civilian who has sufficient sense of the dignity of the moment—not all have—bares his head in respect" (ibid.). The reporter is poetic and passionate about America's new "little brown brothers," in part because they seem to hold a "reverence to the nation" when "not all" of its own citizens have "sufficient sense of the dignity of the moment." For a fleeting moment, Filipinos are used as an exemplar of American citizenship and a foil for those Americans who needed to improve their show of respect for the flag. The writer infuses meaning into the whole scene by connecting past stereotypes with ideas about the meaning of civilization and his own personal vision of what he observes—people consenting, rather than forced, to accept colonial domination. As Rafael points out, "Thus was benevolent assimilation predicated on the simultaneous deployment and disavowal of violence" (1993, 186). It is with a disengaged engagement that the writer and his ethnosympathetic readers were able to take pleasure in Filipinos' apparent patriotism and "intelligent compliance" in their performance of "The Star-Spangled Banner," ignoring and forgetting the violence and coercion that brought Filipinos to America in the first place.

There were some newspaper reports that highlighted the PC Band's musical capabilities without overt racialization, but with a subtle validation of US colonial success in the Philippines. For example, several newspapers repeated the idea that the PC Band gave Sousa's band, arguably America's best, a run for its money. While this could be seen as a marketing technique intended to draw audiences to the concerts, the comparison was repeated many times by the press and was not made with other bands. Sousa himself was quoted as saying that the PC Band was the best band at the fair: "The musicians from the Philippines have made a wonderful hit at the Exposition. Sousa, the bandmaster having stamped them as the best military band he ever heard" (*St. Louis Republic*, November 6, 1904, p. 8, col. 7). An official book published by the Louisiana Purchase Exposition, *The Greatest of Expositions*, remarked of the PC Band, "Of the work of this band, the great Sousa said, 'I am simply amazed. I have rarely heard such playing'" (1904, 226). The PC Band was accepted as musically equal and even superior to other bands at the fair, but this did not contribute to whites considering Filipinos as social equals or capable of political independence. The admiration of whites was possible because Filipinos were represented as possessing "natural" musical abilities rather than skill, and their success as a musical organization was a product of US imperialism. This way of imperial hearing allowed Americans to take credit for Filipinos' tutelage and achievement while ignoring the conditions that brought them there.

Even before the Philippine Exhibit officially opened on June 18, American spectators were fascinated by the activities and behaviors of Filipinos at the Philippine "reservation." Fairgoers were interested in the "weird sound of the ganzas [*sic*; flat gongs] as the Igorrotes pounded them while they danced" (*St. Louis Republic*, April 11, 1904, p. 1, col. 3). But visitors could not distinguish between the different groups of "Igorrotes" and tended to lump all the tribal groups together as "savages." For example, it was the Bontocs rather than the Suyocs who danced and played gongs[18] (Parezo and Fowler 2007, 179). The Tinguians were rarely talked about in the press and reportedly "spurned the Bontocs' dog-meat-eating rituals and considered themselves a superior people" (179). Even though the collective "Igorrotes" were thought of and presented as savages by the American press, the Philippine Exposition board sought to demonstrate that they were capable of being civilized by encouraging fairgoers to observe their daily classes at the school. Roosevelt observed them singing a chorus of "My Country, 'Tis of Thee" during his visit to the fairgrounds. Using musical utterance as proof of benevolent assimilation, Roosevelt exclaimed enthusiastically: "Such advancement and in so short a time!" (quoted in Rydell 1984, 176). Music performed by Filipinos was heard in ways that supported political and social aims, as well as the racial assumptions of fairgoers and the press.

One important music researcher at the fair used an evolutionary model of racial development on the Philippines' "primitive" people to investigate music's origins. Frances Densmore compared her knowledge of Native American music with the similarities she perceived among the "Igorrotes," Aetas, Samal Maranaos, and Lanao Maranaos (Moon 2010, 192).[19] In this paradigm, all cultures were traveling along a single path of evolutionary development that reached its pinnacle in Western civilization. Armed with a moral imperative to preserve their music as the earliest and most primitive form of music, she argued that Philippine tribes were at "the very near beginning of musical expression" (Densmore 1906, 611). Reflecting the general trend of early anthropology as well as the overall evolutionary theme of the fair, Densmore rendered the musical features of Philippine indigenous music as primitive, and thus inferior, because they did not fit the elements of civilized Western music: "The ability to mentally retain a melody and to repeat it at will is a much higher achievement than the original production of a melody. When the melody can be voluntarily repeated, with instrumental accompaniment, it is readily elaborated, and musical progress begins to assume tangible form" (614). Lacking access to a phonographic cylinder, Densmore found it difficult to transcribe songs sung by the "Negritos" (Aeta), "because she was working with musicians who revered improvisational music and often invented songs on the spot" (Moon 2010, 197). She exclaimed that the song "has become crystalized into a remembered melody, but the emotions of love and sorrow are still too wild and uncontrolled to follow twice the same melodic path for vocal expression" (Densmore 1906, 615). Following this line of argument, she assumed that the Aetas' music was primitive because they did not repeat the melody exactly. After analyzing her notation, she realized that the melodic structure was basically the same but that the singers were adding embellishments, which to her imperial ears sounded "very much 'out of tune'" (616). A "young Negrito" told her that the Aeta people improvised the lyrics depending on their observations of the day, including insightful remarks about their American spectators: "how funny that fat American looks sitting in the corner of the theater" (616). Densmore's objective was not to document the feelings and experiences of her subjects at the fair; rather, she aimed to argue, based on racial constructs, that rhythm, for example, evolved from a primitive nonmetric form to the regular rhythmic patterns of civilized Euro-American music: "It is easy to understand how a conventional rhythm can be organized from a free rhythm, but less easy for me to believe that the impassioned cadences of the emotional songs could be evolved in a people of such rudimentary culture and effort, from a set rhythmic form. Such passionate rhythm must always be spontaneous. The white race has well-nigh lost the ability to produce it, and it would be doubly difficult to primitive natures that were accustomed first to singing in regular rhythm. For these reasons I believe that the song without rhythmic unit precedes in point of development the song in regular rhythm" (614). Her conclusions about musical development followed evolutionary theories about race based on assumptions of white superiority.

Turning to the Muslim Filipinos, Densmore concluded that the Moros' musical ensemble, gongs and drum called kulintang, lacked logic and coherence, not because it actually did, but because her imperial ears failed to grasp how kulintang musical structure worked. She writes, "I am convinced that the rhythms have originally no connection with one another, but by repetition in concert they come eventually to coincide at certain points. Every student of primitive music is aware that uncivilized peoples handle combinations of rhythm in a way that bewilders a civilized musician" (Densmore 1906, 626). Listening with imperial ears that rendered the interlocking rhythmic patterns as existing in a "cheerful chaos" and "changing ... according to their fancy," Densmore was unable to make sense of their complexity. If the "civilized" musicologist is bewildered, it is only because the racial or oriental other is uncivilized and chaotic. The power to name and "discover" an organizational structure to the savages' noise-making is only in the hands of the educated Westerner. Her scholarship validated a way of imperial hearing for decades. Densmore only attends to the Philippine bands at the end of her study by lamenting that "the sunset gun is measuring the days until all the Filipino music shall be merged at last in The Star-spangled Banner" (632). While she shows concern for the hegemonic imposition of Western music on colonial subjects, she failed to recognize that the band was an important part of Philippine music-making that existed for centuries before the arrival of the US. In her mind, Euro-American music would eventually assimilate all Filipino music and cause its extinction. This view eradicated the possibility of analyzing Filipino expression in Western forms, because these forms belonged only to whites.

Brass Bands, Ragtime, and Euro-American Musical Hegemony at the Fair

At the time of the LPE, European music represented the highest form of art, a perception that was created, cultivated, and sustained by racial, imperial, and colonial ideologies. While ragtime gained popularity among the masses, it threatened the cultural hegemony of the elite. Because of this, the Bureau of Music of the LPE wanted to emphasize Euro-American musical repertory to minimize the social threat of popular music, with its origins in and association with Black culture. Yet one member, Ernest Kroeger, who was in charge of music programming, disagreed, insisting that the bureau include other musical styles to please the masses of fairgoers (Hylton 1991, 59). He reminded them of the 1893 Columbian Exposition's warning "in the most emphatic manner that a scheme of high-class music at any Exposition would be serious mistake" (Kroeger 1904, quoted in Schwartz and Schwartz 2003, 1). Despite these warnings, the Bureau of Music was determined to educate audiences and "refine" their tastes by emphasizing "high-class" music performed by concert bands. Concert band repertoire typically consisted of arrangements of operatic and symphonic excerpts by European masters such as Wagner, Beethoven, Gluck, Liszt, Mendelssohn, Meyerbeer, Tchaikovsky, and Verdi (Schwartz and Schwartz 2003, 2). American composers, who were often bandleaders themselves (for example, John Philip Sousa, Theodore Moses Tobani, Victor Herbert, and Stephen Foster),[20] composed lighter fare for brass bands, such as marches and arrangements of folk and popular songs, in the style of European classical music (2). Compared to "serious" works for symphony orchestra, these pieces had memorable, simple melodies with lots of repetition, and lively rhythmic sections. Thus, between offering music of entertainment that would please the crowds and music of education that would uphold elite values, the Bureau of Music chose to maintain a focus on arrangements of European classical music played by concert bands, allowing for some popular marches and light classical pieces by American composers. Very few ragtime pieces were programmed or listed in the official programs of the fair (see Schwartz and Schwartz 2003).

Despite these efforts, many Americans were attracted to the new popular music of ragtime and Tin Pan Alley. The excitement, effervescence, and energy—as well as a youthfulness encompassing power, vitality, and kinesthetic intensity (what Gottschild called the "ephebism" of Black expression [2002, 15])—appealed to the novelty-seekers of early twentieth-century America, who were looking for alternatives to the oppressive and limiting social standards of the late nineteenth century. Music became the emotional substance to invigorate young people, the masses, and those who embraced the spirit of innovation, risk-taking, and adventure. Critics of ragtime, however, warned of its detrimental effects, as it was thought to encourage excess, vice, and licentiousness. Elite and conservative whites made a plea to regulate or even prohibit the playing of ragtime at the fair; they argued that ragtime could influence a person's morals in the same way as alcohol. One article reported that "it kills the better understanding.... The plague of trashy music is upon us like a fever epidemic, and its evil effects can be heard at all times and in most places" ("Says Ragtime Is Like Absinthe," *St. Louis Republic*, June 3, 1904, p. 2, col. 5). This article goes on to defend the cultural elite's deference for all things European, even at the expense of promoting homegrown American expression: "America has a low standard of music. . . . [Ragtime music] is poisonous to the youthful mind" (ibid.). It also reveals a disdain for brass band ensembles, instead favoring symphony orchestras: "for all ages of civilization the road to musical refinement has been by way of the stringed instrument, and not by those of percussion or wind" (ibid.). The educated elite favored the music of the symphony, not the middlebrow repertoire of John Philip Sousa or the popular music of the masses. Nevertheless, concert band music of the late nineteenth and early twentieth centuries was deemed to be legitimate and safe by fair organizers because its core repertoire took highbrow European music such as opera overtures and channeled it through a popular middlebrow ensemble, while also including high-spirited American patriotic marches. Despite the PC Band's and Loving's adherence to the tradition of playing Euro-American band music, they were, as racial others, also a novel and welcome variation to the standard American and European military bands, bridging a desire for the unusual while remaining safely within acceptable norms. To appeal to the masses of Americans and also meet the approval of elites, the PC Band excluded ragtime music from its repertoire.

Ragtime music as originally practiced by Black musicians was entirely different from what would become the "ragtime songs" or "coon songs" generated by Tin Pan Alley.[21] Ragtime spread north when New Orleans musicians traveled the Mississippi to Chicago as part of the Great Migration (see Schneider 2006, Milan 2009, and Carney 2012). The earliest published compositions of ragtime appeared in the 1880s and '90s (Berlin 2002, 99), but the style had existed as an oral tradition in Black communities of the post–Civil War era. "Ragging," as invented in the culturally diverse milieu of New Orleans (which included Caribbean musicians), began not as a genre of music, but as a rhythmic style of playing that could be applied to any type of music. Ragtime syncopation emphasized the offbeat, placing emphasis on the second and fourth beats of a four-beat measure, or the second beat of a two-beat pattern.[22] Black musicians could transform any piece by playing it in a rag style, even the marches of Sousa (76). According to Berlin, the "rag" and the syncopated march provided music for a kind of dance music called the two-step (100). When a dance called the cakewalk swept into the ballrooms of the US and Europe, its musical accompaniment also adopted some of the syncopations of ragtime, and soon the terms became interchangeable in the titles of pieces circulated by the music publishers of Tin Pan Alley. As the accompaniment to these dances "adopted the smaller rhythmic divisions of ragtime syncopation, syncopated cakewalks, syncopated two-steps, and ragtime became one and the same" in the minds of most listeners (104). By the 1890s, the term *ragtime* was also conflated with Tin Pan Alley coon songs and minstrel songs (5), and it was this association in particular that led the PC Band to exclude ragtime from its repertoire in the US.

Just before the official start of the fair, the Bureau of Music placed a ban on ragtime, and the PC Band made a vehement statement against the genre:

> FILIPINO MUSICIANS REFUSE TO PLAY RAGTIME. Nauseating ragtime and barbarous coon songs will not be included in the repertoire of the Constabulary Band, which is to furnish music on the Philippine reservation during the World's Fair.
>
> The mere suggestion of ragtime, it is said, will move a member of the Constabulary Band to violence. The Filipino musician turns up his nose at the mention of "Bedelia," according to Lieutenant Walter H. Loving, leader of the Filipino band. The bandsman devotes all his energy to the best classic selections of music. (*St. Louis Republic*, April 23, 1904, p. 8, col. 4)

If the report is accurate, the PC Band's strong reaction is intriguing, given that before arriving in the US, they played some popular songs in Manila, including "Hiawatha" by Moret,[23] in addition to European classical music and American marches. While "Hiawatha" was labeled as a ragtime or two-step work that circulated throughout Asia between 1903 and 1905, it was not a "coon song" like "Bedelia," as I explain below.[24] Coon songs, emerging from the minstrel show, were considered lower-class because of derogatory lyrics and often offensive language. "Hiawatha" held a different connotation in the US compared to the Philippines: not as a socially acceptable popular song but one that belonged to an inferior form of music called ragtime. Loving and the bandsmen may have shifted their repertoire toward "respectable" music to avoid criticism for associating with lower-class music. The distinction between "coon song" and "two-step," both often referred to as ragtime in common parlance, was significant to the band, because they did indeed play a few pieces entitled "two-step" at the 1904 Fair.[25] By omitting pieces labeled as ragtime, especially those associated with coon songs, the PC Band was not rejecting a genre with origins in Black music, but rather those songs that ridiculed and denigrated Black people. As mentioned in the previous chapter, the lyrics of coon songs were often used to insult Black soldiers in the Philippines.

Coon songs and minstrel songs exotified and demeaned racial others "in response to social and political movements—suffrage, abolition, and immigration"—including not only Black Americans but also Germans, Irish, and Chinese (Moon 2003, 31).[26] The coon song "Bedelia" was aimed at mocking the Irish, who were often the subject of scorn in America in the early to mid 1800s (Nowatzki 2007, 163). Irish minstrels soon took up the genre themselves and joined in the ridiculing of Blacks by wearing blackface makeup and using a "negro dialect." By degrading Black people, the Irish shifted attention away from themselves as they sought acceptance in American society. "Bedelia" was composed by the songwriting team of William Jerome and Jean Schwartz in the popular Tin Pan Alley style, which often featured "internal rhymes sung to a catchy melody with a syncopated rhythm and marked by sudden shifts from minor to major modes, and back again. If at times the results sometimes sounded more *klezmer* than Hibernian, no one seemed to mind" (Berlin 2002, 189–90).[27] The lyrics reference stereotypical images of Irishness by invoking place names like Killarney and using the nickname "Emerald Isle" for Ireland. "Bedelia," like many coon songs, minstrel songs, and ragtime songs, satisfied American tastes for the novel, in this case by exotifying Irish women. By the 1850s, depictions of Chinese immigrants appeared in minstrel shows in response to their growing presence in the US, arousing fear over their impact on labor and culture. White actors in "yellowface," who dressed up as caricatured versions of Chinese people and spoke in a mocking accent or pure gibberish, circulated "particular ideas about the Chinese as an unassimilable, inferior race" (Moon 2005, 32). Anti-Chinese sentiments in songs like "Heathen Chinee" and "John Chinaman" helped to "codify stereotypes and expressed fears that led ultimately to exclusionary legislation" (31).[28]

Music about the Philippines also existed in the coon song style. Those that circulated during the time of the Spanish-American and Philippine-American Wars were "crude and offensive," such as the "racially deprecating" "Monkeys Have No Tails in Zamboanga" and "Little Brown Brother," with its chorus, "He [the Filipino] may be a brother of Big Bill Taft, but he ain't no brother of mine" (Walsh 2013, xvii–xviii).[29] Their offensive lyrics "crudely transposed long-held American prejudices and stereotypes onto an unfamiliar Philippine culture" (xviii). As had been the case in political cartoons from the same time period, Filipinos were characterized in similar and often identical ways as Black Americans were in minstrel shows (see Ignacio et al. 2004). Imperial expansion into the Pacific brought American popular music to the Philippines, but the negative regard of music with Black origins was not shared abroad, because it was associated more often with modern American culture.[30] As mentioned earlier, the Black soldier-musicians of the 24th Infantry made money and were popular among Filipinos and Americans by playing minstrel shows during their time in Manila. But in America, the conflation of coon songs and minstrel songs with ragtime may have contributed to Loving and the PC Band's excluding from their programs of all pieces considered ragtime, with the exception of a few refined two-step compositions on which I will elaborate below. By emphasizing Euro-American band music repertoire, the PC Band strategically aligned themselves with acceptable values and norms, much like Black American uplifters who sought to express themselves in elite European arts like classical music.[31]

African American musicians' contributions to European classical music, like those of Loving, are overlooked in music history. Schenbeck's eye-opening book *Racial Uplift and American Music: 1878–1943* sheds light on African Americans' training, careers, and views of music during a time in which they had to advocate for society to regard them as fully equal human beings who were capable of expressing themselves artistically in a genre upheld as the pinnacle of civilized culture. Black classical musicians drew from an elitist, educated version of racial uplift that aimed to win social equality "by stressing respectable middle-class behavior, class distinctions parallel to those in white society" (Schenbeck 2012, 23). By practicing classical European art forms, "many in the black intelligentsia maintained a wary distance from black popular music, in part because of its distasteful proximity to the minstrel legacy" (131). Coon songs were not Black music per se, but offensive songs about Black people. Nathaniel Dett, a Black composer and pianist, wrote in his memoir about the perception of ragtime music in the early twentieth century: "At that time there was little respect for Negro music or its possibilities. To most people, Negro music was merely 'rag time'—something to be amused at, danced to, or employed as a ready-made missile of ridicule if not actual ill will against Negro citizens. At that time, to talk with colored people about Negro music was to embarrass them, since the general attitude of the public toward such music was mildly contemptuous" (Dett, "From Bell Stand to Throne Room," quoted in Schenbeck 2012, 110). Thus, the Black elite's rejection of these songs was not a denunciation of Black culture per se, but a rebuke of the ways that Black people were depicted in these songs. Black elites attempted to refashion their representation in popular culture by highlighting their mastery of "high-class" European music. In my view, Loving used this same approach to make choices in the repertoire of the PC Band. Loving may have rejected ragtime, not as a refutation of a music associated with Black culture, but because of its negative caricaturing of Black people. When jazz emerged shortly after this time period, a negative connotation still tainted its acceptance: "It is important to remember that much coverage in the popular press of what was called 'jazz' in the early twentieth century was sensationalist and based on pejorative race and class tropes. The average white American saw 'jazz' as a threat to his community's morals and safety" (Schenbeck 2012, 142).

Despite the origins of minstrelsy, some Black actors and musicians participated in it because they had few entry points into mainstream entertainment:[32] "Although the opportunity to make a living in the entertainment world appealed to many black musicians, it did not come without severe drawbacks. They inherited white-created stereotypes and felt constrained to play within their boundaries" (Schenbeck 2012, 64). One of most famed actors, for example, was Bert Williams,[33] and one of the most famous songs was "All Coons Look Alike to Me" (1895) by Ernest Hogan. To white audiences, Black actors and musicians' participation seemed to condone minstrelsy and coon songs while infusing them with authenticity: "Worse yet, by impersonating Zip Coon and Jim Crow, they lent credibility to those demeaning character types, receiving praise for their ability to depict white fantasies of blackness" (64). This impersonation was rewarded by white society and not regarded as impersonation or acting at all: "This 'acting' was not considered a matter of talent. Rather it was received as the natural behavior of a spontaneous, musical people, displayed in a way that the performers enjoyed quite as much as the audience. The hard work and genuine ability of individual troupers was seldom acknowledged, because part of the trope of authenticity was the notion of blacks as nature's children" (64). This way of regarding Black talent as natural—and therefore racial—extended to Filipinos, whose "authenticity" was in (seemingly) possessing natural abilities in music and performance to mimic Western forms. To acknowledge that skill, intelligence, and effort, rather than natural ability, were the reasons for the PC Band's success would be to admit that they had the capacity to master the forms of civilization, a view that ran counter to the logics of racism, imperialism, and colonialism.

The National Association of Colored Women, which met during the fair (with the participation of Mrs. Booker T. Washington), also denounced ragtime and coon songs:

> "Coon Songs," "Ragtime Music," and all music of a tropical nature was severely criticized by Mrs. Ida Joyce Jackson of Colorado Springs in her report of the music department of the association. Mrs. Jackson said that all of this class of music, which had become so popular of late with both white and colored people, should be shunned by negroes, as there was not one of the productions that did not hold the negro up to public ridicule. Mrs. Jackson made a strong plea for the general introduction of classic music among her people, and said that much had already been accomplished in that direction. ("Negro Women Taboo Coon Songs," *St. Louis Republic*, July 14, 1904, p. 3, col. 6–7)

Due to the discrimination that they met at the fairgrounds, they thought it wise to hold their meeting at a local church. To the educated members of National Association of Colored Women, ragtime (and its association with coon songs) was one of the ways Black Americans were denigrated, exacerbating their unfair treatment not only at the fair but also in American society.

Even Scott Joplin, "the King of Ragtime," lamented the lyrics of ragtime and coon songs, saying that the texts were "vulgar" and had little to do with ragtime as music: "I have wondered why some composers will continue to make the public hate ragtime melodies because the melodies are set to such bad words." He went on to suggest that "if someone were to put vulgar words to a strain of Beethoven's beautiful Symphonies, people would begin saying: 'I don't like Beethoven Symphonies'" (quoted in Berlin 2006, 36). Joplin never participated in any official performances of the 1904 Fair, but he is said to have visited the fair (inspiring his piece "The Cascades"), and he may have even performed on the Pike, the fair's entertainment zone (Curtis 1994, 138). The fair's official band, which was led by William Weil, performed Joplin's most famous composition, "The Entertainer," on June 21, 1904 (Schwartz and Schwartz 2003, 110), and was the only band to perform a Joplin piece. Despite Joplin's exclusion from official participation at the fair, African American newspaper *Sedalia Weekly Conservator* was very proud of the praises he received in other newspapers, which called him "the most gifted composer of his race," one who "stands in a class by himself as a composer and writer of the American syncopation known as rag-time" ("What They Say about Scott Joplin," *Sedalia Weekly Conservator*, August 5, 1904, p. 1, col. 1). Joplin's refined, composed piano ragtime pieces were nothing like the coon songs of minstrelsy (mis)labeled as ragtime, yet his compositions, along with other performances of ragtime music, were relegated to the Pike's entertainment zone and, but for a few exceptions, not included in the official music programs of the LPE. While no records indicate that Joplin ever met the PC Band, he must have heard of them, and perhaps even attended a performance. However, if he did not see the band in person, it is unlikely that he was aware that Loving was a Black American, since not one of over a hundred articles by St. Louis newspapers identifies his race.

Joplin was probably optimistic at how the fair could showcase African Americans' contributions to society. There were promises of equal treatment to "anyone who has the money" ("The St. Louis Fair at Night," *The St. Louis Palladium*, June 4, 1904, p. 1, col. 4, quoted in Curtis 1994, 140).[34] Black leaders advocated for a Negro Day on August 1 to highlight the contributions of St. Louis's African American community, who made up nearly 10 percent of the population, yet there was little attempt to include any Black leaders in the planning of the fair or its events (Jackson 2004, 99). Although Black workers helped to build the palaces and other structures, they were not hired for steady work (99). When African Americans' financial support was needed, however, they were encouraged to attend: "Driven by a desire to increase attendance, exposition officials adopted an official nondiscrimination policy and invited black St. Louisans to sponsor events that would bring African Americans to the Fairgrounds" (Corbett 1999, 153). Despite this gesture, reports of discrimination soon spread among the African American community, including being denied entry to various concessions and restaurants and barred from white-only fountains, having no access to drinking water at all. To serve their community, Black workers and businesses supplied "off-site services to black visitors, providing lodging, food and drink in their own establishments" (Bundles 2001, 72). Ultimately, Black Americans did not participate in the fair's planning and were represented only in the nostalgic "Old Plantation" exhibit, which was a "portrayal of white imagination designed to make slavery appear desirable" (Parezo and Fowler 2009, 256).

Many groups canceled their planned events or boycotted the fair entirely, as was the case with the 8th Illinois regiment, who originally planned to march in a parade but were told that they would not be allowed to stay on the fairgrounds (Jackson 2004, 99). Eventually "Negro Day" was canceled, and hopes for Black inclusion and involvement in the fair dissipated in the face of the realities of racism and segregation.

While much effort, time, and money were directed to the strategy of racial uplift by elite Black Americans, Schenbeck concludes, "Little evidence had accumulated that investment in uplift ideology, when manifested in cultural production, could or would reap significant concessions from the dominant culture: it was impossible to determine whether the existence of Negro symphonies and string quartets might hasten the passage of anti-lynching legislation" (2012, 131). This effort to argue for and provide evidence of Black Americans' artistic capabilities, and thus humanity, was central to critiquing racism and creating a sense of cohesiveness among elite African Americans, since "black intellectuals could ill afford to abandon an even partially useful strategy given the bleakness of the political climate. Ethnosympathy had severe limitations, but its absence might prove even more deadly" (131). But to ethnosympathetic white listeners, Black performances of European classical music were less appealing—the "cult of authenticity was infected from the very beginning by whites' desires that black culture remain somehow 'pure' (i.e., static)" (33). Black intellectuals like W. E. B. Du Bois denounced this argument as racially restrictive: "What it really means is that Negroes must not be allowed to attempt anything more than the frenzy of the primitive, religious revival" (quoted in Schenbeck 2012, 149). To ethnosympathetic listeners, like the writer of the letter to the editor at the beginning of this chapter, the authenticity of Filipino musicians could only be appreciated by projecting a patriotic sentiment for America onto their skilled performances. An imperial ear attributed the band's exceptional musical skills to the United States' successful tutelage of naturally musical natives.

Despite the cultural elite's scorn for popular music, even President Roosevelt's daughter expressed her fondness for ragtime music. The *St. Louis Republic* reported: "Surrounded by a dozen young women and attracting the attention of a large number of others, Alice Roosevelt did a lively shuffle on the horseshoe piazza of the Casino the other morning. The orchestra struck up a bit of ragtime just as Miss Roosevelt stepped on the plaza, and she could not resist the temptation" ("Society at Summer Resorts," *St. Louis Republic*,

August 28, 1904). Foreign visitors were intrigued by ragtime music as well. Prince Pu Lun, imperial Chinese commissioner to the World's Fair and heir to the throne of China, expressed an interest in ragtime music, and a St. Louis composer, Charles Kunkel, "a great admirer of the Prince," composed a march for him called "Pu Lun Triumphal March" ("Prince Pu Lun Enjoys Ragtime," *St. Louis Republic*, May 9, 1904, p. 8, col. 3). Kunkel visited the prince at his hotel and "said that he would play 'The Cotton Pickers,' by Leroy Hartt, which he selected as a characteristic 'ragtime' composition. He explained to the Prince that the world 'ragtime' might be hard to interpret, but that it really means not bad music but a rhythm peculiar to the negro melodies of the South" (ibid.). Kunkel, a white composer, acknowledged ragtime music's origin as a Black music of the South while also refuting negative perceptions of the genre. While perhaps not as visible to the American public, there were people who were willing to acknowledge Black cultural production and engage in it without the denigrating and comedic aspects. The social contextualization of ragtime linked it to racial difference and forced people to grapple with justifying why they enjoyed it. Presumably, foreigners like the prince had no prior racial and social context for the music—a context created within and between American racial groups—and were drawn to the music as music. As with the "Moros" and the Black porters, music and musical performance created interest across racial lines and provided a space for cross-cultural interaction.

Another development fueling the craze for popular music was mechanical reproduction. While widespread availability of commercial sound recordings was still more than a decade away, mechanical means of reproducing music on phonographs and player pianos were showcased at the 1904 Fair. At the music section of the Liberal Arts building, "automatic pianos rendering 'classic' music" were positioned "only 200 feet away from exhibition phonographs and the sound of one counteracts the effect of the other. While the piano player in the piano section is rendering some Wagnerian classic, the probabilities are that the phonographs are rendering the air with 'Hiawatha,' 'A Hot Time,' and other ever-popular ragtime selections" ("Classic and Syncopated Music Clash at Fair: Phonographs and Automatic Pianos Are So Close Together that Results Are Inharmonious," *St. Louis Republic*, May 24, 1904, p. 8, col. 3). Player piano rolls recorded a live musician by perforating a roll of paper as the musician played, then reproduced this performance by controlling the keys of an acoustic piano. Phonographs recorded sound by etching grooves of sound waves on wax cylinders, which could be played back when amplified (Burgess 2014, 5–11). Intriguingly, both of these musics were mechanically reproduced, yet a distinction of taste is drawn between the two, an example of the clash between clinging to America's European heritage of "classical" music and embracing ragtime as a new kind of syncopated music with Black origins.

Around the time of the St. Louis World's Fair, ragtime was slowly losing its ethnic characteristics and blending into what was considered American popular music.

> Public acceptance of ragtime, as shown by the enormous increase in commercial publications in 1899, was coupled with the gradual absorption of its name and style into the mainstream of American popular music. Ragtime as an exoticism, as a quaint music from the fringes of society, was replaced by ragtime the white American popular music. Through 1902 the vast majority of rag publications still made obvious reference to the music's black origins, usually by the title or cover picture ... and sometimes with the inclusion of a coon-song chorus. In 1903 there was a substantial reduction in the percentage of ethnic depictions, to about 50 percent, and by 1904 reference to blackness in ragtime appeared in only a minority of publications, about 20 percent, the proportions growing smaller in the following years. (Berlin 2002, 123)

As the abusive stereotypes faded in the twentieth century, so did ragtime's identity as rooted in Black music: "This deracialization of ragtime songs was, in fact, viewed by James Weldon Johnson (1871–1938), a prominent writer on black culture, as a theft from the black man" (Berlin 2002, 5–6). References to and omissions of race in music were rarely neutral or simply about music, impacting representations in complex ways in a larger cultural, political, and social context. In all of their performances during the US colonial era, the PC Band and Loving navigated a complicated racialized musical landscape in strategic ways that contributed to their success.

Despite their reportedly vehement public rejection of ragtime music and coon songs in April, the PC Band's repertoire, when examined thoroughly, reveals that they did in fact program a few pieces that would have been considered popular music. In August, Loving arranged a composition called the "Jolliar Two-Step" by Miss Edwina Garrison Tutt, the daughter of a St. Louis patron.[35] In this context, Loving probably arranged the composition for his and the band's social benefit. Three other pieces on the PC Band's programs are called "two-step": Myers's "The Belle of St. Louis, Two-Step" (Schwartz and Schwartz 2003, 172), Onofre's arrangement of "Germinal, Two-Step" by Estrella (193), and Stone's "The Belle of the Philippines, Two-Step" (235). Although these are a far cry from ragtime music's association with "coon songs," they are indeed popular fare, and not at all European concert repertoire. Fred S. Stone's composition is the most interesting because he was a Black Canadian who grew up in Detroit (Milan 2009, 15) and was a well-known ragtime composer. His most popular work is an instrumental entitled "Ma Ragtime Baby," recorded by the Edison Concert Band in 1899 and released in 1905 as an Edison Gold Moulded Record. "The Belle of the Philippines, Two-Step" has light syncopation and a moderate dance-like feel, not unlike a Joplin composition. Two-steps were slower in tempo than piano rags (Berlin 1994, 155), but if played faster, they would have the same stylistic musical elements as other ragtime pieces, including syncopated broken chords, accents on the offbeats, and similar harmonic progressions. Featured on the cover of "Belle of the Philippines" is a refined, well-dressed woman with Caucasian features. Perhaps this piece was acceptable because the lyrics were benign, if generic, with no racially derogatory references: "You are the Belle of the Philippines. The sweetest girl I ever seen. I'd like to have you for my Queen. No girl is fair as the Belle of the Philippines."[36] While "The Belle of the Philippines" and other two-steps were rare in its repertoire, the PC Band's performance of them demonstrates that, despite their earlier rejection of ragtime music, they catered to audiences in their social circle and, like Sousa, used their social and cultural capital to present the music in a refined and acceptable way. William Weil, leader of the fair's official band, programmed the most ragtime pieces of any of the fair's band directors. He programmed Stone's "Belle of the Philippines," as well as compositions by other African Americans, such as Turpin's "The St. Louis Rag" and Joplin's "The Entertainer" (see Schwartz and Schwartz 2003). Like Sousa, Weil's position and social capital allowed him to program ragtime without being tainted by negative musical, social, and racial implications.

It is interesting—and unexpected—to find that the PC Band also performed a few pieces by female composers. In addition to the composition "Jolliar, Two-Step" by Miss Tutt, the band performed "Under the Rose, Waltzes" by Henrietta B. Blanke, Helen May Butler's "Cosmopolitan America, March" (which the composer also performed with her ladies' brass band at the fair), Louise V. Gustin's "Janice Meredith, Waltzes," and Ellen Wright's

"Violets." Perhaps seeing an all-female brass band was influential to my great-grandfather Pedro B. Navarro, because eventually he founded an all-female brass band in the Philippines with his college-age daughters in the 1920s (see Talusan 2009). While the PC Band seemed to align themselves publicly with predominantly male middle-class and elite values, on closer inspection, they played some ragtime pieces (with the exclusion of racially derogatory coon songs) and were willing to be inclusive of Black and also female composers in a popular style.

There was some controversy, apparently, over a piece the PC Band performed called "West Door, H. R." ("'West Door, H. R.' Admired for Its Merit as Well as Name," *St. Louis Republic*, August 3, 1904, p. 8, col. 6). It was written by composer and bandleader Capt. Lem H. Wiley, who had been in charge of the west door of the House of Representatives as a doorkeeper. He wrote the piece "at the time when the Philippine question was under debate in the House of Representatives," likely the period that led up to the ratification of the Treaty of Paris, which approved annexation of the Philippines, Guam, and Puerto Rico by a very narrow margin on February 6, 1899 (see Kramer 2006, 110–11, and Ignacio et al. 2004, 13). At the fair, "considerable curiosity has been aroused by the title, and it has increased as the piece has been heard and admired by World's Fair visitors." Loving was noticeably quick to take up this piece for the PC Band's concerts:

> It is an interesting fact that the first band on the World's Fair grounds to take up and play "West Door, H. R." was the Philippine Constabulary Band. Doctor Loving has been trying it for several days. The piece has proven very popular and has elicited much comment. It is a military march, and may become of semiofficial character with the Philippine people by reason of the circumstances under which it was written and by reason of the popularity it has attained.
>
> The Filipinos take to it as a composition specially suitable to their tastes. "West Door, H. R." was first played in manuscript by the Marine Band at Washington. It was then taken up by Sousa and has been heard at the World's Fair repeatedly during the past week. ("'West Door, H. R.' Admired for Its Merit as Well as Name," *St. Louis Republic*, August 3, 1904, p. 8, col. 6)

The PC Band's performance of this piece resonated with the sentiments of those who supported US colonization of the Philippines, garnering respect from the Marine Band and Sousa, colonial officials, and the American public, since it represented the success of US endeavors. It is curious that the reporter did not use Loving's military title, but instead bestowed on him the title of "doctor." Perhaps he meant to emphasize Loving's education or use the title in a similar way to which bandmasters might be called "professor," but he also obscured Loving's position as a military officer. Notably, he does not mention Loving's race, which would lead many readers to assume that he was white.

A survey of the pieces played by brass bands at the 1904 Fair reveals that some compositions were more popular than others (a list of pieces from the official programs is catalogued in Schwartz and Schwartz 2003). The most often-played composer at the fair was Germany's Richard Wagner, with 570 entries; John Philip Sousa, the first American composer on this list, came in seventh, with 203 entries (Schwartz and Schwartz, ii, iv). The composition receiving an outstanding number of performances was "The Star-Spangled Banner," with 268 entries (iv). The PC Band played it the most times out of any organization (264–70), and this frequency indicates how important it was to emphasize the successful colonization of the Philippines and the assimilation of Filipino subjects. Besides the Philippine bands, only the Mexican Band was not from Europe or the United States.

The St. Louis Fair featured two Native American bands: the Haskell Indian Band and the Government Indian Band (*Government Official Indian Band* 1909). Brass band and military band performance in the US has been used as a disciplining force to align racial wards toward Euro-American values, based on the belief that it had a beneficial influence: "The notion that certain kinds of music could exert a positive moral effect had been in play since the 1830s, but it received renewed emphasis in major American urban centers during the prosperous postwar years, as civic leaders sought ways of channeling and refining the energies of their citizenry" (Schenbeck 2012, 51). The Office of Indian Affairs made careful use of music to assimilate Indian youth in boarding schools, away from their "uncivilized" communities, families, and culture. This was precisely an effort to distance and alienate them from their tribal affiliations, languages, dress and behavior, and history (Troutman 2012, 7), in order for them to acquire the values of "civilized" American society. Sanctioned music was overwhelmingly Euro-American, including brass band repertoire. At the world's fair, the Government Official World's Fair Indian Band performed twice daily and drew large crowds (122). The thirty-five band members were exceptional student musicians drawn from a number of Indian school bands, and they represented several different tribes: the

Pueblos, Pimas, Moquis, Mojaves, Navajos from Arizona and New Mexico; the Chippewas from Minnesota; the Sioux from the Dakotas; the Cherokees, Pawnees, Peorias, Senecas, and Wyandottes from Oklahoma and the Indian Territories; and the Puyallups and Sans Pail from Washington (*Government Official Indian Band* 1909, 3).[37] The Indian Band was also meant to convey the government's successful assimilation and tutelage of America's nonwhites through the performance of brass band music.

Social Engagement with White Society

In addition to the PC Band, the Philippine Scouts Band was also a hit with fair audiences. The Scouts Band was a smaller group, directed by white officer Eugene P. Fischer of the US Army. One enthusiastic young fairgoer wrote:

> The Philippine [Scouts] Band pleased me more than all the rest, they seemed to be natural born musicians. . . . I just felt like cheering to hear those little chaps playing "America," "Star Spangled Banner," [and] "Yankee Doodle." . . . They played these and a lot more of our patriotic songs, just like they had know [sic] them all of their lives and meant every bit of it. . . . I believe people will remember them when others are forgotten. (*The Diary of Laura Merritt*, quoted in Schwartz and Schwartz 2003, 3)

Although she expressed great enthusiasm for the Scouts Band, the teenage girl referred to the grown men as "little chaps," a statement that reflected the absorption of Taft's "little brown brothers" into Americans' parlance in reference to Filipinos. Compared to the frightening, half-naked tribes people displaying "savage" behavior and playing primitive music, the reserved, rational military men playing patriotic songs were not only comprehensible, but also rather endearing to the public. The ethnosympathetic girl applauded the quality of the Scouts Band's performance and made assumptions about the musicians' patriotic intent to take comfort in their benevolent assimilation. This illusion of loyalty to the colonial power was precisely the aim in representations of colonial military bands as instruments of empire.

Yet, American fairgoers were attracted to the Filipino military men for reasons other than music and patriotism. Some white women in St. Louis found them incredibly appealing and desirable socially: "Romantic girls admired then [sic] and took no pains to conceal the fact. They thought the island soldiers were too cute for anything. Because they supposed that none of the soldiers could speak or understand English, the girls permitted themselves to go further with mild flirtations than they would ever have thought of doing with white men, soldiers or civilians" ("St. Louis Color Line Problem at the Fair: Filipino Soldiers Aspire," *St. Louis Post-Dispatch*, July 3, 1904, p. B3). The young women breached racial barriers and social norms by asking the men to write their names on calling cards and accompany them around the exposition, outside of the Philippine Exhibit. The Scouts' commanding officer, Maj. William H. Johnston, freely granted them leave of absence because, from the point of view of the colonial government and the Philippine Exposition board, fraternization with whites was positive, assuming that the troops would become more Americanized and "gain a wider and more intimidating sense of their imperial sponsors" (Kramer 2006, 278). This troubled the *St. Louis Post-Dispatch* reporter because "St. Louis [has] not yet reconciled to seeing white-skinned girls going with brown-skinned men" (July 3, 1904, p. B3). Dressed in khaki and blue with brass buttons, the Scouts' uniform associated them with the US Army, allowing "foolish young girls" to ignore the color line and seek their company: "Their uniforms have drawn to them attentions of a character which they would never have received in their native apparel." To wit, the "tribes who do not wear Uncle Sam's uniforms have not been the recipients of the attentions as the soldiers." Yet, uniform alone was not adequate to explain the women's fascination and desire, for the Scouts man "is in higher favor than any other of the wearers of the uniforms at the Fair. The prettiest girls often turn away from the Jefferson guards to beam upon the dark brown soldier from the Philippines" (ibid.). Not only "foolish young girls," the reported admitted, but also "women of some social standing" pursued the Scouts' company (ibid.). Expressing racial animosity, US Marines "scowl and mutter 'niggers' and soulfully yearn to punch the heads of the presumptuous soldiers and not infrequently jostle and jeer at the colored cavaliers" (ibid.). One article reported that the Marines "went to the Pike intending to start something with the scouts if any of them appeared in company with white women," and that "violence occurred between the Marines and the Scouts when two skirmishes and a general melee took place in front of the Ferris wheel ("Scouts Lose First Battle with Marines," *St. Louis Post-Dispatch*, July 7, 1904, p. 1). A crowd, "composed mostly of women, surrounded [the Scouts] and expressed sympathy for them. The marines were still hostile, and to avoid more trouble, Jefferson Guards made the crowd disperse" (ibid.). While admitting that the white women were associating freely with the Scouts, Marines were "determined to show the Filipinos that the lynch law was not limited to southern blacks" (Rydell 1984, 177). Affection for the Scouts inspired white women to continue socializing with them, despite criticism, physical danger, and increasing restrictions. Jefferson Guards prevented the couples from leaving the fairgrounds, and the women "were much disconcerted by the detention of their escorts, and pleaded with the police to allow the brown soldiers to conduct them to the street car station, if no farther" (*St. Louis Post-Dispatch*, July 17, 1904, p. A8). When a guard volunteered to accompany them, the "young women left the gate, calling back to the protesting scouts that they would meet them on the morrow" (ibid.). Members of the Constabulary also had a fight with or were attacked by white men at the Café Luzon on the Philippine Exhibit grounds, resulting in several injuries as well as the stabbing of a (white) waiter (*St. Louis Post-Dispatch*, July 24, 1904). While the report did not identify the white men as Marines, it blamed the incident on white women with Filipino escorts who were at the "buffet portion of the café" and refused to leave. When the Filipinos were being thrown out of the restaurant, they "drew knives and revolvers" but did not use their weapons. In the fight that ensued, "the women did most of the cutting," and four of them were arrested (ibid.). Situations such as these reveal ways in which Filipino military men and white women broke racial barriers for friendship despite vicious backlash.

These violent encounters did not deter the Filipino military men from having continued contact with St. Louis society, and their commanding officers encouraged the relationship:

> To introduce the little Filipino Scouts to society, Major Johnston is planning to give them a party. The Scouts' party will follow the dancing party given to-night at the Scout camp for the officers of the battalion and their friends.
>
> Major Johnston is anxious that his little soldiers appear in the light of true gentlemen to disabuse the idea that has gone abroad that they are given too much unlicensed flirting with all the pretty girls that visit the camp. ("Scouts Have a Party, Filipino Soldiers to Enter Occidental Society," *St. Louis Post-Dispatch*, July 27, 1904, p. 7, col. 1)

In mid-September the *St. Louis Republic* announced that the Scouts would give a dance for the "St. Louis girls who have so charmed the Filipino soldiers and the native belles of the islands" ("Scouts Give Dance," September 18, 1904, p.1, col.4).[38] In late October, Helen Gould, socialite and teenage daughter of a prominent businessman, was honored at a meeting of the YWCA with a reception attended by six hundred guests, including "many of the Philippine Constabulary and Scouts and Jefferson Guards" (*St. Louis Republic*, October 26, 1904, p. 4, col. 3).[39] She got along well with the Filipino men because she "conversed in Spanish with the Philippine soldiers and displayed marked cordiality in greeting the Jefferson Guards" (ibid.).

The officers and enlisted men of the Constabulary were invited to a musical performance and reception at Forest Park University, an "institution for young girls and women" ("University Girls to Meet Filipinos," *St. Louis Republic*, November 14, 1904, p. 1, col. 5). Earlier in the week, the Constabulary Band had given a concert at the university, and the university staff, especially a Mrs. Anna Sneed Cairns, was inspired to put together a program in honor of the band members. The concert included the staff and students of the university, as well as prominent local musicians, and Miss Helen Gould was invited to attend. The news report stated that "Mrs. Cairns has become deeply interested in the Filipinos, and it is expected that the entertainment to-morrow evening will be one of the most notable in the history of the university.... The students have taken a deep interest in the affair, and have sent invitations to their friends to attend" (ibid.). Ten days later, another reception, on the World's Fair grounds at the Alaskan Pavilion, was held for both the Scouts and Constabulary, and a prominent judge gave a welcome address. Miss Helen Gould was unable to make this event, however, even though the affair was "given by her in token of her interest in the Filipino soldiers" ("Reception for Filipino Soldiers," *St. Louis Republic*, November 25, 1904, p. 10, col. 4). The violence exhibited in July did little to hinder social interaction with the Filipino Scouts and Constabulary. They were still very much in the public eye and were sought-after guests at gatherings of the St. Louis social elite.

The Final Months of the 1904 Fair

The 24th United States Infantry Band, which gained fame in the Philippines before the PC Band was established, arrived at the fair and performed for a week. Loving was well acquainted with the 24th Infantry Band when he was enlisted with them in the US and when he met them again after he arrived in the Philippines (see chapter 1). The 24th USI Band and the PC Band alternated performances at the same events. On October 6, they marched at the Ohio Day parade and played at the reception (*St. Louis Republic*, October 7, 1904, p. 4, col. 3). The *St. Louis Republic* identified the 24th Infantry Band as a "negro organization" but did not mention their time in the Philippines (ibid.). They marched in a parade for Missouri Day on October 11 along with the Scouts, the Constabulary, various national guards from Missouri, and other state infantries and cavalries. While the Berlin Band played a concert in the rotunda, the 24th Infantry Band "played on the outside" (*St. Louis Republic*, October 12, 1904, p. 2, col. 3), maintaining separate racial spaces. On October 19, both the Scouts and Constabulary marched with the 24th and the US Marine Band for the Washington (DC) Day parade (*St. Louis Republic*, October 19, 1904, p. 5, col. 3). Though there were no reports about the interaction between the Black soldiers and Filipinos, I imagine it must have quite cordial, since they knew each other in the Philippines and performed together at several events in St. Louis. Perhaps they found opportunities to discuss and compare their treatment in the US and the Philippines as racialized others. The Black soldiers may have praised Loving for his leadership of the Filipino band, which captured the admiration of America audiences and was held in high esteem by international bandmasters.

In early November, members of the PC Band performed as a fifty-piece orchestra under the baton of Loving. They played at Café Luzon, where patrons could reserve a table for fine dining. The *St. Louis Republic* stated, "This innovation will undoubtedly be highly appreciated by lovers of high-grade music and the many friends of this excellent World's Fair resort" (November 6, 1904, p. 3, col. 7). Loving may have wanted to accentuate the musicians' skills in European music and promote them as a serious musical organization rather than a colonial marching band performing patriotic songs. Liberating the band from its role as an instrument of empire, Loving obliged audiences to hear the Filipinos' musicianship more clearly when they exchanged brass for strings. Switching from a band to an orchestra became a key feature in many future concerts, contributing to the band's fame.

Compared to the PC Band, the Philippine Scouts Band programmed on their official concerts more popular tunes of the day, including ragtime or coon song hits such as "Bedelia" and "Navajo"[40] (*St. Louis Post-Dispatch*, November 27, 1904, p. 4, col. 2). This shows the different approaches to music by the Scouts Band, which was part of the US Army, and the Philippine Constabulary Band, which was part of the colonial government. The Scouts Band had a closer positioning to American culture and a white leader, allowing them to be freer with their choice of music. President Roosevelt was enthusiastic about the performances of both bands. When "the Scouts Band started on the stirring old Irish air of 'Garryowen' the President struck his gloved hands together, and, turning to General Rice, said: 'That's Custer's favorite tune, isn't it? It's a great fighting air and the Seventh Regiment always plays it'" (*St. Louis Republic*, November 27, 1904, p. 4, col. 2). Reports of the president's reaction to the PC Band reflected the pride he had for the band but also for his own accomplishment: "It was a long, earnest gaze which the head of the great American Republic fixed upon the diminutive members of the Constabulary Band. It was the first time that the chief of these people had an opportunity to see the effect of the influence which had made them soldiers of Uncle Sam. They marched with the precision of veterans, and never did any of them look to the right or left." Roosevelt exclaimed, "They are splendid" (ibid.). He looked upon them as if they were his possessions and a demonstration of his imperial triumph. They were not in possession of their own musical capabilities, but rather were "splendid" because of the United States' intervention and efforts. The president attended a class by a Miss Zamora, who "put thirteen naked Igorrotes through their addition and subtraction very briefly." He remarked, "You are doing a great and important work for civilization," as he shook her hand (*St. Louis Post-Dispatch*, November 27, 1904, p. 4, col. 2). A rendition of "America" in English by an "Igorrote chorus" impressed Roosevelt and was further proof of their progress toward civilization (*St. Louis Republic*, November 27, 1904, p. 5, col. 1).

The Legend of the PC Band at the St. Louis World's Fair

The legend of the PC Band's triumph at the fair has endured in the literature and folklore on the band.[41] I first mentioned the legend about the lights going out during their concert in chapter 1 by contextualizing it within the Filipino *banda* tradition called *tambakan*, in which bands competed by playing pieces committed to memory for hours and even days, until one admitted defeat. While I have not found a newspaper report from 1904 that provides an account of this particular concert, I have several theories about which night

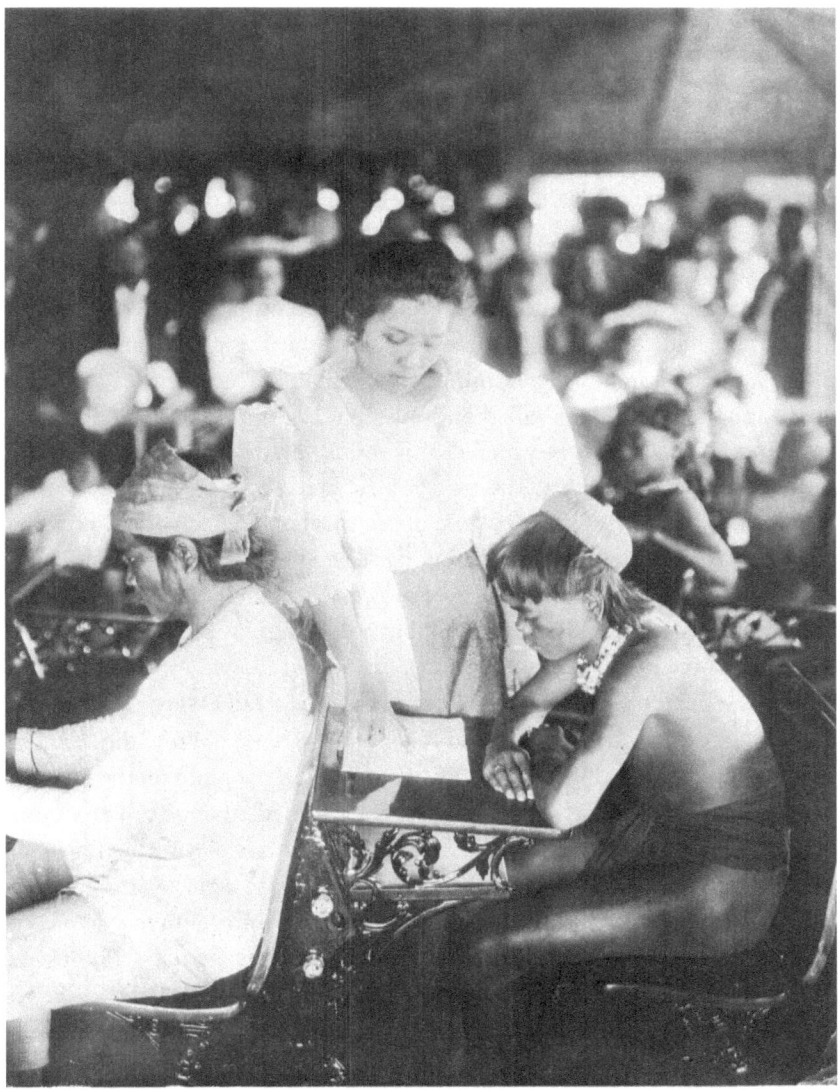

"Miss Zamora, The Native Filipino Teacher Instructing an Igorot Pupil in Reading." (1904 World's Fair, Philippine Reservation). Courtesy of the Missouri Historical Society, St. Louis. http://collections.mohistory.org/resource/145118

it might have taken place. On the night of August 19, 1904, a tornado hit St. Louis, causing a power outage on the fairgrounds (*St. Louis Post-Dispatch*, August 20, 1904, and *New York Post*, August 23, 1904). During this storm, the lights went out at Festival Hall, causing an unnamed band or orchestra (not the PC Band, however) to halt its performance. The audience sat in the dark until someone sang "Dixie" to calm their nerves (*St. Louis Post-Dispatch*, August 20, 1904). Another article, which seems to be a firsthand account, reported, "We were left in total darkness. It lasted for only short intervals between the lightning flashes which, amidst the unbroken roar of thunder, brought the body of the hall [Festival Hall] with the musicians standing mute upon the stage, into ghostly illumination" (*New York Post*, August 23, 1904).[42] Some audience members "called upon the bandmaster to play something—anything. But not a note responded. Any sound to drown out the roar of the thunder and distract the attention from the lightning would have relieved the strain" (ibid.). The audience gave up on this band, which could not play without sheet music, and started singing "The Star-Spangled Banner," "Old Folks at Home," and "Dixie" on their own to calm their nerves (ibid.). On this night, the PC Band was playing at the Philippine Bandstand at 7:00 p.m. (Schwartz and Schwartz 2003, 10). According to my grandmother and others, the band was performing Rossini's *William Tell* Overture when the lights went out, and they continued to play in the dark.[43] While the *William Tell* Overture was not listed on the PC Band's official program on the night of August 19, 1904 (Schwartz and Schwartz 2003, 216), they often took requests from the audience, so it is possible that they played this piece. But, if playing outside in a storm seems improbable, there was also another instance, in which a faulty electrical generator may have caused a power outage at one of their concerts ("Generator in Dispute: Darkness Threatened in the Philippine Reservation at Fair," *St. Louis Republic*, April 14, 1904, p. 5). Still, the PC Band legend demonstrates that, against difficult odds in which the cards were stacked against Filipinos—whether it was a failure of modern electricity, an act of nature, an administrative blunder, or sabotage—they depended on the Filipino *banda* tradition of playing without scores and succeeded through their own capabilities, not with the aid of American tutelage. I continue an analysis of this legend in chapter 5.

In addition to their busy schedule at the fair, the PC Band took several trips to perform concerts at the requests of various organizations. On August 15, the band traveled to Louisville, Kentucky, to perform for the biennial conclave of the Knights of Pythias (*St. Louis Globe-Democrat*, August 15, 1904). In September, the band visited Chicago and Milwaukee, where they were featured at the Wisconsin State Fair. Speaking of their tremendous popularity, Grant Thomas, secretary of the Wisconsin Commission, stated:

> Twenty thousand citizens of Milwaukee, who were attracted by the reputation of the Philippine musicians, attended the opening day of the State Fair, while heretofore the heaviest attendance on the first day has never been more than 2,000. (*The St. Louis Republic*, September 8, 1904, p. 3, col. 6)

Several cities invited the band to perform after the conclusion of the World's Fair, but they declined the offers. Col. Clarence R. Edwards, chief of the Bureau of Insular Affairs, said that the "little Filipinos, who have delighted thousands of World's Fair visitors," all expressed the desire to return home and see their families rather than pursue "good American money" ("Philippine Musicians Will Return to Manila," *St. Louis Republic*, October 8, 1904, p. 4, col. 5). Before they sailed for home from San Francisco in late November, two band members were accidentally left behind in Topeka, Kansas. The *St. Louis Republic* reported that the two men, Pvt. Pedro Navarro (my great-grandfather) and Pvt. Rafael Principe, got off the train to look around the city and were left behind. The two only had twenty cents each and had to telegraph their officers for funds to pay for their expenses until they could take the next train. The transport from San Francisco back to Manila was delayed a couple of days before the two men arrived to join their group (November 30, 1904, p. 1, col. 7).

Aftermath of the 1904 Fair

Filipinos' long history of performing European music was heard by Americans' imperial ear as conforming and assimilating to American values. For Filipinos, the impact of the ways in which American audiences heard the PC Band's performances was both beneficial and disastrous. The Filipino bandsmen found a way to earn a living and receive recognition for work in which they were already skilled and experienced. They were able to travel to the US, play for foreign audiences, meet people, develop friendships, and show pride in themselves and their art. American fairgoers also recognized their musical talent, and socially, the band musicians traversed the color line as guests at several prestigious events. But this achievement did not go far beyond the musical realm, because audiences absorbed the political message that the bandsmen had developed their skills under American tutelage. Because of the shared language of European music and the evolutionary paradigm that was common at the time, very few challenged this idea. Filipinos' musical achievement, creativity, and contributions as Filipinos and equal human beings were inaudible to the imperial ear. Their musical achievement was thus accomplished, but it did little to change the structures of domination that tied them to their unequal position.

The next chapter discusses the PC Band's return to the US five years later. The way that American newspapers minimized the bandsmen's musical skills while emphasizing their natural musical abilities demonstrates an active imposition of white superiority and an ability to control perceptions about the band in particular and Filipinos in general.

3

Hearing with an Imperial Ear: Racializing the PC Band on their Tour of America in 1909

On their yearlong tour of the United States in 1909, the PC Band's performances of Euro-American music garnered them much acclaim and propelled them into the spotlight across the United States. The novel ways that newspapers handled the PC Band's favor with American audiences reveal how they often acted as a hegemonic force to reclaim and reinstate boundaries of race in order to maintain power over America's colonial subjects.[1] Concert reviews gave positive evaluations of music while skewing public perception, casting Filipinos as "little brown men" and "natural" musicians rather than skilled or creative artists. At the turn of the century, "objective reporting" was not the standard, writes Schudson, but rather, "sensationalism in its various forms was the chief development in newspaper content" (1981, 5). Like colonialist European travel writers in Pratt's work (1992), journalists before the 1920s "had relatively little incentive to doubt the firmness of 'reality' by which they lived" (Schudson 1981, 6), affirming colonial and racial ideologies that supported domination over racial others.

The ability to create knowledge about the other—though this knowledge may be nonsensical and ridiculous—is to maintain power and, in this case, to sustain imperialist domination and white hegemony. An important theme in these news reports on the PC Band was the portrayal of Filipino achievement in Western music as aberrant and Filipino musical talent as exceedingly natural—and thus unnatural—so as to cast their music-making as spectacle. A characterization of Filipino musical skill as racial and biological is similar to the way that Blacks were represented from time of slavery as acting from instinct rather than intellect (Hall 1997, 243).² Representing the musical *skills* of the bandsmen as a natural and racial condition of Filipinos was to affix Filipino music-making into a position of lack—lacking true creativity, genius, and uniqueness because it stemmed from instinctive reaction. Musical talent, by this logic, was not a cultural attribute but a racial one, since "culture" is dangerously "open to modification and change" (245), allowing for the possibility of seeing Filipinos as civilized and thus worthy of self-determination. Stuart Hall states that "'Naturalization' is therefore a representational strategy designed to *fix* 'difference,' and thus *secure it forever*. It is an attempt to halt the inevitable 'slide' of meaning, to secure discursive or ideological 'closure'" (245). As a racial attribute, natural musical talent is positioned "beyond history, permanent, and fixed" (245). By ascribing a biological condition of natural musicality to the bodies of "little brown men," news reports engaged in what Hall calls "ritualized degradation" (2003, 245) in order to perpetually contain the Filipino bandsmen's breach of the racial pecking order. Filipino musicians were idealized and sentimentalized as patriotic colonial subjects playing enthusiastic renditions of Sousa marches, but always in condescending and stereotypical ways that fixed them in a subordinate racial position. Images of the bandsmen as constructed by Americans were not only about the PC Band as a musical organization; rather, these images reflected and perpetuated racialized ways of thinking about Filipinos in general, in what Hall calls a "racialized regime of representation" (1997, 249).

To the imperial ear, the identity of "Filipino music" was ambiguous, invisible, and indistinct from Western music. The idea that the Philippines lacked a kind of cultural authenticity was given scientific credibility by newspapers: "Ethnologists have been unable to find anything that resembles a native medley [sic] in the Philippines" (*Washington Times*, April 10, 1909, p. 2, col. 5). Only when transformed by musicians trained in European music could Filipino identity be properly expressed: "There is nevertheless a class of music that is distinctly Filipino. Señor Escamillo [sic] ... an accomplished musician, has captured the vagrant muse of his people as it is given expression in the measures learned from the Spaniard and has prepared a composition he calls 'Songs of the Philippines,' which cannot fail to bring back memories of the sunny, happy isles to all who hear it" (ibid.). The distinctiveness of Filipino music, in this assessment, was developed by, and thereby dependent on, the language of the colonizer for proper recognition. Escamilla's composition, in the mind of the reporter, depicted the Philippines as a place of "sunny, happy" memories rather than as a site of colonial violence or revolutionary action. This representation resonates with the comfortable narrative of benevolent assimilation and encourages listening with a disengaged engagement.

As the PC Band fought against the stereotype of Filipinos as savages by featuring a repertoire of "classical" or "serious" works by European composers, they also unwittingly played into and were "trapped" by a discursive formation (Hall 1997, 263) of Filipinos as savage yet "natural" musicians who could be made semicivilized through the tutelage of Americans. In these ways, cultural and social domination over Filipinos was disseminated and sustained in the cultural sphere through newspapers' reporting and reviewing of the PC Band's musical performances, creating a discourse around Filipino music-making that influenced how audiences perceived the performances of the PC Band with an imperial ear. A racialized regime of representation created "truths" about Filipinos, confirming their difference from the "norm" (i.e., whites). This way of imperial hearing indexes white Americans' feelings, beliefs, and hopes about the Filipino bandsmen, and by extension, Filipinos in general. Rather than hear musical achievement as stemming from the musicians' talent and creative labor, the disposition (Bourdieu 1984) of American listeners led to the hearing of the PC Band as the success of American tutelage, legitimizing US colonization of Filipinos. Concert reviews, circulated in the mass media of newspapers, were the foundation of the discourse through which this dominant reading both reflected and further shaped understandings of the band's performances. My analysis of favorable reviews of the PC Band will support the argument that the positive perception of the band's music-making hinged on its proximity to Euro-American ideals of order, discipline, and willing assimilation to colonial rule. I will also discuss several instances in which the Filipino musicians exercised agency to create space for their self-representation and to encourage recognition of their identity.

Parading Filipinos at the Presidential Inauguration

In 1909, president-elect Taft summoned the PC Band back to the United States at great expense and effort to perform at his presidential inauguration, as proof of his triumph in the Philippines. Afterward, they embarked on a coast-to-coast concert tour of the United States, which was attended by thousands of Americans in major concert halls and popular entertainment venues, before heading to the Alaska-Yukon-Pacific Exposition. Newspapers positively reviewed the band's musical performances while describing them in an orientalist fashion as abnormal and peculiar, for example, sensationalizing their "tribal" diversity while emphasizing their uniformity in appearance. With a few notable exceptions, what was often missing from these accounts was mention of Loving's racial identity, an omission of the success of an African American in a leadership position. In the few instances that his identity was included, mainstream newspapers highlighted Loving's educational achievement as explanation or subjected him to racial ridicule.

On their way to the San Francisco, the PC Band performed at the Nagasaki Hotel for Japanese audiences (*Nagasaki Press*, January 22, 1909). This brief report was critical of the specific musical performance, but these problems were connected not with the band's race but with the weather: "the men were handicapped by the change of climate, their lips and hands being affected by the cold here ... they found it impossible to soften the tones to suit the size of the hall." Nevertheless, the "applause which greeted each item expressed the delight of the audience at the treat provided" (ibid.).

In the US, the purpose of the band's tour was explicitly racial: to give American audiences "the opportunity of correcting their impressions of the Filipinos as half-naked savages, to be exhibited at fairs as curiosities, and of seeing what the islanders themselves consider of their representative organizations" (*Boston Globe*, February 28, 1909, p. 45). Musical performance was part of an agenda to challenge popular racial and colonial stereotypes of Filipinos as unassimilable savages, because these cast doubt on the legitimacy of US involvement in the Philippines, thereby confirming anti-imperialist arguments. Instead, newspapers emphasized Filipinos as "little brown brothers" to anchor the PC Band's success to American intervention in order to bolster US claims of triumph in civilizing the natives.

Despite excitement for the band's upcoming arrival, some American newspapers expressed anxiety about Loving's visit to the White House at the invitation of Taft. The *Hawaiian Gazette*, for example, anticipated a revisiting of the Booker T. Washington "discussions" in 1901, when Washington sat down to dinner with President Roosevelt at the White House and angered many white Southern politicians.[3] The article never stated in overt terms that the cause for concern was that Loving was Black, but the reference to Booker T. Washington made this clear. The tone of the article, entitled "Captain Loving Old Friend of President," did not express outright disapproval, but rather anticipation and caution: "Captain Loving is a sort of Booker T. Washington, a man of conspicuous talent, and one whose name, already famous, will be linked with those of the greatest band directors of the world" (*Hawaiian Gazette*, February 9, 1909, p. 3, col. 5). Loving was called a "personal friend" of Taft, implying an affable relationship, one that justified an exception to strict racial decorum. It was planned that the PC Band would furnish the music for the inaugural ball, where Loving would certainly be "assured of a personal reception at the White House" (ibid.). Loving was a "Southern-born man" who grew up in the Dakotas, where Roosevelt "taught Loving his lessons at night"; he was also a graduate of the Boston Conservatory of Music [*sic*] (ibid.). While Loving was the musical leader of the band and a captain in the insular police of the Philippines, the PC Band would also be accompanied by Col. Mark Hersey, who was a "general supply officer of the Constabulary" and a captain in the regular army, assuring readers that a white man was in charge. As I explain below, guards ultimately prevented Loving from entering the White House complex on at least one occasion during the inauguration festivities. Americans' paternalist racism toward Filipinos did not extend to African Americans, hence the different treatment of the Filipino musicians and Loving at the White House.

The PC Band arrived in San Francisco on the transport *Buford* and went directly to Ye Liberty Theater in Oakland, California (*San Francisco Call*, February 16, 1909, p. 7, col. 2). Without any time to spare, they played that same evening at the Dreamland Pavilion in San Francisco. Walter Anthony, known as a "popular ... dramatic writer" (*The California Outlook*, February 24, 1912, p. 22) for the *San Francisco Call*, reviewed the band's concerts in San Francisco at the beginning of their trip and again several months later before they returned to the Philippines. Anthony's first review was positive, calling the band an "emphatic hit" that with the "thunder of drums, the crash of brass and the swing and sweep of the biggest band that has played in this city will take the most prosaic listener off his feet" (*San Francisco Call*, February 17, 1909, p. 5). He praised Loving, "an American negro," for his "quiet and unostentatious manner. He could not be more modest in his leadership of the Filipinos if he were in Georgia" (ibid.). Referencing racialized social behavior that would have been expected in the South, Anthony projects his values onto Loving, implying that this was the proper way to behave in a color-coded hierarchy: "Every gesture is deprecating, and he leads his bandsmen as though he were conscious of the fact they are brown while he is black" (ibid.). This way of interpreting Loving's gestures as "deprecating" makes Loving's breach of the hierarchy, as a Black person leading brown people, acceptable in Anthony's mind. It is only after disciplining Loving back into his proper racial position that the writer is able to assess his musicianship: "He is a musician. His handling of the great forces in front of him proves that" (ibid.). These ways of representing Loving as a Black person who is "conscious" of proper racial behavior invokes a kind of tokenism in the way American culture "appropriates and uses the images and stories of black Americans" (Cloud 1996, 116). Though he is in a leadership position, Loving's "deprecating nature" reassures white readers that although he is a Black man, he acts in accordance with acceptable social norms. Furthermore, the band played uncontroversial selections: operatic excerpts from Verdi's *La Traviata* and Donizetti's *Lucia di Lammermoor*; their signature piece, Rossini's *William Tell* Overture; and American airs for "patriotic thrills" (ibid.). They pleased a wide audience, not just the concertgoing elite: "It might not have been entirely pleasing to the 'highbrows,' but it was entirely satisfactory to those who have a spinal column and an ability to thrill" (ibid.). While the writer is careful to preserve the racial hierarchy, he is critical of the class hierarchy upheld by "highbrows." Responding to the overwhelming demand by the public, organizers canceled previously scheduled concerts at the Dreamland in order to accommodate two more concerts by the PC Band the next day.

Many purchased tickets prior to the band's arrival, but hundreds more had to be turned away. When the band took the stage, the "musicians were met with instantaneous favor" and enthusiastic applause (*San Francisco Chronicle*, February 17, 1909, p. 7). The band played a "stirring" Sousa march and an "intensely thrilling" *William Tell* Overture. The concert reviewer both complimented and insulted Loving as having a "dignified and pleasing appearance, and, although a negro, his leadership has none of the qualities of his race" (ibid.). Of the Filipino bandsmen, the *Chronicle* reporter expressed surprise at their capability: "at first was difficult to realize that unpretentious little Filipino musicians sent forth the wonderful and splendid volume of sound" (ibid.). Musical performance momentarily intervened to critique colonial racialization that underestimated Filipino capabilities, because while at first it was "difficult" for the reporter, he realized that they could produce "wonderful and splendid" music. Despite what might have resided in the minds of individual audience members like this listener, most newspaper reports shaped the meaning of PC Band's performances to fit colonial and racial agendas of little brown men who were properly assimilated, influencing thousands more readers who were not present at the event, thus developing and sustaining an imperial ear.

In both subtle and overt ways, seemingly positive comments were tempered by making a spectacle of the band, for example, their supposed challenge to America's greatest band leader: "Even in 1904 the Filipinos, in their own estimation at least, outplayed Sousa, and this year they expect to make Sousa's select look like amateurs" (*Boston Daily Globe*, February 28, 1909, p. 45). The PC Band's musical excellence provided proof of US success at civilizing Filipinos: "They are far removed from the Igorrotes of the St. Louis expositions, who ate dogs for the delectation of the spectators" (ibid.). To account for Loving's role, they described him as an "American negro, educated at Harvard [sic] and at the New England conservatory of music" who was "strangely enough, the leader of this band of dusky musicians" (ibid.). The article emphasized Loving's educational background, erroneously stating that he studied at Harvard, to legitimize his "strange" leadership of "dusky musicians." Musicality was racialized to justify colonization—Filipinos, though "untrained," were inherently musical, and when properly disciplined by the United States, even by a member of a subordinate race, could succeed in Euro-American ways: "[Loving's] command over the untrained musicians of his band is marvelous, and he has utilized in a remarkable way the latent musical capacity which is inherent in the island races" (ibid.). The United States' promotion of music had explicitly imperialist purposes in the Philippines: "The intention at first was to get the Filipinos interested in music and so to have another hold on their sympathies which would perhaps be of assistance in establishing American rule" (ibid.). This implied that Americans cultivated Filipinos' interest in music, erasing the very existence of music prior to US rule as well as the cultural heritage of Filipinos. To emphasize the success of this agenda, the report stated, "Pedro Navarro, who holds the proud distinction of being the first Filipino to appear on a concert platform, can do wonders with the piccolo" (ibid.). This, of course, was utter fabrication, given the Philippines' long history in European music and Navarro's musical training from a young age (see chapter 2). Developing the audiences' imperial ear subverted the possibility of hearing the band's performances as evidence of Filipinos' capacity for self-rule, a perspective that would have been a critique of white cultural hegemony.

At the presidential inauguration festivities, the PC Band was given a prominent position. They escorted President Roosevelt with president-elect Taft as they left the White House for the Capitol Building, directly behind a squad of Washington Mounted Police and in front of an escort of veterans of the Spanish-American War (*New York Herald*, February 28, 1909, p. 2, col. 4). The *Boston Globe* also reported that the PC Band was "given a place of honor in the escort of President Roosevelt and Mr. Taft to the capitol and attracted much attention" (March 5, 1909, p. 3). Indeed, newspapers took note of the PC Band's prominent place and its role in drawing attention to Taft's work in the colony: "Immediately behind [a platoon of mounted policemen] came the Philippine Constabulary Band, here from the far-off islands in the Pacific to see raised to the highest office in the land the man who has done and is doing so much for the Filipinos" (*Washington Evening Star*, March 4, 1909, p. 2, col. 2). The PC Band was the only band allowed to play "Hail to the Chief" as they passed the presidential reviewing stand (*New York Herald*, February 28, 1909, p. 2, col. 3–4).

Taft's exceptional positioning of the PC Band demonstrates his preference for emphasizing his own accomplishments in the Philippines over keeping with the racial status quo. The band's prominence, however, did not sit well with everyone. To diminish the band's place of honor, newspapers underscored the men's appearance and demeanor in orientalist ways: "the Philippine Constabulary Bandsmen, in their olive green army overcoats, with scarlet-lined capes thrown back and fresh from their native islands where balm and bloom are natural features seemed ill at ease in the flurrying snow that was driven into their faces and trimmed their uniforms with white" (*Washington Evening Star*, March 4, 1909, p. 2, col. 3). On an unusually cold and snowy day in Washington, DC, where surely many felt the effects of the weather, newspapers did not choose to point out the discomfort of other participants. During the parade, in which several dozen bands passed by the newly sworn-in president, the PC Band was not inserted into its proper place with other "independent military organizations" and was instead inserted between the "Knoxville colored battalion band" and the "Jenkins (colored) Orphan Asylum band" (*Washington Post*, March 5, 1909, p. 9). The following disruption of order was the only one identified among the marching bands by a *Washington Post* reporter: "the Philippine Constabulary Band ... was scheduled to march in the division assigned to the independent military organizations, but owing to an error in formation failed to fall in line" (ibid.). The error in the band's position within the official parade was not attributed to a malfunction on the part of the system or its management, but rather to the failure of the yet undisciplined natives, who were "delayed in reaching their points of assembly" (ibid.). The placement of the PC Band, I believe, was a deliberate act to communicate that Filipinos, like children, were orphaned (by mother Spain) and adopted by American institutions in order to be developed into productive but properly subordinated members of society. The representation of Filipinos as belonging with the "colored" wards of the state sustained the *doxa* or taken-for-granted reality of white domination (Bourdieu 1977, 165) by preventing a breach of the racial order. In this case, the racial gatekeepers of the press were not in the highest position of power, since the president himself put the band in a place of prominence, nor were they of the general public, who took pleasure in the band's music-making, for when the PC Band finally marched by the president, "it did not take long for the crowds recognize the famous musicians, and they received a tremendous ovation" (*Washington Post*, March 5, 1909, p. 9). Newspapers, nevertheless, played an important role in simultaneously celebrating the Filipino musicians for their music while making sure they were properly subordinated both physically and symbolically when they threatened to exceed their place in the colonial and racial hierarchy.

After the grueling parade in the blizzard, the PC Band performed at the White House for the inaugural ball celebrating the new president and important guests. Newspaper reports of the event focused mainly on the décor, the elite guests, and the women's elaborate ball gowns. The *New York Press* marveled that the "ball was the finest picture of the kind Washington ever has seen, and Old World diplomats enthusiastically declared it equaled in impressiveness and beauty any display in their experience in Europe" (March 5, 1909, p. 2, col. 4). A chorus of five hundred members, an orchestra, and the US Marine Band were "concealed behind plants in the gallery" while they provided music for the affair (ibid.). Although anecdotal accounts and Philippine sources both attest that the PC Band played at the White House during the inaugural ball (Bañas 1924, 30; Flores 1976, 74), the ensemble was not named in any major newspapers. All that is mentioned is that an "orchestra of 125 pieces" alternated with the US Marine Band (*Boston Globe*, March 5, 1909, p. 1, col. 3.). A published report to the chairman of the

The Philippine Constabulary Band at the White House, Clarinet, Cornet & Euphonium soloists. *The Evening Star*, April 10, 1909, p. 8. Barr-Farrhan P.P.C.C.

inauguration committee, however, confirms that a contract was given to the PC Band, proof that they were indeed the unnamed "orchestra" at the ball (Stellwagen 1909, 149). While Philippine sources state that the PC Band was the first non-US band to perform at an inaugural ball, the list of "firsts" on the Joint Congressional Committee on Inaugural Ceremonies website does not credit the PC Band with this honor, thus erasing their contribution.[4]

Anticipation over Loving's visit to the White House, as mentioned earlier by the *Hawaiian Gazette* ("Captain Loving Old Friend of President," February 9, 1909, p. 3, col. 5), culminated in the racist treatment to which he was subjected on at least one known occasion. One account by Flores provides some insight: "Something happened to dampen the happy occasion for Loving: just before the parade, some of the senior officers tried to prevail on him to pass himself off as a Cuban officer attached to the US Army" (1976, 74). Loving refused by saying, "No. When I march my band down Pennsylvania Avenue, there will be friends of mine down there calling out my name. And when they call out, 'Walter!' what do I tell them? That I'm not Walter Loving but a Cuban officer? No, I cannot, will not hide my identity" (74). My granduncle Bienvenido was told by his father, Capt. Navarro, that guards prevented Loving from entering the White House grounds, even though he was in uniform. The

"Filipinos were very sad," he said, and Navarro had to conduct the band in Loving's place (Interview with author, 1998). This ill-mannered treatment provides further insight into why the PC Band was inserted into the wrong section of an otherwise well-executed inauguration parade. While Loving's papers at Howard University do not contain any personal accounts of these racist encounters, Flores writes that Loving was "disrespectfully treated" by a captain and several lieutenants at the 1904 St. Louis Fair (1976, 74). Loving's grandchildren, Walter Loving III and Edith Loving Lucas, recall a story that while on a ship traveling to San Francisco (likely in 1939), Walter Sr., Edith, and Walter Jr. and his wife Mary were ignored and poorly treated "because of their race" (Personal communication with author, 2021). However, when they docked, Col. Loving was greeted with such acclaim that the attitude on the ship changed to one of respect. Bandsmen who went to the 1939 Golden Gate Exposition recall that they were prevented from participating in one parade even though they were in position waiting to be inserted (Richardson interview, 1980). Instances like this show that, while the band was being celebrated, they also experienced acts of racial aggression and interference that barred them from full inclusion in prominent events.

Over the next two days, four concerts took place as part of the inaugural festivities. The PC Band played on the morning of March 5 in conjunction with the Haydn Male Chorus of Utica, New York, and on the evening of March 6, they were joined by the Taft Glee Club and the Musurgia Glee Club. The US Marine Band also performed concerts on the evening of March 5 and the afternoon of March 6. The *Washington Post* expressed great amazement that the PC Band gave a concert "rivaling that of the Marine Band," especially since Americans "expected to hear an untrained organization of 'little brown men,' with a limited comprehension of music, and no great capabilities for interpretation" ("Throngs at Concerts," March 6, 1909, p. 9). They were also surprised that the "Oriental musicians . . . have no freak instruments among their number" (ibid.), despite the fact that they were a military band, a musical ensemble that was familiar to Americans. Colonial, racial, and orientalist stereotypes about Filipinos clearly influenced the audience's assumptions about the band. Yet, with this shift to focus on their performance, the moniker "little brown men" appears in quotes, as if to call it into question or at least express hesitation at its usage. The audience was "agreeably surprised," and before the grand march from Verdi's *Aida* was half over "it was clear to everyone that the musicians from the archipelago were talented. An ovation greeted the first number, and because of the intense enthusiasm manifested by the 7,000 men and women in the audience, many additional selections were added to the scheduled program" (ibid.). Loving dispensed with formality to please the audience and to show off the band's skill. My great-grandfather is complimented here, notably not as a "little brown man" with natural talent, but as a fine musician: "Señor Pedro B. Navarro, piccolo soloist, showed that he was a finished artist by playing the divertissement for piccolo by Green in a most acceptable fashion" (ibid.). The review comes dangerously close to realizing the talent of Filipinos as artists who did not mimic but *rivaled* the US Marine Band, and also noted the soloists' musicianship.

During one concert, the "audience seemed unusually pleased" by a medley of Filipino airs "especially arranged by one of the members" ("Thongs at Concerts," *Washington Post*, March 6, 1909, p. 9).[5] By performing this medley, the band called attention to its Filipino identity in a format that was recognizable and acceptable to their audience, an expression of civilizational attainment that did not erase their cultural identity. It was only by expressing themselves in the language of the colonizer that they could be recognizable as capable of civilization; however, by doing so, their cultural *distinctiveness*—and thus authenticity—was obscured to the imperial ear. Instances in which the PC Band included Filipino composers in its repertoire were acts of agency that voiced pride in Filipino culture, examples that were more obvious to audiences than acts such as playing from memory, a skill developed from their own *banda* tradition. For example, a collector named Jacob Greenwald reported to the *Desert News* of Salt Lake City that the PC Band, among all the bands at the inaugural parade, "eclipsed everything in line in all Washington, and, in fact, anything he ever listened to. Those men play without a single score—everything from memory" (March 15, 1909, p. 2, col. 6). The PC Band played a concert entirely of works by Filipino composers at the 1904 Fair, the "first of the kind ever given" in the US (*St. Louis Republic*, July 24, 1904, p. 1, col. 6). I will highlight several more instances in which the PC Band played compositions by Filipino composers to express pride in their identity.

A lengthy concert review in the *Washington Post* recounted that as soon as the band started the Overture to *Zampa* by Herold, "the audience was comparing the band with the Marine Band. The Oriental musicians played with a dash and confidence that permitted of none but favorable criticisms" (March 7, 1909, p. 6, col. 1–3). The review continues with rare, specific insight into their playing style: "The excerpt from 'La Gioconda' and 'First Heart Throbs' showed

Pedro Navarro, Chief Musician of the Philippine Constabulary Band. *Washington Times*, April 10, 1909.

that the band from the archipelago was equal to the demands of fine and light shading as well as being able to play the broad fortissimo portions of the heavy march numbers" (ibid.). While this review was positive and complimentary of the band as a whole, it chose to make a spectacle of one performer: "Señor Hipolito de la Cruz, a very little man handling a very large bass horn, played a fantasia for the tuba with great success" (ibid.). Nevertheless, his musical skills are acknowledged by the reviewer: "Before his solo, it would have been difficult to imagine so much delicate harmony being extracted from such a heavy instrument. Señor de la Cruz's playing was heartily appreciated and enjoyed, and great applause was given him" (ibid.). For American audiences, hearing the Filipinos' performance live was crucial to overturning prevailing stereotypes and recognizing them as fine musicians, even if temporarily: "That the Filipino bandsmen established themselves in the hearts of Washington music lovers and thousands of visitors by their initial concert on Friday was amply attested yesterday afternoon when between 5,000 and 6,000 men, women, and children gathered in the vast hall to listen to its second recital" (ibid.). Loving's choice of repertoire demonstrated that he catered to the crowd's musical desires in order to endear the PC Band to his American audiences, and that he allowed the musicians to showcase their extraordinary musical abilities as soloists: "Yesterday's program was entirely different from Friday's, and proved the versatility of the 'little brown men.' Their selections were varied and numerous, many encores being interspersed between the scheduled pieces" (ibid.). It is interesting to note here that after a detailed discussion of their fine musical performance, the phrase "little brown men" appears again in quotes, exhibiting some hesitation or reservation about its flagrant use.

Musical performance, in instances like the one above, allowed the band and its audiences to transcend racial barriers and critique stereotypes. Reviewers say that audiences appreciated the band choosing compositions that catered to their tastes, and that they requested that the ensemble play their favorite pieces. Soloists pleased crowds with their remarkable command of their instruments, producing "delicate" melodies even from heavy instruments like the tuba, as well as "fine and light shading" and "broad fortissimo" (*Washington Post*, March 7, 1909, p. 6, col. 1–3). Only three recordings of two pieces (both compositions by Filipino composers) provide insight into their musical style. "La Sampaguita" by M. Ruiz is available on an Edison cylinder recording from 1910, and another version, dated 1915, was recorded on a Columbia 78 rpm record, with the piece "La Bella Filipina" on the other side.⁶ While early sound recording technology could not capture the scope and breadth of all the musical subtleties of this large ensemble, one can hear on these recordings the source of some of the points that concert reviewers made. The band had a command of dynamic contrasts, often swelling from a delicate *piano* to grand *forte* in unity at dramatic moments. They had a flare for the use of rubato, accelerating and holding back the melody for expressive effect. Fast rhythmic gestures are light and quick, and triplet passages are synchronized as if one instrument was playing by itself. One can only imagine how they would have sounded live.

Descriptions of audiences' reactions to live concerts of the PC Band seemed to hold the possibility of upending stereotypes and critiquing messages blatantly supporting imperialism. As the band's popularity grew among the DC public and a few reports called into question the infantilizing, racial epithet of "little brown men" by putting the phrase in quotes, there was nevertheless a noticeable increase in most newspapers' use of the phrase without quotes.⁷ This moniker strongly counteracted the band's success in rivaling or even exceeding American bands and rescued the belief in white superiority from flaws and failures. This label, in conjunction with an emphasis on Filipinos' "natural" musical abilities, praises the United States' role in developing their racial inheritance: "Naturally they are musicians, and their ability has been directed and organized by Capt. Loving" (*The Meriden Weekly Republican*, March 18, 1909, p. 3, col. 4). Filipinos were so naturally talented that they could be "chosen at random by Capt. Walter H. Loving, the musical director, and their success furnishes a substantial index to the capacity of their race" (*Washington Times*, April 5, 1909, p. 10, col.1). The outrageous story that Loving chose the men at random and shaped them into superb concert musicians bolstered the claim that US colonization could fashion any Filipino into a proper colonial subject, because the "members of the band are all average Filipinos, taken from the Tagalog, Viscayan [*sic*], Ilocano, Bicol, and Pampangueno people" (ibid.). The PC Band's accomplishment was attributed to American intervention so that audiences could feel gratified by the United States' delivery on its promise of successfully civilizing the natives and making them productive subjects. The few notable exceptions demonstrate that if audiences had not developed an "imperial ear," they might have comprehended how skillful and talented Loving and the bandsmen were in developing such a large and varied repertoire and connecting with their audiences through exciting performances of crowd-pleasing music.⁸

From Washington, DC, the band traveled to New York, where they performed in a circus arena called the Hippodrome on March 7. The advertisement for this venue reads: "Every Week Brings More Novelties to the Only Great Show." The *New York Times* reported that the Hippodrome audience gave them a "rousing reception" (March 8, 1909, p. 4, col. 2). Audiences responded enthusiastically to the lively, energetic performances by the band, animated by their perception that America had accomplished the impressive feat of civilizing Filipino savages, because members of the band who "seven years ago had never seen an instrument now play Wagner and Beethoven" (ibid.). This demonstrates how the "only great show" exploited images of Filipinos as savages at the St. Louis World's Fair to influence the American public's expectations and perceptions. It was impossible that anyone in the band had "never seen an instrument before," even if the newspaper meant this only with regard to the youngest musician, who was then nineteen years old. The statement implies that Filipino musicians in general had never heard of band instruments until the US colonized them just seven short years earlier and miraculously transformed them into some of the finest band musicians in the world. The reporter describes the Filipinos in orientalist fashion, being from different tribes yet inexplicably appearing identical: "As for the men themselves, they all look much alike, and every one of them is a pure blood Filipino, most of them being recruited from the Tagalog, Visayan, Bicole [sic], Ilocano, and Pompangan [sic] tribes of Luzon and the Visayas" (ibid.). Although being from diverse tribes, the "little brown men" appeared identical and friendly in their "natty" Constabulary uniforms, and they were loyal to the United States, as was evidenced by the fact that "in the eight years of its existence [the band] has yet to advertise for a deserter" (ibid.). An unnamed officer traveling with them stated that "they were extremely proud of their organization" and loyal to Taft, whom they called "the big Governor." Taft was the "only man on earth," said the officer, that "these little fellows would have tramped through that blizzard for" (ibid.). There is no mention of the conductor's racial identity, even though they note that Loving was a well-known army musical conductor (ibid.). Certainly, in this circus-arena venue catering to a popular audience, the promoters could have capitalized on this additional sensational and exotic aspect of the band, yet the *New York Times* chose to omit his racial identity, which was to imply that he was white.

On March 8, the PC Band performed at the Academy of Music in Brooklyn, known today as the Brooklyn Academy of Music. The *Brooklyn*

Daily Eagle highlighted that the "little brown brothers" were eighty-six Malay musicians who played during President Taft's inauguration. When the blizzard struck, they persevered: "With that true soldier discipline that has made the Philippine constabulary famous, they simply sawed wood and said nothing" (March 8, 1909, p. 5, col. 6). Descriptions like this sensationalized the bandsmen, making them seem aberrant, but nevertheless portrayed them as faithful, disciplined soldiers. This depiction is in stark contrast to the one describing their discomfort in the cold weather in the *Washington Evening Star* (March 4, 1909, p. 2, col. 3). Again, the report made no comment on Loving's race, while accentuating the band as "Malay musicians."

From New York, the band headed to New England to play in major concert venues for elite audiences. In New Haven, Connecticut, two concerts took place on Saturday, March 13. The *New York Age*, a Black newspaper, was very complimentary of Loving, although the reporter called him "Mr." instead of using his military title, "Capt.": "The distinguished leader, who so gracefully conducted this band of eighty-six pieces, is Walter Howard Loving, an American Negro, and a native of Minnesota [*sic*]" ("Filipino Band at New Haven," March 18, 1909, p. 3, col. 4). The reporter noted, "Never before perhaps did wealth, society and rank turn out as they did to the concerts given by the world-famous Philippine Constabulary Band at the Hyperion playhouse" (ibid.). But amid the band's success, tragedy struck. In New Haven, three young bandsmen, José Mediavello, Rosendo Stalsquez, and Lomberne Martine, died due to asphyxiation from a gas lamp heater. One of the men blew out the light before bed, and all three were found unresponsive and remained in a coma for a few days before dying (*New York Times*, March 19, 1909, p. 1, col. 12). I am sure that this greatly saddened Loving and the men of the band, but they had to go on and complete their tour.

After New Haven, the band proceeded to play in Boston's Symphony Hall on March 16, 17, and 21. Here they entered the sacred venue of elite culture and performed both as a band and an orchestra. While all of the *Boston Daily Globe* and *Boston Globe* articles mention Loving's military position and education, only two of the six news reports identify his race. The "singularly interesting character of [the band's] members and the prominence the organization has gained by the intelligence, patience, and devotion of its leader, Capt. Loving, in his very successful work in the development of the native Filipinos" (*Boston Daily Globe*, March 14, 1909). The bandsmen were "taught and trained by Loving, a graduate of the New England conservatory"

(*Boston Globe*, March 16, 1909). Only after the third concert did the *Boston Globe* report that Loving was an "Afro-American" and a graduate of the New England Conservatory of Music, "where he made a special study of military band instruments in addition to his work in the regular musical courses" (March 19, 1909). Local pride was expressed by pointing out that Loving studied at the New England Conservatory. Furthermore, audiences in Boston may have had different motivations to celebrate Loving, because his success legitimized the North's fight in the Civil War, proving that America could give a member of its most oppressed race the opportunity to reach a highly respected position. The article provides a comprehensive account of the band's accomplishments but also repeats a trope about Filipino natural musicality honed by American tutelage:

> By Commissioner Taft's permission Capt. Loving selected at random about 100 men from the Tagalog, Visayan, Hocano [*sic*], Bicol and Pampangueno nations in 1902, and immediately began their musical instruction. Eighteen months after these native Filipinos were called together they appeared at the St. Louis exposition, and in the competitive test of the bands engaged there the Constabulary band was awarded the second prize, taking the lead of Sousa's band and the Grenadier Guards Band of London in the competition, and nearly equaling in the opinion of the judges of the famous Garde Républicaine band of Paris. The band is the official band of Manila, and now has a repertory of 1000 classical and modern selections. (*Boston Globe*, March 19, 1909)

The claim that in eighteen months Filipinos could have reached the level of the world's finest band with a repertoire of a thousand pieces comes dangerously close to laying bare the illusion of white superiority, yet an imperial ear reclaimed its dominance by believing that the United States trained and civilized a randomly selected group of natives.

On the last concert in Boston, the PC Band was given a series of "test compositions" to prove that they were actually playing music and not simply mimicking it by ear. Since the 1800s in Britain, test pieces were a tradition among brass bands, a standardized way of comparing bands to each other (Herbert and Barlow 2013, 163; Herbert 2000, 54). When they sight-read the test compositions of classical and modern works expertly, the *Boston Globe* exclaimed that "the 'little brown men' have proved their musical intelligence and industry beyond all question" (March 21, 1909, p. 39). It is significant

Philippine Constabulary Band at Boston Symphony Hall, 1909. Courtesy of the Moorland-Spingarn Research Center, Manuscript Division, Howard University, Washington, DC.

here that the newspaper shifts from referring to the bandsmen as natives to employing the term "little brown men," though in quotes, suggesting tentativeness about its usage. Although Boston audiences felt compelled to test the band's skill, the reviews indicate that for the moment, listeners were able to hear past race to understand the band's true musical merits. Boston was the center of American anti-imperialist activity,[9] and this may have changed the way audiences heard the band, veering away from prescribed ways of listening driven by racialist and imperialist sentiment. While Boston's musical elite may have been hesitant to hear the band at first, the audience at the last concert "was a large one and more in proportion to the merits of the band than those which attended the preceding concerts here" (*Boston Daily Globe*, March 22, 1909, p. 3). After the test pieces and the many encores that followed, the band chose to showcase a "potpourri of Filipino airs" that the reviewer called "unusual and interesting" (ibid.). The description seems a bit dismissive, but this shows an act of agency on the part of the bandsmen, who were reminding the American audience that Filipinos could not only play Euro-American music but also produce music of their own. Thus, they made space to express pride in their own heritage and tradition.

Emulating the Philippines in Washington, DC, at the "American Lunetta"

When the Tafts returned to the US, they were clearly influenced by the musical life of the Philippines. Helen Taft's earliest musical events as first lady prominently featured the PC Band (Gould 2010, 79). The first concert of her husband's presidency took place on April 6, 1909, at the White House with many distinguished guests. The PC Band's concert program included pieces in a wide variety of styles: the Filipino composition "Potpourri of Filipino Airs" by Antonio Escamilla; arrangements of piano pieces, including the *Moonlight* Sonata by Beethoven and Paderewski's Minuet No. 1; opera excerpts, including their signature piece, Rossini's *William Tell* Overture, the "Dance of the Hours" from *La Gioconda* by Ponchielli, the sextet from *Lucia di Lammermoor* by Donizetti, and the *Poet and Peasant* Overture by Austrian composer Franz von Suppé; and light classical pieces, including "First Heart Throbs" by Richard Eilenberg and "Amoureuse," a waltz by Rodolphe Berger (155). The band ended the program with "Suite de Valses 'España'" by a famous

Filipino composer, Juan de S. Hernandez (Santos 2005, 184). Surprisingly, two popular music pieces also appeared on the program: "Rose Mousse" by Auguste Bosc and "By the Suwanee River" by W. H. Myddleton, each featuring catchy, repetitive melodies and rhythmic accompaniment. Also known as "A Darky's Dream by the Swanee River," Myddleton's lightly syncopated and racialized piece could be considered ragtime music, a departure from their rejection of ragtime in 1904.[10] Since the band was hosted by Mrs. Taft, perhaps they considered this venue a safe one in which to incorporate popular pieces, including one that could be considered ragtime, albeit composed by European-born composers. Absent were Sousa's pieces (including the band's usual "Stars and Stripes Forever") and pieces by American-born composers. By showing off a widely varied repertoire and omitting their usual patriotic numbers, the bandsmen distanced themselves from a representation of Filipinos as having been assimilated under US colonial tutelage. Loving's name does not appear on the concert program (see Gould 2010, 155) or in mainstream news reports, so it is unclear if he conducted this concert.

The next day, Mrs. Taft hosted visiting Japanese commissioners, the Japanese ambassador, the US secretary of the Navy, several US senators and representatives, and many more prominent guests for a dinner in the state dining room. The *Washington Times* reported, "There was an innovation in the way of music, the Philippine Constabulary Band furnishing the programme" (April 7, 1909, p. 6, col. 4). While an honor such as this would have usually been given to the US Marine Band, the PC Band instead was given the chance to perform at a high-profile international and presidential event. Only the *Afro-American* reported that it was indeed Loving that conducted the band at the White House: "Captain Lovering [sic] and his band ... played before the President and a distinguished audience a night or two previous in the East Room of the White House" (April 17, 1909, p. 1). Other newspapers deliberately omitted Loving's name when reporting on the band's concerts at the White House.

Helen Taft was an active supporter of music in the Philippines while her husband served as governor-general and played a role in advocating for the creation of the PC Band. Gould writes that, while "the Tafts shared some of the prejudices of white Americans towards blacks and other minority groups," in Manila, "the couple refused to draw 'the color line'" and attended many social occasions in which they "treated the members of the island aristocracy as social equals" (2010, 14–15). The Tafts returned to the US with this perspective, affording the PC Band a place of honor during the inauguration and at concerts at the White House. In the Philippines, Mrs. Taft enjoyed concerts at Luneta Park, where Americans and Filipinos gathered frequently to listen to performances, saying that it was an institution "whose usefulness to society in the Philippine capital is not to be overestimated" (quoted in Gould 2010, 15). As first lady, she wanted to create for Washington, DC, "what the Luneta was to Manila" (quoted in ibid., 46). An article entitled "Music Will Recall Luneta at Manila" stated, "What President and Mrs. Taft are trying to do for Washington in the establishment of a public meeting place in Potomac Park, where band concerts will be given frequently, all Spanish cities have had for generations. The Luneta at Manila is famed the world over for the excellence of the music that is played nightly and the gorgeousness of the sunsets. To listen to the Constabulary Band and watch the ever changing cloud effects is said by one artist to be worth the discomforts of a trip around the world" (*Washington Times*, Saturday, April 10, 1909, p. 2). The music planned by the band was typical of their "high-class" selections, including Wagner, Handel, Strauss, and Verdi, but without any of the popular pieces that they included at the White House concert: "The Constabulary Band has made the Luneta famous, and the fame is real and genuine because the kind of music the band has given has been the real and genuine kind. The popular demand is for music of the highest type today because Captain Loving and his eighty musicians have shown the people the attractiveness of this class of compositions" (ibid.). The PC Band also planned to include a medley called "Songs of the Philippines" as "representative of the type of music the band is accustomed to playing in the evenings on the Luneta in Manila." To account for this departure from standard European repertoire, the report explains, "While ethnologists have been unable to find anything resembling a native medley [sic] in the Philippines there is nevertheless a class of music that is distinctly Filipino." The composer Antonio Escamilla, a man of political importance as a former aide to General Aguinaldo, was able to capture the "vagrant muse of his people" (ibid.) in the composition. In this way, the reporter compliments Filipinos as possessing a class of music that is distinct, while simultaneously excluding their cultural production as "real and genuine," thus disciplining them back into their proper subordinate place.

Newspaper accounts of the opening of what was dubbed the "American Lunetta" bandstand in Potomac Park discussed the PC Band's prominent role.

One article announced that "Philippine Musicians Will Open the American Lunetta," with a photo of clarinet soloist Baldermero Ian Juan (*Washington Times*, April 16, 1909, p. 4, col. 2–3). To honor this auspicious occasion, the mayor of Tokyo sent four thousand trees as a gift to line the drive (*Washington Times*, April 17, 1909, p. 3, col. 7). The location of the bandstand was criticized, however, because "unlike the Luneta [in the Philippines] . . . the Potomac Drive is far from the centre of things and accessible only to those who can afford to maintain automobiles or carriages. That the public is not expected to interfere with society's weekly meet was indicated to-day by the conspicuous absence of benches or seats for the accommodation of those who had plodded wearily the long distance to the affair" (*New York Times*, April 18, 1909, p. 2). Concerts such as these were important to the city's musical life because, at the time of Taft's presidency, Washington, DC, did not have its own symphony orchestra and relied on visiting organizations (Gould 2010, 77). A very poetic and patriotic description of the "American Lunetta" performance appeared in the *National Tribute*:

> The Philippine Constabulary Band gave the musical program in the pretty bandstand. The closing number was *The Star-Spangled Banner*. At the first notes the President stood up in his auto and removed his high hat, and Mrs. Taft also promptly arose. Every officer, every diplomat stood at salute, and the men present all removed their hats, as the inspiring strains of our beautiful National air spread out over the Potomac, reaching to the distant shores, where Arlington stands with its mighty dead asleep under the over-arching trees. The dead who died for the Star-Spangled Banner. Over there the sun was just setting in a sea of red and amber, and the flag which floats all day over the heroes asleep was gently lowered as the martial strains floated about it. (*National Tribute*, April 22, 1909)

While it was ironic that a colonial military band performed for this American patriotic moment honoring those who died for the flag—albeit not those who died defending the sovereignty of the Philippines—an imperial ear was able to disregard the band's Filipino identity, seeing them as supplying music for the occasion, and as passive recipients of American ideals that had reached their "distant shores." As an instrument of empire, the PC Band's image was most valuable when it served as an exemplar of Filipinos' consent to US benevolence and tutelage.

Two instances in which the PC bandsmen sang rather than played are remarkable moments in which the musicians created a space to express themselves in their own way. The band gave a concert at the Belasco Theater, and the "house was well filled with Washington music lovers who attested by generous applause and demand for encores their appreciation of a well-arranged and varied program" (*Washington Times*, April 12, 1909, p. 6, col. 6). A similar narrative repeated that the band benefited from American leadership, since the musicians demonstrated "a remarkable aptitude in rendering Old World music, with which they were more or less unfamiliar a short time ago" (ibid.). In addition to the band's ability to play European compositions, "One of the attractive departures in last night's program was several songs in the native Filipino tongue, demonstrating that the 'little brown men' can sing as well as play" (ibid.). Surely, the musicians could play their native songs on their instruments, so why did they sing at this moment? Was it spontaneous or deliberate? Even if it was a rare spur-of-the-moment occurrence, I believe singing must have resulted in a very intimate and emotional expression of themselves as Filipinos. By singing, they were distanced from their professional training as instrumentalists whose musicianship was mediated by their instruments, whether string or brass. They sang with the timbres of their own voices to allow for the expression of deep personal feelings that may have resulted from homesickness for their families, exhaustion from endless concerts demanding perfection, grief from the deaths of their fellow bandsmen, and the pressures of being in the public eye in ways not of their own choosing or preference. Singing in their own imperfect voices rather than producing well-trained sounds through their instruments may have been risky, for it exposed less-expert musical execution, but I think that they took this risk for its greater emotional force. The band musicians likely sang these native tunes in unison, not arranged with Western harmonies, and with less than perfect aesthetic control, because no other documents or stories indicate that they ever practiced as a chorus. While I have no doubt that the bandsmen could sing adequately enough, they were not trained singers in the way that they were professional instrumentalists. Nevertheless, in its musical imperfection, the moment allowed them to bare their *loób*, or inner self, and resulted in what I can only imagine as a profound moment of unity, cohesion, and pride. By singing songs in their "native Filipino tongue," they created a physical, aural, emotional, and cultural space for themselves in America as Filipinos, shedding their instruments of empire for the sound of their own voices.

A few articles report on bandsmen off the concert stage, mainly in orientalizing ways that made a spectacle of them. While in Washington, the band took time off and toured the city while staying at the barracks. They were quite visible to the DC public, and the *Washington Post* ran an article that mocked and infantilized them while simultaneously complimenting their musical talents. Rather than simply calling them "little brown brothers," the *Post* extended the moniker to "Little Brown Step Brothers as Bandsmen" (*Washington Post*, April 18, 1909, p. M10). By calling them stepbrothers, the article removed the positive implication of "brothers" (a shared parentage), suggesting instead an obligatory relationship. The headline subtly implies that they were not actual bandsmen, but only acting *as bandsmen*. The report complained that it was not "an easy task to chaperon 86 stepsons of Uncle Sam, few of whom have ever been beyond their native lands"—an erroneous claim, since many of the men had been to St. Louis a few years earlier. The article could have also pointed out that the band performed in Japan and Hawaii before arriving in the United States, but this was concealed to paint the men as naïve, sheltered, and primitive.

Capt. Asa F. Fisk, a white officer who was in charge of the bandsmen, appears in a large photo in the middle of the article. Mention of Loving as the band's conductor does not appear until the end of the article, which mostly highlighted Fisk's role as leader of the group because he had served and lived in the Philippines for eleven years and spoke most of the native dialects: "to Capt. Fisk is due much of the success of the present tour of the band.... [He] worked unremittingly to give them all the benefits that could possibly be derived from such a trip" (ibid.). The outing becomes a racialized spectacle by comparing Fisk to the "old woman who lived in a shoe, and had so many children she did not know what to do." Her troubles, however, were "mild compared to the funny little mishaps which have befallen Capt. Fisk and his Oriental charges." The men "spoke broken English," and Capt. Fisk had "to 'ride herd' to gather in the scattered members of the party." The article makes contradicting statements about the bandsmen by claiming that they had an "Oriental gravity which prevents them from showing any extravagant appreciation of the good times they have been having." Yet, at other times, they "showed mild symptoms of excitement," for example, during a theatrical performance at the Hippodrome in New York, in which they "broke their impassivity to rise to their feet and applauded the gyrations of one of the dancers" (*Washington Post*, April 18, 1909, p. M10). This description plays into an orientalist stereotype that was prevalent in American popular culture: the passive yet unscrupulous Asian male who concealed a sexual deviancy that threatened to erupt unexpectedly.[11]

Newspapers were not always consistent in the ways that they racialized the bandsmen, but they often wrote about them to emphasize their otherness. Filipinos either exceeded or fell short of being "normal" Americans in the way that they "displayed an attachment to the institutions of the adopted country, which argues that they are, even now, good Americans" ("Little Brown Step Brothers as Bandsmen," *Washington Post*, April 18, 1909, p. M10). If this statement cast doubt on whether or not they were actually "good Americans" or simply mimics of Americans as "little brown stepbrothers," musical performance was used as evidence of their adopted patriotism. When the bandsmen passed in front of the statue of Washington on Wall Street, they "played 'The Star-Spangled Banner' in a way no American band could excel, [and] they received an ovation from the crowd that had gathered to listen" (ibid.). While their playing was superlative, it was only due to involvement of the US: "The present perfect ensemble playing of the band is the more remarkable when one remembers that seven years ago not one of its members had the smallest smattering of musical knowledge. Today they are accomplished performers, each bandsman playing several instruments in addition to that which he has adopted in the military band and in the symphony orchestra" (ibid.). In moments that threatened to exceed Filipinos' "assigned script . . . as docile US colonial subjects" (Burns 2013, 7), the bandsmen were subjected to ritualized degradation (Hall 2003, 245) to repress their autonomy and agency. Adding to the witness of their music-making, the band's military uniforms also attested to aspirations that audiences took for an acceptance of benevolent assimilation: "In their natty uniforms the bandsmen make a fine appearance and give their American fellow-citizens an excellent impression of the Filipino at his best" ("Little Brown Step Brothers as Bandsmen," *Washington Post*, April 18, 1909, p. M10). Like other newspapers, this report provides specific details of the bandsmen's "tribal" backgrounds as being of "Tagalog, Visayan, Ilocano, Bicol, and Pampangueno types." While the men were identical in their military uniform, their phenotypical distinctiveness seemed to have been apparent to the reporter: "The racial characteristics of the various peoples which are united in the Philippines Islands are distinctly visible in many of the bandsmen" (ibid.). When Loving as the leader is finally mentioned in the last third of the article, he is not identified as an African American. Instead, his role in training the musicians is highlighted: Loving "has not had a difficult task to train his musicians, for the Filipino is a born musician. His love for melody is instinctive; his sense of rhythm is unerring" (ibid.). This, once again, downplays Loving's efforts and the Filipinos' talent and labor, because the men were "natural" at playing music and training them was not a "difficult task." Their success was not theirs: it was a gift of American colonial tutelage in civilizing the natives—though by its own admission, it was not a task that was difficult to accomplish.

The reporter then speculates on the history of music in the Philippines to support this final claim. At the "time of Magellan," "troubadours" strolled through the country "chanting war ballads and extolling their gods" on a "crude guitar" called a "codyapi" and a "balalone" or "hollow wood cylinder, played as a drum" (ibid.). This so-called balalone isn't a drum, but only played "as a drum," in the same way that the "little brown stepbrothers" acted "as bandsmen." However misinformed, this description seems to derive information from someone, perhaps a bandsman or Loving himself, who was able to describe some aspects of Philippine music. While completely omitting the history of European music and the Philippine band music tradition, there is one reference to "old Spanish waltzes" that the band played with "fire and abandon." While music of the pre-Spanish era is rendered primitive, warlike, and pagan, the Filipinos' playing of old Spanish waltzes was emotional and fiery, invoking a "semi-civilized" state (ibid.). Finally, this article references what would become part of the legend of the PC Band. At the 1904 St. Louis Fair, the band "took honors over famous competitors like Sousa's Band, the Mexican National Band [*sic*], and the Grenadier Guards Band" in a competition, perhaps an unofficial one, which "divided the judges on the question of its equality with the Garde Républicaine from France" (ibid.). While this article did not mention this occasion as the one on which the legend about the lights going out during their performance was based, it does corroborate a story about an event in which the PC Band took second place after the Garde Républicaine.[12]

In late April, the PC Band marched with the Washington High School cadets of Fort Myer at the cadets' special request. The regiment of high school cadets, "being without overcoats, was withdrawn from the parade inauguration day by the board of education" (*Washington Times*, April 5, 1909, p. 9, col. 4). The parade was very important to the school: it seems that Col. Burton R. Ross, commander of the cadet corps, and assistant superintendent Percy M. Hughes called Taft to personally request that he view the cadets' parade. The cadets themselves raised $300 to "secure" the PC Band, with Capt. Oyster "making up the difference, and increasing the amount to $400" (*Washington Times*, April 5, 1909, p. 9, col. 4). On April 20, the high school cadets marched on the north side of Pennsylvania Avenue from Market Place to Seventeenth Street, from which all vehicles were cleared. The PC Band headed the honorable procession while President Taft and Col. Ross watched them from horseback, although Ross was injured when suddenly his "horse slipped and threw him to the ground" (ibid.). The *Washington Times* reported that the PC Band "was the object of every small boy's interest along the route," and that ten thousand people watched them march on this occasion (April 21, 1909, p. 14, col. 1). Even though an enormous crowd came out to see the band, the newspaper chose to single out small boys' fascination with the bandsmen in a way that resonated with characterizations of the Filipinos as "little brown men." The president complimented the cadets as doing "credit to the entire school system of the District" (ibid.). It is remarkable that Taft was willing to show his concern for the boys by taking the time to review them, and also that the cadets themselves raised money to march with the PC Band, out of many available bands in Washington, DC. This unofficial and unique event expresses the meaning and importance of the PC Band with the public, outside of more politicized contexts that deployed the band as an instrument of empire.

The PC Band gave a farewell concert to its Washington audiences and was again lavished with praise. The *Washington Herald* noted that the music was executed with "exact precision" and a "harmonious blending of instruments" that called forth a "fine appreciation of the spirit" of each piece (April 26, 1909, p. 2, col. 2). Capt. Loving was "generous" with his encores in response to the "unstinted applause" of the audience (ibid.). The standout piece again, however, was not a European selection, such as Paderewski's Minuet or Donizetti's Sextet from *Lucia di Lammermoor*, but Sousa's "Stars and Stripes Forever": "That Sousa still remains a popular favorite was simply attested by the enthusiastic manner in which the last-named march was received." Moreover, the piece itself was perceived to be universal in meaning: "'The Stars and Stripes' is a martial air of enduring qualities, and the Filipino Band played it last night with inspiring dash and enthusiasm" (ibid.). The band's skill in playing this popular favorite was not due to their musical acumen but to their enthusiasm for its American patriotic sentiment.

After their farewell concert, the PC Band played a few more times due to audience demand before leaving Washington, DC. A special program was given during a weekday afternoon to accommodate federal employees; it consisted entirely of special requests by the audience, who were "eager to hear their favorite selections played by the little brown men" (*Washington Times*, April 28, 1909, p. 16, col. 3). The way the reporter renders the Filipinos' music-making gives the impression that music-loving audiences wanted to hear pieces played as interpreted by the PC Band, but the newspaper casts it racially—audiences wanted to hear "little brown men" play them. This reduces the men's popularity with the public to the level of spectacle. However, it is clear that the band's concerts were sought out enthusiastically by music lovers: days before this concert, audiences at the Belasco Theater filled the band's program with requests "embracing everything from classical to light opera" (*Washington Herald*, April 26, 1909, p. 2, col. 2). Despite what may have been genuine appreciation for the band's musical skills and creative labor, newspapers played a crucial role in depicting the band as a racial spectacle.

On April 30, the band played at a reception at the YMCA. The program was covered in the *Washington Times*, and the article contained orientalist, infantilizing, and condescending comments: "The work of the band is interesting in the extreme at all times, for the little brown men from the far-off islands are musicians" (April 30, 1909, p. 2, col. 2). Despite this praise, the reporter objected to the arrangement of "sacred" pieces: "Captain Loving chose as the concluding number of his program an arrangement of selections from 'Carmen.' Whether the number as presented by him was his own or the arrangement of someone else is not known, but it was not altogether pleasing. The familiar setting of the opera, as played by bands and orchestras, has left little to be desired in the way of arrangement or orchestration, and that of yesterday was not a happy form" (ibid.). He went on complain that "the beautiful song of Michaela was arranged to march time, and other unpleasant liberties were taken with Bizet's score" (ibid.). Perhaps this was a veiled criticism of Loving for taking creative liberties with the score of a venerated European composer and altering the correct way of execution "as played by bands and orchestras," a statement that conceals the normative whiteness of bands and orchestras to emphasize their universality. Nevertheless, this detail provides an account of Loving as an arranger for band music, not simply orchestrating scores but also adding his own creativity to them, despite the fact that his creative labor ran against the grain of the sacralization of European music. The reporter was more complimentary of clarinet soloist Sergeant Potenciano del Rosario: "The young musician played one of the most brilliant numbers ever heard on the concert stage here.... His performance of the number brought a storm of applause" (ibid.). The band was given dinner and a reception in their honor and treated to an athletic exhibition. At the end of the evening, the bandsmen "sang their native songs and played a number of selections" (ibid.). Here again the bandsmen chose to sing rather than play, not because of their skills as singers, but to intimately communicate, lay bare, and make clear the heritage of their native songs by using their bodies and voices, unmediated by their instruments, to express themselves as Filipinos.

Collaborating with Washington, DC's Elite Black Community

While Taft and others who supported the United States' imperial endeavor in the Philippines sought to contextualize the PC Band in ways that confirmed the successes of benevolent assimilation and colonial tutelage, Black elites emphasized Loving as demonstrating the success of racial uplift and as proof of Blacks' capability to be equal with whites. When Loving arrived in DC, members of the African American community mobilized quickly to plan a concert with the PC Band. Newspapers reported that Loving "has many friends here, and they flocked to Convention Hall last evening to show by their presence that they rejoiced in the success of their friend" (*Washington Evening Star*, April 10, 1909, p. 8, col. 3). Several well-respected musicians in the Black community, including Will Marion Cook, James Reese Europe, and Mary L. Europe, were affiliated with the Samuel Coleridge-Taylor Choral Society, among whose supporters was Frederick Douglass. In a little-known event, Loving and the PC Band collaborated in a joint concert with the choral society at the Convention Hall for Washington's Black elites on April 9. The chorus performed under the direction of "Prof. John T. Layton" (the title of professor was often used for Black bandmasters [Cunningham 2007, 22]) and several of DC's most famous Black classical musicians (*Washington Times*, April 10, 1909, p. 2, col. 5). While the relationship between Filipinos and African Americans during the Philippine-American War has been the focus of several scholars (Gatewood 1987, Miller 1981, Cunningham 2007, and Marasigan 2010), none has attended to their interaction in the US during this time period. This concert provides a glimpse into their rare but significant collaboration, which demonstrated their level of achievement in classical music.

Elite, educated African Americans turned to a strategy of racial uplift—to advocate for equal rights by demonstrating that their capacities were equal to whites—in part by engaging in the artistic and musical world of white elites: "Many hoped to rehabilitate the Race's image—and win social equality—by stressing respectable middle-class behavior, class distinctions parallel to those in white society, and an ethos of service to the less fortunate ('Lifting as we Climb')" (Schenbeck 2014, 23). The Samuel Coleridge-Taylor Choral Society promoted the works of Samuel Coleridge-Taylor, a British composer of African ancestry, who became popular in the US with his composition *The Song of Hiawatha*. Several choral societies performed parts of the larger work, including *Hiawatha's Wedding Feast* and *The Death of Minnehaha* to high acclaim. Americans were not only impressed by Coleridge-Taylor's music, they also were "intrigued by the thought that a person of African heritage could be the idol of London audiences" (McGinty 2001, 199). American music-lovers' positive response was strongly influenced by Coleridge-Taylor's background as a *British* person of African descent, thus demonstrating that American society's anxieties and fears of Blacks were directed very specifically at African Americans. In 1904, President Roosevelt received Coleridge-Taylor at the White House (211) with none of the heated debates and racial backlash that followed Booker T. Washington's dinner with the president just a few years earlier (Davis 2012). Celebrating the composer's musical success "brought much-needed inspiration and encouragement and helped to reinforce ideas of economic self-sufficiency and artistic creativity" among Black communities, who were subjected to violent backlash against their political rights, civil liberties, and economic prospects (McGinty 2001, 200). Three thousand people, two-thirds of whom were among the city's prominent African Americans, attended a concert in 1904, in which the choral society was accompanied by the orchestra of the United States Marine Band, performing *The Song of Hiawatha* (211). It is significant that the famous composer chose to launch his 1904 tour of the US with a concert given by Washington, DC's elite Black community. Given Coleridge-Taylor's popularity with white audiences, I do not think this gesture was out of necessity nor merely coincidental. The concert was a momentous event culturally, but also socially and politically, for its level of collaboration between Black and white Americans. Rather than highlight the multiracial collaboration of performers, however, news reports focused on the musical significance of the concert as the debut of an exciting new composition. The *Evening Star* referred to Coleridge-Taylor as "the eminent English composer" without the racial qualifier of Black or African (November 18, 1904, p. 15, col. 5). Only subtle reference to his racial difference is made: "In this production Mr. Taylor made his first public appearance in America, and the reception tendered him was as cordial and enthusiastic as ever greeted a composer of whatsoever creed or color" (ibid.). By contrast, the news report racialized the chorus as "composed exclusively of colored vocalists, led by a composer and conductor of their own race; the colored people were in the majority in the audience, but there were present also many prominent members of the Washington social and official life" (ibid.). These "prominent members" were not described as white, but this is implied or assumed. Concert reviews praised the chorus, although in racially specific ways, but criticized the US Marine Band: "The chorus of two hundred responded almost instinctively to every move of the conductor's baton, and the harmony would have been unbroken but for the occasional bad work of the orchestra. This unfortunate feature was commented upon because the musicians were all members of the Marine Band orchestra" (*Evening Star*, November 17, 1904, p. 14, col. 3). In this case, I found it surprising that the newspaper critiqued the musical performance of the Marine Band based on the music itself, even going so far as to criticize them while praising the Black performers, albeit drawing on stereotypes of Black musicality, such as that they responded "instinctively" rather than skillfully to the conductor's baton. It is also meaningful that the two organizations, while segregated into their respective groups, came together to perform this work in a momentous cross-racial collaboration, a point that was downplayed in the article. Other newspapers commented more explicitly on the implications of Coleridge-Taylor's success for American race relations: "Almost every review of a concert of Coleridge-Taylor's music in the United States . . . would contain a reference to race, and writers frequently took considerable pains to extract from his circumstances lessons in race relations for both black and white Americans" (McGinty 2001, 200). Coleridge-Taylor was both proof of the success of and a model for Black racial uplift through his artistic capabilities: "Hiawatha mania had a distinct relationship to the cause of racial uplift, and the contribution of the S. Coleridge-Taylor Choral Society to this relationship should not be underestimated" (203).

Similar to their aim in highlighting Coleridge-Taylor as a person of African descent, DC's elite Black community promoted Loving's achievement as a leader, officer, and person of prominence as the director of the Philippine Constabulary Band. While Loving's situation was rare, it was not wholly unique; his contemporaries were well-known Black classical musicians and music critics in the African American community (see Southern 1971, Schenbeck 2014, Reid 1995, Berlin 1994, Lefferts 2013, McGinty 2001). Like Loving, middle-class and elite Blacks engaged in European classical music to distance themselves from the derogatory way that the American public characterized "Negro" music through ragtime and its association with minstrelsy. As mentioned earlier, Black elite musicians like R. Nathaniel Dett stressed poise and discipline in musical performance, and reviews of his concerts noted that his "dignified expression" exemplified the "better class of Negroes" (quoted in Schenbeck 2014, 121). This strategy, however, had the unintended consequence of erasing racial specificity in musical performance and confirmed the universality of European arts (120). Despite his accomplishments in classical music, Dett's choice of repertoire lacked authenticity in the minds of some audiences: "what whites heard was not necessarily what they wished to hear from a Negro" (23). Some white progressives were more interested in "authentic" Black expression, such as spirituals, that appealed to "their own negative attitudes toward an increasingly materialistic, industrialized contemporary America" (23). Choral groups like the Fisk Jubilee Singers found a warm reception among white and Black audiences who appreciated Negro spirituals rendered in a European choral style. Black audiences, however, familiar with antislavery struggles listened differently to this genre, regarding "spirituals with some distaste, since they served as reminders of enslavement" (112). White audiences, on the other hand, "managed to ignor[e] most of the double-coding" in Negro spirituals and instead "valoriz[ed] the Christian themes" (112). This is similar to what Cruz (1999) describes in his work as ethnosympathy, and what I call an imperial ear, one that heard Filipino music-making in Euro-American band repertoire as a validation of US colonization, while dismissing other interpretations of Filipino capabilities and their long history with European music. By being wary of the popularity of spirituals, Black elites declined to endorse what whites upheld as "authentic" Black music and instead showed great enthusiasm for the works of a British composer with African ancestry.

Black classical musicians, who were encouraged by respected European composers like Antonín Dvořák, were enthusiastic about embracing themes and musical elements from Black music within the forms and structures of European art music (see Schenbeck 2014, 113). Loving, and perhaps the PC Band musicians, shared the perspective of this generation of classically trained Black musicians who embraced "hybrizing projects" (132), as is evidenced by the band's inclusion of compositions by Filipino composers. While both Loving's and the bandsmen's primary musical language was already Western, the compositions they chose to play safely inserted ethnic and cultural elements in a way that was not offensive to their largely white audiences or to Black elites.[13] While uplift strategies encouraged pride among African Americans for their equality with whites in terms of capability and capacity, racial uplift in music was not powerful enough, by itself, to change a whole system of institutionalized racism in all sectors of society. Similarly, the PC Band's musical popularity would do little to change the minds of most Americans, who believed that Filipinos in general were inferior in every other way.

The following two articles approach the significance of the PC Band's collaboration with the Coleridge-Taylor Society concert differently. The *Washington Times* seemed apathetic about the performance and interjected that "throughout the program, which contained many compositions by American writers, the band played with spirit and dash" (April 10, 1909, p. 2, col. 5). This report showed little enthusiasm for the symbolic purpose of the concert, which was to demonstrate Blacks' (and Filipinos') achievement in a "civilized" form, but instead assured readers that there were many compositions by "American writers," implying white Americans. While the inclusion of works by (white) American composers should have been utterly unremarkable, the reporter thought it noteworthy to emphasize, in response to the predominantly Black chorus, Coleridge-Taylor's identity as a British composer of African heritage, and the presence of the Filipino band musicians. In this way, mentioning that the program "contained many compositions by American writers" is not just a statement of fact, but racially coded commentary within a "racialized regime of representation" (Hall 1997, 249). That the reporter used the word *writer* rather than *composer* seems to indicate that he was not particularly musically educated, and he seems to know little about the S. Coleridge-Taylor Choral Society, blandly stating that "the work of the choral society, which is interesting at all times, was particularly pleasing in a series of numbers including several of Coleridge-Taylor's 'Hiawatha'" (ibid.). There is no mention of either Loving's or Layton's racial identities, undermining attention to Black leadership and achievement by most white readers.

A *Washington Herald* concert review, compared to the other reports, was much more detailed about the musical performance without making racial implications. The reviewer pointed out that Loving conducted the band without the aid of a written score: "In directing the band numbers without score, as well as in the good taste displayed in granting encores, Capt. Loving demonstrated his thorough musicianship; this, together with his dignified manner of conducting, accounts for the favor into which he has come" (April 10, 1909, p. 16, col. 3). The description of Loving as "dignified" would have met the approval of the Black elite, because it was a representation of the "better class" of Blacks to white society. Both elite Blacks and whites approved of Loving not only because of the type of repertoire that he chose for the PC Band but also because of his refined behavior and generosity toward his audience in granting encores. To whites, Loving was nonthreatening, assimilated, and "useful" in providing music that they desired—a model for other Blacks. This positive moment for Black and white interaction vis-à-vis Filipino involvement is reflected in the way the article referred to the choral society as "local favorite" (ibid.) without further qualifying it as a favorite among Blacks or whites, symbolically connecting two otherwise racially divided communities. The choral society often performed for racially mixed audiences (Badger 1995, 24) and provided a space for their shared love of music. This particular article focused on the music rather than on the spectacle of the "little brown men": "Of special interest was the tuba solo, Catozzi's 'Beelzebub,' given by Sgt. Hipolito De La Cruz. This instrument, which is a familiar sight to band audiences, is rarely heard as a solo instrument" (April 10, 1909, p. 16, col. 3). This neutral description stands in sharp contrast to an earlier, orientalized, deprecating depiction of de la Cruz in the *Washington Post*: "Señor Hipolito de la Cruz, a very little man handling a very large bass horn" (March 7, 1909, p. 6, col. 3). By juxtaposing these two descriptions of de la Cruz, we can see the lens through which each characterization materializes. Throughout the rest of the article, there were no overt racialized comments: "in all their work credit was reflected up their director, Prof. Layton, who has been actively identified with musical life in this city for many years. . . . Great credit is due Miss Mary L. Europe for her excellent work at the piano as accompaniment for the choral society" (*Washington Herald*, April 10, 1909, p. 16, col. 3).[14] The choral society performed the excerpts from *Hiawatha*, but it was Mary L. Europe that accompanied them, not the PC Band. Save for excerpts from *Hiawatha's Wedding Feast*, the PC Band performed pieces in their regular repertoire, including the *William Tell* Overture, the Intermezzo from *Cavalleria Rusticana*, "First Heart Throbs," the Sextet from *Lucia di Lammermoor*, and finally the "The Star-Spangled Banner." This joint concert had a variety of pieces, from "serious" works to more popular band selections (without ragtime, however), with a final rousing patriotic march. The concert's significance lay in Loving's and the Filipinos' engagement with the musical audiences of the elite Black community, rather than in being a cohesive musical program for its own sake.

In contrast to the explicitly racialized descriptions of the band in most articles, James Campbell, writer with the *Afro-American*, highlighted Loving's and the band's musical successes. He stated that the band won "golden opinions" and that the choral society joint concert was a "magnificent success" (April 17, 1909, p. 1). Campbell laments that only when a Black person accomplishes an exceptional achievement do newspapers take notice: "Now and then it is that the daily papers of Washington forget themselves long enough to make mention, in complimentary terms, of some laudable achievement of the Negro, but generally there must be extraordinary cause for this sense of duty" (ibid.). The remarkable ensemble from the Philippines "under the direction of Capt. Walter Lovering [sic] . . . simply thrilled the audience of two thousand people gathered there, with its rendition of popular airs and the most classical music, and the press on the day after was simply teeming with words of praise" (ibid.). However, Campbell notes that other significant events, especially in terms of racial achievement, were "totally ignored by the white press: that Captain Lovering [sic] and his band also played before the president and a distinguished audience" in the East Room of the White House in April (ibid.). Perhaps Campbell observed this, because he writes, "The President was extremely forceful in his praise, expressing himself in no uncertain terms as to what he thought of the noted musical organization, and before bidding them adieu he shook the hand of every member of the band and wished them further successes" (ibid.). However, despite this praise and musical appreciation, Campbell reveals that not much help was extended materially: "the financial end of the enterprise of bringing this band to Washington during inaugural week has been trying to find the right string to pull which will compensate it for the trip here. Apparently some government red tape has gotten mixed up with Uncle Sam's pursestrings, and the inadvertent pulling of the former has resulted in producing but $660 of the $5,000 promised by the Inaugural Committee, with the result that much inconvenience has been caused thereby" (ibid.). Campbell sincerely hoped that, before the band returned home in September, "the depleted treasury of this organization will have been attended to" (ibid.). The band encountered a similar lack of sufficient funds during 1904, and this explains why some members of the band at first refused to return to the United States in 1915. Despite his misspelling of Loving's name, Campbell's account provides much-needed insight into the struggles of the PC Band that were not mentioned in mainstream newspapers. Washington's Black community continued to honor Loving after the Coleridge-Taylor Choral Society concert. On April 21, they gave him a reception at the Second Baptist Church, of which he was a member when he attended the "Colored High School" (M Street High School), and claimed that he was born in Washington, DC, even though he was born in Virginia (*Washington Herald*, April 21, 1909, p. 2, col. 4). Loving was given a "gold-mounted ivory baton" by the teachers of M Street High School, where he graduated in the class of 1892, and he used it to conduct the band's performances (*Washington Times*, April 29, 1909, p. 3, col. 1).

The *Freeman* confirms that many in the Black community were not aware that Loving was African American: "It may not be generally known that the director of the famous Philippine Constabulary Band is a colored man. He is noticeably of Negro extraction, and right from home, the States. He is Captain William [sic] Loving, formerly of the Twenty-Fourth Infantry Band" (March 27, 1909, p. 7, col. 3). This shows the impact of newspapers that frequently omitted Loving's race, leading most readers to assume that he was white. The reporter of the *Freeman* also seems to think that some of the bandmembers were Black: "From what is learned, the much greater number of the big company are Filipinos." He emphasizes the bond between Blacks and Filipinos: "from the fellowship that seems to prevail they [Filipinos] are not averse to the Negro race. In fact, during the recent war the Filipinos often expressed surprise in that they were fought by colored men; they said they were of their race, [and] consequently should stand by them. Intermarriage with the Filipinos is common" (ibid.). To Black Americans, the PC Band represented a successful collaboration between Filipinos and Blacks, not necessarily the outcome of American tutelage or benevolent assimilation.

The *Afro-American* reflected on Loving's contributions and noted the importance of the politics of representation: "Of all the colored men who have gone to the Philippine Islands not one has gained such fame as Walter Loving. He broke into new fields, into unexplored forests. He sought and succeeded in breaking over racial lines and as a result comes back to his native land as the leader of a band composed of eighty-five men of the Malay race" (May 8, 1909, p. 6). Loving was an "Afro-American of fine presence, attractive physique and winning personality" who won the "unstinted praise of the music loving people of Washington" (ibid.). Rather than focus solely on the PC Band and briefly mention its conductor only by name, like most mainstream newspapers, the article highlighted Loving as the "central figure, the promoter, in fact, the creator of this band," called by "musical critics of high repute as one of the world's greatest bandmasters" (ibid). While the article noted that the bandsmen were of the "Malay race," it did not claim that Loving trained a randomly selected group of naturally musical Filipinos, nor did it attribute the band's success to American colonial tutelage. Citing Dunbar's poem "When de Colo'ed Band Comes Marching Down the Street," the report notes that it "would not be an exaggerated description of the Filipino band" (ibid.). While the article boasted that among the crowd were the president, Mrs. Taft, and other distinguished guests who "gathered to hear this band of 'little brown men,'" the phrase is presented in quotes rather than standing as a statement of fact, and the only instance in which any articles by Black newspapers included this phrase. Other reports described the men as "Filipino musicians," and, in one case, "young and fine-looking Filipinos" (*New York Age*, March 18, 1909). Accounts like this provided much-needed contrast to the negative ways that the band was represented, and it is noteworthy that these observations are made through the lens of African American reporters.

Amusement Zones in Atlantic City, New Jersey

From May to the end of August, the PC Band was contracted by Captain Young's Million Dollar Pier in Atlantic City, New Jersey. They performed with circus and variety acts, including "Prince, the largest and finest specimen of lion in captivity; Steve Miaco, the clown; The Sea Lion Band, a novelty act" (*New York Times*, June 14, 1909, p. 1). During the band's engagement, the *New*

Poster of the Philippine Constabulary Band for Young's New Million Dollar Pier, 1909. Courtesy of Robert E. Loving Lucas, from the Edith Loving Collection.

York Times reported that there was a mutiny of Philippine Constabulary troops in Davao, a town "largely settled by Americans engaged in the hemp trade" (ibid.). Much surprise was expressed, because there was "almost unanimous ... praise of the natives' soldierly qualities and loyalty to the colors," and this was the "first serious outbreak in the constabulary since its organization nearly ten years ago." No one could "offer a guess at the reasons which prompted the men to mutiny" (ibid.), leaving it up to the reader to believe that this was nothing more than one anomalous occurrence from an otherwise loyal and placated organization of native police upholding American authority. When asked about the men of the PC Band, "officers who accompanied them" reassured the public that they were not like these mutineers against US rule and attested "proudly to the fact that ... not a single case of desertion had occurred" (ibid.).

The PC Band was very popular with Atlantic City crowds. To fill the demand for their concerts, Atlantic City managers paid heavy fines to the managers of the band's tours of the West to keep them until the end of the season in September: "The Philippine Constabulary Band has made such a hit in Atlantic City that arrangements have been made to extend its stay at the resort until September ... managers in Atlantic City paid a large sum to cancel the other contracts and retain the services of the band throughout the summer season" (*Washington Times*, June 17, 1909, p. 3, col. 2). The band was playing to thousands of spectators twice daily, yet the crowds could not get enough of their performances. While the US government and white American media may have profited symbolically from representations of the band at world's fairs, concert promoters profited financially from the band's concerts, even at the expense of canceling the contracts of other performers.

In June, the African American newspaper *New York Age* reported on the band in Atlantic City, providing a large photograph of Loving. The report highlighted Loving as an "American Negro officer" who impressed the current president and trained the eighty-four Filipino men. "Captain Loving and his band have been idolized by large crowds at Atlantic City" (August 12, 1909, p. 4, col. 3–4). No other news reports during their stay in Atlantic City identified Loving's race, yet details about the bandsmen's race proved interesting to readers. All summer they had been an "integral part of the Boardwalk crowds" on the Million Dollar Pier, and while at first, "people came ... out of curiosity to see the little brown men who were so high in favor with President Taft, [they] remained to listen to the splendid music of eighty pieces which filled the pier with a melodious volume of sound, not equaled by any musical organization that has been here this Summer" (*New York Times*, September 5, 1909). While the musical account was very favorable, the band's movements in public were made a spectacle: "The Filipinos have been packing up all week, and in every store one could see them buying toys and baby carriages and Yankee labor-saving inventions, and it was funny to watch them seriously examining the big blonde dolls that open and shut their eyes. All of these purchases are intended for happy little brown children in the Philippines 'bosky,' to whom they will appear wonderful indeed" (ibid.). Note the contrast of the "little brown men" examining the "big blonde dolls," a metaphor for the way white Americans might imagine Filipinos gazing back at them, positioning whites as superior. There is a stark contrast, a deliberate one, that praises the music and entertainment provided by the PC Band, while disciplining them back into a subordinate position by reiterating the infantilizing image of "little brown men" in contrast to the "big blonde dolls." Loving's role is erased by identifying only Capt. Asa Fisk, Maj. Gurney, and Mr. George Sellner as being in charge of the band. Nevertheless, "Atlantic

City was sorry to see them go, for they made a most favorable impression in every way" (ibid.).

A New Jersey newspaper headline exclaimed, "A Band or Orchestra? Little Brown Men Switch from Brass Instruments to Strings" ([1909?], clipping in Walter Howard Loving Papers, Howard University). Symphonic music was not alien to Filipinos, nor was technical mastery of several instruments a sensational circus trick. This perception reduced the musicians' ability and original thought to the level of mere mimicry. The belief that natives could only imitate their colonial masters is "construed as a sign of inferiority borne out of racial difference" (Rafael 2000, 34). Loving, whose race is not mentioned, was given "all credit to the wonderful success of the Symphony Orchestra" ([1909?], clipping in Walter Howard Loving Papers, Howard University). Loving, turning the attention to the band musicians' accomplishments, "only referred to his artists, whom he holds the greatest in the world and equal to anything in the musical line" (ibid.). I appreciate Loving's acknowledgement, since it was the Filipino musicians who trained each other on stringed instruments. Loving's instrument was cornet, and though the idea of training the musicians as both a band and orchestra may have been his, it was brought to fruition by men of the band like Navarro, who played both flute and violin, and Gayetano Jacobe, a violinist who trained others in the band on strings. The newspaper, not Loving, however, again attributes their skills to race: "Philipinos [sic] are natural born musicians and characteristically of the ambitious sort" (ibid.).

Newspaper reporters and concert reviewers did the job of reinforcing racial ideologies in order to shield the American public from breaches of hierarchy. They drew on their habitus about their own superiority to rationalize how it was possible that Filipinos, as racial inferiors, could attain such a high level of cultural achievement. Bourdieu explains that practices produced by the habitus are a "strategy-generating principle enabling agents to cope with unforeseen and ever-changing situations" (1977, 72). Their habitus structured their new experiences to conform to a belief in racial superiority, even when these experiences seemed to suggest the opposite and negate their own claims: "If they seem determined by anticipation of their own consequences, thereby encouraging the finalist illusion, the fact is that, always tending to reproduce the objective structures of which they are the product, they are determined by the past conditions which have produced the principle of their production, that is, by the actual outcome of identical or interchangeable past practices, which coincides with their own outcome to the extent (*and only to the extent*) that the objective structures of which they are the product are prolonged in the structures within which they function" (72–73). In this way, audiences easily believed and continued to affirm that Filipino achievement in "civilized music" was the direct result of their natural abilities harnessed by American tutelage, rather than the result of Filipino capability. For this reason, despite the success of Filipino musicians in the civilized cultural space of the concert hall, musical recognition did not translate into a widespread repudiation of the unequal treatment of Filipinos.

In the hundreds of newspapers reports that I scoured, only a handful of mainstream newspapers identified or mentioned Loving's race. When Loving's identity as an African American was omitted, the famed conductor ceased to be a Black person in the minds of American readers, because it was assumed that he was white. By contrast, the ethnicities or "tribes" from which the Filipino bandsmen came were often listed meticulously in reports. The few reports that mentioned Loving's racial identity emphasized his educational background and position as an American officer, rather than highlighting his achievement as a Black person in a highly racialized American society. By not mentioning Loving's race, newspapers effectively erased from view, in the minds of thousands of readers, his achievement as an African American in leadership, music, and the military.

The Alaska-Yukon-Pacific Exposition of 1909, San Francisco, and Hawaii

After their contract in Atlantic City ended, the band proceeded to Seattle, Washington, to participate at the Alaska-Yukon-Pacific Exposition (henceforth AYP). Along the way, they performed in Chicago, Cincinnati, Madison, and Denver, where they took a special train over the Union Pacific line for Portland on September 11 (*The Standard*, September 11, 1909, p. 6, col. 2). There was little excitement for them when they stopped in Pendleton, Oregon: "The train was in command of Jack O'Neill . . . who will see that the dusky and diminuitive [sic] musicians reach the metropolis of the state in safety" (*Daily East Oregonian*, September 14, 1909, p. 8, col. 2). They were seen as embracing the paternalistic relationship with the president, and by extension, the United States: "When President Taft was governor of the

Philippines he became greatly interested in the clever musicians, and the bandsmen have a high regard for 'Tio Guillermo,' which in Filipino lingo means 'Uncle Bill'" (*Daily Capital Journal*, Salem, Oregon, September 15, 1909, p. 9, col. 1). They had not their own language, but instead a "lingo," orientalizing them as exotic racial others.

The PC Band was expected to be a visible participant at the AYP exhibition by leading several parades. Local newspapers were excited about their arrival and announced it on their front pages (*Tacoma Times*, September 15, 1909, p. 1, col. 1). After factually reporting the activities of the band, from the inauguration to their concert tours, the *San Francisco Call* repeated the sensationalized ways of depicting the band, even though they had been in their city months earlier and performed for the public: "Strange as it may seem, it is nevertheless the fact that many of the members of the band had never seen an occidental band instrument until seven years ago; yet now there is not a member of the organization that does not play at least two. Thus a symphony orchestra is a possibility, it is claimed, and the bandsmen present, side by side, the masterpieces of military and martial music, with those of the classic writers for orchestra" (September 19, 1909, p. 29, col. 3). While the article expressed some doubt about the fantastic ability of primitives to quickly learn band and orchestral instruments, it nevertheless accepts this as truth because of the relentlessly reiterated stereotype about Filipinos' natural musicality.

Arriving at the AYP Exposition, the band stayed for two weeks, much shorter than their monthslong participation at the 1904 Fair. Much changed in the aftermath of the St. Louis Fair, and due to Filipino objections to the exhibiting of Igorots, the Bureau of Insular Affairs and President Taft hesitated to allow these controversial exhibits again (Rydell 1984, 195). Ultimately, exhibits of tribal people were not incorporated into the official Philippine Exhibit, but shows by private entrepreneurs were allowed because of their popularity with the American public. An Igorot Village–Barbaric Tribes exhibit took place on the Pay Streak (the Seattle exposition's version of the St. Louis World's Fair's Midway) rather than the War Department's Philippine Building, which displayed ethnological photographs, artifacts, and commodities. The Philippine Constabulary Band's role was to present a positive image of the Philippines in order to counter the negative representation of the "savage" Igorots. The PC Band's brief stay was highlighted by Taft's visit. As an example of the United States' positive

Philippine Constabulary Band at the Alaska-Yukon-Pacific Exposition, 1909. Courtesy of the Moorland-Spingarn Research Center, Manuscript Division, Howard University, Washington, DC.

influence in the Philippines, the band headed the parade at the opening of the exhibition, and the president "applauded [the band] several times as it passed back and forth before the reviewing stand" (*The Sun*, October 1, 1909, p. 4, col. 1). The PC Band symbolized Taft's achievement of civilizing Filipinos, and thus he always recognized them publicly and enthusiastically.

On Thursday, September 30, the *San Francisco Call* reported that the PC Band would play on campus at the Greek Theater in San Francisco the following week. The report did mention Loving by name—but without identifying him as an African American officer—and described him as a graduate of the New England Conservatory who was handpicked by Taft to lead the band. It repeats the myth that "none of the 85 members of the band at that time had the slightest knowledge of music, but their development has been phenomenal" (September 30, 1909, p. 8, col. 3). On October 1, the PC Band arrived in San Francisco at the Southern Pacific station on a train especially chartered for them. They were in a rush because the "managers of the Seattle Exposition . . . kept [the band] so long in that city" that it was "unable to reach Berkeley on time by a regular train" (*San Francisco Call*, October 2, 1909, p. 17, col. 3). This demonstrates that the PC Band was in high demand at the AYP and was required to stay as long as possible by exposition officials, who even chartered special transportation for them. The PC Band was met by a group of Filipino students at UC Berkeley, and the press called it "a reunion," because some of the PC bandsmen had "friends among the students of the university from their native lands" (ibid.). This statement disrupts the framing of the bandsmen as uneducated natives, for the Filipino students came from an elite class, but this kind of information was rare to hear about the men, and thus largely unavailable to the American public. The students took the musicians on a tour of Berkeley in carriages. Two concerts were given in Berkeley at the Harmon Gymnasium, both in one day. The program contained classical pieces by Wagner, Hume, Paderewski, Weber, Liszt, and Donizetti, as well as a potpourri of "Filipino Airs" by Escamilla (ibid.). The program did not have any of the typical patriotic marches by Sousa and instead emphasized more serious works by European composers. This omission of patriotic marches was a departure from their concerts for general audiences, which often served to highlight American patriotism and inspire a connection with audiences, for whom proof of the Philippines' compliance and enthusiasm about US rule was essential as well as expected. For their countrymen, the PC Band played not only a composition by a

Filipino composer but also European classical pieces that emphasized their level of playing as equal to the world's finest bands.

In the week that concluded the band's tour of the US, venues scrambled to fit in as many concerts as possible. San Francisco audiences demanded to hear the PC Band as an orchestra: "Considerable disappointment was felt here last February because this city did not have the pleasure of hearing the musicians as an orchestra. They are a symphony orchestra as well as a brass band, every one of the eighty-six playing at least two instruments. The fact that it proved so interesting and meritorious as a band will surely make the orchestral portion of Monday afternoon's concert of additional interest" (*San Francisco Chronicle*, October 3, 1909). This particular article meticulously lists the pieces that were going to be performed: European classical works such as Beethoven's *Moonlight* Sonata, excerpts from Wagner's *Lohengrin* and Verdi's *Rigoletto*, and Catozzi's grand fantasia for tuba, *Beelzebub*. Only one Sousa march appears—not "The Stars and Stripes" but "Hail to the Spirit of Liberty." The band promised to play many encores and requests by audience members, stated the reporter, so it is not entirely known what they played in addition to the listed selections. Additionally, they "promised many Spanish and Filipino pieces" (ibid.) to express their musical and cultural heritage. In this way, they made space in their program to express their cultural identity and did not solely cater to the audience's desires to hear popular pieces by European and American composers. They were able to ask for the audience's indulgence without *hiya* (shame of embarrassment), because by granting the audience's requests and showing appreciation, they had succeeded in creating an *utang* (a social debt) to be repaid in kind. Despite a list of their accomplishments—serving as escort of honor for President Taft, performing for the state dinner and other White House events, and having taken the "grand prize at the St. Louis Exposition five years ago"—the PC Band was still likened to "a fond child in the eyes of the President," who was credited with organizing them. The band's "biggest success," stated the *Chronicle*, was playing to Atlantic City crowds, in which "more than 769,000 paid admissions" were recorded (ibid.). The band covered major cities of the United States, except for the deep South, and played in New England and New York, as well as the Midwest, in Cincinnati, Chicago, Madison, and Denver, before arriving in Seattle and San Francisco. Amid all these details and accomplishments, Loving's name is glaringly absent, and thus his contributions as an African American in an esteemed leadership position are made invisible.

The Filipino People 3, no. 7 (Washington, DC: March 1915): 4. PC Band at the Panama-Pacific International Exposition.

Music critic Walter Anthony, having reviewed the PC Band earlier that year, wrote about the band's final concerts in the *San Francisco Call* ("Week's Music Is of Novel Nature," October 3, 1909, p. 24, col. 1). He likened the band's popularity to a kind of "martial take over"—certainly influenced by the fact that they were the band of the Philippine Constabulary, but also related to the ongoing skirmishes in the Philippines threatening to hijack US control: that summer, there had been a well-publicized mutiny of Philippine Constabulary men in Mindanao. Anthony speculated: "San Francisco, it is expected, will surrender to the Filipinos today. The little brown men who kept Uncle Sam busy for a season or two of skirmishing are expected to take us captives. Their victory will be celebrated with martial music, and the weapons will be instruments of melody" (ibid.). He summarizes general attitudes circulating in newspapers toward the band: "To drop the overworked metaphor, the Constabulary band is an authentic musical organization, combining the brightness of a huge military band and the softer and more alluring qualities of the orchestra" (ibid.). Anthony's style of description makes this feat seem magical rather than skillful: "the band drops its wind instruments and assumes the strings and qualities of an orchestra at will" (ibid.). In this way, the band becomes a machine that can be commanded to switch instruments and assume the qualities of an orchestra, rather than outstanding musicians who could skillfully play multiple instruments. Despite all the details about the Filipino band, their music, and concerts, there is no mention of Loving at all.

An article appearing in the *San Francisco Chronicle* was less complimentary, reminding readers of the band's visit in February at the Dreamland Rink. The band had greatly improved since then: "None of the little crudities of the former concerts were in evidence yesterday, and the keenly critical auditors more than ever were pleased to vote affirmatively as to the musical merits of the little brown musicians" (October 4, 1909, p. 5). But while complimenting the "improvement" of their musical skills, the writer mocks them as military men: "Filipinos, they say, are notoriously bad sailors, and their thirty-two days on a storm-tossed sea last January placed them at a musical disadvantage" (ibid.). Regarding their musical aesthetic: "A little too great tendency to rubato and an exaggerated slowness in andante and adagio movement occasionally mar the otherwise good leadership of the conductor, who really excels in the briskness of his lively tempi and in his marked and beautiful shading.... [The] crescendos and diminuendos which he obtains from his band are of noteworthy merit" (ibid.). This concert review echoes others that reference the band's command and control of musical dynamics and shading, qualities that can be heard on two extant recordings. The band "generously interspersed" extra pieces that were requested by the "delighted" audience (ibid.). The article mentions Capt. Loving, "under whose capable leadership ... the playing of the eighty-six clever little Filipinos met with its well-deserved appreciation," but without identifying his race. This and other omissions had the effect of obscuring the achievement of an African American leader for the vast majority of readers.

Following the ensemble's final concert in San Francisco, Walter Anthony wrote another article, but this time on the Constabulary musicians as a symphony orchestra. His piece selectively commingles musical critique with racialization: "As an orchestra, the little brown brothers are not so satisfactory" (*San Francisco Call*, October 5, 1909, p. 5, col. 1). His use of the moniker in this context, rather than being a statement of opinion or a repetition of convenience, emphasizes their flaws as racialized musicians. He continues with a fair critique that the violins were out of tune, but says, overall, that their performance was admirable: "The Wagner harmonies proved a bit too dissonantal [sic], and the high soaring violins in the grail motive wavered away from accuracy. However, for an 84-man combination the result was praiseworthy and promising" (ibid.). Anthony hears a single moment in which the violins were off pitch as a sign that signified[15] Filipinos' lack of ability to reach the highest level of civilization: "Wagner will remain a generation or two ahead of the Philippine musical consciousness for some years to come" (ibid.). To his ear, and in his mind, the Philippines and "Philippine consciousness" had not yet achieved the capability to interpret the pinnacle of European music. The band, however, played pieces well in their own musical tradition, according to Anthony: "What was more interesting and better played was the selection of Filipino melodies. These showed the touch of the Spanish throughout—in the bolero movement with which the number begins for instance" (ibid.). Also, light opera and American marches came easily for the band, "Suppe's overture to 'Pique Dame' was played by the band in crisp and catchy manner and the Sousa march which opened the program—'Hail to the Spirit of Liberty'—was done with dash and precision" (ibid.). In this piece of musical criticism, Anthony heard the band's mastery of light opera, marches, and their own traditions in a more or less fair way, but when it came to Wagner, he heard a failure to master the highest form of "serious music." The PC Band was primarily a concert band, and as an orchestra, while excellent, was likely less practiced at stringed instruments than a full-time symphony orchestra. Anthony, while mostly complimentary of the band, engaged hearing with an imperial ear to safeguard the loftiest pieces of European music for Euro-Americans.

In her book on classical musicians of Asian heritage, Grace Wang discusses how a "so-called international standard" in Western musical performance should be understood as "culturally specific and emerging out of a long Western/U.S. tradition of normalizing and valorizing the standards and techniques of Europeans and white Americans as universal, authentic, and raceless" (2015, 15). Wang emphasizes that in the US, the "obfuscation of racialized beliefs through praise, unspoken assumptions, and veiled language has created a musical environment in which race is simultaneously visible and underground" (85). Filipino band musicians navigated a highly racialized environment in the arena of Euro-American classical music at a time when race was more explicitly referenced. Anthony was not just suggesting that the Filipino musicians and "Philippine musical consciousness" could not grasp the finer points of Wagner, he was also implying that they had not reached the achievements of whites as a race. Completely missing from Anthony's exposition on the state of "Philippine musical consciousness," however, was Loving. Loving's racial identity would have complicated Anthony's conjecture about Filipinos' level of sociocultural evolution in music by opening a discussion about Black culture, and thus it was left out of the discussion.

President Taft attended the concert, "where he was greeted by a throng which filled the great amphitheater. The Filipino constabulary band, which was with the President at Seattle, provided music" (*The Evening Telegram—New York*, October 5, 1909, p. 16, col. 5). Taft gave a brief speech and was escorted by a troop of the US Cavalry. The PC Band's musical success helped to support Taft's assertion that "we have done something for the Philippines. At least in 10 years we have brought about justice to those islands in admitting them to free trade with the United States. It did not seem at the time that we of the Philippine commission left to visit them that a bright future could exist. I can well remember the fog of uncertainty that we looked into as we left this Golden gate and turned our prows toward the Philippines. It was dark before us then" (*San Francisco Call*, October 6, 1909, p. 1, col. 4). He affirms his role in the improving the Philippines but also legitimizes his presidency: "If anyone had said at that time that that trip would land me in the presidency of the United States I would have thought he was either a falsifier or a fool. It would seem a long way around to take a journey of 10,000 miles to reach the White House, but that's where it landed me" (ibid.). Thus, as an instrument of empire, the PC Band served Taft's purpose—they were the embodiment of Taft's (and the United States') work in the Philippines, which ultimately helped him attain the presidency of the United States.

Taft bid farewell to his "pet organization" as they departed from San Francisco Bay on the transport *Thomas* (*Los Angeles Times*, October 6, 1909, p. 11). As the ship set sail, he pulled up to the vessel on the cutter *McCulloch* and waved goodbye. The PC Band waved back from the bridge of the *Thomas*, and as they played "Hail to the Chief," the president "shouted across the water to the khaki-clad soldiers: 'Good-by [sic], boys; I wish you a pleasant voyage'" (ibid.). It was a momentous occasion, with American flags waving as the PC Band sailed for the open ocean. Taft was asked by Capt. Butt, another American who had spent years in the Philippines, "Does it make you feel homesick, Mr. President?" Taft answered, "Indeed it does. . . . I would give anything if I were going with them" (ibid.). The *Yakima Herald* of Washington State reprinted this article with the heading "Homesick for Philippines" (October 6, 1909, p. 1, col. 1). Notably, Butt and Taft referred to the Philippines as "home," a rare but rather touching moment of affection for the colony. A training ship at the Yerba Buena station give Taft a twenty-one-gun salute as the ship carrying the PC Band sailed for the far reaches of the US empire.

On their way home, the PC Band stopped in Hawaii to perform for the queen. Several advertisements announced their upcoming concerts to ensure that their fans were aware of their arrival: "Never was a prettier or more appropriate tribute paid Her Majesty, Queen Liliuokalani, than that offered last evening when the Philippine Constabulary band marched out to Washington Place to play the Queen's own composition, Aloha Oe" ("Filipinos Pay Honor to Queen," *Hawaiian Gazette*, October 15, 1909, p. 3, col. 4). The band surprised her by arranging her composition for their group, an act that required musical knowledge and skill from each member:

> The Queen received Captain Loving and Mr. Sellner, the manager of the band, who informed her that the men of the band had learned the piece from hearing it played while here last February; that each of the eighty-six men had written his own orchestral part for his individual instrument, and that they had asked to be allowed to render it for her.

The arrangement of her composition was not only a musical endeavor, but one meant to honor the queen:

> Her Majesty thanked them in a most gracious manner, and Captain Loving stepped down, raised his hand, and the first notes of the plaintive melody of Aloha Oe were carried out among the palms. Her Majesty's face lighted up with a pleasant smile, and throughout the piece she sat with clasped hands, listening intently until the last low note had died away, when she warmly applauded.

Not only did the band play her composition, but they also expressed their own traditions, as well as representing their connection to the US:

> After the Hawaiian selection the Filipinos played a medley of their own native music, to which the Queen was an attentive listener, and, when the band struck up the Star-Spangled Banner, Her Majesty was the first to arise. After the national anthem the boys stood with bared heads and curtsied to the Queen, who bade them a gracious aloha. ("Filipinos Pay Honor to Queen," *Hawaiian Gazette*, October 15, 1909, p. 3, col. 4).

The band played two concerts at the Orpheum on Oct. 14, and also played as a symphony orchestra the next day. They presented a concert entirely of audience requests: "Honolulu's music-lovers are up in the very best in the music line, for the first half of the program closed with a Wagnerian selection" (ibid.), which was considered "serious art music." The audience was so delighted that each of the pieces generated an encore; that is, they were played twice: "the encore numbers received the larger rounds of applause, especially Mendelssohn's Spring Song and La Paloma. But it was when the band struck up the opening airs of Aloha Oe that they audience rose to its feet to cheer" (ibid.). The report describes the men in different ways than mainland newspapers: "Of the eighty-six members of the organization, each one plays as many as two instruments, the organization being a symphony orchestra as well as a brass band. These musically-gifted Filipinos have more than fulfilled the expectations of President Taft, through whose offices they were organized eight years ago, in the Philippines, while the President was governor-general of the islands" (ibid.). They are described as "musically gifted" rather than "naturally musical," and entirely missing are references to "little brown men," identical except for being from "different tribes," with no previous knowledge of music but civilized by Americans. While I'm not suggesting that Hawaiian audiences had no racial biases, this article focused much more on the band's musical excellence, rather than emphasizing colonial and racial ideologies to explain the band's success.

Another Hawaiian report focused on Loving as the reason that the band was the "greatest musical success in the history of Honolulu."

> Never was there a more enthusiastic audience than that which greeted these phenomenal artists. Every number was applauded and Captain Loving was generous in his responses with encores. Old airs seemed like new ones and those with which the local people were especially familiar were hardly recognized, so melodious were the notes struck. . . . People in the audience seemed to regret they could not have the band here always and others who cared little for the music ordinarily heard took on new life and bought tickets for the concerts which followed that given in the afternoon. Too much cannot be said of the conductor, Captain W. H. Loving and his ability as a leader. Perfection marked every note, every artist in his part. (*Hawaiian Star*, October 14, 1909, p. 9, col. 2)

Although this reporter does not mention his race, he characterizes Loving as an American leader in control of Filipinos: "Captain Loving is clever. To many who have seen Sousa and listened to his musical achievements the former gets the laurels, both for his work of training eighty-four Filipinos, which was stupendous, and the marvelous skill and perfect ease and composure with which he directs the members of his band" (*Hawaiian Star*, October 16, 1909, p. 3, col. 5). I do not think that in this case the absence of Loving's racial identity was necessarily a way to conceal that he was Black. His leadership provided him with symbolic capital (Bourdieu 1984) that allowed him to traverse racial boundaries that were more rigidly enforced on the US mainland. In Honolulu, as in Manila, Loving had greater social mobility and visibility as a conductor than he did on the mainland.

Newspaper reports in Hawaii and their focus on music provide a foil for the kind of overt racialization that framed the bandsmen on the mainland. None of the articles published in Hawaii referred to them as "little brown men." Newspapers in different areas of the mainland United States reveal the dominant political agenda of representing the band in ways that affirmed an ideology of white superiority by emphasizing Filipino natural abilities over their skills and training in music. Rendering the Filipinos as natural musicians removed their equality and made them inferior, because skill, creativity, and mastery were the sole purview of whites, who were considered the most civilized. If the PC Band was heard to be musically superior, then it must be due to the harnessing of those natural abilities by American leadership and tutelage, and in this way white superiority was protected. Loving's race was downplayed, invisibilized, and explained away by highlighting his education. In this way, the work of colonial domination is achieved not only through actual violence but also through symbolic violence, so that Filipino and Black collaboration and achievement are invisibilized, and recognition as equals with white Americans is withheld. Uncovering and making visible this symbolic violence that developed the imperial ear is one step toward undoing its invisible power.

Contextualizing the PC Band in the Philippines

Back in Manila, the PC Band was placed into a different context. While they were the most famous musical ensemble in the country, they were certainly not the only one, and they were often compared to other Filipino bands. During the first Manila Carnival of 1908, they took second place in a band competition, losing first place to a local band. The Manila Carnival was first organized by an American, Capt. Langhorne, who planned to exhibit "'half-naked' Igorot tribesmen" and amusements (McCoy and Roces 1985,

23). Anticipating that this theme would end up becoming a "colonial freak show," governor-general James Smith put his cabinet's secretary of commerce, Cameron Forbes, in charge, to create a festival that would celebrate Philippine American progress (23). An intense rivalry ensued between American and Filipino participants, especially in choosing a carnival queen, and a decision was made to select two queens—one American as "Queen of the Occident" and one Filipina as "Queen of the Orient" (24).[16] Teodoro M. Kalaw, Filipino intellectual and bureaucrat (Mojares 2006, 17), wrote, "On Sunday, everyone played *William Tell*. The best player was the Banda de Pasig, which was repeatedly applauded. This band has already garnered laurels abroad. Although the Constabulary Band had more instruments, more men, two directors, more time to rehearse, the Pasig Band did better" (*El Renacimiento*, March 1, 1908, quoted in Katigbak 1983, 129). Whether or not the bands were judged on musical merit alone, Kalaw accentuates the triumph of native ingenuity over the advantages of an American-sponsored organization with more resources. Band competitions, in this way, were venues to safely express Filipino nationalist sentiment and resist American superiority.

In Manila, Loving was part of the elite American community of politicians, military officers, and businessmen.[17] While I am not sure whether other African Americans were invited to social events by the colonial administration, Loving's name appeared in the society pages of the *Cablenews-American* (1907–20) as the conductor of the PC Band—which provided music for the balls—rather than as a guest. Perhaps elite guests demanded that only the PC Band perform for their events, but I suspect there are other reasons. After the Philippine-American War, approximately 1,200 Black veterans remained in the Philippines to work and raise families with Filipina wives in both rural areas and in Manila (see Marasigan 2010, chapter 7). The only Black publication in the Philippines, *The Philippine Weekly* (1903), reported that Black veterans continued to face prejudice and discrimination after their service, for example, referring to "white-American owned newspapers whose editors had refused to give them space in their columns" (Marasigan 2010, 433). Loving was a celebrated member of the Manila American community, yet he was likely treated in ways not always socially equal to whites during this time.

4

Sounding Philippine Nationalism at the Panama-Pacific International Exposition of 1915

> Constabulary band goes to the exposition. The musicians apparently do not care to make the trip. How their pay will be handled[?] (*La Democracia*, December 12, 1914)

During preparations for the Panama-Pacific International Exposition (henceforth PPIE), members of the PC Band expressed grave concerns about how the colonial government would adequately support them. The high profile and favor they had with music-loving audiences across the globe was not reflected in their financial compensation. The Philippine newspaper *La Democracia* explained that

> the majority of the musicians who compose the band have no desire to go to Panama [the Panama-Pacific International Exposition], for fear of not getting enough to eat, under actual circumstances, as it is known that the Constabulary have ordered that but 50% of their salary be delivered to them while in America, the other half to be assigned to their respective families.
>
> We have had occasion to speak with some of them, and they have manifested that the half of their salary will not suffice for their expenses in America, more so, when it is understood that there it is more necessary. If

these rumors are correct, what will the Government do? (*La Democracia*, December 12, 1914).

The band's initial refusal demonstrates that the opportunity to travel to and perform in the United States was not sufficient motivation for them to participate at the PPIE; the men's concerns were material, practical, and individual rather than solely patriotic—either for the Philippine colony or the American flag. Eventually, they were convinced and embarked on the long trip overseas. The numerous activities of the PC Band at the PPIE demonstrate that they participated in a number of venues, both within and outside of the exposition, including midway attractions at the Joy Zone and benefit concerts for the San Francisco community. Some of these concerts may have been in addition to their official work for the PPIE, and they likely did not benefit financially from them. For all their work in official and unofficial capacities, the PC Band was not recognized properly for their crucial participation. Just as women's and African Americans' contributions have been overlooked in official publications and newspaper reports of the PPIE, I take seriously Markwyn's assertion that scholars must seek to understand activities and interactions left out of most reports and examine the ways that the "visual and performative aspects of fairs . . . are absolutely integral to understand the way visitors *experienced* expositions" (2010, 171). I will analyze a few newspaper articles on the PC Band that reveal clues about how audiences recognized their contributions, compared to the lack of acknowledgement of the band in official reports and most other newspaper articles.

When the PPIE opened on February 20, 1915, San Francisco newspapers announced excitedly the arrival of the Philippine Constabulary Band, which had been a musical sensation in their city five years earlier. By increasing the band's members from eighty-three to ninety, Loving created visibility for the ensemble, and newspapers boasted that it was "the largest military band in existence" (*San Francisco Chronicle*, February 16, 1915, p. 1). Since their last visit, the PC Band's reputation had been firmly established, the Philippine-American War had ended, and the Jones Bill, a landmark proposition granting the Philippines increased independence, was close to being approved. Because of these developments, the PC Band was contextualized in the debate over the future of the Philippines as both an example of Filipinos' capacity for and progress toward civilization, and of the pressing need of the US to continue its work in civilizing Filipinos and protecting its interests in the Philippines.

Technological Progress, Masculinity, and Eugenics at the PPIE

The Panama-Pacific International Exposition of 1915 was the last of the Victorian-era fairs in form, style, and function (Rydell 1993, 15). It was promoted to celebrate the completion of the Panama Canal and the rebuilding of San Francisco after the fire of 1906. Both the PPIE and its counterpart in San Diego, the Panama-California International Exposition (1915–17), were led by "directors ... [who] sought to preserve the people's faith in the idea of progress—with all its interlaced connotations of technological advance, material growth, racism, and imperialism—and to reshape that faith with particular reference to the challenges posed by domestic and international turmoil" such as immigration, women's right to vote, and the outbreak of WWI (Rydell 1984, 219). One response to the perceived threat of unwanted immigrants was a promotion of eugenics—in the exhibits of the Race Betterment Foundation hosted by the Palace of Education—to "improve" the human race and prevent white racial deterioration caused by intermarrying with lesser races (225). In addition to controlling race and gender in the nation, another theme of the PPIE was the conquering of the Western hemisphere through masculine might: "the exposition provided evidence—visual, spatial, and ideological—of the efficacy and efficiency of America's transgressions of its national borders" (Moore 2010, 76). The exhibits, architecture, and spatial layout of the fair were "celebrated as the manifestation of the United States' imperial prowess and revitalized national manliness" (76). US dominance over internal and external people, land, and technology provided a roadmap for what Theodore Roosevelt called "the future highway of civilization" (quoted in Moore 2010, 76). Sarah Moore's examination of the visual constructions of the fair shows how the design and layout "functioned as a visual agent of regulation and social meaning," leading to a Social Darwinist logic of white masculinity as the apex of civilization (76). Moore argues that, in part, the fair's exhibits transformed a reading of "feminine nature to masculine natural resource" (88). The ways that the fair redirected the meaning of women's, African Americans', and Filipinos' participation worked to emphasize the triumphs of white masculinity over people, land, and technology.

Abigail Markwyn's study of women's participation at the PPIE analyzed the variety of ways that fairgoers "encountered the idea of 'Woman' and a promotion of women's interests as a sex at every turn" (2010, 170). These encounters were both due to and in spite of the lack of a designated "Woman's Building" that in past fairs relegated women's activities to a circumscribed space. While suffragists and women's organizations created alternate spaces from which to advocate for their place as valuable citizens in the nation, representations of white womanhood in exhibits served several purposes—to uphold and accentuate white manhood with a rendering of women's femininity and beauty, to emphasize respectable white womanhood through the participation of the Woman's Board, and to titillate crowds at the Joy Zone with the fetishized allure of "exotic" women (172). Statues like the *Pioneer Mother*, which was sponsored by the Woman's Board, "asserted the dominance of the white middle class in California culture, erasing the presence of nonwhites in the state and the culpability of white women for the results of the conquest" (180). By defining the white woman as the mother of pioneers, the statue "erased the experiences of the many other women who lived in California" (181). This representation emphasized the "link between white women, civilization, and nation building" to advocate that women were "ready for inclusion in the national polity" (181). However, white suffragists' insistence on inclusion was not for the equal treatment of all people—they strongly objected to the fact that President Wilson extended the vote to Filipino men but not to white women. A political cartoon that was on display in one exhibit expresses their complaint. Mr. Wilson, depicted with two heads, smiles toward a childlike Filipino man who bows his head to him, while the other face directs a "vacant smile" to a respectable adult white woman (175–76). The cartoon shows Wilson extending voting privileges to a physically, racially, and socially unequal Filipino male, while the woman depicted as an adult is denied the same rights. This asserted that Filipinos were unworthy of the vote because of their racial inferiority, and that white women, though not the same as men physically because of gender, were nevertheless equal in whiteness. Neither party, however, was equal politically to the white male president, who held the power to grant or deny them privileges. While white women embraced and upheld assumptions about white racial dominance, they found spaces to object to their unequal treatment as a gender and to argue for inclusion in the nation. An "International Suffrage" meeting that featured a session on women's suffrage globally included speeches from nonwhite women, including Mrs. Ch'en Chi, the wife of the commissioner general to the Exposition from China; Rouva Mayi Maya from Finland; Coodalook Eide, an Alaskan Inuit; and Neah Tagook, an Alaskan Indian (176).

These women were featured in a photo in a *San Francisco Chronicle* article about the event in their respective native regalia. By showing the nonwhite women in cultural dress, this photo emphasized the white women's role in "civilization work," what Louise Newman identified as their claim to social power in the nineteenth century (176). Markwyn notes that in honoring these nonwhite women, the photo seems to represent a "curious paradox" (176); however, I think that white suffragists need not appear in the photo because the reader's gaze has naturalized them as the progressive benefactors of women who are marked culturally and racially as being in need of "civilization work." Pratt's analysis of European travel writing illuminates the ways in which "the (lettered, male, European) eye that held the system could familiarize ('naturalize') new sites/sights immediately upon contact, by incorporating them into a language system" in which the "European observer himself has no place in the description" (1992, 31–32). As these examples show, the activities of white women in "some ways reinforced and in other ways challenged the official narratives of the fair" (Markwyn 2010, 184). Markwyn emphasized the need to analyze the experiential aspects of the fair, and that women's participation in face-to-face encounters generated important interactions to "convey their vision of politically active public womanhood to large numbers of people in a short time" (177). Similarly, the PC Band's participation at the fair was far more essential than official publications and most newspapers asserted. We turn now to the ways that the activities of the PC Band reveal that the goals and progress of the empire were not possible without the labor of racial others, and how the subsequent erasure of that labor was made to emphasize white men's domination over racial others.

Bill Brown's argument in his examination of how the fair celebrated man's triumph over machine is useful for understanding how racialized labor had to be erased for this glory to be achieved. Examining popular science fiction during this time period, he writes, "Technology, far from being dependent on scientific neutrality, is and has been an objectification of division within society—in this case, an objectified preservation of divisions that have been politically (if not socially) overcome" (1993, 132). The celebration of the creation of the Panama Canal Zone (what Brown calls a "prosthetic extension" of the US in a "mechanical institution of hemispheric domination" and the "technological and technocratic control over the global flow of good" [134–35]) depended on the erasure of the labor of racialized others, some thirty to forty thousand "white and negro" men, primarily West Indians (146).

This expurgation is mostly clearly illustrated in a famous poster from the PPIE, which depicts a muscular, naked Hercules pushing apart the massive land masses that stood in the way of progress with only the strength of his body, in a way that "occults the mechanical achievement by refiguring the decade-long canal construction as the gesture of the individual, who is *whole* without being *part* of a labor, technological, or military force—without being a 'tool of the government'" (146).

While the portrayals of white men's victories like the one demonstrated by the Hercules poster erased from view the labor of racialized men, eugenicist exhibits relegated these men to racially subservient roles in order to emphasize the evolutionary progress of white men. Eugenics was the topic of several papers at the International Purity Congress and the Education Congress; its use was an attempt to address the "problem" of immigration and the threats that nonwhites posed to the white race (Rydell 1984, 224). In the United States Department of Labor exhibit, a motion picture about Ellis Island "made it clear that the composition of the white ethnic population of the United States was changing" for the worse (226). Especially in California, these exhibits provided the "intellectual underpinnings for mass support for the immigration restriction laws of the 1920s, which placed limits on European immigration, fixed racial quotas on other immigrant groups, and, by 1927, excluded Asians altogether" (226).

Black Americans and Asian Immigrants in California

In her article on African Americans at the PPIE, Lynn M. Hudson argues that the exposition in San Francisco was an important event in that it made a statement about African American contributions to the state and the nation (2010, 27). The exposition took place at a time when Jim Crow, the popularity of eugenics, and the political and social marginalization of African Americans and other racial groups were at their height. The California Chapter of the National Association for the Advancement of Colored People (NAACP) was established during the year of the fair, but at the same time the play *The Clansmen* and the racist film *The Birth of a Nation* were popular among audiences in San Francisco. The film played in the Bay Area for the duration of the exposition, despite California's NAACP pressuring the mayors of both Oakland and San Francisco to ban it (31). Ethnological exhibits on race (such as the Race Betterment booth in the Palace of Education), the Congresses on Eugenics hosted by the Race Betterment Foundation (founded by cereal magnate John H. Kellogg), and the leadership of the former president of Stanford University, David Starr Jordan, gave credibility and legitimacy to white supremacist ideas (Rydell et al. 2000). California was "fast becoming a center of eugenicist thought and practice, a place where racial purity was championed and race mixing despised" (Hudson 2010, 32). The "staging" of race in and around the PPIE, Hudson argues, supported racist and nativist visions of the nation (44). Thousands of California's African American residents "might have seen the PPIE as a chance to ... challenge the tenets of Jim Crow at the same time as their rights were mocked in the theater and on film" (44). To fill in the gaps about African Americans' participation, Hudson focuses on the writings of Delilah L. Beasley (1871–1934), who was the first Black woman columnist for two major newspapers in California—the *Oakland Tribune* and the Black newspaper *Oakland Sunshine* (26). By providing eyewitness accounts of the PPIE, Beasley sought to "make black people visible" and in this way "joined the ranks of other African Americans, including Booker T. Washington and W. E. B. Du Bois, who recognized fairs and expositions as essential locations for demonstrating and representing the talents of black Americans" (36). Beasley's work is crucial to understanding the impactful ways that African Americans contributed to the exposition—contributions that were left out of the accounts of most mainstream news reports.

African Americans were barred from participation at the fair on their own terms, and the most visible representations of them were negative and demeaning caricatures in exhibits in the Joy Zone. A "Dixie Land" concession featured "real old plantation melodies and dances done by real plantation negroes" (*San Francisco Chronicle*, February 24, 1915, p. 4). The concession's elaborate facade featured an enormous and frightening caricature of a "negro" taking a bite out of a gigantic watermelon (ibid.). The "African Dip" allowed fairgoers to toss a ball at a target that dunked an African American seated at the booth into a pool of water, and the "Sperry Flour" included Black women dressed up as stereotypic "mammies" who served the crowds pancakes (Hudson 2010, 38). Al Jolson's popular blackface personification of "Gus" was especially popular with Joy Zone audiences (*San Francisco Chronicle*, June 6, 1915, p. 24). African American fairgoers felt unwelcome and menaced at the international exposition.

Civil rights leaders and lawyers wrote letters to San Francisco mayor James Rolph to advocate for equal treatment in public places. They argued that Black fair attendees should not have to "walk mile after mile until they come to some 'Jim Crow snack house'" to obtain food and drink, and that they only desired to be "accorded the same civil treatment accorded to decent, responsible members of other races" (quoted in Hudson 2010, 34–35). Despite the protest, no action was taken by officials except for denial, and the fair carried on, with a small number of Black workers and fairgoers receiving ill treatment from the concession stands and restaurants both inside and outside the fairgrounds (Hudson 2010, 34). In response to discriminatory hiring practices at the PPIE, the Colored Non-Partisan League wrote a letter to PPIE president Charles Moore (33). Moore never responded, but two weeks later, PPIE secretary R. J. Taussig replied to the league that "speaking officially, the Exposition has not at any time drawn a color line," and as proof of nondiscrimination, cited that a number of "colored men" were employed at the fair (quoted in Hudson 2010, 34). Despite a handful of Black workers, there were no Black guards at the fair, and Taussig's excuse was that only veterans of the Spanish-American War had been hired, even though African Americans had also fought in the war (34). African Americans planned a "Negro Day" and invited Booker T. Washington to speak, but the event never materialized (38). Yet, African Americans found ways to participate and make visible their contributions to the state and nation.

On November 13, Abraham Lincoln Day, a military parade marched through the PPIE. Beasley noted that "the Negroes led the day," since at the head of the entire parade was an African American bandmaster leading Black soldiers of the 9th Cavalry, the 24th Infantry, and the Buffalo Soldiers, who fought in the Spanish-American War, followed by white bands including the US Marines and Cavalry (Beasley 1918, 240). A few days earlier, the 24th Infantry also "acted as Special Escort to the Liberty Bell," which was leaving for its return trip to Philadelphia (240). Beasley wrote that the Black military men "behaved like gentlemen" during their stay at the PPIE, which lasted from summer to fall (240). Their contributions, however, were not highlighted by major newspapers, nor by the fair's official publications.

Loving was an important figure for African Americans at the fair; his presence challenged negative depictions and characterizations of the Black community. One Black newspaper noted with pride: "One of the great and most popular features of the Frisco Exposition is the Philippine Constabulary

Band of one hundred musicians under the leadership of Captain Walter H. Loving, the only Negro bandmaster of the world who holds the rank of captain.... We were especially proud of Captain Loving because he is a member of the Missouri jurisdiction of Masons and has been our District Deputy in the Philippine Islands for several years" ("The Colored Americans Making Good in the Far West," *Kansas City Sun*, November 27, 1915, p. 1). Few other references to Loving noted his achievement as an African American, and this erasure paralleled another one: A contest to name the fair was won by an African American girl, Virginia Stephens, who submitted the name "Jewel City" (Hudson 2010, 41). Since no effort was made to highlight Stephens as an African American, most never knew that she was Black, and this effectively expunged an important contribution by African Americans. To make her identity known, Black women's clubs, which were the only ones from the Black community allowed to participate, presented Stephens on a float along with a large banner announcing her accomplishment during Alameda County Day. Two floats, one sponsored by the Colored Women's Clubs and another carrying seventy-five schoolchildren "dressed in uniform and waving American and Bear flags," marched proudly past the offensive exhibits at the Joy Zone (41). In this way, Hudson argues, "black club women indicated their desire to merge the politics of family and respectability with the tropes of nationalism and patriotism" in order to insist on their belonging to the nation and to their state (41). Especially meaningful was that the "scores of children atop flowery floats signaled a refutation of the claims of eugenicists that African Americans were incapable of 'healthy' reproduction and bred deficient racial stock" (42). Despite a large crowd of spectators who witnessed the event, newspapers like the *San Francisco Chronicle* did not report on these floats and effectively concealed their participation from most of the public. This erasure by the mainstream press, similar to what Loving and the PC Band faced, invisibilized the contributions and successes of racial others to the fair and to society at large.

While the participation of African Americans at the PPIE was largely ignored by the press, exhibits by Japan and China managed to negotiate for their representation, albeit in limited ways. In California, Asian immigrants were the target of violence, and in population they outnumbered African Americans. Despite reservations about anti-Asian sentiment in California, local residents of Japanese and Chinese heritage "perceived the fair as a place from where nations could assert identities that would help improve the status of Chinese and Japanese Americans in California" (Markwyn 2008, 446). Japanese official Matsuzo Nagai, acting consul general of Japan in San Francisco, informed Moore in 1911 that "offensive depictions of Japan would cause friction" (446). Japan also wished to use the fair to showcase itself as a modern nation, as did China. But both parties were also "aware of the potential risks of attending an event in anti-Asian California," including bills forbidding Asian immigrants' access to citizenship, thus preventing them from owning land (446). Exposition officials mobilized against the bills, motivated by a desire for Japan and China to participate in the fair. Although PPIE president Charles Moore attempted to shut down the negative stereotypes to which China and the Chinese community in San Francisco objected, concessionaires on the Joy Zone still managed to draw on stereotypes to attract crowds, and the fair became a place for struggles over representation. A concession called Underground Chinatown had its name changed to Underground Slumming on the direct orders of Moore. Despite this gesture, the public still understood "slumming" to be code for "the popularly known practice of white men and women visiting Chinatown in search of a salacious view of the degenerate lifestyle found there" (463). Compared to other concessions, many of which were struggling financially on the Joy Zone, Underground Slumming made a profit. The stereotypes attracted visitors by offering them comfortable if salacious representations of racial others in their midst. On the other hand, Japan did not protest its particular representation in the Japanese Village, which was full of quaint traditional icons, such as geishas serving tea and manicured gardens. Even though Japan was "trivialized," as Rydell notes, Japanese officials did not protest, because the trivialization of Japan's culture was similar to those found in concessions that featured European cultures (464). Japan and China put on their own respective exhibits that highlighted their progress, but only Japan was able to draw on traditional aspects of its culture as the basis for continued progress: "These tactics reflect the fact that Japanese officials did not face stereotypes that associated ancient Japan with decay or decadence, as white American stereotypes of China did" (457). The respective approaches of Chinese and Japanese officials to representation had to consider the stereotypes they were trying to battle in addition to projecting the image they deemed appropriate. Similarly, Filipino officials navigated complex racial and imperial messages to represent themselves to the American public. The PC Band played a crucial role in this affair.

The PC Band at the PPIE

While journeying to the United States for their third visit, the PC Band performed again in Japan and were "enthusiastically received by the American Ambassador to Japan at concerts in Kobe and Yokohama" (*San Francisco Chronicle*, February 16, 1915, p. 1). This particular report gave accurate details about Loving's life, and rather than obscure his racial identity, identified him as "a full-blood American negro" (ibid.). This peculiar verbiage reflected the spread and popularity of racial evolutionary theories generated by exhibits at previous world's fairs (Rydell 1984, 222), as well as the PPIE's central theme of eugenics.[1]

Much planning went into the musical programs, and officials again chose to emphasize European and American military-style bands, despite their waning popularity among the public. Ragtime was all the rage, and the rise of jazz as America's popular music was just on the horizon. A letter to the editor in the *San Francisco Chronicle* exemplifies the tension between the masses' desire for popular music and the elites' control over concert programming. The writer lamented the banning of ragtime music at concerts at the Golden Gate Park: "Ragtime may not be classic, but it is what the San Francisco people want" (*San Francisco Chronicle*, February 23, 1915, p. 6). The people to whom the letter referred specifically were the "wage-earning class, the people with families who cannot afford to select the amusements that their more favored brothers may enjoy," but who, with their applause, "will prove that ragtime music is the most popular with the multitudes who visit the Park concerts on Sundays" (ibid.). Despite this plea, the PPIE, in its official concerts and programs, chose to highlight Euro-American concert fare and patriotic band music rather than the ragtime and Tin Pan Alley selections enjoyed by the masses of Americans. The most famous concert bands in the world, including the PC Band, were named in the *San Francisco Chronicle*: Sousa's band, Cassasa's band, Garde Républicaine of Paris, Creatore's band, Thaviu's band, Conway's band, Boston Band, and the Philippine Constabulary Band (February 7, 1915, p. 54, col. 5). Despite the honor of being among this elite group, the PC Band would not be included in a concert of an "all-star massed-band" combining the official exposition band, Sousa's band, and the Garde Républicaine. They were allowed to play only before the massed band concert, segregated from the main event. While the PC Band was known for its world-renowned playing, it would be excluded physically, materially, and symbolically from the highest forms of recognition at the PPIE. As they had obscured African Americans' and women's contributions, mainstream newspapers also downplayed the significant ways that the PC Band participated at the PPIE. Filipinos sought to make their presence known through the Philippine Exhibit, which through their representation argued for their level of civilization as worthy of self-government.

The Philippine Exhibit was largely organized by Filipino politicians and elites of the Philippine Board, including president Dr. Leon Ma. Guerrero and members Dr. Francisco Liongson and Fabian de la Rosa, chief of the Fine Arts Exhibit (Panama-Pacific International Exposition 1915, 87). Filipino organizers sought to project a message of progress in the Philippines and portray the country as an emerging nation rather than a subjugated colony of the United States. The exhibit, as stated by the board in a three-hundred-page document, was intended to "spread information on the cultural and other conditions of the Filipinos, the progress they have made in the last decade and a half, and the immense industrial and commercial opportunities they offer" (3). Ten thousand square feet of space in the Palace of Education was dedicated to an exhibit on Philippine education curated by the Philippine Bureau of Education, and a special lecture called "A Visit to the Philippines" took place to educate American fairgoers about the commercial goods that the country could produce. The exhibit demonstrated how American-based education was used for the needs of industry, showcasing Filipinos transforming native materials into crafts. A large model of a standard school of reinforced concrete built by the insular government was on display to showcase progress in the islands and "pointed out that the United States pays nothing toward Philippine Education," because the municipal, provincial, and insular legislature of the islands acquired the necessary funds (Ryan 1916, 58). The Philippines could manage internal affairs such as education on its own. Strikingly absent were the ethnological exhibits of past expositions, which had displayed Filipinos in various stages of civilization. Instead, European-style paintings, a vast library of books on the Philippines by Filipinos, exhibits of agriculture and education, and, of course, the musical performances of the Philippine Constabulary Band were featured to emphasize progress in the Philippines and their readiness for independence. In this way, the PC Band was meant to exemplify and emphasize the achievement of the Philippines as a developing nation—a marked difference from previous representations of the PC Band as exemplifying the pacification and tutelage of "savages" by the United States.

When the Philippine Building was dedicated on February 26, Dr. Leon Guerrero, president of the Philippine Board, and Dr. Francisco Liongson of the commission spoke at the dedication (Todd 1921, v, 3, 311). The purpose of the Philippines' participation, according to the Philippine delegation, was to "give a new idea of the islands as they are under American rule" (*San Francisco Chronicle*, February 24, 1915, p. 4, col. 2). It was reported that Guerrero made a plea for independence by "pointing to the exhibits in the building, which [they] declared were proof in part of the intelligence, industry, and civilization of the insular possessions" (*San Francisco Chronicle*, February 27, 1915, p. 5). He outlined the history and growth of the islands under American rule, stating graciously but firmly, "We are thankful that we have been permitted to accomplish these strides without the loss of dignity that belongs to the race" (ibid.). He commented on the significance of the Philippine Building in the scheme of the fair as a metaphor for the Philippines' position in the world: "You are present at the dedication of this building, insignificant, perhaps, when compared with the magnificent palaces which have arise [*sic*] here, but if you contemplate it as a symbol of a new civilization in the Orient, assuredly you will discover in it something more than that which presents itself to the eye" (ibid.). Guerrero's argument, though somewhat understated, insists that audiences focus on the accomplishments of Filipinos, which, while they did not yet measure up to American and Western civilizational achievements in obvious ways, were no less significant as the Philippines prepared for independence.

Commissioner Guerrero delivered his speech in Spanish; it was translated for the crowd by Charles Morales, director of the exhibits from the Department of Mindanao and Sulu. President of the PPIE Charles Moore responded to Guerrero politely, stating that "Americans love the Filipino people and regard their accomplishments and aims most highly. The sentiments they hold toward us are most cordially reciprocated" (*San Francisco Chronicle*, February 27, 1915, p. 5). Judge William Bailey Lamar, chairman of the US National Committee, countered, "Fate, destiny, Providence, have it what you will, placed our flag in the Philippines. Having been there once, we stay there forever—not as a conqueror, but as the guardian of the Filipino people and as their friend. And as their friend, adviser and protector we will remain" (ibid.). In this response, Lamar assured the audience, and Filipino politicians, of the continued friendly but steadfast involvement of the US. The Philippines' participation at the PPIE was especially urgent, Kramer writes, since "the most significant domestic U.S. struggle over sovereignty in the Philippines since the end of the Philippine-American War" took place between 1912 and 1916 (2006, 351). Manuel L. Quezon, who was the resident commissioner, missed this important event to attend discussions in Washington, DC, about the Philippines in the US Senate (*San Francisco Chronicle*, February 26, 1915, 4). The PC Band performed during this ceremony, and one reporter, an eyewitness, noticed that behind them stood "a group of pretty Filipinos girls" (*San Francisco Chronicle*, February 27, 1915, p. 5), directing attention away from the lofty messages of politicians to a gendered, sexualized representation of the Philippines.

Former president Taft supported the continuation of US administration in the islands because he had invested so much in the Philippines and built his political career on the success of US colonization. Despite his efforts to prove his achievement, he lost his 1912 bid for a second term to Woodrow Wilson. When the Senate Committee debated the administration bill for Philippine independence in early 1915, Taft maintained that Filipinos were not ready for self-rule and that the Philippines would transform into an oligarchy, giving the most privileged and wealthy complete control, thus risking the liberties and rights of the lower class ("Shall We Turn Filipinos Loose?," *Los Angeles Times*, January 4, 1915, p. II4). The *Los Angeles Times* supported continuation of US rule by arguing that "Filipinos are not a united people; they are divided into hundreds of tribes, some of which are in a state of unmitigated savagery. Many of them are fairly intelligent, but few are educated, and practically all—as a race—are lazy, unclean and shiftless" (ibid.). This view reflected California's general disdain for its Asian population and the nativist and xenophobic attitudes that helped to pass the Immigration Act of 1917, known also as the Asiatic Barred Zone, and later the Immigration Act of 1924, which included the Asian Exclusion Act. The racialized stereotypes of "lazy, unclean and shiftless" were also common ways that Blacks were characterized. It would be unwise to turn Filipinos "loose," the *LA Times* claimed, because most of the "savage tribesmen" would "cut each other's throats and fight for loot" (ibid.). The report warned that any American commercial interests would fall to raiding and burning within thirty days of the US military's withdrawal, and that the Philippines would become lawless "just like Mexico" (ibid.). Negative stereotypes that drew on images of the savagery and shiftlessness of racialized others bolstered support for continued US administration. The article advocated for continuing the "work of educating, protecting and civilizing" Filipinos until they could prove themselves fit for self-rule (ibid.). In this context, the PC Band at the PPIE was a visible exemplar for both sides of the argument, as Filipino nationalists could argue that Filipinos had the capacity for self-rule, and US imperialists, alternately, could argue that the US should continue their work to civilize Filipinos.

On May 1, the exposition celebrated May Day concurrently with Philippine Day. A series of "novel sports" were held, in which fifty Filipino youth climbed a greased bamboo pole to "reach the American flag that floated from the top" (*San Francisco Chronicle*, May 2, 1915, p. 33). This symbolized Filipinos comically attempting to reach up to the level of Americans with much difficulty and without dignity, like a "greased pig at a county fair" (ibid.). Correlating Filipinos with animals, infantilizing them, or sexualizing women as "pretty girls" (*San Francisco Chronicle*, February 27, 1915, p. 5) contributed to ritual degradation (Hall 2003, 245), sustaining a "regime of representation" (232) to legitimize their continued treatment as a subjugated race unworthy of equality. The PPIE powerfully "staged race" (and gender) in exhibits, events, and newspaper reports as Filipinos struggled to gain support for independence.

Yet, there are moments in some articles where one can catch glimpses of the PC Band's musical authenticity. Walter Anthony, a music critic who had written at least two articles about the PC Band's performances in 1909, wrote one such review in the *San Francisco Chronicle*. While he expressed skepticism about the PC Band's talents during their earlier visit, Anthony had a more favorable view of the band in 1915. He states that, since their last visit, "the organization has made remarkable progress in all respects of tone quality, attack and dynamic capacity" (March 11, 1915, p. 5). While the headline reads, "Leader Loving Is Sousa of Manila," Anthony specifies that Loving is a "colored" person: "Loving may justly be called 'the colored Sousa of the Philippines,' for he has martial energy in the military music and an orchestral sense of delicacy in the concert offerings" (ibid.). Anthony enthusiastically remarked that while the band won only second prize at 1904 St. Louis Fair, this time the "fine organization of Philippine musicians will be a stubborn contestant for first honors" (ibid.). It is notable that Anthony no longer describes the bandsmen as "little brown men." His appraisal of the band's music-making is detailed: "Particularly fine is the reed department of the band. The clarinet tone is almost as fluent as though it were a violin section, and the quality of tone is mellow, not shrill and full of color. This was discovered beautifully in Durand's well-known 'First Waltz' [Auguste Durand's E-flat-major Waltz, Op. 83].... Deep sonority characterized the band in an excerpt from 'Aida,' and the leader's control was splendidly disclosed in Victor Herbert's fanciful and wayward 'Badinage'" (ibid.). Anthony's in-depth musical criticism of the band's performance is rare, because few newspaper reports included any rich descriptions or critiques about musical aesthetics. His assessment of the reed section as mellow and fluent as a violin section reflects the band's superlative treatment of timbre in orchestration. He reveals that the band was not merely one that performed patriotic marches, but one that was capable of handling the fine orchestral qualities of waltzes and overtures excerpted from symphonic music.

Yet, there was still skepticism about the musicians' abilities among band conductors at the fair, and the band was challenged to prove its skill by responding to a "test piece" that they sight-read in public for the first time. The purpose, presumably, was to prove that they had the skill to read and interpret composed music competently, rather than mimicking the music by ear. The ability to read music notation was considered civilized in the minds of Western-trained musicians, while playing without notation or by ear was not. The piece the PC Band was given to sight-read was even more challenging because it was a new march by Walter Wolff, a local composer whose music the PC Band would not have had access to before the exposition. Anthony remarked, "Though not difficult nor intricate in scheme, it might tax the capacity of any good band to play it well without a rehearsal. Loving had a right to be proud of the way his men acquitted themselves, though there was a measure or two when the trombones were not quite certain which way their Sousa-like melody was proceeding" (*San Francisco Chronicle*, March 11, 1915, p. 5). He concludes, "While the Constabulary Band of ninety pieces may lack something of the refinement of the French band under Pares' direction, it will likely be as popular with the masses who love the militant and brave in music" (ibid.). Again, tension between the masses and educated elite audiences was emphasized, reflecting general tensions in society that were about not only race but also class. Testing the band's capacity to execute and interpret a piece on their own—thus "acquitting" themselves of the charge of mimicry—also seemed analogous to probing if Filipinos had the capacity to govern themselves appropriately.

The PC Band played the most concerts out of any ensemble at the fair, often performing three concerts a day, at 12:30 p.m., 2:00 p.m., and 8:00

p.m. Other bands, like the US Marine Band, typically played one concert per day, or occasionally two. Only Sousa's band played three concerts a day during his nine-week visit, but the PC Band played for the duration of the fair, from February to December. While they were in demand by organizers and audiences, they were not recognized adequately for their participation by official publications. Their musical labor contributed to the many needs of the PPIE, but in order to emphasize the glory of white supremacy at the fair, that labor, like that of other nonwhites and women, had to be invisibilized and erased from recognition.

Unlike the 1904 Fair, in which the PC Band was relegated to the bandstand at the Philippine Reservation, the ensemble played at number of diverse venues at the PPIE. They performed at the Scottish Rite Hall at the corner of Van Ness Avenue and Sutter Street, and Loving's full name was mentioned in the news article, without any negative or positive markers of race, thus concealing the achievements of an African American leader (*San Francisco Chronicle*, March 20, 1915, p. 4). The band's program included Wagner's Vorspiel from *Das Rheingold*, Sousa's *At the King's Court* suite, selections from Verdi's *La Traviata*, and Liszt's *Second Hungarian Rhapsody*—pieces in their standard concert repertoire of "high-class" music and Sousa marches. When the US hosted an international ball for the US vice president and other dignitaries, the PC Band furnished the music, along with the Official Exposition Orchestra (*San Francisco Chronicle*, March 24, 1915, p. 5). Though the Official Exposition Orchestra could have provided the music by itself, the PC Band may have been included due to their popularity and also as proof of the United States' success in the Philippines. In the eyes of Philippine nationalists, this was also an opportunity to demonstrate the achievement and capacity of Filipinos. The view to which audience members subscribed very much depended on their orientation as supporters of Philippine independence or continued US rule.

Sometime in mid-May, Loving became suddenly ill while he was conducting at the Court of the Universe. He signaled to the chief musician to take over, and without missing a beat, Pedro Navarro "mounted the podium, took the baton, and completed the concert" (Richardson 1982, 17). On May 12, Loving was still listed as the conductor in publications of the band's programs, but by May 17, Navarro's name had replaced Loving's in the published program as the conductor (*San Francisco Chronicle*, May 12, 1915, p. 1, and May 17, 1915, p. 1). Filipino journalist Maidan Flores comments that this was a "sinister move to scrap [Loving's] name as conductor of the Band—but this did not prosper. The Filipinos were too grateful and loyal to him to allow it" (1976, 75). The *Washington Herald* reported that Capt. Loving had to leave the exposition to receive treatment at Fort Bayard, New Mexico (May 22, 1915, p. 2, col. 3), and, coincidentally, this was the place where he had started his military career in 1893. During Loving's several months of convalescence, Edith McCary, the daughter of Loving's old army friend Michael McCary, wrote cheerful notes that were delivered to him regularly (Richardson 1982, 17). The two, whose age difference was some twenty-four years, eventually fell in love and married in 1916.[2] Sgt. Navarro took over as interim conductor of the band, which continued to win acclaim for its excellence.

Just as Loving left for New Mexico, Sousa's band arrived at the exposition to perform from May 22 to July 24 (*San Francisco Chronicle*, February 7, 1915, p. 54, col. 5). As he did in 1904, John Philip Sousa again declared the PC Band "easily the best band at the Exposition" (quoted in Flores 1976, 75), even while Loving was not there to lead the band. Sousa conducted the PC Band playing his famous march "Stars and Stripes Forever" and declared, "When I closed my eyes, I thought it was the U.S. Marine Band playing" (quoted in Flores 1976, 75). This was the highest praise that Sousa could bestow on the Filipino bandsmen. With his eyes closed, domestic and colonial constructions of race were erased, allowing him to properly hear the band's artistic abilities, which, in his mind and imperial ears, rivaled but did not surpass Americans' musical achievement. By casting the Filipino musicians as superb mimics of the US Marine Band rather than skilled musicians, he avoided a breach of racial-colonial ideology and constructed Filipinos as imitators but not masters of Western music, a cultural pinnacle of civilization. Sousa was so excited on one occasion that he embraced Navarro, calling him "my friend, my little brown brother" (quoted in Flores 1976, 75).[3] His fondness for the Filipino musicians and praise for their musicality was formed by and expressed in an unequal colonial relationship that highlighted the ways US tutelage purportedly civilized Filipinos.

An extravaganza for music lovers was held in May, including concerts by the PC Band, Sousa's, Cassasa's, Conway's, and the Columbia Park Boys' bands (*San Francisco Chronicle*, May 30, 1915, p. 29). A chorus of 150 voices and the Exposition Orchestra performed Brahms's *Requiem*. Commenting on the tension between "classical" music and popular music at the fair, Sousa stated, "I mix the classics with the popular" (*San Francisco Chronicle*, June

6, 1915, p. 24). Sousa was keenly aware of his position as a band leader but also as a businessperson: "I know, as every other musician knows who ever tried to sell music to the public, that no one can make a financial success purveying a single kind of art to the dear public. Even such an institution as the Boston Symphony Orchestra has to have somebody back of it who is willing and able to 'dip into his pocket' to keep the organization going" (ibid.). Sousa included "classic music," but also a tune popular with WWI soldiers, the "Tipperary."[4] For Sousa, musical performance had nationalistic implications as well. He created his own arrangement of *Tannhäuser* and played it to the approval of Berlin critics—those who were most familiar with and invested in respecting Wagner's style—even though they were "naturally likely to be jealous of an American treatment of a Wagnerian composition" (*San Francisco Chronicle*, June 6, 1915, p. 24). This "American treatment" of European forms was an argument for the capability of the United States to participate on an international platform, on par with the cultural power of European nations. Whether Sousa's assessment was accurate or not, he had the power to convey this message of white American superiority, which was supported by the aims of the larger exposition.

The massed band concert took place in June, bringing together Sousa, Conway, and Cassasa's groups in the Court of the Universe (*San Francisco Chronicle*, June 18, 1915, p. 3) without the participation of the PC Band, which played only before the event. Sousa conducted the 140 instrumentalists of the combined groups, including an arrangement of what the *San Francisco Chronicle* called a "scenic symphony" on a platform at the Court of the Universe. Much pageantry, decoration in national colors, and themes such as "American proclaiming liberty to the world" were celebrated with a fanfare of trumpets and brass as a shot was delivered on cue "by wireless" from the platform (ibid.). The program began with "My Country, 'Tis of Thee" and Sousa's suite *The Dwellers in the Western World*, including the movements "The Red Man" (which incorporated his version of "Indian" themes), "The White Man," and "The Black Man" (which used light syncopation to represent Black music). After these pieces, which reflected the eugenicist categorizations of race at the fair, the massed band suddenly paused, and "From off to the east of the Court of the Universe came the plaintive notes of a fife, with recurrent intervals of drumbeats. The crowd turned, and down the steps from the archway came a Continental drummer and fifer, marching through the gardens and to the platform" (ibid.). Columbia approached in her chariot and took her throne while "The Star-Spangled Banner" played. The Philippines and Filipinos were absent from Sousa's depiction of the racial others of the "Western World,"[5] and the PC Band participated not as part of the event but rather on the periphery, a metaphor for Filipinos' place in US history and American society.

Education Day featured schoolchildren, with dancing, singing, and "merry doings" (*San Francisco Chronicle*, October 12, 1915, p. 11). One hundred girls dressed as Lady Columbia led a flag demonstration around the Liberty Bell, and the Columbia Park Boys' Band played. While the children sang patriotic songs, they were accompanied by the PC Band rather than the Exposition Band. While it is unclear why the PC Band rather than other bands performed for this event, one could interpret this as representing the value of American education for the instruction of youth as well as for America's colonial wards.

While military parades, educational exhibits, official programming, and benefit concerts were part of the PC Band's activities at the PPIE, they also participated in events at the Joy Zone. Like the Pike at the 1904 St. Louis Fair, the Joy Zone was not part of the official exposition, but an entertainment area run by concessionaires who profited from exciting exhibits with exotified themes. Joy Zone Day featured concessionaries in procession, pageantry, and showmanship, culminating in the blowing up of an imitation battleship and exploding mines. Especially thrilling was a mock battle between Maoris and Samoans, both of whom "struggled on the platform for supremacy, [as] tribal cries from the rooters for each made the air weird" (*San Francisco Chronicle*, May 28, 1915, p. 1). Cash prizes were given to exhibits like "Japan the Beautiful" and the "Streets of Cairo" that displayed "reclining princesses on soft Oriental couches." For "displays on foot," the PC Band won top honors (ibid.), but their participation was part of an elaborate presentation that, rather than celebrate their musical performance, used their racialized bodies as exotic visual attraction.

The PC Band participated in "Portola Day," celebrating Don Gaspar de Portola, Spanish governor of California, who was the "first to view San Francisco Bay" (*San Francisco Chronicle*, October 24, 1915, p. 35)—since native people were removed from this narrative. A great barbecue took place on the Joy Zone along with a parade on the exposition grounds, culminating in a grand ball later that evening as a thousand people enjoyed barbecue with "Spanish trimmings" (ibid.). Going along with this theme of Spanish influence was music furnished by the PC Band and a program of vaudeville numbers "all flavored with Spanish features" (ibid.). Portola was a fitting figure to represent the city because he "offered a nostalgic trip to a mythological past, rather than a glorification of any particular segment of San Francisco society. Yet, Portola's Hispanic background was apparently too remote for sustained public identification" (Robin 2018, 21). The PC Band may have represented a vague connection to Spanish heritage, but it is more likely that their purpose was to provide musical labor for an event that was outside the official exposition's programming. It would have been interesting to know what vaudeville numbers they performed, since these were outside of their typical repertoire of European music and American marches, demonstrating that they could play other genres of music.

On May 23, the PC Band played outside of the fairgrounds to give a concert in Oakland for the School Women's Club at Oakland Auditorium, for the benefit of public-school children (*San Francisco Chronicle*, May 24, 1915, p. 8). The PC Band was not just interested in promoting their own musical achievements, but also strove to provide concerts outside of the fair and their official duties. I suspect that they did not benefit financially from their performances outside of the fair's official programs, and extra engagements like this may have been one of the reasons that PC Band members hesitated to participate in the exposition. Nevertheless, benefit concerts had been part of the PC Band's history since their inception, and they carried on even after Loving retired for the first time in 1916 (see next chapter).

At the end of October, a letter to the editor appeared in "The People's Safety Valve" in the *San Francisco Chronicle*. The writer felt irked that while cups, plaques, and medals were given for every occasion and participating organization, the PC Band did not receive its due recognition:

> Is not the Philippine Constabulary Band to be honored? These incomparable musicians, under their two wonderful leaders [Loving and Navarro], have given pleasure to millions of people since opening day of the exposition. Such band music we have never before heard, and shall not again hear unless they pay us another visit. I am sure there are many who would be glad to contribute toward some souvenir which these musicians might bear with them to their island home as an appreciation from us of the treat they have given. There is to be a Philippine day soon; could not the Constabulary Band in some way be specially honored upon that occasion? (*San Francisco Chronicle*, October 27, 1915, p. 16)

While this letter shows that some enthusiastic fairgoers appreciated the contributions of the PC Band, little effort on the part of fair officials was made to recognize their impact on the public. Less than a week later, another letter pressed that if the PC Band should receive an award, then the Guatemalan marimba band should also get one: "The eager crowds drawn daily to the Guatemala building by the Marimba Band (where standing room is at a premium), is proof of the hold they have on the public. They played with great physical endurance because they stood, not seated, and played without notes." Moreover, "their courteous response to encores, the wonderful time, coupled with the fascinating Spanish music, go to make a unique whole which places them in a class apart" (*San Francisco Chronicle*, November 3, 1915, p. 18). The writer added that concerts at the Guatemala Building were always free, unlike some of the official band concerts at the exposition. The writer puts the two bands on the same level, equals in music but also in the ways that their contributions were unrecognized formally. These two letters to the editor point out the unequal treatment by the fair, but also that there was an appreciation by audience members who witnessed them in person. By taking into account how this fairgoer experienced the Guatemalan band, an assumption about the superiority of playing music by reading written scores is challenged; moreover, the interaction between the marimba musicians and the audience was forged by their "courteous response to encores," in a way similar to the PC Band's playing of audience requests. Perhaps others recognized the role of the two bands in pleasing their audiences, but these voices were not heard, nor did they have the power to change the actions of fair organizers or representation by mainstream newspapers.

In Boston, a different Filipino band played in October 1915. They were the Philippine Band of the USS *Georgia*, and they played for the benefit of the Manila Society of the "Gota De Leche" (*Boston Daily Globe*, October 31, 1915, p. 8). They included some standard band pieces by composers such as Paderewski and Auber, but also pieces representing their Philippine identity, such as Araullo's Filipino Waltz "Papa Y Chating [*sic*; Chiting]." While this concert is outside of the scope of my study, this rare finding shows that a Filipino military band other than the Constabulary and Scout bands performed in the US during this time period.

As the weather got colder and the PPIE was winding down, a concert featuring orchestras and bands playing light classical music was held; participating ensembles were the PC Band, Thaviu's band, the Columbia

Park Boys' band, Casanassa's band, and the Exposition Chorus of two hundred voices, as well as two school groups. The famous conductor and composer Victor Herbert performed with his orchestra, offering light concert fare such as "Babes in Toyland," "The Sleeping Beauty and the Beast," and "In Bohemia" (*San Francisco Chronicle*, November 4, 1915, p. 1). Herbert's performance is listed as "Popular concert" (rather than simply "Concert") in the programs (ibid.). This denotes how the fair organizers distinguished between "popular" music of the masses and "classical" music of the elite. Between official exposition concerts, benefit concerts outside the exposition, and participation in the Joy Zone, the PC Band performed at more events than any band at the exposition.

Philippine Day at the Fair

Philippine Day was celebrated on November 3 with an official dedication of the Philippine Pavilion. It was an important occasion for Filipino officials to demonstrate their readiness for independence. Several important guests attended, such as San Francisco mayor James Rolph and PPIE president C. C. Moore, who presented Quezon with a box of tower jewels and planted a Philippine pine tree on the grounds. Manual L. Quezon, then a delegate to Congress, and Dr. Leon Ma. Guerrero, president of the Philippine Board, gave speeches in front of the Philippine Pavilion. In his speech, Quezon stated, "The United States in eighteen years has done much for the Philippine Islands and yet the Filipino is misunderstood in this country. Many think he is a naked semi-savage. The type of native brought to the St. Louis Exposition is largely responsible for this. We have participated so largely here because we wanted you to know us better" (*San Francisco Chronicle*, November 4, 1915, p. 1). While Quezon lamented the display of "semi-savages" in the 1904 Fair, he did not deny this characterization but rather marked a distinction between civilized Filipinos like him and so-called savages. To this point, Kramer writes, "Not all the inhabitants of the Philippines were placed on the same evolutionary track: while evolution was said to characterize U.S. colonial time, Christians and non-Christians were progressing not only at different rates but in different directions. Evolutionary colonial progress, in fact, might widen rather than diminish difference among the islands' inhabitants" (2006, 201). Quezon urged the American public to get to know "us" better, by which he meant civilized, assimilated Filipinos. He cited the Philippine Commission and PC Band as examples of Filipinos who were already civilized prior to US rule:

> Great things have been done by the United States in the Philippine Islands, but no government could have converted a savage, naked people, in ten years, into such citizens as you see represented here in the persons, say, of the Philippine Commission.... And in enumerating the splendid features of that participation I do not forget the much-applauded Philippine Constabulary Band. Nothing of your representation here will linger longer than the memory of the band and its distinguished leader.[6]

Quezon argued that the capacity and level of civilization obtained by Filipinos should motivate the US to grant them independence, but he did not advocate for the rights of all nations to self-determination, nor for the rights of all persons, including "naked savages," for protection and inclusion under the law. Rather, he affirmed US directives that only "civilized" people, as defined and approved by civilized Americans, could be considered for self-governance. As part of this report on the dedication, a picture of a Filipino baby named "Little Consuela Losada" is shown in a baby basket draped with a US flag. The use of this picture, rather than a photo of the esteemed members of the Philippine Board, was for the purpose of representing Filipinos as being in a state of infancy, still in need of swaddling by the US. While Filipino politicians took the opportunity to advocate for Philippine independence and demonstrate their level of civilization through proximity with Euro-American social and cultural norms, their message fell on deaf ears. The dedication was followed by a polite luncheon, ball, and reception attended by Quezon, Guerrero, Moore, and other exposition officials, and the Philippine Constabulary Orchestra provided the music.

Not long after Philippine Day, the *New York Times* published an article that contested the Philippine Commission's optimistic outlook for the Philippines. In a letter to the editor, Robert Frothingham wrote about "Our Losing Game in the Philippines" (November 10, 1915, p. 12). He criticized governor-general Harrison's announcement of Manuel Quezon's promotion from Filipino commissioner to the US to governor-general in 1913, calling it "one of the most amazing and inexplicable blunders a white man could have made in an Oriental country" (ibid.). He felt that the natives were not ready for an increased measure of self-rule and that there was "dissatisfaction among all the residents with business interests over the removal of well-trained American officials from public service to make place for inexperienced Filipinos" (ibid.). Since his visit, he claimed that he kept in touch with friends who reported that "conditions have grown steadily worse" (ibid.). Using music as an example of these conditions, he asked, "Is it any wonder that doubt, uncertainty, and business depression reign on every hand? Is it any wonder that the Filipino band has ceased to play 'The Star-Spangled Banner' on the Luneta every evening and has substituted 'Aguinaldo's March' because the natives refuse to salute the flag?" (ibid.). The loss of white cultural superiority was lamentable: "Need we be surprised at the news of insurrections among the natives when a Filipino can elbow an American off the sidewalk with impunity in the city of Manila?" He insisted that the US maintain its rule over the Philippines to continue the "marvelous strides made by this island since the American occupation . . . [that] never cost the Government of the United States a dollar" (ibid.). The tune of "Aguinaldo's March" was particularly subversive because Gen. Emilio Aguinaldo commissioned Julian Felipe to compose "Lupang Hinirang" at the time of the Philippine Revolution against Spain, when Filipinos declared independence on June 12, 1898. Eventually, it would become the national anthem of the Philippines. The tune was banned for several years, but nevertheless musicians played it at the 1904 Fair:

> In one of the buildings a Filipino man and woman played respectively a guitar and harp. When they had finished a Filipino in the doorway said in excellent English, "That is the march of Aguinaldo, the Filipino who fought so hard for his country and who gave the Americans such trouble to capture him," to which the American in charge added, "And it's only recently that they've been allowed to play that again." (*New York Daily Tribune*, August 22, 1904, p. 7, col. 1)

While Filipinos had few ways to contest their treatment, musical examples such as this provided an opportunity to express nationalist sentiment in a subtle way. The man's complaint that Filipino bands by 1915 substituted "Aguinaldo's March" for "The Star-Spangled Banner" at Luneta Park, where Americans and Filipinos gathered for music, shows the changing attitudes toward American rule in the Philippines.

The End of the Exposition and Return to the Philippines

During the final festivities of the PPIE, the PC Band received an exposition medal: "The Philippine Constabulary band, which has entertained so many thousands at daily concerts during the exposition period, was accorded formal recognition yesterday. Director Frank L. Brown voiced the appreciation of the exposition management at formal ceremonies in the court of Abundance and presented Captain W. H. Loving, the conductor, with a bronze medal" ("Philippine Band Gets an Exposition Medal," *San Francisco Chronicle*, December 1, 1915, p. 1). Despite all their work, they were not awarded a gold medal but given bronze and an "Honorable Mention." There was ample acknowledgement by ordinary citizens and by famous conductors like Sousa, but not by the Exposition Board. This act overlooked the band's contribution and kept them subordinate to American and European bands—not because of their incompetence, for indeed they were popular with the public and other bandmasters, but because of racial oppression and colonial tyranny. What is preserved and protected in the traces of history, the musical resonances of empire, is that the Philippines remained unrecognized even for achievements that challenged claims that they were not civilized enough to earn the right to self-determination.

The closing of the exposition was a grand affair with fireworks and pageantry. Again, the PC Band performed an important role. When the "The Star-Spangled Banner" "burst upon the air, played by the Philippine Constabulary Band. To his feet every man came, head bared and lowered, hand clasping hand in a great surge of feeling" (*San Francisco Chronicle*, December 5, 1915, p. 25). As the piece finished, "guns of warships in the harbor boomed forth the Presidential salute of twenty-one guns." At midnight, fireworks lit the sky and a "bugle sounded taps from the Tower. On the minute of midnight, a switch was thrown extinguishing all the exposition lights." More fireworks flashed, and the word *Finis* in light bulbs lit the Tower of Jewels as a three-hundred-person chorus sung "Auld Lang Syne" (ibid.). It is interesting that this particular report focused on the participation of the PC Band, because the Exposition Band played the same music concurrently. They were mirror parts of the ceremony that took place at exactly at the same time, on opposite ends of the exposition, to accommodate the large crowds. The Exposition Band played their program at the racetrack, and the Philippine Constabulary Band performed the same program at the Court of the Universe. "All the actors in the allegorical part of the Court of the Universe programme are being rehearsed to give a flawless performance. Seven characters are to be presented—a Boy Scout, a journalist, a laborer, a cowboy, a surveyor, a soldier and a sailor. Their mission is to convey President Wilson's sentiment to places where mechanical means of transmission cannot carry it" (*San Francisco Chronicle*, December 1, 1915, p. 1). A technology that could broadcast simultaneously the official fair event was not yet invented, and thus the PC Band was a stand-in for the Exposition Band at a ceremony that was similar but not the same, part of it yet separate. As they had been doing all along, the PC Band during the last days of the PPIE played more than any other band:

> Throughout the day, the various famous bands which have assisted at all important functions throughout the exposition's life, rendered their farewell concerts at the different points within the grounds. The Philippine Constabulary and Cassasa's bands assisted at the noon-day closing ceremonies. Thaviu's band gave a concert to a large audience at the Fillmore bandstand at noon. The Philippine Constabulary band gave an exceptional concert in the Court of the Universe at 2 o'clock and a farewell concert from 6 to 8 o'clock at the Fillmore street stand. (*San Francisco Chronicle*, December 5, 1915, p. 22)

While the labor of racialized others, in this case the PC Band's musical labor, was necessary to pull off a grand celebration of (white) man's achievement, it was erased from its central role in that achievement and relegated to the footnotes of history. Like the erasure of racialized labor from the images of the Panama Canal's triumph, the PC Band's role in this event functioned as what Brown called a "prosthetic of empire," labor that was needed in service to the triumph of white men.

The PC Band made their way back to Manila on the transport *Sherman*, and on their way home, they stopped in Hawaii. A local newspaper called the band the "winner of first prize [*sic*] at the San Francisco exposition [who] played every day under the leadership of its director, Capt. Walter H. Loving" (*Honolulu Star-Bulletin*, December 14, 1915, p. 8). Here this detail took a different meaning, because it effectively erased Navarro's management over the band for most of the fair and highlighted American leadership. It is worth noting also that the newspaper's report of the discomfort of the journey due to the weather did not single out and racialize the Filipino bandsmen as a "bunch of sick monkeys" as the *San Francisco Call* did in 1904 ("Brings Famous Filipino Band," *San Francisco Call*, April 16, p. 4, col. 6). Instead, it was neutral: "The organization is returning to Manila.... Steaming time here from San Francisco was 7 days.... For the first three days of the voyage high seas made nearly everyone on board 'dead to the world,' but after that the ocean became calm as a lake, and the remainder of the trip was uneventful and delightful" (*Honolulu Star-Bulletin*, December 14, 1915, p. 8). The PC Band had fans in the city: "Famous Philippine Constabulary Band will play tonight," and through "the courtesy of Capt. Walter Howard Loving, acting at the request of Mayor Lane, Honolulans will have an opportunity tonight to hear a long program by the PC Band, one of the most famous of all the musical organizations which played at the San Francisco fair" (*Honolulu Star-Bulletin*, December 14, 1915, p. 8). Although the PC Band was recognized by their music-loving audiences, they did not receive sufficient official recognition to create a lasting name for themselves in America as one of the greatest musical organizations of their time.

5

Musical Resonances of Empire: The Golden Gate International Exposition and the End of an Era

The Panama-Pacific International Exposition of 1915 marked the end of an era for the Philippine Constabulary Band. They would not return to the US until twenty-four years later, when much about the relationship between the Philippines and the US had changed. The period before WWI represented a particular era, in which the US had great investment in projecting its vision of civilizing the Philippines to the American public and to Filipinos. By the time they participated in the Golden Gate International Exposition (henceforth GGIE) in 1939, the PC Band had come to symbolize the readiness of the Philippines to govern itself.

To round out my study, I outline the rest of Loving's career in the Philippines and his significant place in Philippine history as it moved toward independence from the United States in the years before WWII. Upon returning to the Philippines from the PPIE, Loving retired from the PC Band and handed the baton to its first Filipino conductor, Capt. Pedro B. Navarro.[1] A few years later, Loving came out of retirement to revive the PC Band, from 1919 to 1923, after which he handed the baton to then Lt. Alfonso J. Fresnido. In 1937, he came out of retirement a second time to bring the newly formed Philippine Army Band to the GGIE. When the band returned from San Francisco, Col. Loving and his wife Edith Loving stayed in the Philippines until they were incarcerated by the Japanese during occupation of the Philippines (1942–45). Loving was killed just as the US military returned to take back the Philippines at the end of the war and the *Afro-American* announced his death on March 10, 1945. I include transcripts of recorded interviews conducted by Dr. Claiborne T. Richardson in 1980 with surviving musicians of the band who went the GGIE, in order to understand how the Filipino bandsmen themselves narrated their experiences and their memories of Loving. Finally, I end by reflecting on the legacy of the Philippine Constabulary Band today with interviews of the descendants of Loving, Navarro, and Fresnido who were the conductors of the pre-WWII PC Band.

Handing the Baton to Filipinos

When Loving retired for the first time in 1916, he turned over the leadership to Pedro B. Navarro, the first Filipino conductor of the PC Band. Navarro had been assistant conductor and chief musician for ten years and also served as interim conductor for several months when Loving had to leave the Panama-Pacific International Exposition for health reasons. On Monday evening, January 17, 1916, a farewell concert was given for Maj. Loving at the Luneta (*Cable-News American*, January 28, 1916, front page). Music historian Raymundo C. Bañas witnessed this historic event:

> [What] gave me a strong impression that evening, which I considered to be the climax was this: a few bars before that sentimental piece, "Auld Lang Syne" ended, without any previous notice, Maj. Loving gave the baton to Navarro, who at once put aside his piccolo and stood before the band and conducted it until the program was ended. Navarro's receiving of the baton was followed by an incessant applause of the public, showing their love for him who was the right man to take Maj. Loving's place. (Bañas 1924, 32)

To commemorate Loving's leadership of the PC Band, Manila's American community came together to raise funds for a parting gift. A committee was appointed and given authority to receive contributions from the public (*Cable-News American*, January 12, 1916, p. 1). Several thousand music lovers attended the concert, and they witnessed the presentation to Loving of a gold watch and chain and a purse of gold coins. Afterward, they waited in line to shake his hand one last time (*Cable-News American*, January 18,

1916, p. 1). The paper published vice governor Gilbert's speech in full, but only summarized Loving's parting speech. Gilbert expressed that Loving's departure inspired a "poignant grief" to the community: "We, the citizens, will need you. Regardless of race or color; regardless of religious or political views; regardless of station, high or low, we will need you. We are selfish; we want you back. Be assured that if your health permits, we will have you back. You belong to us" (ibid., p. 8). Indeed, Loving and the PC Band provided a bridge between various groups in the Manila community through a shared love of music, but they also represented the positive outcome of an often-contentious debate about the benefits of US colonization. While music may not have erased all differences—for to disregard "race or color" and "station, high or low" is to also acknowledge these divisions—Loving was embraced as a "friend" by the Manila community (ibid.). Loving was "visibly moved" by these words and expressed that he hoped to return someday to visit "old friends and acquaintances" (ibid.).

While the newspaper did not print Loving's speech, it was preserved on two typewritten pages among his papers at the Moorland-Spingarn Research Center at Howard University. In this rare find, Loving expresses his sentiments in his own words: "I would belie my feelings if I failed to express my deep regret at this parting ... it is no trifling incident to part with friends, many of whom have supported me in my work from the beginning" ("To the People of Manila and the Philippine Islands," Walter H. Loving Papers, Box 113-1 to 113-3, Manuscript Division, Moorland-Spingarn Research Center, Howard University). He was "deeply appreciative" of the support of not only friends but also the US military: "I take this occasion to mention the fact that when the organization of a Constabulary Band was still in the projective state, it was the army that came forward and loaned us the instruments to begin our work" (ibid.). He thanked the officials of the Philippine government as a source of "cordial relations" and "generous cooperation" during his years of service: "I feel that I owe to them and to the people in general a debt of gratitude that can never be measured because it has been through them that I have been able to realize the culminating ambition of my life" (ibid.). Demonstrating his knowledge of Filipino culture, Loving chose to use the term "debt of gratitude"— a common Filipino value, expressed as *utang na loób*—when referring to his supporters in the Philippines. But, he also includes some often-repeated tropes about Filipino musicality: "It is a far cry back to that day in October,

1902, when the Constabulary Band made its first public appearance in Manila. Even at that early day I had faith in its future for I was aware of the latent musical genius of the Filipinos" (ibid.). The broad generalization is tempered by indicating that there was effort as well as a long tradition on the part of the musicians, who also benefited from exposure to the world's best bands: "I have faith in the future of the Constabulary Band, with its membership drawn from a race which possesses the essential traditions and temperament of musicians; with the experience gained by contact with great musical organizations abroad, and with a competent director who is a thoroughly trained musician, there is no reason why the band should not progress in the future as it has progressed in the past" (ibid.). This is the closest that Loving comes to making any statement about race, though he does not mention anything about the supposed innate musicality of African Americans. In any case, he had faith that the Filipino bandsmen could continue on their own, and that their success was not contingent on American leadership. He chose a Filipino, not an American as their next leader, but sensed some tension around the succession of leadership: "I would ask that my successor be given the same generous support that has been accorded me, to the end that he may have a fair opportunity to prove his fitness. Let the public remember that any discouragement coming to him in the early stages of his responsibility could easily spoil a career that might otherwise be successful" (ibid.). I think Navarro was chosen as successor because of his long service to the band, his musical capabilities, and his proven leadership during Loving's leave. There is also a parallel in this choice to the way that Filipino leadership was developing in the colony, and, for this reason, I think that Loving may have supported independence in the Philippines, although he anticipated criticism in its early stages. Of Loving's choice of a Filipino successor, Antonio C. Hila writes: "This gesture could not have been more fitting and relevant to the time as the spirit of 'Filipinization,' or the gradual withdrawal of the Americans in favor of Filipinos in the colonial government, was at its height" (2004, 83).

An earlier letter of Loving's reveals that he had a different opinion about choosing a leader, at least at the time. In 1907, Loving strongly advised Emmett J. Scott, who lobbied Taft to replace white bandmasters of Black regiments with Black chief musicians (Lefferts 2013, 156), that a director should not be appointed from the ranks of the regiment:

The Chief musician should be a man unknown to the members of the band. It is because the men will have a tendency not to pay proper respect to a man cut out of their own ranks. You cannot expect to drink, fall asleep and eat with a crowd of men and then after a quick ascension expect these men to pay you due respect. While on the other hand, if a new man comes to the regiment bearing a good reputation as to conduct and ability, the men will be forced to respect him. But if a man goes to a regiment knowing no more than the man he is supposed to teach, his days will be numbered by both men and officers. (Loving, Manila, Philippines, May 10, 1907; letter quoted in its entirety in Lefferts 2013, 174–75)

While Loving is emphatic in his opinion that a leader should be chosen from outside of the regimental band, one wonders if the need for capable leader "bearing a good reputation as to conduct and ability" was even more urgent because of the stakes involved in advocating for Black bandmasters. He continues, and although he doesn't specifically say "white officers," this is understood in the context: "The officers especially will pick out every little flaw to make good their objection to colored Bandmasters" (ibid.). This letter hints at Loving's unique experience of being the sole Black officer in the Philippine Constabulary. Although he advocated for the fair treatment of African Americans and Filipinos, he also believed in following protocol and working with the system. For example, Marasigan points out an incident that occurred in 1904: Loving put the entire band under arrest for refusing to play until they were granted their fair pay, but at the same time, he sympathized with the musicians and loaned them money until the matter received attention by government and fair officials (2010, 376–77). As one bandsman explains below, Loving was encouraged to escape house arrest during WWII but refused because he promised to report to the Japanese officials. These examples indicate that while he worked within the system and within the rules, he also believed in fairness. Above all, in the words of his grandson Walter H. Loving III, Col. Loving stood for "honor, dignity, and hard work" (Personal communication with author, 2021).

After Loving's farewell concert, Sgt. Navarro was appointed second lieutenant and assumed the position as Loving's successor and the first Filipino conductor of the Philippine Constabulary Band on February 20, 1916. Wade H. Hammond of the 9th US Cavalry Band (and the first African

American bandmaster in the US military) sent a letter to Navarro: "I wish to congratulate you upon the splendid success of the concert of the band and orchestra ... your people have every reason to be proud of you" (quoted in Bañas 1975, 104). Under Navarro's direction, the PC Band continued Loving's excellent work and maintained its reputation as the leading band of the Philippines and Asia. It was active in the colonial life of Manila, performing weekly concerts at the Luneta and raising money for the Mary Johnston Memorial Hospital. The hospital's director, Dr. Rebecca Parish, "expressed her sincere gratitude to Capt. Navarro and the Band" (104). In another memorable concert, the PC Band played a program of Spanish airs to honor Manila's Spanish residents (104). In this way, the band demonstrated that it was not merely a symbol of American colonial rule, but it also made efforts to benefit Manila's multicultural society.

While Navarro continued Loving's work in keeping the PC Band at the highest level of musical performance, he also expanded the band's repertoire by regularly performing his own compositions, including "Enharmonica-Cromatica March" (*Cable-News American*, February 17, 1916, p. 8). His original compositions brought a Filipino nationalist dimension to the PC Band's character and also highlighted his provincial identity in such pieces as "Liga Ilocana" and an arrangement of "Popular Songs of Ilocanos" (ibid.). Ever the musical perfectionist and disciplinarian, Navarro disliked noisy children at the Luneta's outdoor concerts and even filed a complaint with the chief of police, asking that they be moved away from the bandstand while the concert was in progress (*Cable-News American*, March 26, 1916, p. 6).[2] Navarro continued Loving's strict and disciplined style during rehearsals, partly because of his own character, but also because of his many years as Loving's apprentice. Indeed, Walter H. Loving III remembered his grandmother Edith (Mrs. Loving) and his father Walter, Jr. describe Col. Loving as a "perfectionist" who often said, "If it's worth doing, it's worth doing right" (Personal communication with author, 2021).

Toward the end of 1917, after twenty-two months of serving as bandleader, Navarro resigned (or was forced to resign) as conductor. So far, no written sources have explained the exact reasons for his departure, but according to his daughter Irene (my grandmother), the story is quite scandalous. During a banquet for then senate president Manuel L. Quezon, the PC Band was made to play continuously for hours without food or a break. Frustrated, angry, and concerned about his men, the defiant and hotheaded Navarro ordered the PC Band to pack up and leave during the politically significant celebration. He brought the men to his house, where they rested and ate a proper meal. Needless to say, Quezon and his staff were enraged by Navarro's actions. For his rebelliousness, the story goes, Navarro was removed from his position and sent to the front lines of the provinces of Cavite, Bataan, Masbate, Camarines Norte, and Baguio. From 1918 until his retirement in 1924, he was on active duty and rarely saw his family in faraway Manila. In the midst of his loneliness and excommunication, he turned his attention to composing music, not only for band but also for strings and piano (Bañas 1924, 100–101).[3] From then on, Navarro never played with the PC Band again, although he kept in touch with Loving, and his friends and former colleagues. Navarro never publicly explained the reasons for his sudden resignation as band director and is it still a mystery in the history of the PC Band. When questioned by Bañas in an exchange of letters, the only ones to survive in Navarro's own words, he seemed evasive: "I am sorry indeed that I will not be able to answer these questions for being lack of memorandum [sic] of the past, some of the questions are so hard to comply with and they are impossible to [describe] them as requested and to give you a full explanation" (Navarro 1919 and 1920). Navarro promised to give Bañas an interview when he visited Manila, but never contacted him. In another letter, Navarro apologized for missing his interview: "Sorry indeed for not having interviewed with you during my last stay in Manila as was intended and to give you a [sic] better information about this matter" (Navarro 1919 and 1920). Meanwhile, Lt. José Silos filled Navarro's position as director, but "cooperation between the conductor and the members deteriorated and the Band suffered as a consequence" (Bañas 1975, 105). This may have been due, in part, to the sentiment regarding Navarro's dismissal or the fact that Silos was an outsider to the PC Band's membership, a choice that went against Loving's recommendation (Bañas 1924, 33). Loving may have understood this to be the case—that the PC Band's members wanted a leader from within their own ranks—and this may be why he took a different approach than the one he advised Scott to take in his 1907 letter.

When Loving retired as a major, he returned to the US, settled in Oakland, California, and married Edith McClary in August 1916. They had their only child, Walter Jr., on May 2, 1917 (Richardson 1982, 19). Even though retired from the military, Loving looked for ways to involve himself in US political life. In September 1917, Loving was recruited to work as a civilian for the

Military Intelligence Section of the War College Division of the Army's General Staff to monitor the nation's "racial situation" (Cunningham 2007, 16). Former president Taft refused Loving's request for a letter of introduction, despite the years of service that the PC Band gave to him. Eventually, Loving acquired a letter of recommendation from Army chief of staff Maj. Gen. James Franklin Bell, who commanded the Philippine Department from 1911 to 1914 (16). As part of Loving's work, he warned the government that Harlem, a center for Black intellectuals and activists, was "the fountain head of all radical propaganda among Negroes" and recommended vigilant surveillance (quoted in Cunningham 2007, 18). Nevertheless, Cunningham states that Loving advocated for fair treatment of African Americans in the military and was against segregation (18).[4] Richardson also highlights the positive recommendations Loving made toward providing Black military men with more opportunities: "Loving felt that the time had come to put colored officers in command of colored troops" (Richardson 1982, 20). In his advocacy for fair treatment, equal opportunity, and an end to segregation in the military, Loving was committed to working within the current government rather than seeking alternate routes influenced by "radical propaganda" (Cunningham 2007, 18).

Loving's belief in transforming the system from within played a role in his commitment to the PC Band's band excellence as a musical organization steeped in the repertoire of established Euro-American band music. His approach was one that represented the social and political possibilities of racial uplift for both African Americans and Filipinos, advocating for equality from within existing racial and colonial systems, not in radical ways outside them. Loving's choice of repertoire, while influenced by his background in European classical music, reflects his esteem for respectable, moral, and dignified behavior as well as self-control, discipline, and a strong work ethic. The military brass band and a repertoire of Euro-American concert music enabled Loving to express these ideals and values, a strategy that led to successful collaboration with colonial rule but ultimately did not radically alter the structures of control over Filipinos or Blacks. In the realm of musical performance, a strategy of racial uplift contributed to advocating for equality but did not overturn the system that kept domination in place.

The Great War ended in November 1918, and Loving's service with the Office of Military Intelligence concluded in August 1919. Not long after, Manuel Quezon, president of the Philippine Senate, requested that Loving return to the Philippines to revive and lead the PC Band once again (Richardson 1983,

20; Cunningham 2007, 18). The *Philippines Free Press* proclaimed, "He is back again. Major Walter H. Loving, the man who made the constabulary band—the band, which it might almost be said, 'made Manila famous'" (quoted in the *New York Age*, April 10, 1920, p. 6. col. 4). This statement of Filipino sentiment toward Loving and his role as leader is interesting because it confirms that the PC Band's purpose was not only musical but politically significant, providing recognition for Filipinos. Since Loving's retirement, the *Philippine Press* explained, the PC Band, "while still keeping up a fine standard, has never been quite the same. It has lacked the magic touch of the master. Nor is this any particular reflection on Filipino leadership, for even in the United States, with all its plentitude of band leaders, it would be difficult to find a man qualified to relieve him and maintain an equal standard of excellence" (quoted in the *New York Age*, April 10, 1920, p. 6., col. 4). The *Philippines Free Press* recognized Loving's exemplary leadership but was also careful to state that it was not because he was American but because he was exceptional and irreplaceable as a band leader. I think this article gives Loving the proper credit he deserved as a musician, musical director, and leader, while carefully positing that the band's condition was not a failure of Filipino leadership or capability. By contrast, Flores writes, although he does not cite a source, that the band had deteriorated without Loving and was "a trifle better than an ordinary street band" (1976, 76). Many people who supported a continuation of US rule would have been oriented toward viewing the band's decline as proof of Filipinos' incapacity to govern themselves, and the *Philippines Free Press* clearly did not want the situation to be perceived that way as most Filipinos supported independence from the US.

The first concert given by the PC Band took place just two months after Loving's return, on January 1, 1920, at the Luneta (Bañas 1924, 33). Bañas provided an eyewitness account of Loving's return: "He arrived at the Luneta a few minutes before 6 o'clock; while he was approaching the band, he received the tumultuous applause of the people, which did not cease until he with his baton, stood before the band to begin the first number of the evening's concert. Every piece was applauded by the public" (33–34). Because Loving did not intend to stay in the Philippines indefinitely, he prepared Alfonso J. Fresnido, chosen from within the band's membership (and who went to the PPIE in 1915), as his successor. Loving sent Fresnido to the Dana Music Institute in Warren, Ohio, to study conducting (Bañas 1924, 34; Richardson 1982, 19–20). Loving attempted to secure more work with the Military Intelligence Division in the US, but no offers materialized (Cunningham 2007, 19), and he stayed in the Philippines for the next four years. Navarro reunited with Loving in 1920 during his brief visit to Manila from the front lines (Bañas 1924, 101).

When it was time for Loving to return to the US, members of the PC Band, including Fresnido, urged him to stay:

> We, the undersigned musicians, having been informed of your proposed departure for January 22nd, 1922, have the honor to request that our petition be heard to reconsider your decision for the sake of the honor, prestige and discipline of our band.
>
> We do not mean to say that we lack confidence in our men, but past experiences show that, without your valued management and direction of the band, it was impossible to have harmony, teamwork, cooperation and discipline among us.
>
> We feel that if you will leave us forever it is likely that many of us will be compelled to resign rather than see that the prestige which we have acquired during your stay with us is lost thru [sic] inefficiency of your successor who may not have as much experience as yours from which we learned a great deal.
>
> Trusting you will give this petition your careful and kind consideration. (Walter Howard Loving Papers, Box 113-1 to 113-3, Manuscript Division, Moorland-Spingarn Research Center, Howard University)

The letter is careful to state that, while the band had confidence in their men, they needed Loving and feared that many would resign after his departure. This sentiment may have also reflected an anxiety by some Filipinos over the transfer of power to Filipino leadership. Either way, the fact that Fresnido, as Loving's successor, signed this request, shows how much the band respected and valued Loving as a conductor over any political reasons.

Loving decided to return to the US, and a final concert took place on November 23, 1923, when the baton was handed to the band's second Filipino conductor, Lt. Alfonso J. Fresnido. Bañas's account stated that "the public came nearer the stage and greeted him by an incessant applause" (Bañas 1924, 34). Under Fresnido, Bañas hoped that "by having [he] who is a Filipino as the band conductor, I think, its members will be inspired to work still harder to maintain the standard of the band" (ibid.). He compared the two Filipino

Capt. Alfonso J. Fresnido, conductor of the Philippine Constabulary Band. Raymundo C. Bañas, *Pilipino Music and Theatre*, rev. ed. (Quezon City: Manlapaz Publishing, 1975), 95.

conductors, writing with nationalistic sentiment and optimism, not only for the band, but for the Philippines:

> Never has the band won the most exalted love of the whole public than it did at its splendid concerts on the Luneta when the Filipino, now Capt. Navarro was the conductor. Nevertheless, under proper direction of Lieut. Fresnido, the band will continue to achieve more. The Philippines are very proud to own this band whose incomparable success have been due to the effort exerted by Maj. Loving, Capt. Navarro, together with the cooperation of its members who aspire to see its splendor shine over the civilized countries of the World. (Bañas 1924, 35)

The direction and success of the band under Filipino leadership resonated with similar hopes for the independence of the Philippines generally. Bañas's words nodded to American intervention through Loving but also expressed confidence that Filipino leadership was the proper direction for the band in particular and the Philippines in general. Having turned over control of the band to Filipinos, Loving returned to Oakland with his family in 1924. He was appointed as a major in the Officers' Reserve Corps and bought real estate in Oakland.[5]

As circumstances of US colonization changed, so did the meaning of military brass band performance. I argued in previous chapters that Euro-American band music was a bridge and a shared language between Filipinos and Americans in the early stages of colonization, allowing for aural and visual representation of a successful alliance between colonizer and colonized subjects. As Filipinos gained a foothold in their struggle for independence after 1915, brass band music became a political battleground between white Americans and Filipinos. In 1922, an article appeared in the *LA Times* reporting that the performance of the US national anthem in Manila was "causing friction between American soldiers and Filipinos, according to Dr. T. H. Padro Detavera [sic],[6] Filipino member of the first Philippine commission during the Taft regime" (September 7, 1922, p. 12). During the PC Band's weekly concerts at the Luneta, some Americans were incensed that Filipinos in the audience did not remove their hats while the US national anthem played. American soldiers went so far as to snatch the hats off the heads of the offenders, including those of city officials. In his letter to the editor, de Travera vehemently asserted that to "establish as ritual the playing of the national march at every concert by the band only causes friction between peaceful individuals and persons who, just because they wear the uniform, consider themselves as of their sovereign country and treat Filipinos as an autocratic sovereign treats his subjects" (ibid.). American patriotism and Filipino nationalism collided at the PC Band's concerts when they included the ritual playing of the US national anthem to sonically reinforce an aura of US rule in the Philippines. Filipinos' refusal to remove their hats revealed their rejection of American social and political authority, and it is this act, rather than colonial rule itself in the minds of Americans, that caused the "disorder." When confronted by physical enforcement of American patriotism, Filipinos demanded respect by objecting to the frequency with which this act of subordination and subservience to US colonial authority was repeated through the ritual of playing the US national anthem. As mentioned earlier, some bands chose to play "Aguinaldo's March" rather than

"The Star-Spangled Banner" at concerts in Luneta Park. The role and meaning of musical performance in the colony shifted as political circumstances changed, and, once an instrument of empire, band performance explicitly expressed Filipinos' resistance to colonial rule.

The first appearance in an American newspaper of the legend in which the PC Band performed in the dark at the 1904 St. Louis Fair appeared just two years after the above *LA Times* report. The *Poughkeepsie Eagle News* (as well as two smaller newspapers) ran the article "Exhaustion Brings End to Musical Marathon" (December 16, 1924, p. 8). The article reported that two rival brass bands in Pasig City had an unusual contest that tested musical skill and physical endurance, ending with the intervention of the Philippine Constabulary. One band from the *barangay* (district) of Tinajeros in Malabon City and another from Kawit, a municipality in the province of Cavite, battled each other, starting on Friday evening and ending Sunday morning, when authorities were sent in to stop the battle: "There were no judges of the affair, it being the custom in these contests for the bands to play until one admits defeat, frequently from exhaustion" (ibid.). An important requirement of the competition was that all the pieces had to be played from memory, without any written scores. The explanation for this was a tradition dating back before US colonization: "Playing from memory has been an acquisition of Filipino musicians from Spanish times. Recalling an incident at the St. Louis Exposition in 1904, where the Philippine Constabulary band played, a member of that organization said that the lights went out one night, while the band was giving a concert, and that the audience was amazed when the music continued without a break" (ibid.).[7] While I have no doubt that the 1904 event occurred, it does not seem to have been regarded as significant until decades after the St. Louis Fair, and it was not written about in any US or Philippine newspapers in 1904 that I could find. Newspaper reports in 1909 about the PC Band's tour frequently referred to a competition in 1904 in which the band took second place after the France's Garde Républicaine, but the detail that they played in the dark is absent (see chapter 3). These may have been two separate occasions that were merged into one story, making the legend all the more grandiose when Loving returned to the Philippines to revive the band in 1938. I will elaborate below.

In 1925, a news article reported that a ban had been placed on jazz music in Constabulary concerts at Camp Crame in Quezon City. Responding to these criticisms, Gen. Rafael Crame instructed Lt. Fresnido to "refrain from jazz music at public concerts" to placate "certain 'intellectual' quarlers [*sic*; quarrelers] against the frequent jazz numbers" (*Niagara Falls Gazette*, December 21, 1926, p. 28, col. 4). This ban proves that the PC Band did eventually play jazz, though not under Loving's or Navarro's leadership. There was pushback, not from the entire Manila public necessarily, but from those whom the article refers to as "'intellectual' quarlers." The presence of quotes around *intellectual* snubs this elitist position, one that objected to the presence of culturally inferior music that was popular among the public. The criticism likely came from elite members of Manila society who were more invested in portraying the Philippines in a "civilized" way than appealing to the masses. I would not be surprised if Navarro was among those who were against playing a popular musical style instead of the "classical" fare.[8] Criticisms by the cultural elite of Manila were not necessarily a rejection of jazz's Black origins. Rather, jazz acquired new meaning in 1920s colonial Asia, a fascinating topic treated by Schenker (2016)—what he calls "imperial pop." For example, composer Francisco Santiago championed musical nationalism[9] among Filipinos and was concerned that older folk forms, ones that predated American colonization, would be "drowned out by the rhythms and melodies of U.S. popular music" (Schenker 2016, 184). "It is sad to say," Santiago wrote, "that the genius of the native composers did not escape the baneful influence of the new environment, as evidenced by their adoption of Americans airs, from the old cakewalk, the noisy march of Sousa, and the deafening and somewhat distorted jazz" (quoted in Schenker 2016, 184). Jazz represented not only the sound and culture of American imperialism to some Filipinos, but also gave rise to fears about how composers abandoned folk traditions and gravitated toward popular, commercially viable genres—what Santiago called "cheap dance music" (quoted in Schenker 2016, 186). The resonance of American music in the empire was not only cultural and political, but also increasingly commercial (see Schenker 2016, especially chapter 3). The perceived threat did not emanate from a fear of Black culture or Black people—in this case, it was an objection to pervasive American influences at a time when there was a strong movement toward Philippine independence.

More than a decade would pass before the PC Band was referred to again in American newspapers. In 1935, they were mentioned briefly, when they played during the landing of the *China Clipper* in Manila, after its eight-thousand-mile journey from Alameda, California, carrying the first load of airmail over the Pacific Ocean (*Geneva Daily Times*, November 29, 1935,

p. 1, col. 4). While news about this historic event focused on the success of aviation, it was also significant for bringing attention to the Philippines' status as a commonwealth, which recently had replaced the US insular government. The clipper carried a letter from President Franklin D. Roosevelt to Manuel Quezon, the newly inaugurated first president of the Philippine Commonwealth. Attesting to the PC Band's vital role as part of the emerging Philippine nation, the *Geneva Daily Times* reported: "The thrilled onlookers of many races, cheered when the Philippine constabulary band struck up the native and United States national anthems" (ibid.). Some of the "onlookers of many races" may have cheered for the Philippine national anthem in recognition of the rising nation, while others may have applauded for the US national anthem as representing the continued presence of the US in the Philippines. Regardless, the recognition of a "native" national anthem reflected the changing political landscape of the Philippines as it moved toward independence.

Loving's Return and the PC Band Legend

In 1936, the Philippine Constabulary was absorbed into the Philippine Army as the Constabulary Division, and the PC Band officially became the Philippine Army Band (Cunningham 2007, 19). In 1937, Loving requested permanent retirement status with a pension from the Philippine Legislature, effective as of his last retirement date, November 1923 (Richardson 1982, 21). Instead of granting his pension, however, Quezon insisted that Loving return to the Philippines once more, this time with the rank of lieutenant colonel in the Philippine Army, to prepare the Philippine Army Band for the Golden Gate International Exposition. The *Pittsburgh Courier*, an African American newspaper, proudly announced his promotion: "An artist, scholar and gentleman, Lt. Col. Loving is a credit to his people and his country" (March 19, 1938, p. 4, co. 3). On October 16, 1937, the Loving family, including twenty-year-old Walter Jr., sailed for the Philippines. Philippine newspapers and magazines in Spanish, Tagalog, and English captured Loving's popularity among different sectors of Manila society.[10]

While announcements of Loving's return to the Philippines in 1937 were abundant, along with brief histories of the band's founding and their tours of the US, none of these early articles mentioned the PC Band legend from the 1904 St. Louis Fair. The first mention of the legend, to my knowledge, did not appear until March 1938, five months after Loving arrived, when the Philippine Army Band (henceforth PA Band) performed its first concert under his direction at the Luneta. An article by I. T. de León explained that the purpose of Loving's return was to restore the band to its past glory, but with a renewed purpose: to "conquer the world" and make the band "equal to none" (*Philippine Herald*, March 12, 1938). He provided a lengthy and detailed account of the legend:

> Now, for a bit of interesting history: At a concert program one night during the world's exposition in 1904 at St. Louis, Missouri, the Philippine Constabulary Band was playing the first number, an Overture. Before the selection was over the lights at the Philippine village all of a sudden went out. The music however went on despite the darkness that enveloped the entire section of the exposition grounds with several thousands of people gathered to witness the concert. After the Overture, another piece was played, which was followed by another, and still another until the whole program that lasted an hour was finished in the dark.
>
> The feat created a sensation. The story made good newspaper copy. More than that, members of the famous Sousa Symphony Orchestra [*sic*] were there including the master himself. Also present were C.J. Conn, manufacturer of the internationally known Conn instruments, Le Febre, the first saxophone player that played in the United States, and other celebrities of the music world. That night gave the first Constabulary Band's name and fame that have lasted to this day." (I. T. de León, *Philippine Herald*, March 12, 1938).

If this version is accurate—and it may have come from Loving himself—the details about an electrical outage occurring on the Philippine exposition grounds and Sousa attending the concert both coincide with problems over a faulty electrical generator in April as well as Sousa's visit (see chapter 2). This version does not mention a band competition in which the PC Band took second place after the Garde Républicaine, suggesting that these were two separate events that later merged into one story.

The PC Band legend was repeated months later in an article entitled "The Loving Touch" in the *Philippines Free Press* (July 2, 1938). This particular clipping, found among Loving's papers at Howard University, is interesting because someone, perhaps Mrs. Loving, made notations on several passages.

Walter H. Loving, Bandmaster. Foto News (January 1938).

A scribble mark seems to obscure—but also inadvertently draws attention to—what looks like the word *Negro* in this section: "In summoning him from the tranquil peace of his second retirement in Oakland, California, President Manuel L. Quezon paid signal tribute to the executive as well as creative ability of the [crossed out] musician" ("The Loving Touch," *Philippines Free Press*, July 2, 1938, p. 36). Whoever crossed it out may have objected to the term *Negro* or the way it was used to qualify "musician." Out of twenty-four news clippings from Philippine periodicals during this time period, this was the only article that referred to Loving's racial identity. This omission in Filipino newspapers was not to deliberately erase Loving's achievements as an African American like most American newspapers; rather, it was not deemed significant to his popularity or success as a renowned and beloved bandmaster in the Philippines. Loving was an American, but one who was embraced as one of their own by Filipinos. Other markings underline that the PC Band won *first* prize at the PPIE in 1915, which is not accurate because they were awarded only a bronze medal and an honorable mention (see chapter 4), and bracket the account of the PC Band legend, highlighting its significance. The "Loving Touch" article elaborates on the legend first presented by the above *Philippine Herald* article of March 12, 1938, by stating that the PC Band played for not one but three hours in the dark. It adds another detail: "to *control his men* Colonel Loving tied a white handkerchief to his baton and continued to direct his band" (ibid.; emphasis mine). The article's usage of the phrase "control over," rather than a neutral phrase such as "direction of," the musicians echoes a sense of imperial domination over native subjects, implying that they are unruly and need to be ruled. Such ways of representing the band as an instrument of empire continued to resonate in the colony even when it aspired to portray itself as a nation and an independent people. It was this singular event, the *Philippines Free Press* claimed, that led the PC Band to international fame: "When the lights were finally turned on the audience broke into salvos of applause. Though the band was awarded only second place, Loving remembers the incident as the most thrilling in his life. Fair-goers at the St. Louis exposition were so crazy about the Filipino musicians that they were reported to have said: 'When the constabulary band is not playing, there is no fair'" (ibid.). The detail about the band winning second place at this event may have led to other retellings of the legend that conflate the concert in the dark with a competition in which the PC Band took second place after the Garde Républicaine. Again, my argument here is not about the veracity of the legend, but its greater significance in 1938, when the PC Band was trying to recapture its former glory and the Philippines was moving toward national independence.

I think that there are other ways to interpret this legend, challenging the myth that Filipinos were incapable of self-rule without the aid of the US. Specifically, I wonder how useful the handkerchief of the conductor was if indeed they played in "total darkness" ("The Loving Touch," *Philippines Free Press*, July 2, 1938, p. 36). This detail seems to make it appear that an American leader was in control when conducting the band, which was not absolutely necessary, because they would have continued without this symbolic white handkerchief, relying on their *banda* tradition and musical skills. Ileto's work on *pasyon* (epic narratives) provides insight to understanding the retelling of this legend when he notes that, in many Tagalog sources, there is an "apparent disregard for accurate description of past events;" nevertheless, it presents an opportunity to "study the workings of the popular mind" and pay close attention to the cultural context of those who tell the stories (1998, 11). I've heard the PC Band legend recited by many Filipinos, but their descriptions leave out the handkerchief of the conductor while highlighting the musicians' capabilities to sidestep an act of sabotage, or prevail despite an act of nature, and outshine other bands, including the most venerated international organizations. In our interview, Emilio N. Gamalinda and Virgilio Ruiz Fresnido both recounted the power outage as an act of sabotage by the "Americans" or other bands who wanted either to embarrass the Filipinos or wanted them to fail, yet they won first place (July 15, 2018). In these retellings of the legend, not only did the band overcome adversity and beat out the other bands, but they were also properly recognized by fair officials (representing Americans in general) for their skill, talent, and musical prowess, while other bands could not shed their dependency on written scores. Recall in chapter 2 that a frightened audience was disappointed that other bands stopped playing when the lights went out during a storm at the 1904 World's Fair. The legend expresses that Filipinos did not succeed by economic or educational superiority, but by a tradition they possessed before Americans came. This emotional retelling is almost like the performance of a *pasyon* that inspires one to feel validated by the wealth of one's own traditions. Ileto encounters a similar attitude in *Pasyon Pilapil*, in which "social status based on wealth and education has no real value" because it is damaging to the "individual *loób* (inner self), which is where the true worth of a person lies" (1998, 15). Like the *pasyon*, retelling the story allows one to safely vent ill feelings, like resentment of circumstances beyond one's control, and rejoice in a moment of reclaiming one's dignity. The legend is most meaningful to me because, no matter the exact details, the bandsmen continued their own *banda* tradition in the US, and succeeded, not as instruments of empire, but as musicians in their own right.

The appearance of the legend in 1938 may have also been practical, an attempt to garner more financial support for the band. The "Loving Touch" article expressed great concern that Quezon, while professing to support the band, vetoed a bill allotting 2 million pesos to finance its tour of the US, including a trip to the New York exposition. The writer urged, "If the government's finances will not allow expenditure of money on such a worthwhile investment, some interested person could make arrangements with the U.S. war department in Washington and have the band go to America on one of the army transports, at very little expense" ("The Loving Touch," *Philippines Free Press*, July 2, 1938, p. 36). Indeed, many "believe that all the traditional exhibits should be omitted and that the constabulary band alone should represent the Philippines" (ibid.) at the two world's fairs. The article's recounting and embellishment of the legend bolstered the argument for giving the band more resources from the government and encouraged support from the people.

For his comeback and the revival of the PC Band, Loving wrote a piece called "Marcha de los Colectivistas" to honor Quezon and his political party.[11] Quezon had the band perform concerts outside of elite Manila society to cultivate political support among the poor, to demonstrate concern for them.

An unidentified newspaper indicated that "President Quezon has ordered the Philippine military band [to give] concerts in various sectors of the city where the poor ... live" ([December 8?], 1938). A portable platform was constructed to accommodate the band's performances in Sampaloc, Osmeña Park, Plaza Moriones, Tondo, and Plaza del Pan in San Nicolas. There were numerous high-profile concerts for the city's political and social elite. On December 3, 1938, the PA Band gave a symphony concert at the Metropolitan Theater with distinguished guests in the audience, including "First Lady" Aurora Quezon and officials of the commonwealth. On Christmas Day, they played a concert including excerpts from Handel's *Messiah* and other Christmas favorites, the Overture to Rossini's *Stabat Mater*, and the Spanish march "Los Banderilleros" by Volpatti (*Philippine Herald*, December 25, 1938). Concert programs like this did very little to highlight Americanness or American patriotic spirit. Rather, the musical choices expressed a vision of a multicultural Filipino society in Manila that was possible without American rule.

The Golden Gate International Exposition was held in San Francisco and concurrently in New York, and the band was scheduled to perform in New York after San Francisco. Before leaving for the San Francisco, the band's membership was increased to one hundred musicians by special order. It is not clear whether this was Loving's decision or Quezon's, but the choice to increase the band to such a large size seems more symbolic than musical, making the band outstanding and conspicuous among other bands. Loving, now sixty-six years old, was the last of the thirty men who formed the original band in 1902 and the only one to have gone to St. Louis in 1904. Of the 1909 PC Band's members, only two musicians were still active: Sgt. Daniel Fajardo and Sgt. Restituto de León. Of the 1915 group, only eleven men, including Lt. Fresnido, participated in the 1939 Golden Gate International Exposition ("The Loving Touch" *Philippines Free Press*, July 2, 1938, 36).[12]

The 1939 Golden Gate Exposition in San Francisco, California

Despite the PA Band's renowned reputation, American conductors were still skeptical about the ensemble's musical skills. At the GGIE, Edwin Franco Goldman, conductor of the famous Goldman Band, "questioned the musicianship of the Filipinos," and he asked them to sight-read his own newly composed piece "Golden Gate March" (Richardson 1982, 22). The idea that

Philippine Constabulary Band on Treasure Island, 1939. Golden Gate International Exposition Postcard. Photo courtesy of Kathryn Ayres, Vice President, San Francisco Bay Area Post Card Club.

Filipinos were natural musicians was a well-known stereotype, and sight-reading music would prove if the Filipino musicians had the skills to play "civilized" music, not simply mimic playing it. Reportedly, Goldman was so impressed when they expertly sight-read the piece that he no longer doubted their musicianship.[13] Goldman later traveled to the Philippines on a USO tour in 1946, and he conducted the Philippine Army Band, which was then under the direction of Col. Antonino Buenaventura (Richardson 1982, 27). Another American bandmaster, Cznera C. Lafler, was so inspired by the band that he wrote a piece entitled "Philippine Constabulary Band March 1939" (Walsh 2013, 279).

Dr. Claiborne T. Richardson, an African American music historian who wrote an article about Loving, traveled to the Philippines in 1980 and conducted an interview with elderly members of the Philippine Army Band who went to the 1939 Fair.[14] During the hour-long interview, the bandsmen answered in English but made comments to each other in Tagalog. I transcribed the interview, translated the Tagalog comments, and shared my analysis with Dr. Richardson. Musician José Bascon talked about a troublesome incident that occurred at the 1939 Fair:

> When we were arriving in San Francisco, the head of the exposition power [?]to us that he is making the band stay there at Fort Basilio. And Col. Loving had already vacate the [inaudible] living in his apartment. So, the colonel rejected the offer of the head of the exposition. On the occasion of this . . . when we arrived about a day before the opening of the parade. At the time of the parade, we are in the corner of the street waiting to be inserted, but the parade finished without us being inserted [*chuckling*]. Because of the head of the union. (Interview with Richardson, 1980)

Several members interjected comments such as "the head of the union" in reference to why they were not inserted in the parade. Someone added that the head of the exposition was "trying to have power over us," and that he was forcing the band to stay somewhere that they did not want to stay. Col. Loving, having already made arrangements for the band's stay, rejected the offer by the head of the exposition. In the bandsmen's accounts, they stated that the "head of the union" was upset by Loving's refusal and found ways to undermine the band's participation. Another theory might be that this had something to do with the Musicians' Union—similar to the situation at the 1904 Fair when the PC Band was not allowed to play outside of the Philippine Exposition grounds.

While many of the members were elderly at the time of this the interview and were not very specific about the events, they did have a clear memory of Loving's gracious manner. Russ Valderon, a baritone player, said,

> When we were in the States, I liked the way he treated us, Col. Loving. We were served well. We played at the exposition . . . I have nothing to say. We were living there very quietly . . . we were served well by the colonel at the house . . . complete. (Interview with Richardson, 1980)

Loving's grandchildren confirm that while Col. Loving may have been a strict disciplinarian, he also had a "soft-side" in his personal relationship with others (Personal communication with author, 2021).

While in San Francisco, Filipinos living in Oakland "honored and welcomed" Loving and the band at a dinner dance on March 25 at the Bohol Island restaurant (*Philippine News* of Oakland, California, May 1939). Pictured seated at a long table were Col. Loving and Mrs. Loving, with important members of the Filipino community, including Sofronio

Dulay, manager of the restaurant; Dr. Laena, band physician; Laureto A. Lagpacan, editor-publisher of the *Philippine News*; Miss Salome Corcino, *Philippine News* Queen;[15] and Miss Leonora Rivera, "princess of the World's Fair" (ibid.). The Stockton Filipino community arranged for the band to perform at Stockton High School for the benefit of the Filipino Scholarship Fund at the College of the Pacific (*Lodi News-Sentinel*, Stockton, California, May 26, 1939, p. 2, col. 1). The article made it a point to state that the program planned for them was different from the music at the GGIE and would be "akin to a symphonic program" (ibid.). The president of the college, Dr. Tully C. Knoles, was "enthusiastic over their appearance" and bought a large block of seats (ibid.). These invited performances suggest that for Filipino communities in Northern California, the band was a point of pride and honor. As a famous musical organization from the Philippines, it may have served as an example of the cultural success and capabilities of Filipinos, especially since they faced discrimination in California. Local California newspapers ran short articles on Loving and the PA Band[16] (although many still referred to them the Philippine Constabulary Band), and Filipinos in California would have known about the Philippines' participation in the GGIE as well as the reputation of the PA Band.

Filipinos came to the US as *pensionados* in the early twentieth century.[17] Through government sponsorship, 289 students, mostly young men from the Filipino elite, attended American universities from 1903 to 1911 (Baldoz 2011, 44), and some of them visited the 1904 World's Fair (see chapter 2 and also Kramer 2006, 274). A much larger wave of Filipino laborers migrated to the West Coast after the 1924 Immigration Act (or Asiatic Exclusion Act) barred immigrant labor from other Asian countries. Many of these laborers came to Stockton, California, for agricultural work and because of Stockton's proximity San Francisco (Mabalon 2013, 61–62).[18] By 1930, there were approximately thirty thousand Filipinos in California, a third of whom were in the Stockton area, making it the "crossroads of early Filipina/o America" (62). Filipinos came from a variety of regional backgrounds, including Visayan, Ilocano, and Tagalog, and on the fields, they were brought together: "Ilocanos who had come as sakadas from the sugar plantations of Hawai'i cut asparagus next to Tagalog pensionados studying for their PhDs, and Illonggo and Ilocana/o schoolteachers sowed celery seed and topped onions next to teenage provicianas/os from Capiz, La Union, Tarlac, and Pangasinan who aspired to be doctors and engineers" (63). A small number of these agricultural workers included students attending the University of California, Berkeley, and the University of the Pacific (63), and even if they were able to find jobs other than agricultural work, most worked as domestic servants because of rampant nativist racism. Mabalon argues that the "racialization, exploitation, and degradation they experienced in the fields brought these Ilocana/o, Visayan, and Tagalog immigrants together, allowing them to transcend and challenge differences of region, class, and language and view their experiences collectively and themselves as part of a larger racial or ethnic community" (63). Mobs often bombed and burned living quarters, lynched men seen with white women, and killed many Filipinos who had once believed in the American dream as told to them by schoolteachers in the Philippines (see Mabalon 2013, especially chapter 2).[19] The Tydings-McDuffie Act of 1935 effectively made Filipinos aliens and thus ineligible for New Deal relief programs during the Great Depression (107). By 1939, Filipinos had already been forming groups to protest and strike, and the Stockton-based Filipino American Laborer's Association (later renamed the Filipino Agricultural Laborer's Association) formed and became "the most powerful Filipino American union ever to emerge in the United States" (99).

While thousands of Filipinos in Northern California came together to unionize, they were still divided along lines of region, language, and social class, as well as ideology (Malabon 2013, 103). Many of the taxi dance halls (where single Filipino workers expended their wages by paying mostly white working-class women for a minute-long dance) were criticized by conservative Filipinos as promoting vice, taking the wages of workers, and stoking anti-Filipino violence (135). Observers from the Philippines perceived that the reputation of these venues reflected poorly on Filipinos and the Philippines, impairing the movement for Philippine independence. For example, J. R. Fernandez urged Quezon to do something about them "for the sake of the country," and Jorge Bocobo,[20] while studying at University of Southern California, organized protests by Filipinos who opposed taxi dance halls (Bernardo 2014, 68). He lamented that Filipinos in America were beguiled by "the superficial things of American civilization," including cabarets and "barbaric and primitive" jazz music (quoted in Mojares 2006, 23–24). Many Filipinos associated jazz not with Black culture, but with the undesirable context of the taxi dance hall.[21] When the Rizal Social Club, a taxi dance hall, opened in 1937, the Filipino community of Stockton, the same group that invited the PA Band to perform, passed a resolution "denouncing the club and sent it to local officials, business groups, women's groups, and local ministers" (Mabalon 2013, 135).

The question of the Philippines' independence from the United States was being pushed from various sides during this time. Nativist groups and agribusiness concerns in the US supported Philippine independence as a way to exclude Filipino immigration and end the "privileged" status of Philippine imports, and Filipino nationalist politicians advocated for national sovereignty (Baldoz 2011, 156–57). After the Tydings-McDuffie Act passed in 1934, Baldoz argues, Filipinos "living in the United States remained an outcast population living on the margins of American society" (2011, 193). The PA Band's visit to Stockton was a significant occasion, connecting the Philippines with Filipinos in California and providing an opportunity to counter prevalent racial stereotypes. The PA Band played "serious art" music, "akin to a symphonic program" (*Lodi News-Sentinel*, Stockton, California, May 26, 1939, p. 2, col. 1) to demonstrate Filipinos' cultural attainment of and alignment with "civilized" Euro-American values. As discussed earlier, a mastery of European art music was part of the ideology of racial uplift and a demonstration of the respectability of African American educated elites. The PA Band and Loving provided expressions of Filipino and African American identities that differed from negative portrayals in American culture, connecting the goals of educated Filipino Americans and African Americans in a strategy of racial uplift.

A lengthy article on Loving appeared in the African American periodical *Silhouette Pictorial Magazine*; it took special pride in the "Virginia-born Negro, founder of the now famous Philippine Army Band, one of the opening features of the Golden Gate International Exposition" (May 8, 1939). The article seems to come from an interview with Loving, having details of his military career and education as well as facts about the band's earlier tours. The article states, "The great bandmaster's organization is a symphonic band that has achieved 'extremes of power and pianissimo beyond the gamut of an orchestra.' His repertoire includes Wagner, Haydn, Bizet, Sibelius, and Bach" (ibid.). This article no longer highlights Loving and the band as successes of US colonization but focuses on Loving's musical achievement as an African American bandmaster and his recognition as a musical leader and conductor. If this came from an interview with Loving, I believe that this is how Loving wanted to be remembered—for his contributions to excellence in music. Yet, to African Americans as well as Filipino Americans, the PA Band's successes were more significant than the appreciation of superb music: they were a rejection of negative racial stereotypes and proof of Filipinos' and African Americans' capabilities.

Another newspaper reported on Loving's long career with the band in "Virginia-Born Negro Is Famed as Bandmaster" (*Sunday Morning Star*, Wilmington, Delaware, August 20, 1939; reprinted in *Knickerbocker News*, Albany, New York, September 11, 1939, p. 12-A, col. 1). It confirms that few among the American public knew that Loving was Black: "One thing which only a comparative few are learning, however, is the story of its remarkable conductor, Lieut.-Col. Walter Howard Loving, Virginia born Negro, educated in Washington, D.C. and graduate from the New England Conservatory of Music in Boston" (ibid.). Because of Loving's leadership, the band of "110 members ranks immediately after the United States Marine band as the second-best organization of its kind" (ibid.). However, no one in the Philippines could take his place: "Loving has retired three times, but as no other conductor could be found to keep the orchestra up to his standards he eventually resumed the directorship" (ibid.) Loving's musical leadership is highlighted, and entirely missing are tropes of "little brown brothers" and "natural musicians," and a detailed list of the bandsmen's "tribal" affiliations. While the emphatic racialization of the PC Band rampant in newspaper reports of previous visits disappeared as the United States' need to justify colonization faded, a belief in Americans' necessary leadership of Filipinos, however, was still implied. Nevertheless, both African Americans and Filipinos living in the US highlighted Loving and the PA Band as examples of the cultural achievements of their respective communities. One unnamed newspaper stated that a bronze bust of Col. Loving was displayed at the Philippine Exhibit created by Guillermo Tolentino (Walter Howard Loving Papers, Box 113-1 to 113-3, Manuscript Division, Moorland-Spingarn Research Center, Howard University), who would later become a national artist of the Philippines.[22] This bust was an expression of Loving's, and the PC Band's, esteemed place in the making of Philippine national symbols.

The PA Band never made its trip to New York and was ordered back to the Philippines by Quezon. Newspaper and magazine articles in the Philippines blamed Quezon for the unexpected return. The *Philippines Free Press* complained that "the band was scheduled to visit the New York fair, but the government refused to pay $30,000 for the trip. The band is expected back by July 23" (July 7, 1939). The *Manila Bulletin* stated that the Philippine

Exposition would continue at the Golden Gate until its close in December, but without the band's participation: "the plan [to go to New York] did not materialize because the Commonwealth government declined to pay for the trip" (June 30, 1939). Since no army transport was available until October, the band was instructed to take a commercial steamer home to Manila, because there was "practically no fund to maintain the band" (*The Commerce*, June 30, 1939). A Filipino tabloid in Tagalog called *Jaliba* reported that one of the members died in Honolulu on the way home but did not state his name (July 25, 1939). Reporting on the band's arrival in Manila, the *Tribune* stated that they played "Home Sweet Home" as "the giant liner was steaming alongside of Pier 7" (July 26, 1939). The ensemble received a huge round of applause from the crowd that gathered to welcome them home. Despite the band's early return, newspapers and tabloids reported that the trip was successful. Loving was quoted as saying, "Everything came out as expected. . . . We'd a fine time and I believe our band gave the American exposition-goers a swell time, too" (ibid.).[23] Mrs. Loving, as well as their son Walter, now a young man, accompanied the band on the return trip to Manila. At some point, Walter Jr. returned to Oakland, but Col. and Mrs. Loving were imprisoned by the Japanese during World War II.

Loving was remembered by the children of several band members. Col. Honorado Pedro, son of band member Artemio Pedro, remembers their homecoming at the pier: "The first time I saw Col. Loving, when I was ten years old upon their arrival from the Golden Gate Exposition. I went to the pier, and I was only young, a small boy like that, and he even had a dog taller than I am at the time. And I was afraid of that dog [but] . . . [Loving] talked to me, 'How are you, boy?'" (Interview with Richardson, 1980). This interaction with the famed bandmaster made such an impression on Pedro that he eventually became conductor of the PA Band, retiring in 1982, just after the interview with Richardson. Leonor Navarro, daughter of Capt. Navarro, remembers the Lovings visiting the house of her father, showing that the Lovings had a convivial relationship with the bandsmen and their families: "At dinnertime, we eat and he [Loving] has to lecture the Old Man [Navarro]" (ibid.). From these few stories, it seems that Loving was kind to and respected by the families of his men. The men interviewed by Richardson strongly agreed that Loving wanted the leader of the band to come from within its ranks, not from outside of the organization: "He [Loving] used to train an individual from within the band. He is not in favor of getting an officer outside from the band. He prefers to have an officer develop within the band, coming from the lines" [several members say yes in agreement] (ibid.). Demonstrating their high level of musicality and expertise, the band members had to train on both a brass instrument and a stringed instrument. Col. Pedro and his father were both violinists who trained on a brass instrument, and Capt. Alejandro T. Romano was a trombone player who was sent by Loving to "study with Conductor Alexander Lippay who was conductor of the Manila Symphony to finish his violin course" (ibid.).[24] By having each member train on both brass and strings, Loving cultivated the PC Band's signature style of a concert band sounding like a symphony orchestra. His conducting style was not flamboyant or ostentatious; his descendants note that Loving "made use of slight cues to the musicians rather than showy use of his body, hand, or arms" (Personal communication with author, 2021). By employing this subtle style, Loving focused the audiences' attention on the music and the musicians, not the conductor's showmanship. For all his accomplishments with the PC Band, Loving's greatest contribution to music is that of an outstanding conductor, one who deserves recognition among the famous bandmasters of history.

World War II, Internment, and Death

Japan invaded the Philippines in December of 1941, just a few weeks after the attack on Pearl Harbor. Philippine and US forces withdrew to the Bataan Peninsula and declared Manila an open city. During occupation, the Japanese army rounded up all of the Americans and imprisoned them. While the Philippine Army Band dissolved, other brass bands were put together by the Japanese for official functions. Fresnido's son Virgilio, who was fifteen years old at the time, remembered how his father came to conduct a band organized by Japanese officials.[25] In 1942, a Japanese officer moved in next door to their home in Manila, after a German Jew who had been living there moved away.[26] Capt. Fresnido had been hiding inside the house for almost a year, fearful of what the Japanese would do to him and his family if they found out that he was part of the Philippine Army: "He didn't go out much, he's afraid someone will recognize him ... and put my father with the rest of the war prisoners" (Interview with author, 2018). Members of the band, like Fresnido, were "not included when [Gen. Douglas] MacArthur moved his soldiers to the mountain of Bataan because he is not train[ed] as a fighting soldier—all he knows is music to lead his band on parade" (ibid). Somehow the Japanese officer found out that Capt. Fresnido was hiding in the house and came looking for him. This officer knew Fresnido by name because he had seen the PA Band perform in San Francisco in 1939. According to Virgilio, the officer said to Fresnido in English, "Your band are [sic] magnificent. I want you to play for our generals and diplomat. I know your band is Philippine Constabulary Army [sic]. Your profession is music instrument. Everybody love to listen to music. Nobody like to listen to gunfire. Music is to enjoy and relax while you're listening to good sound of music in your ears. If you can play for MacArthur, you can play for us too" (ibid.). The officer gave Fresnido a book of Japanese songs and asked Fresnido to arrange them for band. Virgilio remembers that "it didn't take long to complete because he's been doing it many times. When he writes, sometimes I watched him writing new songs in his room, [but] no one is allowed to make noises or you'll get yelled [at]" (ibid.). Virgilio remembers that the officer "respected my father and they became good friends. He brought us grocery and knows what kind of food we eat. Mr. Hitashi is very educated, and he studied in one US university during peacetime. He spoke English like any American man. During the war, they worked together" (ibid.). Brass band music, as an instrument of empire under US rule, was also utilized by the Japanese to represent Filipino collaboration with the new colonizers.

A big concert was held on Japanese Navy Day on May 27, 1943; several bands were featured at the Luneta. Capt. Fresnido led the Metropolitan Constabulary Band in a performance of *Genroku Hanami Odori* that he likely arranged for band (Bañas 1975, 243). Each band played arrangements of Japanese compositions in addition to the Japanese national anthem. Bañas wrote, "It was a splendid military event and every band tried its best to perform its part well" (1975, 243).[27] In some ways, Filipino music under Japanese occupation flourished, because the Japanese encouraged their musical creativity as long as it fit with the aims of the Pan-Asianism and Southeast Asia Co-Prosperity Sphere, which emphasized an Asian identity devoid of the more blatant and decadent influences of American entertainment—music of dance halls and *bodabil* (vaudeville) (Santos 1992, 95). Santos writes that a "nationalist program in Philippine music, as conceived and implemented by the Japanese imperial government, consisted of the encouragement and promotion of Filipino compositions, Filipino artists, the rediscovery of pre-Western cultural roots and a musical thinking based on the concept of a 'New Philippines'" (1992, 96). Despite the fact that this process "aimed to project the Filipinos at centerstage in the artistic field [it] was actually a scenario wholly scripted and directed by the Japanese" (96). While American band music like the patriotic fare of Sousa was banned, European concert pieces by classical composers like Beethoven and light operatic music by Verdi and Puccini were sanctioned, along with classical Filipino genres such as *sarsuela* and *kundiman*, as well as new compositions for symphony (98). Despite the "lofty objectives" of the Japanese (aimed at emphasizing Filipinos' Asian roots in new compositions and "reorienting the Filipino artists on their pre-Western musical heritage and the importance of oriental culture"), Santos argued that the agenda largely failed because there were very few available resources on both indigenous Philippine music and the music of other Asian countries (99).

The use of music to influence Filipinos during US rule was successful in part because of Filipinos' long history with European music. However, this strategy failed during Japanese occupation because of the incongruence of, on one hand, Filipinos' orientation toward Western music as the hallmark of civilization, and on the other, the promotion of the idea that Japanese music, and by extension, Japanese culture, was superior: "While the Japanese found it prudent to invoke the use of Western musical idioms to reach to the Filipino musicians and music-loving public, their mastery of the language fell short of the level of proficiency of the Filipinos" (Santos 1992, 100). Western band music, a genre and tradition in which Filipinos were superlative in all of Asia, failed to testify to Japanese cultural superiority and authority because, to Filipinos' ears, "the so-called music of Japan that [Japanese composer] Yamada and his team introduced in the Philippines were crudely-crafted compositions trying to fuse Japanese scales and modes with Western harmony" (99). Thus, hybridized Japanese and European music for band was ineffective as an instrument of empire in the Philippines.

Filipinos' mastery in European forms allowed some composers to embed subversive elements in their music. When Felipe Padilla de León was asked by Japanese officials to set a poem by Catalino S. Dionisio to music, it became the "martial and spirited 'Awit sa Paglikha ng Bagong Filipinas,' more commonly known as 'Tindig, Aking Inang-Bayan,' which served as a national song especially during the time when the Philippine National Anthem was prohibited" (Samson 1976, 116). After the war, de León was investigated by US authorities for this perceived act of collaboration with the Japanese, but was cleared. Samson writes, "His defense was that he did his silent resistance against the enemy through his music which made use of the Philippine National Anthem as the underlying motif of his marches especially during the time when Filipinos were forbidden to sing the anthem" (116). The first few notes of the melody of "Awit sa Paglikha ng Bagong Filipinas" gestures to the opening notes of "Lupang Hinirang," and many heard this as a reference to the national anthem. Filipino composers could "easily weave these materials into the over-all musical fabric quite unobtrusively and with a measure of artistic finesse" (116), and composition in Western forms bolstered by Filipino composers' mastery of them subtly expressed resistance to Japanese rule.

The Lovings were interned at Santo Tomas University along with some three thousand American, British, and foreign civilians. Because of Loving's declining health and advanced age (sixty-nine years old), they were later released and permitted to stay at their residence under house arrest in the Ermita district of Manila. Loving promised to report to the Japanese authorities twice a week, and he kept his word. Clarinetist José Baldevarona described Loving's life during the war:

> I always went to his house in Mabini St. [Ermita]. I said to him . . . that was October, before the Americans came here in 1944, "Go out of Manila, stay in the province." He didn't do that because he is reporting to the Japanese army during that time. I told him to escape because it's very dangerous here in Manila. He knows General Castañeda. He knows him [so] he can survive there [in the province]. He doesn't like because he said he's reporting [to the Japanese]. I told him to forget that because he cannot [survive] here anymore. But he still insisted. So, after December, there is a mass . . . roundup. He was killed, I think, in Luneta . . . because the Japanese took all the people here in Mabini and bring to them Manila to be put in fire there. But, luckily, he did not reach Manila and he was killed. That was going to Manila hotel from Luneta. . . . Sometimes I brought them sugar, food. He gave me money to buy food, he paid for it. I carr[ied] the sack of rice to the third floor [*laughter*]. (Interview with Richardson, 1980)

Richardson affirmed Mrs. Loving's gratitude toward Filipinos by telling the interviewees, "That's very beautiful because Mrs. Loving remembered this, but she couldn't remember [who]. Also, she recalled that many would go to Santo Tomas and do the same thing, bringing food. So, she really recognizes and recalls the little things that you've done" (ibid.).

My grandaunt Leonora, youngest daughter of Capt. Navarro, provided her memories of Loving during Japanese occupation:[28]

> When it comes to the last days of Loving, the one thing I could contribute—because I was young then—I was the only one going with him [Navarro] in Mabini Street. They used to meet. What a very pathetic view of two old men embracing as if husband and wife.... And I was the only one who witnessed it.... We gave some things to Col. Loving. In return he gave us plenty of food, coffee ... because we were hungry then [*laughs*]. And Mrs. Loving is also to be commended because she was managing the Casa de Oro then. (Interview with Richardson, 1980)

Loving continued to have close ties with his men during Japanese occupation. They did what they could to comfort each other and did their best to stay alive, even offering to help the Lovings escape.

When US forces returned to take back Manila on February 2, 1945, they dropped bombs and raided the city. The Japanese set fire to Intramuros to destroy the city, and much was lost, including records of the PC Band. Sadly, Fresnido was killed in one of these raids along with other family members, including his youngest son. Virgilio recounts that they were

> hiding with us on our block where our houses used to be before the bombing. There are seventeen bodies in all when we buried them on the same long hole we dug. We put a marker on each body, [and] when the fighting calmed down, we will transfer the bodies to a regular cemetery. One month later, we went back to dig the bodies and we saw the place had been bulldozed. The ground was flat and there was no way to pinpoint where the bodies were. I have a feeling the bodies had been swept [away] when [the Americans] run the bulldozer on the spot where the bodies were. It really hurt my heart, my feeling, because we didn't have bodies to give a decent funeral. (Interview with the author, 2018)

In a 1986 interview, Mrs. Loving recounts the last days with her husband during liberation:

The Japanese came and burned everything. Oh, you should have seen my house, and all that burned with it, including this portrait of my husband by Fernando Amorsolo! We were running, running for nine days. Now the order, which came directly from Japan, was *Matar y Destruir* (Kill and Destroy). Walter and I kept running until we got to Plaza Ferguson and here, the Japanese caught up with us. We were separated. He was brought to the Manila Hotel, and I was sent off to join the other women. (Moreno 1986, 24)[29]

Although she never saw her husband again, she recounted how a few former bandsmen told her of Loving's last moments:

Gen. Yamashita went to the prison camp and told the men "I will give you 5 minutes to run." Many did and they were shot while running. Col. Loving told the General (his knees were failing by then), "I'm too old to run but if I die, I die an American." And with that he was beheaded. So you see, my husband lies somewhere in Philippine soil, I don't know where but that's where he is. I understand that the American dead were separated from the others but because Col. Loving was dark, he was left among the Filipinos.[30] (Moreno 1986, 24)

After his death, Loving was placed among the Filipinos and was never returned to the US. It was reported that his body was buried somewhere at the Luneta, the site of the PC Band's triumphant concerts.

Mrs. Loving returned one last time to the Philippines, now an independent nation, in 1952, under President Magsaysay, to celebrate the Golden Anniversary of the Philippine Constabulary Band (souvenir program, 1952). The concert honored not only Col. Loving but the conductors who succeeded him: Capt. Pedro B. Navarro, Capt. Alfonso J. Fresnido, and Lt. José Silos. My investigation of the Philippine Constabulary Band ends here, but the PA Band has a rich history after this time period (Hila 2004, 85–87). Capt. Alejandro T. Romano was the only surviving junior officer of the PA Band after the war's end, but he could not revive the band. Col. Honorado S. Pedro recalled, "Unfortunately, he [Romano] has no guts to assemble the surviving members. It was Col. Buenaventura who was then a lieutenant who was recalled from Baguio to assemble the surviving members" (Interview with Richardson, 1980). Buenaventura founded what would become the First Armed Forces Band, Philippine Army. Capt. Campaña organized and conducted the postwar Philippine Army Band at Camp Crame until 1962. Lt. Col. Honorado S. Pedro took over and served as its leader until 1982 ("Parangal Concert 1980," Brochure of the 78th Anniversary of the Philippine Constabulary Band). A seventy-eighth anniversary concert took place under the Marcos regime, and it is clear that the PC Band's prestigious history was meaningful in expressing Philippine nationalism. Ferdinand Marcos wrote that the PC Band "reflects a service-oriented organization dedicated to public welfare.... I enjoin the members of the PC Band to carry on the good name and tradition of their organization" (ibid.). Imelda Marcos emphasized the band's cultural significance: "It is heartening to learn that it contributes toward the cultural development of our people through concerts" (ibid.). Then Maj. Gen. Fidel V. Ramos stated that the PC Band's "remarkable achievements ... have brought honor and prestige not only to the Constabulary but to the entire Filipino race as a whole" (ibid.). While most Americans heard the PC Band's excellent performances as proof of US benevolence and tutelage, Filipinos heard them as proof of their own achievements and capabilities in their own musical traditions.

Walter H. Loving Jr. continued his father's legacy by serving in the US military. He enlisted during WWII and served for 2 ½ years before entering Officer Candidate School in Fort Benning, Georgia. He was commissioned as an infantry officer in June 1945 (Cunningham 2007, 19). During the Korean War, he was an artillery captain and later joined the National Guard. Sometime in the 1950s, he visited the Philippines with his wife, Mary Elliot Loving, and his daughter, Edith (Personal communication with author, 2021). In 1969, he retired as a colonel and passed away in California in 1998 (ibid.).

Conclusion: Hearing Filipinos

My analysis of the PC Band's musical performances in the context of US-Philippines relations brings to light the contradictory and ambivalent ways that Filipino musical labor and cultural production were represented and heard with an imperial ear. The ways that newspapers described the Filipino musicians had a powerful influence on audiences: "In modern societies, the different media are especially important sites for the production, reproduction and transformation of ideologies ... [I]nstitutions like the media are particularly central to the matter since they are, by definition, part of the dominant means of *ideological* production. What they 'produce' is, precisely, representations of the social world, images, descriptions, explanations and frames for understanding how the world is and why it works as it is said and shown to work" (Hall 1997, 82). When the PC Band musicians were cast as "little brown men," newspapers communicated the Filipinos' inferiority to "big white men," despite celebrating them for their musical performance. Representing the bandsmen in this way fixed racial-colonial meaning to their performances and was the overwhelming way in which they were understood by people reading these news reports. Stuart Hall explains, "Representation is a practice, a kind of 'work,' which uses material objects and effects. But the *meaning* depends, not on the material quality of the sign, but on its *symbolic function*. It is because a particular sound or word *stands for*, *symbolizes*, or *represents* a concept that it can function, in language, as a sign and convey meaning—or, as the constructionists say, signify (sign-i-fy)" (25). "Little brown men" as "natural musicians" were linked and became an "iconic sign" that in its "form, [bears] a certain resemblance to the object, person or event to which [it refers]" (20). This iconic sign contained some truths—Filipino musicians were shorter in stature, a range of brown skin tones, and talented musicians; they were not, however, biologically predetermined to always or only be those things. This trope in its frequent repetitions over time became fixed in the minds of audiences, with the result that, "after a while, it comes to seem natural and inevitable" (21). A way of hearing Filipino music-making became what Foucault analyzes as a discourse, because the sign, as well as what it signifies, "never consists of one statement, one text, one action or one source," (44) but emerges from a variety of sources and utterances with a similar message. Hearing Filipinos in this way especially when they perform Euro-American repertoire is part of a larger *episteme* (a way of thinking that appears "across a range of texts, and as forms of conduct, at a number of different institutional sites within society" [44]) that positions Filipinos as colonial subjects and racial others in a subordinate position compared with whites. This position sustains a project of white hegemony, a form of power that works ideologically to attain the consent of others and impose ways of thinking and behavior to dominate them (see Gramsci et al. 2008). By making Filipinos appear inferior, despite their musical achievements, whites could enforce their superiority across a number of avenues in their control including print media, concerts, and expositions. Throughout this book, I argued that the prevalent ways that newspapers and world's fairs characterized the musicians of the Philippine Constabulary Band and their excellent musical performance in the familiar and celebrated genre of band music played an important and overlooked role in the United States' empire-making and racial domination of the early twentieth century.

The PC Band's performance of European classics and American patriot fare mitigated anxieties over the early twentieth century's social transformations by continuing some dearly held traditions from the nineteenth century through the bodies of brown men and a Black leader. Brass ensembles like John Philip Sousa's band were popular with middlebrow audiences while providing the allure of "high-culture" by including symphonic and operatic excerpts and confirming those values. The playing of patriotic marches by the PC Band bolstered Americans' national pride and belief in the United States' fulfillment of benevolent rather than coercive assimilation. The figure of the Filipino as "little brown brother," patriotic, disciplined, behaving properly, and providing safe, pleasurable music to white Americans served to mitigate fears of the invading foreign other and provided a contrast to the threatening domestic other, Black Americans. Lisa Lowe writes, "Throughout the twentieth century, the figure of the Asian immigrant has served as a 'screen,' a phantasmatic site, on which the nation projects a series of condensed, complicated anxieties regarding external and internal threats to the mutable coherence of that national body: the invading multitude, the lascivious seductress, the servile yet treacherous domestic, the automaton whose inhuman efficiency will supersede American ingenuity" (1996, 18). To quell these fears, the Filipino bandsmen were presented as the model-minority-in-the-making prior to the great influx of educated professionals from Asia in the post-1965 era: "Stereotypes that construct Asians as the threatening 'yellow peril,' or alternatively, that pose Asians as the domesticated 'model minority,' are each equally indices of these national anxieties" (19). The marching Filipino bandsmen enthusiastically playing American patriotic marches, and even Loving himself as their leader, provided some comfort to the American public, assuring them that their racial wards could "behave" as proper subjects included in American society as long as they remained in a subordinate racial position. With their superb musicianship, Loving and the PC Band succeeded in this colonial/racial context, not despite their racialized otherness, but because of it. Like Asian American artists today, the PC Band had "visibility and prominence ... celebrated and turned against them" (Wang 2015, 3) by strategies of white dominance that capitalized on, benefited from, and took pleasure in their musical performances while excluding them in most other ways.

The PC Band's musical performances were an important context in which American audiences negotiated the conflict between desire and domination in the colonial fashioning of Filipino identity. Colonial discourse and its exercise of power, explains Bhabha, articulates ambivalent forms of difference that are "realized as multiple, cross-cutting determinations, polymorphous and perverse, always demanding a specific and strategic calculation of their effects" (1984, 67). Desire of fine musical performances and the domination of Filipinos' cultural production by controlling its meaning resulted in ambivalence: "Such an articulation (of difference) becomes crucial if it is held that the body is always simultaneously (if conflictually) inscribed in both the economy of pleasure and desire and the economy of discourse, domination and power" (67). My analysis of the discourse surrounding the PC Band's performances confirms Bhabha's assertion that this form of discourse is "crucial to the binding of a range of differences and discriminations that inform the discursive and political practices of racial and cultural hierarchization" (67). A way of viewing Filipinos that emphasized colonial benevolence and assimilation placed them in the "imperial order" (Pratt 2008, 3) of early twentieth-century America and gave meaning, substance, and value to their performances within this order. These explanations and frames for understanding benefited American audiences and allowed them to consume Filipino production and labor while safely keeping Filipinos (and also Blacks) in their subordinate place. This framing of the PC Band, the Filipino bandsmen, and Loving in newspapers engaged a number of novel and inventive ways, confirming Pratt's stipulation that "imperial thinking continues to renew itself and mutate with great resilience" (3). News reports painstakingly listed the Filipinos' "tribal" diversity, but completely omitted Loving's racial identity. They claimed that Loving randomly selected Filipino men who had never seen Western instruments before and miraculously transformed them into superb soloists and musicians who could play the most highly regarded concert pieces of their time. A centuries-old tradition of European music, proof of a level of civilization, was erased from the history of the Philippines.

The ways that musical performance was deployed served extramusical purposes in the contexts of American colonialism and Filipino nationalism. But ultimately, the strategy by Filipino nationalists—arguing that Filipinos were civilized because of their mastery of a "civilized" musical language— bought into a system that was designed to keep them dominated. No matter how successful Filipinos became in politics or music, they remained in a subordinate position compared to whites in the perception of most Americans. White cultural superiority was kept at the forefront by repeating that the Filipinos were "natural musicians" who were trained by Americans, referring to them in ways that ridiculed or made them a spectacle. The promise of meritocracy and of "giving" Filipinos independence once they "earned" it by proving they were civilized was not, after all, a real promise, but rather a glass ceiling to contain racial others while maintaining the veneer of America's most lofty ideals. The trope of benevolence that American imperialists adopted in order to hide the hypocrisy of colonizing the Philippines, while purportedly supporting freedom and equality, had to include Filipinos while exercising domination over them. This logic allowed white American audiences to praise the musical capabilities of the PC Band while simultaneously preserving a sense of superiority. Their repertoire of "civilized" Western music did not inspire the majority of American society to realize the profound contradiction that the PC Band represented in this racial logic. I began this project with the naïve assumption that a popular band playing for hundreds of thousands of Americans should have cast doubt on the derogatory stereotypes meant to dominate and subordinate nonwhites, both the Filipinos and also Loving as a Black American, but of course this never materialized because of the power of newspapers to sustain Americans' imperial ear.

Nevertheless, newspaper articles on the PC Band can be read against the grain of tenacious racial ideologies, and I offered interpretations of these to fill a gap in knowledge about early Filipino music-making in the United States. American audiences enthusiastically responded to the PC Band's style of performance, demonstrating that there was something specific and unique about the PC Band that captivated listeners and fueled desire, not only or always imperialist or racial, but sometimes personal and emotional. The PC bandsmen and Loving interacted with their audiences and allowed them to request their favorite pieces, endearing themselves to Americans and expressing their deep commitment to excellent musical performance. These requests to hear the PC Band's interpretation of favorite pieces would often take more time than the actual concert program itself. The band's interpersonal approach and skill in musical interpretation are clear in this account: "Every number was applauded and Captain Loving was generous in his responses with encores. Old airs seemed like new ones and those with which the local people were especially familiar were hardly recognized, so melodious were the notes struck" (*Hawaiian Star*, October 14, 1909, p. 9, col. 2). Loving pleased audiences who wanted to hear the band's interpretation of their favorite pieces, but in doing so, he also radically transformed, if momentarily, the band's racial positioning. The Black bandmaster and brown musicians were seated on the concert stage above a white audience who had to appeal to the band to grant their request. In this encounter, Loving and the Filipino musicians interacted with white audiences in a way that breached the norms of a racially segregated and stratified society, altering the power dynamics that dominated them and making themselves heard as exceptional musicians.

If we engage in "disobedient listening" (Balance 2016, 4), we might hear the Filipinos' challenge to the white supremacy. With their own skills and capability, they could capture the style of famous bands, paying homage to them while also disputing their superiority. Sousa's compliment, "When I closed my eyes, I thought it was the U.S. Marine Band playing" (quoted in Flores 1976, 75), while conducting the PC Band's performance of "The Star-Spangled Banner," demonstrated that the musicians rendered the US Marine Band's style to perfection, but it was certainly not the only way they could have interpreted the piece. Other reporters commented that the PC Band played "The Star-Spangled Banner" "in a way no American band could excel" (*Washington Post*, April 18, 1909, p. M10). Some surprisingly insightful letters to the editor or opinion columns that I discussed went against the grain of dominant ideological views of Filipinos, demonstrating that certain Americans did come to conclusions that were not intended, perpetuated, or disseminated by the government or mainstream media: "No man with an ounce of appreciation in his soul could hear [the Philippine Constabulary Band] without being convinced that the 81 men who compose its membership are far above the ordinary in both intelligence and sentiment" ("Filipinos at the St. Louis World's Fair, Wonderful Music Rendered Daily by Islanders on Plaza of Philippine Building," *Bourbon News*, Paris, Kentucky, August 30, 1904, p. 3, col. 1 and 2). A few concert reviews provided insight into the band's excellent playing style: "Particularly fine is the reed department of the band. The clarinet tone is almost as fluent as though it were a violin section, and the quality of tone is mellow, not shrill and full of color" (*San Francisco Chronicle*, March 11, 1915, p. 5). Performing on brass instruments as well as strings, the PC Band validated their skills and talents as musicians who were capable of handling orchestral and symphonic music, not just patriotic fare. To demand that audiences hear them, the Filipino musicians sang their native songs on a few occasions, shedding their instruments to articulate their innermost sentiments through imperfect, but intimate voices.

Old notions still resonate after the colonial era. Referring to Filipino musicality as natural abstracts Filipinos as biological entities possessing racial ability, and thus Filipino musicians need not be judged in the same way as white performers, because their success is not the product of education, hard work, and skill but simply a natural state of being Filipino. Racialized accolades bestowed on performing Filipino bodies and their musicality work to control and limit their autonomy, equality, and recognition. When cast as mimics, Filipinos' contributions in Euro-American forms are invisibilized, and this cultural invisibilization of Filipino achievement is still felt by many. Yet, Filipinos are also hypervisible as spectacles when viewed through the lens of a white gaze, whether they are "little brown men" playing Western music, "splendid dancers" of the taxi dance hall, "dog-eaters" in world's fairs, shoe-hoarders in a country of starving people, or orange-clad inmates dancing to the Michael Jackson hit song "Thriller" on YouTube.[31] Bhabha's use of Fanon's analysis of exoticism as a form of simplification is helpful to understanding the paradox of Filipino cultural visibility/invisibility: "There is on the one hand a culture in which qualities of dynamism, of growth, of depth can be recognized. As against this, [in colonial cultures] we find characteristics, curiosities, things, never a structure" (Fanon 1970, 35, quoted in Bhabha 1984, 84). The exotification of Filipino performance by affirming that all Filipinos are "natural musicians," construct Filipino musicians as an object for the white gaze and a product of colonialism, and in this way, continues to frame how Americans hear with an imperial ear.

I am still curious about how the members of the PC Band themselves understood early twentieth-century American racial logic when they were confronted by it, and what made the relationship between the Filipino bandsmen and their legendary African American conductor so special and different from this hegemonic enforcement of race. Did Loving and the bandsmen reject a racial hierarchy that assumed that they could not achieve a mastery of "civilized" music because of their confidence in their musical talent? Or was there ever an internalization of white superiority in ways

Aida G. Kasman, Emilio N. Navarro, Maj. Gilbert Ramos, and author with photo of Capt. Pedro B. Navarro at Camp Crame, Philippines, 1999. Courtesy of Mary Talusan.

they didn't realize, seeing themselves as the beneficiates of US colonial rule? Bourdieu emphasizes that, "when the dominated apply to what dominates them schemes that are the product of domination, or, to put it another way, when their thoughts and perceptions are structured in accordance with the very structures of the relation of domination that is imposed on them, their acts of *cognition* are, inevitably, acts of *recognition*, submission" (Bourdieu 2001, 13; emphasis in original). Perhaps there is "always room for a *cognitive struggle* over the meaning of things of the world" (13) and Loving and the Filipino musicians asserted pride in their cultural identities when they were able, and, at other times, played along on their instruments of empire as a means of agency. Under Loving's creative musical leadership and generous spirit, and with dedication to his men, Filipinos brought their cherished *banda* tradition, cultivated in the celebratory atmosphere of town fiestas, to the US during a time of intense political and racial tension. Their labor was the "cultural work" (Wong 2004, 170) that made them popular and highly acclaimed with their fans, but it was often silenced with the racialized hearing of an imperial ear. Despite this, in a glorious moment when they continued

Walter H. Loving Jr. with wife Mary Elliot Loving and daughter Edith visiting the Philippines during the 1950s. Courtesy of Edith Loving Lucas.

to play in the dark with the use of musical scores, they relied on their *banda* tradition, not American tutelage or technology, to overcome adversity. As the PC Band once did, Filipinos in the worldwide diaspora continue to make music, perform, and express themselves, critiquing and challenging the symbolic violence engendered in old stereotypes and tropes with their creativity, skills, and ingenuity.

NOTES

Introduction

1. Variations on the term *Filipino* include Filipina/o, Pilipino/a, and more recently, Filipinx. For the purposes of this work, I chose to use "Filipino" and "Filipino American" for consistency. I intend the terms to be gender-neutral and inclusive of complex and multilayered identities when discussing Filipinos and Filipino Americans generally.

2. He attended New England Conservatory not Boston Conservatory. They are two separate institutions.

3. For a more thorough treatment of Loving's life and military career, see Richardson 1982, Cunningham 2007, Marasigan 2010, and Yoder 2013.

4. Taft is credited with introducing the term "little brown brothers" to refer to Filipinos. It was both inclusive and condescending, infantilizing Filipinos by portraying them as diminutive, othering them as nonwhite, and including them in the American family, but only in a subordinate position. See also Kramer 2006, 200.

5. I use the term *white*, rather than Anglo-American or Euro-American, deliberately to analyze racialization. Throughout this book, "white" does not refer to a specific ethnicity or national origin, but rather to an American racial construction deployed to enforce social, political, and cultural power over nonwhite "racial others." "Whiteness," Lipsitz writes, "is a social fact, an identity created and continued with all-too-real consequences for the distribution of wealth, prestige, and opportunity" (1998, vii). Also, see Haney-López 2006 for a history of the legal construction of "white" in the US.

6. During the revolution against Spain, the use of the term *Filipino* shifted from meaning a Spaniard born in the Philippines to referring to natives and *mestizos* or those of mixed ancestry. See Francia 2014 for a more thorough discussion.

7. For works that more thoroughly treat the politics of imperialist and anti-imperial debates during this period, see Hoganson 1998, Raphael 2000, Shaw and Francia 2002, Ignacio et al. 2004, Kramer 2006, and McCoy 2010.

8. In addition to the standard brass and percussion instruments of a marching band, Sousa included a larger section of reed instruments, such as clarinet, oboe, and bassoon, to give the brass band a more orchestral timbre. This larger ensemble is referred to as a concert band.

9. See Bourdieu 1984 for his influential concept of symbolic forms of capital.

10. For more on the spread of American popular music to Asia in the early twentieth century, see Schenker's dissertation (2016).

11. See Schenbeck's notable book *Racial Uplift and American Music* (2012) for detailed histories of African American musicians and the larger context of early twentieth-century American music.

12. See Gatewood 1972, 1975, and 1987; Powell 1998; and Marasigan 2010 about the treatment and comparison of Black soldiers and Filipinos in the Philippines.

13. Densmore was an American anthropologist and comparative musicologist who is considered an early ethnomusicologist. For more on her work and the racialization of music at the 1904 Fair, see Moon 2010.

14. This type of assimilation and subordination also became the basis for the "model minority" myth that has characterized Asian Americans since the mid-1960s.

15. *Utang na loób* means "sense of inner debt or gratitude," and *hiya* translates into "shame." See David 2013 for a more thorough discussion of Filipino cultural values and psychology.

16. See Campomanes (1992, 53) on the United States' historic amnesia with regard to imperialism in the Philippines.

17. For a discussion of the concept of "colonial mentality" and Filipino psychology, see David 2013.

18. For an important work on Filipino working-class men and the creation of masculinity in the 1920s and '30s, see España-Maram 2006.

19. The band members left no personal written accounts of their tours, to my knowledge. Loving's papers at Howard University are mostly official letters and reports from his time with the Office of Intelligence.

20. Tito Ed, who is of Tausug heritage, inspired me to become a scholar.

21. https://www.britannica.com/biography/Benigno-Aquino-Jr (accessed October 11, 2019).

22. Dr. Claiborne T. Richardson, an African American music scholar, traveled to the Philippines to conduct these interviews in 1980.

23. Schenker discusses former PC Band musicians like Nicanor Amper who were able to build careers outside of the Philippines because of the band's reputation (2016, 122–24 and 133–34).

Chapter 1

1. America's investment in this icon of nationalism became a point of political contention when "Nuestro Himno" was released in 2006; it was based on the melody of "The Star-Spangled Banner." While some heard it as "a multicultural demonstration of U.S. patriotism," others cast it as a "disloyal act of blasphemy" (see Garrett 2008, 3). The response was not just about the reinterpretation of the song, but also the political climate engendered by the immigration policies of George W. Bush's administration.

2. By contrast, in Central Java, brass band music mixed and hybridized with indigenous gongs and drums (Herbert and Sarkissian 1997, 171). Another example of hybridization is brass bands in East Africa that accompany an indigenous dance called *beni ngoma* (Ranger 1975, 65, cited in Herbert and Sarkissian, 174).

3. Irving describes this account at length (2010, 220–21). He cites the master's thesis of Maria Patricia Brillantes-Silvestre for a translation and analysis of the text. See Irving 2010, 327n29.

4. A clarion is a type of narrow tubular trumpet commonly found in the Middle Ages in Europe (Randel 2003, 183).

5. This skill and demonstration of prowess by Filipino musicians was not limited to town brass bands. In the taxi dance halls of the 1920s and '30s, Filipino jazz band musicians played continuously for hours—almost a hundred songs a night—often without musical scores (see Parnes 1999, 65). España-Maram writes that musicians had to be familiar with a minimum of five hundred songs, as well as skilled in sight-reading the latest tunes (2006, 123; see also Vedder 1947).

6. For a thorough and detailed analysis of the revolution against Spain, see Ileto 1998 and 1999.

7. Ironically, the song "All Coons Look Alike to Me" was written by African American composer, Ernest Hogan. I will discuss the participation of Black musicians in ragtime in chapter 2.

8. Marasigan notes that twenty-nine Black soldiers allegedly deserted and perhaps a dozen joined the revolutionaries (2010, 33).

9. Loving went to the same high school as the renowned composer-conductor James Reese Europe, but I did not find any evidence that the two knew each other personally. Europe is famous for having sparked a craze for ragtime music worldwide when he went to France during WWI as leader of the 369th Regiment Band (known as the Harlem Hellfighters). Like Loving, he was trained in European music, but because there was little work for a Black violinist in New York, he turned to writing more profitable "coon songs" for Tin Pan Alley and performing ragtime (see Badger 1995).

10. For more on Black soldiers in Cuba, see Hoganson 1998, 131–32; Kaplan 1993; and Gatewood 1972, 1975, and 1987. After Cuba, they proceeded to the Philippines as the first group of Black soldiers to arrive (Marasigan 2010, 43).

11. The "wild tribes" to which the journal refers are the indigenous natives inhabiting what is now referred to as the Cordillera Mountain region of the Philippines. I think the writer of the journal chose to refer to them as "wild tribes" rather than "insurgents" or "insurrectos" because that would implicate the danger closer to home—those who did not accept US rule.

12. His wife, Helen "Nellie" Taft, attended as well and was an avid music lover. She played a key role in inviting the PC Band to the White House in 1909 (Gould 2010, 15–16).

13. Typed letter. Office of the Provincial Board/Province of La Union, San Fernando March 13, 1902, Chief of the Philippines Constabulary, Manila. No. 371. Walter Howard Loving Papers, Box 113-1, Folder 4, Manuscript Division, Moorland-Spingarn Research Center, Howard University.

14. I gathered this information from my grandmother Irene and her siblings and corroborated it with Bañas's book (1924, 98–101).

15. This was explained to me by my grandmother (Navarro's daughter) Irene Navarro Gamalinda, my granduncle Bienvenido Navarro, and my uncle Emilio N. Gamalinda.

16. Some Black regulars and volunteers remained in the Philippines even after they were discharged (Cunningham 2007, 11; see also Marasigan 2010, 359), but it is not known if any musicians continued to perform in Manila.

17. Handwritten letter from Loving to Roosevelt, October 14, 1901. Walter Howard Loving Papers, Box 113-1, Folder 2, Manuscript Division, Moorland-Spingarn Research Center, Howard University.

Chapter 2

1. The other band to which he refers is the Philippine Scouts Band.

2. See Frith (1996, chapter 6) on conceptions of African music as primitive.

3. For an important scholarly work that analyzes how music listeners infuse value into musical choices, see Frith 1996.

4. See *The Forbidden Book*, edited by Ignacio, de la Cruz, Emmanuel, and Toribio, for examples of the comparisons between Filipinos and Blacks, Filipinos and Native Americans, and Filipinos, Hawaiians, and Puerto Ricans.

5. This word is of course a misnomer. I keep the spelling used in 1904 to refer to how Americans regarded Philippine indigenous groups of the Cordillera and not to the actual people or groups themselves. This is not to reinscribe the error but to flag that this word was a historical construction. To refer to the culture or people themselves, I use the ethnolinguistic names such as Bontoc or Kalinga.

6. Firsthand accounts written by the bandsmen or Loving himself of the PC Band's visits to the US have never been located. The interviews conducted by Dr. Richardson in 1980 with the elderly band members who went to the 1939 Golden Gate International Exposition are the only firsthand accounts (see chapter 5).

7. While I use the term *Filipino* as an umbrella term to refer to fair participants from the Philippines, ideas about what "Filipino" meant were just beginning to develop in the years after 1898. Most Filipinos at the fair did not regard themselves as people with a common national heritage, what Anderson calls an "imagined community" (1984). For example, some cultural-linguistic groups had long histories of fighting each other, many of the "tribal" peoples fought against the Constabulary or Scouts, and members of the colonial military had themselves been fighting against US forces just a few short years before the fair.

8. For official publications of the Louisiana Purchase Exposition, see Hanson 1904, Louisiana Purchase Exposition 1904, and Louisiana Purchase Exposition Co. 1904.

9. There were 38 Bagobos, 41 Negritos, 114 Igorrotes, and 100 Moros, compared with the 431 Scouts and 280 Constabulary (Rydell 1984, 171–72).

10. "Moro" was typically considered to be a derogatory name for Muslim Filipinos when used by Spanish officials and Christian Filipinos. Nowadays, it has been recontextualized by Muslim Filipino political organizations to stand for unity among the various cultural and linguistic groups in the southern Philippines, but is not, however, a common name by which they describe themselves. Most often, Muslim Filipinos refer to themselves as Muslims, or by their specific ethnolinguistic group, for example, Maranao, Magindanao, or Tausug.

11. This popular "ragtime" song was written by Neil Moret (aka Charles N. Daniels), an American composer, and published as sheet music in 1902 by Whitney Warner Publishing Company of Detroit (Berlin 1994, 48).

12. Despite this "privilege," most Scouts chose to return home by the end of the fair. The Philippine Exposition reported that of the 301 Scouts scheduled to be discharged on September 30, almost half chose to go home, while the rest reenlisted and stayed until

January to clean up before returning to the Philippines (*Report of the Philippine Exposition Board* 1904, 28).

13. The name of the transport vessel was *Sherman* rather than *Sheridan*. The five hundred men of the 11th US Volunteer Cavalry were returning from active duty in Manila and heading to Iowa.

14. For a discussion on how Asian Americans have historically been excluded from discussion about race in the US, see Ancheta 2010.

15. See Edward Said, *Orientalism*. For application of this concept to Asians and Asian Americans see Lee 1999 and Moon 2005.

16. See Vicente L. Rafael, "White Love: Census and Melodrama in the U.S. Colonization of the Philippines," in *White Love and Other Events in Filipino History*, 17–51.

17. Kramer writes that "non-Christian" was the colonial regime's adaptation and awkward translation of the Spanish-colonial use of *infieles* or "infidels" (2006, 211).

18. Style of music was just one difference. Each also demonstrated cooking methods using copper vessels and different styles of tapestry weaving.

19. Densmore is considered a pioneer of comparative musicology and the beginnings of modern-day ethnomusicology, as well as a pioneer female researcher.

20. Some included immigrants from Europe who grew up in the US, as in the case of Tobani.

21. Today, ragtime music is most often associated with a piano genre made famous by the likes of Scott Joplin, "the King of Ragtime" (Berlin 2002, 1–2).

22. European "classical" music placed greater emphasis on the first and third counts of a four-beat measure, or the first beat of a two-beat pattern. To some like Densmore who considered European rhythmic styles to be more "civilized," this approach would have seemed more primitive.

23. Guevara's (1970) compilation of concert programs in Philippine newspapers from 1862 to 1918 shows that the PC Band played "Hiawatha" at concerts in the Binondo district (*Manila Times*, July 15, 1903) and at the Luneta (*Manila Times*, July 20, 1903).

24. See Schenker for an analysis of the global circulation of "Hiawatha." He explains that sheet music of Sousa's marches and blackface minstrel songs were sold in music stores in Manila before the arrival of the US (2016, 59). Not only were Filipinos familiar with Euro-American military brass music before US colonization, they were also familiar with Euro-American popular music, refuting the claim that these genres were introduced only when Americans arrived.

25. As mentioned earlier, "Hiawatha" was taught to the Moros on the train by a porter, likely an African American.

26. For an analysis of the consumption of blackface minstrelsy among the white working class, see Lott 2013.

27. Klezmer is a style of music based on Jewish folk tradition. For a history of Jewish immigrants' participation in minstrelsy, see Rogin 1998.

28. For more about Asian Americans in popular culture, see also Lee 1999. For the connections between Black Americans and Chinese immigrants during this time period, see Aarim-Heriot 2006.

29. Though long forgotten today in music history, Walsh's (2013) important work documents some 1,400 songs related to or referencing the Philippines produced during the US colonial period.

30. See Schenker's dissertation (2016) for the ways that white Americans living in Asia engaged in ragtime and Tin Pan Alley songs, what he calls "imperial pop," to express modernity.

31. See Schenbeck (2012) regarding Black uplifters and music. While he doesn't mention Loving specifically, Loving's education in European classical music and disapproval of ragtime and its negative connotations fits their approach.

32. See the documentary *Vaudeville* by Fenster et al. 1999.

33. For a biography on the complexities of Williams's life and work, see Chude-Sokei 2006.

34. See also Bundles 2001, 72.

35. *St. Louis Globe-Democrat*, August 6, 1904, p. 2, col. 5, and also *Music Trade Review* (n.d., August 1904): 21. No recording exists as far as I am aware.

36. The piece was published in 1903 by the Whitney Warner Publishing Company. To view the original score, see https://digitalcollections.detroitpubliclibrary.org/islandora/object/islandora%3A208468 (accessed January 16, 2020). To hear a recording, visit http://cylinders.library.ucsb.edu/.

37. Their names, short bios, and a group photo are printed on page 4 of the brochure.

38. The hosts were a company of Ilocano men under the command of Lt. Charles E. Dority.

39. For more information on Gould, see the New York Historical Society Museum and Library website: http://dlib.nyu.edu/findingaids/html/nyhs/gould/gould.html.

40. An "Indian Characteristic March & Two-Step" by Egbert Van Alstyle. See Amundson 2017, 58.

41. While no comprehensive list of all the band members at the 1904 Fair is available, there is a list of members who received medals, diplomas, and honorable mention in the *Report of the Philippine Exposition Board in the United States for the Louisiana Purchase Exposition* (Philippine Exposition Board, 1905), 157–58. A remarkably clear photo of the PC Band with Loving is available at the St. Louis Public Library. I recognize my great-grandfather in the front row on the far right of the photograph, holding his piccolo.

42. Newspaper clippings on the St. Louis World's Fair at the St. Louis Public Library. The original clippings are gathered and pasted into an old book, and the page numbers are cut off.

43. In honor of this event, Navarro's grandson Emilio N. Gamalinda named his son Rossini Peter Gamalinda.

Chapter 3

1. See Richardson 2007, 35–37, for a discussion about the role of journalism in the maintenance of hegemonic power.

2. See also Frith 1998, especially 141.

3. See Davis (2012) for an analysis of Washington's White House visit and the backlash that ensued.

4. Another "first" is that this was the first time a first lady accompanied her husband on the return ride from the Capitol to the White House. See https://www.inaugural.senate.gov/31st-inaugural-ceremonies (accessed December 29, 2020).

5. My great-grandfather may have arranged this medley, because his arrangements of Filipino folk songs were often programmed on concerts in the Philippines after he took over the band from Loving.

6. See http://www.library.ucsb.edu/OBJID/Cylinder8469 for the Edison recording. I purchased a rare Columbia record on eBay, but have not found any other extant recordings.

7. Newspapers in Hawaii and African American newspapers did not use this diminutive at all.

8. The repertoire of the PC Band was reported to comprise over one thousand pieces. From my own knowledge as a classically trained musician, and from discussions with concert band specialists, it is clear that their choice of pieces represented some of the finest in band repertoire of the day.

9. See Anti-Imperialist League 1899 and Legaspi 1973.

10. All three pieces were available on major labels by known bands during this time. "Rose Mousse" was recorded by Sousa's band under Arthur Pryor (see https://www.loc.gov/item/jukebox-5574). "Amoureuse" was recorded by Sousa's band under Walter B. Rogers (see https://www.loc.gov/item/jukebox-121828). Eilenberg's "By the Suwanee River" was recorded by Author Pryor's band (see https://www.loc.gov/item/jukebox-121444, accessed March 3, 2020).

11. For works that attend to orientalist stereotypes of Asians, especially the Chinese, in popular culture during this time period, see Lee 1999, Garrett 2004, and Moon 2005.

12. I could not find a 1904 report of this competition, in which the PC Band took second place. While the Mexican Artillery Band, the Grenadier Guards Band, and the Garde Républicaine Band performed at the fair at the same time (from September through October), Sousa's band attended the fair from April to June, and could not have participated in a competition with the others (Schwartz and Schwartz 2003, 7).

13. A number of well-known Black composers of the time, by contrast, employed other strategies. Will Marion Cook, James Reese Europe, Bob Cole, J. Rosamond Johnson, and James Weldon Johnson incorporated the rhythms of ragtime and other musical conventions of minstrelsy-derived popular songs (without the racist words or subject matter) in their works of popular music. Drawing on their symbolic capital as college-educated and conservatory-trained musicians, they "still employed melodic and rhythmic Africanisms that rooted their music in ethnic identity" (Schenbeck 2014, 95).

14. Mary L. Europe was the younger sister of famed bandmaster James Reese Europe.

15. See Hall's discussion of Saussure's semiotic approach to representation (1997, 30–36).

16. The Filipina queen was Pura Villanueva, the future Mrs. Teodoro M. Kalaw, who came from a distinguished family from Iloilo (McCoy and Roces 1985, 25).

17. For an article on Americans in Manila, see Gleeck 1977.

Chapter 4

1. Hrdlicka's ideas about racial progress, despite Franz Boas's important critique of this approach in *The Mind of Primitive Man*, sparked interest in eugenics as a way of "improving the human stock" (Rydell 1984, 223).

2. I will discuss Edith Loving further in the next chapter.

3. Flores does not cite a particular source for this, but it may have been a well-known story among band musicians. My uncle Emilio Gamalinda, Navarro's grandson, who spent a lot time with Navarro as he conducted various bands in his later years, recounts the same story. In Tito Emil's version, Sousa calls Navarro "my little brown friend."

4. The full title is "It's a Long, Long Way to Tipperary."

5. Native Hawaiians, Puerto Ricans, and Pacific Islanders under US territorial rule were also absent from Sousa's composition.

6. The speech was reproduced in its entirety in the article "The Philippines at the Panama Exposition," *The Filipino People* 3, no. 7 (Washington, DC: March 1915): 7, 23.

Chapter 5

1. See Talusan 2018a for a detailed biography of Navarro.

2. Navarro's grandson Emilio remembers that whenever a musician made a mistake during rehearsals, Navarro knew exactly who he was and would throw his baton at him.

3. He founded several bands, including the National University Band, Banda Malabon, Banda Ligaya, and the Banda Puti of Malabon (see Bataclan 1977 and Talusan 2018a).

4. See Cunningham 2007 for detailed discussion of this time period in Loving's life as it relates to African Americans during WWI. He analyzes Loving's correspondence with US military officials and provides scholarly studies on the surveillance of African Americans.

5. For more details on Loving's life in Oakland, see Cunningham 2007 and Yoder 2013.

6. Dr. T. H. Padro de Tavera.

7. This also appears in the *Buffalo Express*, December 14, 1924, p. 1, col. 4.

8. Programs of the PC Band's concerts published in the *Cablenews-American* in 1916 under Navarro's leadership were mostly classical pieces from composers like Wagner, Liszt, Rossini, and Verdi, and compositions by Sousa.

9. See Castro 2011 for a discussion of musical nationalism.

10. See Walter Howard Loving Papers, Box 113-1 to 113-3, Manuscript Division, Moorland-Spingarn Research Center, Howard University. Many of the clippings, but particularly those from 1937 through 1939, were likely gathered and donated by Mrs. Loving with the assistance of the Philippine Press Clipping Bureau Inc. I also gathered clippings from this time period from *Foto News* at the Ayala Museum in Makati (see *Foto News*, October 31, 1937; November 15, 1937; January 1, 1938; and February 1, 1939).

11. A piano score of this piece is archived in the Walter Howard Loving Papers, Manuscript Division, Moorland-Spingarn Research Center, Howard University.

12. Clippings from the *Philippines Free Press* found in Walter Loving Papers at Howard University. The Lovings had a subscription while living in Manila, and Mrs. Loving must have collected these during her time there to preserve her husband's legacy. Newspaper clippings and other memorabilia were passed on to Loving's grandchildren, Edith Loving Lucas and Walter H. Loving III (Personal communication with author, 2021).

13. Recall from chapter 3 that a similar incident happened in Boston in 1909, when the PC Band was subjected to a series of test compositions to prove that they could read music.

14. I contacted Dr. Richardson in 2000 and he graciously sent me a cassette tape of the interview. On the recording, the band members who introduced themselves were José Baldevarona of Makati; Russ Valderon (?) of Mandaluyong; José Bascon-Santa Rosa of Laguna, trombone; Francisco Bautista of Malabon, baritone sax; Mrs. Fresnido, wife of Capt. Fresnido, and Nelia, Fresnido's daughter; Leonora Navarro, daughter of Navarro; and Mariano Baldevarona of Cavite. Sadly, Dr. Richardson passed away in 2020 before I could give him a copy of this book.

15. Corcino was the *Philippine News* queen contestant for Rizal Day. For more information on Rizal Day queen contests in the Filipino American community, see Mabalon 2013, chapter 4, and Jamero 2015.

16. Announcements of the band's concerts appeared in the *Oakland Tribune*, the *Berkeley Daily Gazette*, the *Oxnard Daily Courier*, and the *Bakersfield Californian* (archived at NewspaperArchive.com).

17. Filipinos first landed in Morro Bay, in what is now California, in 1587, aboard a Spanish galleon. In the late 1700s, a Filipino fishing village was founded in St. Malo, Louisiana. Filipinos also fought in the American Civil War, for the North. See http://philusnavy.tripod.com/fabroscw.htm (accessed October 2, 2017) for original sources, including Massachusetts state rosters, New Hampshire rosters, and pension records at the National Archives in Washington, DC.

18. I would like to acknowledge the unexpected and sad passing of Dr. Dawn Mabalon on August 14, 2018. Her contributions and dedication to Filipino American studies and to the community are exemplary. I dedicate this chapter to her. See https://history.sfsu.edu/content/passing-dr-dawn-bohulano-mabalon (accessed October 2, 2018).

19. See Carlos Bulosan's famous novel *America Is in the Heart* (2006), first published in 1946.

20. Bocobo played an important role in the movement for Philippine independence and served as president of the University of the Philippines, Diliman.

21. For more detailed accounts of the taxi dance hall and its significance among Filipino Americans, see Pareñas 1998, España-Maram 2006, Burns 2008, and Bernardo 2014. For a study of music in California's Filipino communities during this time period, see Parnes 1999. Music in taxi dance halls is also discussed in Cressey 1932 and Vedder 1947. Their repertoire included blues, waltz, the foxtrot, and swing (see España-Maram 2006, 124).

22. Tolentino eventually created the seal of the Republic of the Philippines and designed the Bonifacio Monument in Caloocan City (NCCA.gov).

23. A Spanish-language periodical quoted Loving as saying, "Pasamos muy buenos ratos y creo que la banda brindo horas muy placenteras a los que acudieron a la exposicion" (*El ?*, July 26, 1939). "We had a good time, and I think the band brought many very pleasant hours to those who came out to the exposition" (translation by Alonso Nichols). Clipping in the Walter Howard Loving Papers, Howard University.

24. Lippay was a Viennese conductor who founded the Manila Symphony Orchestra in 1926 (http://www.manilasymphony.com/about-us, accessed September 23, 2018).

25. Virgilio Ruiz Fresnido was born in 1928. I met him in June of 2018, at the age of ninety, when I united him with my uncle, Navarro's grandson, Emilio N. Gamalinda, eighty-eight years old. I interviewed them together on video, and they reminisced about their youth under Japanese occupation of the Philippines. Tito Emil passed away a few months after this interview.

26. They lived in the Ermita district, Dakota Street, not far from Manila Bay.

27. Apparently, "Pedro B. Navarro . . . could not come," but the Ligaya Band was there and performed *Dai-Nippon No Uta* (Bañas 1975, 243). Navarro composed a piece called *The Rising Generation*, which my uncle Emilio said he heard performed at the Luneta. The score is in my possession.

28. When I met her in 1996, she was elderly and sick, and did not speak. On the tape, I was surprised at the force and power of her voice. She expressed a strong opinion that historians of the band and the musical community in the Philippines no longer recognized Navarro's contribution to the PC Band's history.

29. A photocopy of the Moreno 1986 article was in the Walter Howard Loving Papers, Howard University.

30. Like the members of Virgilio Fresnido's family, Loving's body was likely swept away when US forces bulldozed the area of debris, along with the remains of loved ones.

31. I am making reference to the stereotype from the 1904 World's Fair, Imelda Marcos, and the more recent viral YouTube videos of the dancing inmates at the Cebu Provincial Detention and Rehabilitation Center, which first appeared in 2007.

BIBLIOGRAPHY

Aarim-Heriot, Najia. 2006. *Chinese Immigrants, African Americans, and Racial Anxiety in the United States, 1848–82.* Urbana: University of Illinois Press.
Amundson, Michael A. 2017. *Talking Machine: A History and Catalogue of Tin Pan Alley's Western Recordings, 1902–1918.* Norman: University of Oklahoma Press.
Afable, Patricia O. 2004. "Journeys from Bontoc to the Western Fairs, 1904–1915: The 'Nikimalika' and their Interpreters." *Philippine Studies* 52 (4): 445–73.
Agawu, Kofi. 2016. "Tonality as a Colonizing Force in Africa." In *Audible Empire: Music, Global Politics, Critique*, edited by Ronald Radano and Tejumola Olaniyan, 334–55. Durham, NC: Duke University Press.
Alidio, Kimberly A. 2001. "Between Civilizing Mission and Ethnic Assimilation: Racial Discourse, U.S. Colonial Education and Filipino Ethnicity, 1901–1946." Ph.D. diss., University of Michigan.
Ancheta, Angelo N. 2010. "Neither Black Nor White." In *Asian American Studies Now*, edited by Jean Yu-Wen Shen Wu and Thomas Chen, 21–34. New Brunswick, NJ: Rutgers University Press.
Anderson, Benedict O. 1991. *Imagined Communities*, rev. ed. London: Verso Press.
Anderson, Warwick. 1995. "'Where Every Prospect Pleases and Only Man Is Vile': Laboratory Medicine and Colonial Discourse." In *Discrepant Histories: Translocal Essays on Filipino Cultures*, edited by Vicente L. Rafael, 83–112. Philadelphia: Temple University Press.
Anderson, Warwick. 2006. *Colonial Pathologies: American Tropical Medicine, Race, and Hygiene in the Philippines.* Durham: Duke University Press.
Anti-Imperialist League. 1899. *Address Adopted by the Anti-Imperialist League, February 10, 1899; Report of the Executive Committee of the Anti-Imperialist League, February 10, 1899.* Boston, MA: Anti-Imperialist League. (https://archive.org/stream/addressadoptedby00anti/addressadoptedby00anti_djvu.txt, accessed January 26, 2020).
Appadurai, Arjun. 1996. *Modernity at Large: Cultural Dimensions of Globalization.* Minneapolis: University of Minnesota Press.
Attali, Jacques. 1985. *Noise: The Political Economy of Music.* Minneapolis: University of Minnesota Press.

Badger, Reid. 1995. *A Life in Ragtime: A Biography of James Reese Europe*. New York: Oxford University Press.
Baker Jr., Houston A. 2000. Foreword to *Music and the Racial Imagination*, vi–vii. Edited by Ronald Radano and Philip V. Bohlman. Chicago: University of Chicago Press.
Balance, Christine Bacareza. 2016. *Tropical Renditions: Making Musical Scenes in Filipino America*. Durham: Duke University Press.
Baldoz, Rick. 2011. *The Third Asiatic Invasion: Empire and Migration in Filipino America, 1898–1946*. New York: New York University Press.
Bañas, Raymundo C. 1924. *The Music and Theater of the Filipino People*. Manila: printed by the author.
Bañas, Raymundo C. 1975. *Pilipino Music and Theatre*, rev. ed. Quezon City: Manlapaz Publishing Company.
Baraka, Amiri (LeRoi Jones). 2002. *Blues People: Negro Music in White America*. New York: Perennial.
Bataclan, Lt. Col. Augusto C., ed. 1997. *Philippine Bands*. Manila: M.G. Zabat Jr.
Bateson, Gregory, Don D. Jackson, Jay Haley, and John H. Weakland. 1962. "A Note on the Double Bind." In *Communication, Family and Marriage*, edited by D. Jackson, 154–61. Palo Alto, CA: Science and Behavior Books.
Beasley, Delilah L. 1918. Letter to the editor [W. E. B. Du Bois]. *The Crisis* 15, no. 5. https://books.google.com.
Berlin, Edward A. 1994. *King of Ragtime: Scott Joplin and His Era*. New York: Oxford University Press.
Berlin, Edward A. 2002. *Ragtime: A Musical and Cultural History*. Lincoln, NE: iUniverse.
Bernardo, Joseph A. 2014. "From 'Little Brown Brothers' to 'Forgotten Asian Americans': Race, Space, and Empire in Filipino Los Angeles." Ph.D. diss., University of Washington.
Bhabha, Homi K. 1994. *The Location of Culture*. London: Routledge & Kegan Paul.
Bierley, Paul E. 1986. *John Philip Sousa, American Phenomenon*, rev. ed. Columbus, OH: Integrity Press.
Boonzajer Flaes, Robert M. 2000. *Brass Unbound: Secret Children of the Colonial Brass Band*. Amsterdam: Royal Tropical Institute.
Bourdieu, Pierre. 1977. "Structures, Habits, Power: Basis for a Theory of Symbolic Power." In *Outline of a Theory of Practice*, translated by Richard Nice, 159–97. Cambridge: Cambridge University Press.
Bourdieu, Pierre. 1984. *Distinction: A Social Critique of the Judgment of Taste*. Translated by Richard Nice. Cambridge, MA: Harvard University Press.
Bourdieu, Pierre. 2001. *Masculine Domination*. Cambridge: Polity.
Breitbart, Eric. 1997. *A World on Display: Photographs from the St. Louis World's Fair, 1904*. Albuquerque: University of New Mexico Press.
Brown, Bill. 1993. "Science Fiction, the World's Fair, and the Prosthetics of Empire, 1910–1915." In *Cultures of United States Imperialism*, edited by Amy Kaplan and Donald E. Pease, 129–63. Durham, NC: Duke University Press.
Brownell, Susan, ed. 2008. *The 1904 Anthropology Days and Olympic Games: Sport, Race and American Imperialism*. Lincoln: University of Nebraska Press.
Buangan, Antonio S. 2004. "The Suyoc People Who Went to St. Louis 100 Years Ago: The Search for My Ancestors." *Philippine Studies* 52 (4): 474–98.
Bulosan, Carlos, and Carey McWilliams. 2006. *America Is in the Heart: A Personal History*. Mandaluyong, Philippines: Anvil Publishing.

Bundles, A'Lelia Perry. 2001. *On Her Own Ground: The Life and Times of Madam C. J. Walker*. New York: Scribner.

Burgess, Richard James. 2014. "The Phonograph." In *The History of Music Production*, 5–11. New York: Oxford University Press.

Burns, Lucy Mae San Pablo. 2013. *Puro Arte: Filipinos on the Stages of Empire*. New York: New York University Press.

Campomanes, Oscar V. 1992. "Filipinos in the United States and Their Literature of Exile." In *Reading the Literatures of Asian America*, edited by Shirley Geok-Lin Lim and Amy Ling, 49–78. Philadelphia: Temple University Press.

Camus, Raoul F. 2001. "Military Music: North America." In *New Grove Dictionary of Music and Musicians*, edited by Stanley Sadie and John Tyrrell, 687–91. New York: MacMillan Press.

Cannata, Amanda. 2014. "Articulating and Contesting Cultural Hierarchies: Guatemalan, Mexican, and Native American Music at the Panama-Pacific International Exposition (1915)." *Journal of the Society for American Music* 8 (1): 76–100.

Cannell, Fenella. 1995. "The Power of Appearances: Beauty, Mimicry, and Transformation in Bicol." In *Discrepant Histories: Translocal Essays on Filipino Cultures*, edited by Vicente L. Rafael, 223–58. Philadelphia: Temple University Press; Manila: Anvil Publishing.

Cannell, Fenella. 1999. "Beauty and the Idea of 'America.'" In *Power and Intimacy in the Christian Philippines*, 203–26. Cambridge: Cambridge University Press.

Carney, Court. 2009. *Cuttin' Up: How Early Jazz Got America's Ear*. Lawrence: University of Kansas Press.

Castro, Christi-Anne. 2011. *Musical Renderings of the Philippine Nation*. New York: Oxford University Press.

Certeau, Michel de, and Steven Rendall. 1984. *The Practice of Everyday Life*. Berkeley: University of California Press.

Chude-Sokei, Louis. 2006. *The Last "Darky": Bert Williams, Black-on-Black Minstrelsy, and the African Diaspora*. Durham, NC: Duke University Press.

Clevenger, Martha R., ed. 1996. *'Indescribably Grand': Diaries and Letters from the 1904 World's Fair*. St. Louis: Missouri Historical Society Press.

Cloud, Dana L. 1996. "Hegemony or Concordance? The Rhetoric of Tokenism in 'Oprah' Winfrey's Rags-to-Riches Biography." *Critical Studies in Mass Communication* 13 (2): 115–37.

Cojuangco, Margarita R., Rene R. Cruz, Guillermo T. Domondon, Ramon E. Montaño, and Cesar P. Nazareno. 1991. *Konstable: The Story of the Philippine Constabulary, 1901–1991*. Manila: ABoCan.

Corbett, Katharine T. 1999. *In Her Place: A Guide to St. Louis Women's History*. St. Louis: Missouri Historical Society Press.

Cordova, Fred, Dorothy Laigo Cordova, and Albert A. Acena. 1983. *Filipinos, Forgotten Asian Americans: A Pictorial Essay, 1763–circa 1963*. Dubuque, Iowa: Kendall/Hunt Publishing.

Cressey, Paul. 1932. *The Taxi-Dance Hall: A Sociological Study in Commercialized Recreation and City Life*. New York: Greenwood Press.

Cruz, Jon. 1999. *Culture on the Margins: The Black Spiritual and the Rise of American Cultural Interpretation*. Princeton, NJ: Princeton University Press.

Cunningham, Roger D. 2007. "'The Loving Touch': Walter H. Loving's Five Decades of Military Music." *Army History* 64: 5–25.

Curtis, Susan. 1994. *Dancing to a Black Man's Tune: A Life of Scott Joplin*. Columbia: University of Missouri Press.

David, E. J. R. 2013. *Brown Skin, White Minds: Filipino-American Postcolonial Psychology.* Charlotte, NC: Information Age Publishing.

Davis, Deborah. 2012. *Guest of Honor: Booker T. Washington, Theodore Roosevelt, and the White House Dinner that Shocked a Nation.* New York: Atria Books.

Densmore, Frances. 1906. "The Music of Filipinos." *American Anthropologist* 8, no. 4 (October–December): 611–32.

Dines, Gail, and Jean McMahon Humez. 2003. *Gender, Race, and Class in Media: A Text-Reader.* Thousand Oaks, CA: Sage Publications.

Dyreson, Mark. 1998. *Making the American Team: Sport, Culture, and the Olympic Experience.* Urbana: University of Illinois Press.

Elarth, Harold H. 1949. *The Story of the Philippine Constabulary.* Los Angeles: Globe Print.

Ellis, Mark. 2001. *Race, War, and Surveillance: African Americans and the United States Government during World War I.* Bloomington: Indiana University Press.

España-Maram, Linda. 2006. *Creating Masculinity in Los Angeles's Little Manila: Working-Class Filipinos and Popular Culture, 1920s–1950s.* New York: Columbia University Press.

Fanon, Frantz. 1970. *Toward the African Revolution.* Harmondsworth, UK: Penguin Books.

Fermin, Jose D. 2004. *1904 World's Fair: The Filipino Experience.* Diliman, Quezon City: University of the Philippines Press.

Fenster, Rosemary Garner, Greg Palmer, Ben Vereen, Tamar Hacker, Gary Gibson, Susan Lacy, et al. 1999. *Vaudeville.* New York: Winstar TV & Video.

Flores, Maidan. 1976. "The 'Loving' Band." In *Philippine Constabulary Diamond Jubilee, 1901–1976,* 72–77. Manila: Philippine Information Office

Foucault, Michel. 1972. *The Archaeology of Knowledge.* New York: Pantheon Books.

Foucault, Michel. 1977. "Nietzsche, Genealogy, and History." In *Language, Counter-Memory, Practice: Selected Essays and Interviews,* edited by D. F. Bouchard, 139–64. Ithaca, NY: Cornell University Press.

Fosler-Lussier, Danielle. 2015. *Music in America's Cold War Diplomacy.* Oakland: University of California Press.

Francia, Luis H. 2014. "From Indio to Filipino: Emergence of a Nation, 1862–1898." Chap. 3 in *History of the Philippines: From Indios Bravos to Filipinos.* New York: Overlook Press.

Frith, Simon. 1998. *Performing Rites: On the Value of Popular Music.* New York: Oxford University Press.

Gaines, Kevin K. 1996. *Uplifting the Race: Black Leadership, Politics, and Culture in the Twentieth Century,* 2nd ed. Chapel Hill: University of North Carolina Press.

Garafalo, Reebee. 2011. *Rockin' Out: Popular Music in the U.S.A.* London: Pearson.

Garrett, Charles Hiroshi. 2004. "Chinatown, Whose Chinatown? Defining America's Borders with Musical Orientalism." *Journal of the American Musicological Society* 57 (1): 119–74.

Garrett, Charles Hiroshi. 2008. *Struggling to Define a Nation: American Music and the Twentieth Century.* Berkeley: University of California Press.

Gatewood Jr., Willard B. 1972. "Black Americans and the Quest for Empire, 1898–1903." *Journal of Southern History* 38, no. 4 (November): 545–66.

Gatewood Jr., Willard B. 1975. *Black Americans and the White Man's Burden, 1898–1903.* Urbana: University of Illinois Press.

Gatewood Jr., Willard B. 1987 [1971]. *"Smoked Yankees" and the Struggle for Empire: Letters from Negro Soldiers, 1898–1902.* Reprint. Urbana: University of Illinois Press.

Gilbert, James Burkhart. 2009. *Whose Fair? Experience, Memory, and the History of the Great St. Louis Exposition.* Chicago: University of Chicago Press.

Gleeck Jr., Lewis. 1977. *The Manila Americans 1901–1964*. Manila: Carmelo and Baumann.
Goehr, Lydia. 1994. "Political Music and the Politics of Music." *Journal of Aesthetic and Art Criticism* 52 (1): 99–112.
Golay, Frank H. 1997. *Face of Empire: United States-Philippine Relations 1898–1946*. Manila: Ateneo de Manila University Press.
Golden Anniversary of the Philippine Constabulary Band. 1952. Souvenir Program. Philippines.
Gonzalves, Theodore S. 2010. *The Day the Dancers Stayed: Performing in the Filipino/American Diaspora*. Philadelphia: Temple University Press.
Gottschild, Brenda Dixon. 2002. *Waltzing in the Dark: African American Vaudeville and Race Politics in the Swing Era*. New York: Palgrave.
Gould, Lewis L. 2010. *Helen Taft: Our Musical First Lady*. Lawrence: University of Kansas Press.
The Government Official Indian Band: Organized by the U.S. Government Expressly for the Louisiana Purchase Exposition, St. Louis, 1904. 1909. Chicago: Hollister Brothers, Engravers and Printers.
Gramsci, Antonio, Quintin Hoare, and Geoffrey Nowell-Smith. 2008. *Selections from the Prison Notebooks of Antonio Gramsci*. New York: International Publishers.
Guevara, Leticia. 1970. "References to Music in Periodicals 1862–1918 at the National Library." MA thesis. University of the Philippines, Diliman.
Hall, Stuart. 1980. "Encoding/Decoding." In *Culture, Media Language*, edited by Stuart Hall, Dorothy Hobson, Andrew Love, and Paul Willis, 128–38. London: Hutchinson.
Hall, Stuart, ed. 1997. *Representation: Cultural Representations and Signifying Practices*. London: Open University.
Hall, Stuart. 2003. "The Whites of Their Eyes: Racist Ideologies and the Media." Chap. 10 in *Gender, Race, and Class in Media: A Text-Reader*, edited by Gail Dines and Jean McMahon Humez. Thousand Oaks, CA: Sage Publications.
Hammond, David. 2013. "Soft Powering the Empire." *RUSI Journal* 158 (5): 90–96.
Haney-López, Ian. 2006. *White by Law: The Legal Construction of Race*. New York: New York University Press.
Hanson, John Wesley. 1904. *The Official History of the Fair, St. Louis, 1904: The Sights and Scenes of the Louisiana Purchase Exposition*. United States: s.n.
Herbert, Trevor. 2000. "Nineteenth-Century Bands: Making a Movement." Chap. 1 in *The British Brass Band: A Musical and Social History*, edited by Trevor Herbert. Oxford: Clarendon Press.
Herbert, Trevor, and Helen Barlow. 2013. "The Empire and Other Foreign Fields." Chap. 11 in *Music and the British Military in the Long Nineteenth Century*. Oxford: Oxford University Press.
Herbert, Trevor, and Margaret Sarkissian. 1997. "Victorian Bands and Their Dissemination in the Colonies." *Popular Music* 16 (2): 165–79.
Hoganson, Kristin L. 1998. *Fighting for American Manhood: How Gender Politics Provoked the Spanish-American and Philippine-American Wars*. New Haven, CT: Yale University Press.
Hudson, Lynn M. 2010. "'This Is Our Fair and Our State': African Americans and the Panama-Pacific International Exposition." *California History* 87 (3): 26–45, 66–68.
Hurley, Victor. 1938. *Jungle Patrol: The Story of the Philippine Constabulary*. New York: E.P. Dutton.
Hylton, John. 1991. "Music at the Louisiana Purchase Exposition." *College Music Symposium* 31: 59–66.
Ignacio, Abe, Enrique de la Cruz, Jorge Emmanuel, and Helen Toribio. 2004. *The Forbidden Book: The Philippine-American War in Political Cartoons*. San Francisco: T'Boli.

Ileto, Reynaldo Clemeña. 1998 [1979]. *Pasyon and Revolution: Popular Movements in the Philippines, 1840–1910*. Fifth printing. Quezon City: Ateneo de Manila University Press.

Ileto, Reynaldo Clemeña. 1999. *Filipinos and Their Revolution: Event, Discourse, and Historiography*. Quezon City: Ateneo de Manila University Press.

Ileto, Reynaldo Clemeña. 2002. "The Philippine-American War: Friendship and Forgetting." In *Vestiges of War: The Philippine-American War and the Aftermath of an Imperial Dream, 1899–1999*, edited by Angel Velasco Shaw and Luis Francia, 3–19. New York: New York University Press.

Irving, D. R. M. 2010. *Colonial Counterpoint: Music in Early Modern Manila*. Oxford: Oxford University Press.

Isaac, Allan Punzalan. 2006. *American Tropics: Articulating Filipino America*. Minneapolis: University of Minnesota Press.

Jackson, Billy. 1991. *Didn't We Ramble On: The Black Marching Band*. New York: Filmmakers Library. VHS, 14 minutes.

Jackson, Robert. 2004. *Meet Me in St. Louis: A Trip to the 1904 World's Fair*. New York: HarperCollins Publishers.

Jacobson, Matthew Frye. 1998. *Whiteness of a Different Color: European Immigrants and the Alchemy of Race*. Cambridge, MA: Harvard University Press.

Jacobson, Matthew Frye. 2000. *Barbarian Virtues: The United States Encounters Foreign Peoples at Home and Abroad, 1876–1917*. New York: Hill and Wang.

Jamero, Melissa Jeanne. 2015. "The Mystery of Pacita Todtod: Filipino American Actress, Singer, Journalist, and Community Leader in the 1940s." MA thesis, University of California, Los Angeles.

Johnson, E. Patrick. 2003. *Appropriating Blackness: Performance and the Politics of Authenticity*. Durham, NC: Duke University Press.

Jun, Helen Heran. 2011. *Race for Citizenship: Black Orientalism and Asian Uplift from Pre-Emancipation to Neoliberal America*. New York: New York University Press.

Kaplan, Amy. 1993. "Black and Blue on San Juan Hill." In *Cultures of United States Imperialism*, edited by Amy Kaplan and Donald E. Pease, 219–36. Durham, NC: Duke University Press.

Katigbak, Maria Kalaw. 1983. *Legacy, Pura Villanueva Kalaw: Her Times, Life, and Works, 1886–1954*. Manila: Filipinas Foundation.

Kramer, Paul. 1999. "Making Concessions: Race and Empire Revisited at the Philippine Exposition, St. Louis, 1901–1905." *Radical History Review* 73: 74–114.

Kramer, Paul, 2006. *The Blood of Government: Race, Empire, the United States, and the Philippines*. Chapel Hill: University of North Carolina Press.

Lafler, Czerna C. 1939. *The Philippine Constabulary Band*. N.p.: George F. Briegel.

Laurie, Clayton D. 1989. "The Philippine Scouts: America's Colonial Army, 1899–1913." *Philippine Studies* 37: 174–91.

Lee, Robert G. 1999. *Orientals: Asian Americans in Popular Culture*. Philadelphia: Temple University Press.

Lefferts, Peter M. 2013. "U.S. Army Black Regimental Bands and the Appointments of their First Black Bandmasters." *Black Music Research Journal* 33 (2): 151–75.

Legaspi, Edelwina C. 1973. *The Anti-Imperialist Movement in the United States, 1898–1900: With Special Emphasis on the Role of the Anti-Imperialist League*. Quezon City: University of the Philippines.

de León, Felipe Padilla, ed. 1977. *Philippine Bands*. Manila: National Band Association of the Philippines.

Levine, Lawrence W. 1988. *Highbrow/Lowbrow: The Emergence of Cultural Hierarchy in America*. Cambridge, MA: Harvard University Press.
Lewis, Robert M. 2003. *From Traveling Show to Vaudeville: Theatrical Spectacle in America, 1830–1910*. Baltimore: Johns Hopkins University Press.
Lipsitz, George. 1998. *The Possessive Investment in Whiteness: How White People Profit from Identity Politics*. Philadelphia: Temple University Press.
Lott, Eric. 2013 [1993]. *Love and Theft: Blackface Minstrelsy and the American Working Class*. New York: Oxford University Press.
Louisiana Purchase Exposition. 1904. *The Greatest of Expositions Completely Illustrated: Official Publication*. St. Louis: Official Photographic Company.
Louisiana Purchase Exposition Co. 1904. *Manual of the Louisiana Purchase Exposition, World's Fair, Saint Louis, 1904. Containing Lists of Officers and Committees of the Company and of the Commission, the Acts of Congress, the By-Laws of the Corporation, and Other Information*. Saint Louis: Louisiana Purchase Exposition Company.
The Loving Touch. N.d. Directed by Raul T. Silos. Produced by Gregorio S. Cendaña. Documentary film. Philippine VTR Cassette Project, 44 min.
Luther, Catherine A., Carolyn Ringer Lepre, and Naeemah Clark. 2012. *Diversity in U.S. Mass Media*. Chichester, West Sussex: Wiley-Blackwell.
Mabalon, Dawn Bohulano. 2013. *Little Manila Is in the Heart: The Making of the Filipino American Community in Stockton, California*. Durham, NC: Duke University Press.
Maceda, José. 1973. "Music in the Philippines in the Nineteenth Century." In *Musikkulturen Asiens, Afrikas und Ozeaniens in 19. Jahrhundert*, edited by Robert Gunther, 215–32. Regensburg, Germany: Gustav Bosse Verlag.
Manalansan, Martin F. 2003. *Global Divas: Filipino Gay Men in the Diaspora*. Durham, NC: Duke University Press.
Manalansan, Martin F., and Augusto Fauni Espiritu. 2016. *Filipino Studies: Palimpsests of Nation and Diaspora*. New York: New York University Press.
Marasigan, Cynthia L. 2010. "'Between the Devil and the Deep Sea': Ambivalence, Violence, and African American Soldiers in the Philippine-American War and Its Aftermath." Ph.D. diss., University of Michigan.
Markwyn, Abigail. 2008. "Economic Partner and Exotic Other: China and Japan at San Francisco's Panama-Pacific International Exposition." *The Western Historical Quarterly* 39 (4): 439–65.
Markwyn, Abigail. 2010. "Encountering 'Woman' on the Fairgrounds of the 1915 Panama-Pacific Exposition." Chap. 9 in *Gendering the Fair: Histories of Women and Gender at World's Fairs*. Champaign: University of Illinois Press.
Matherne, Neal D. 2014. "Naming the Artist, Composing the Philippines: Listening for the Nation in the National Artist Award." Ph.D. diss., University of California, Riverside.
McCoy, Alfred W. 2009. *Policing America's Empire: The United States, the Philippines, and the Rise of the Surveillance State*. Madison: University of Wisconsin Press.
McCoy, Alfred W., and Alfredo Roces. 1985. *Philippine Cartoons: Political Caricature of the American Era, 1900–1941*. Quezon City: Vera-Reyes.
McCoy, Alfred W., and Francisco Antonio Scarano, eds. 2010. *Colonial Crucible: Empire in the Making of the Modern American State*. Quezon City: Ateneo de Manila University Press.
McGinty, Doris Evans. 2001. "'That You Came So Far to See Us': Coleridge-Taylor in America." *Black Music Research Journal* 21 (2): 197–234.
Metcalfe, Rochelle. 1979. "I Heard That . . ." *Sun Reporter* 36 (13): 22. https://mgetit.lib.umich.edu/go/6333213.

Milan, Jon. 2009. *Detroit: Ragtime and the Jazz Age.* Charleston, SC: Arcadia Publishing.
Miller, Richard E. 1981. "Black American Troops in the Philippines." *American Historical Collection Bulletin* 8, no. 4 (January).
Mojares, Resil B. 2006. "The Formation of Filipino Nationality under U.S. Colonial Rule." *Philippine Quarterly of Culture and Society* 34 (1): 11–32.
Moon, Krystyn R. 2005. *Yellowface: Creating the Chinese in American Popular Music, 1850s–1920s.* New Brunswick, NJ: Rutgers University Press.
Moon, Krystyn R. 2010. "The Quest for Music's Origin at the St. Louis World's Fair: Frances Densmore and the Racialization of Music." *American Music* 28 (2): 191–210.
Moore, Sarah J. 2010. "Manliness and the New American Empire at the 1915 Panama-Pacific Exposition." In *Gendering the Fair: Histories of Women and Gender at World's Fairs*, 75–94. Champaign: University of Illinois Press.
Moreno, Cherie M. Querol. 1986. "Col. Walter Loving Remembered." *Mr. & Ms.* (special edition): 23–24.
Murphy, Gretchen. 2010. *Shadowing the White Man's Burden: U.S. Imperialism and the Problem of the Color Line.* New York: New York University Press.
Navarro, Pedro B. 1919 and 1920. Letters to Raymundo C. Bañas. National Archives of the Philippines.
Ng, Stephanie. 2005. "Performing the 'Filipino' at the Crossroads: Filipino Bands in Five-Star Hotels throughout Asia." *Modern Drama* 48 (2): 272–96.
Nowatzki, Robert. 2006. "Paddy Jumps Jim Crow: Irish-Americans and Blackface Minstrelsy." *Éire-Ireland* 41, nos. 3 and 4 (Fall/Winter): 162–84.
Ocampo, Anthony Christian. 2016. *The Latinos of Asia: How Filipino Americans Break the Rules of Race.* Stanford, CA: Stanford University Press.
Panama-Pacific International Exposition Board. 1915. *The Philippine Islands: Their Industrial and Commercial Possibilities; The Country and the People.* Manila: Panama-Pacific International Exposition Board of the Philippines. https://babel.hathitrust.org/cgi/pt?id=uc2.ark:/13960/t9862nko2&view=1up&seq=9, 18.
Panama-Pacific International Exposition. 1915. *Official Catalogue of the Department of Fine Arts.* The Wahlgreen Company. https://library.si.edu/digital-library/book/official catalogoopana.
Paredes, Ruby R. 1988. "Introduction: The Paradox of Philippine Colonial Democracy." In *Philippine Colonial Democracy*, edited by Ruby R. Paredes. Southeast Asia Studies 32. New Haven, CT: Yale University Press.
Parreñas, Rhacel Salazar. 1998. "'White Trash' Meets the 'Little Brown Monkeys': The Taxi Dance Hall as a Site of Interracial and Gender Alliances between White Working Class Women and Filipino Immigrant Men in the 1920s and 30s." *Amerasia Journal* 24 (2): 115–34.
Parezo, Nancy J., and Don D. Fowler. 2009. *Anthropology Goes to the Fair: The 1904 Louisiana Purchase Exposition.* Lincoln: University of Nebraska Press.
Parnes, Samuel Will. 1999. "A History of Filipino Rondalla Music and Musicians in Southern California." Ph.D. diss., University of California, Los Angeles.
Philippine Constabulary Band (Banda de la Constabularia Filipina). 1910. "La Sampaguita" by M. Ruiz. Edison Amberol: 8018. http://www.library.ucsb.edu/OBJID/Cylinder8469.
Philippine Constabulary Band. 1913. "Sampaguita." New York: Columbia Phonograph Company. 78 record.
Philippine Constabulary Band. 1913. "La Bella Filipina." New York: Columbia Phonograph Company. 78 record.

Philippine Exposition Board. 1905. *Report of the Philippine Exposition Board in the United States for the Louisiana Purchase Exposition.* Washington, DC: Bureau of Insular Affairs, War Department.

Poblete, JoAnna. 2014. *Islanders in the Empire: Filipino and Puerto Rican Laborers in Hawai'i.* Urbana: University of Illinois Press,

Powell, Anthony L. 1998. "Through My Grandfather's Eyes, Ties that Bind: The African American Soldier in the Filipino War for Liberation, 1899–1902." Paper originally presented at the 1997 National Conference of African American Studies and Hispanic and Latino Studies in Houston, TX.

Pratt, Mary Louise. 1992. *Imperial Eyes: Travel Writing and Transculturation.* New York: Routledge.

Prentice, Claire. 2014. *The Lost Tribe of Coney Island: Headhunters, Luna Park, and the Man Who Pulled off the Spectacle of the Century.* Boston: New Harvest.

Quizon, Cherubim A. 2004. "Two Yankee Women at the St. Louis Fair: The Metcalf Sisters and Their Bagobo Sojourn in Mindanao." *Philippine Studies* 52 (4): 527–55.

Radano, Ronald Michael, and Philip V. Bohlman. 2000. "Introduction: Music and Race, Their Past, Their Presence." In *Music and the Racial Imagination*, 1–53. Chicago: University of Chicago Press.

Radano, Ronald Michael, and Tejumola Olaniyan. 2016. *Audible Empire: Music, Global Politics, Critique.* Durham, NC: Duke University Press.

Randel, Don Michael. 2003. *The Harvard Dictionary of Music.* Cambridge, MA: Belknap.

Rafael, Vicente L. 1988. *Contracting Colonialism: Translation and Christian Conversion in Tagalog Society under Early Spanish Rule.* Manila: Ateneo de Manila Press.

Rafael, Vicente L. 1993. "White Love: Surveillance and Nationalist Resistance in the U.S. Colonization of the Philippines." In *Cultures of United States Imperialism*, edited by Amy Kaplan and Donald E. Pease, 185–218. Durham, NC: Duke University Press.

Rafael, Vicente L. 1995a. "Mimetic Subjects: Engendering Race at the Edge of Empire." *Differences: A Journal of Feminist Cultural Studies* 7 (2): 127–49.

Rafael, Vicente L. 1995b. "Colonial Domesticity: White Women and United States Rule in the Philippines." *American Literature* 67, no. 4 (December): 639–66.

Rafael, Vicente L. 2000. *White Love and Other Events in Filipino History.* Durham, NC: Duke University Press.

Rehrig, William H., Paul E. Bierley, and Robert Hoe. 1991. *The Heritage Encyclopedia of Band Music: Composers and Their Music.* Westerville, OH: Integrity Press.

Reily, Suzel Ana, and Katherine Brucher. 2016. *Brass Bands of the World: Militarism, Colonial Legacies, and Local Music Making.* London: Routledge.

Richardson, Claiborne T. 1980. "Interview with Members of the 1939 Philippine Constabulary Band under Col. Loving." Camp Crame, Quezon City (October 15).

Richardson, Claiborne T. 1982. "The Loving Band." *The Black Perspective in Music* 8 (2): 3–28.

Richardson, John E. 2007. *Analysing Newspapers: An Approach from Critical Discourse Analysis.* London: Red Globe Press.

Ricoeur, Paul. 1991. "Mimesis and Representation." In *A Ricoeur Reader*, edited by Mario J. Valdes, 137–55. Toronto: University of Toronto Press.

Robin, Ron. 2018. *Signs of Change: Urban Iconographies in San Francisco, 1880–1915.* New York: Routledge Library Editions.

Robinson, Henry S. 1984. "The M Street High School, 1891–1916." *Records of the Columbia Historical Society, Washington, D.C.* 51: 119–43.

Rogin, Michael Paul. 1998. *Blackface, White Noise: Jewish Immigrants in the Hollywood Melting Pot*. Berkeley: University of California Press.
Rubio, Hilarion F. 1977. "Introduction: A Brief Survey of Band Development in the Philippines." In *Philippine Bands*, edited by Lt. Col. Augusto C. Bataclan, 4–5. Manila: M.G. Zabat.
Ryan, William Carson. 1916. *Education Exhibits at the Panama-Pacific International Exposition, San Francisco, California, 1915*. U.S. Government Printing Office.
Rydell, Robert W. 1984. *All the World's a Fair: Visions of Empire at American International Expositions, 1876–1916*. Chicago: University of Chicago Press.
Rydell, Robert W. 1993. *World of Fairs: The Century-of-Progress Expositions*. Chicago: University of Chicago Press.
Rydell, Robert W., ed. 1999. "Editor's Introduction." In *Why the Colored American Is Not Included in the Columbia Exposition*, by Ida B. Wells, Frederick Douglass, Irvine Garland Penn, and Ferdinand L. Barnett. Originally published 1893. Urbana: University of Illinois Press.
Rydell, Robert W., John E. Findling, and Kimberly D. Pelle. 2000. *Fair America: World's Fairs in the United States*. Washington, DC: Smithsonian Institution Press.
Said, Edward W. 1979. *Orientalism*. New York: Random House.
Samson, Helen F. 1976. *Contemporary Filipino Composers: Biographical Interviews*. Quezon City: Manlapaz Publishing.
Santos, Ramón P. 1992. "Nationalism in Philippine Music during the Japanese Occupation: Art or Propaganda?" *Panahon ng Hipon* 2: 93–106.
Santos, Ramón P. 2005. *Tunugan: Four Essays on Filipino Music*. Quezon City: University of the Philippines Press.
Schenbeck, Lawrence. 2012. *Racial Uplift and American Music*. Jackson: University Press of Mississippi.
Schenker, Frederick J. 2016. "Empire of Syncopation: Music, Race, and Labor in Colonial Asia's Jazz Age." Ph.D. diss., University of Wisconsin-Madison.
Schneider, Mark Robert. 2006. *African Americans in the Jazz Age: A Decade of Struggle and Promise*. Lanham, MD: Rowman and Littlefield.
Schudson, Michael. 1981. *Discovering the News: A Social History of American Newspapers*. New York: Basic Books.
Schwartz, Richard I., and Iris J. Schwartz. 2003. *Bands at the St. Louis World's Fair of 1904: Information, Photographs, and Database*. Colonial Heights, VA: Richard I. Schwartz and Iris J. Schwartz.
Scott, James C. 1990. *Domination and the Arts of Resistance: Hidden Transcripts*. New Haven, CT: Yale University Press.
Scott, William Henry. 1982. *Cracks in the Parchment Curtain and Other Essays in Philippine History*. Quezon City: New Day Publishers.
See, Sarita Echavez. 2009. *The Decolonized Eye: Filipino American Art and Performance*. Minneapolis: University of Minnesota Press.
Shaw, Angel Velasco, and Luis Francia. 2002. *Vestiges of War: the Philippine-American War and the Aftermath of an Imperial Dream, 1899–1999*. New York: New York University Press.
Small, Christopher. 1998. *Musicking: The Meanings of Performing and Listening*. Hanover, NH: Wesleyan University Press.
Smith, Brian F. 2004. *Bandstands to Battlefields: Brass Bands in 19th Century America*. Gansevoort, NY: Corner House Historical Publications.

Sousa, John Philip, and Paul E. Bierley. 1994. *Marching Along: Recollections of Men, Women, and Music*. Westerville, OH: Integrity Press.

Southern, Eileen. 1971. *The Music of Black Americans: A History*. New York: W.W. Norton.

Spivak, Gayatri Chakravorty. 1994. "Can the Subaltern Speak?" In *Colonial Discourse and Post-Colonial Theory: A Reader*, edited by Robert Williams, John Patrick, and Laura Chrisman, 64–111. New York: Harvester Wheatsheaf.

Starr, Larry, and Christopher Waterman. 2018. *American Popular Music: From Minstrelsy to MP3*. 5th ed. New York: Oxford University Press.

Stellwagen, Edward J. 1909. *Final Reports of Chairmen of Committees to Edward J. Stellwagen, Chairman of the Committee in Charge of the Inauguration of William Howard Taft as President of the United States and James Schookcraft Sherman as Vice-President of the United States: At Washington, D.C., March 4, 1909*. Washington, DC: Inaugural Committee.

Suppan, Armin, and Wolfgang Suppan. 2001. "Military Music: Europe from the Middle Ages." In *New Grove Dictionary of Music and Musicians*, 683–87. New York: MacMillan Press.

Takaki, Ronald T. 1989. *Strangers from a Different Shore: A History of Asian Americans*. Boston: Little, Brown.

Tan, Arwin Q. 2014. "Reproduction of Cultural and Social Capital in Nineteenth-Century Spanish Regimental Bands of the Philippines." *Humanities Diliman* 11 (2): 61–89.

Talusan, Mary. 2004. "Music, Race, and Imperialism: The Philippine Constabulary Band at the 1904 St. Louis World's Fair." *Philippine Studies Quarterly* 52 (4): 499–526.

Talusan, Mary. 2009. "Gendering the Philippine Brass Band: Women of the Ligaya Band and National University Band, 1920s–1930s." *Musika Jornal* 5: 33–56.

Talusan, Mary. 2013. "Music, Race, and Imperialism: The Philippine Constabulary Band at the 1904 St. Louis World's Fair." In *Mixed Blessing: The Impact of the American Colonial Experience on Politics and Society in the Philippines*, edited by Hazel M. McFerson, 146–70. Westport, CT: Greenwood Publishing Group.

Talusan, Mary. 2018a. "Capt. Pedro B. Navarro," in *Cultural Center of the Philippines Encyclopedia of Philippine Art, Volume 7: Music*, edited by José Buenconsejo, 630–31. Manila: Cultural Center of the Philippines.

Talusan, Mary. 2018b. "Hearing with an Imperial Ear: Racializing the Philippine Constabulary Band and African American Conductor Lt. Walter H. Loving." In *Philippine Modernities, Commemorating 100 Years of UP College of Music*, edited by José Buenconsejo, 165–86. Manila: University of the Philippines Press.

Todd, Frank Morton. 1921. *The Story of the Exposition: Being the Official History of the International Celebration Held at San Francisco in 1915 to Commemorate the Discovery of the Pacific Ocean and the Construction of the Panama Canal*. New York: Published for Panama-Pacific International Exposition Co. by Putnam.

Troutman, John William. 2012. *Indian Blues: American Indians and the Politics of Music, 1879–1934*. Norman: University of Oklahoma Press.

Tuohy, Sue. 2001. "The Sonic Dimensions of Nationalism in Modern China: Musical Representation and Transformation. *Ethnomusicology* 45 (1): 107–31.

Vazquez, Alexandra T. 2014. *Listening in Detail: Performances of Cuban Music*. Durham, NC: Duke University Press.

Vedder, Clyde Bennett. 1947. "An Analysis of the Taxi-Dance Hall as a Social Institution, with Special Reference to Los Angeles and Detroit." Ph.D. diss., University of Southern California.

Vergara Jr., Benito M. 1995. *Displaying Filipinos: Photography and Colonialism in Early 20th Century Philippines*. Quezon City: University of the Philippines Press.

Walsh, Thomas P. 2013. *Tin Pan Alley and the Philippines: American Songs of War and Love, 1898–1946; A Resource Guide*. Lanham, MD: Scarecrow Press.

Walter Howard Loving Papers, Box 113-1 to 113-3, Manuscript Division, Moorland-Spingarn Research Center, Howard University.

Williams, W. H. A. 1996. *'Twas Only an Irishman's Dream: The Image of Ireland and the Irish in American Popular Song Lyrics, 1800–1920*. Urbana: University of Illinois Press.

Wang, Grace. 2015. *Soundtracks of Asian America: Navigating Race through Musical Performance*. Durham, NC: Duke University Press.

Wong, Deborah. 2004. *Speak It Louder: Asian Americans Making Music*. New York: Routledge.

Yamomo, MeLê. 2018. *Theatre and Music in Manila and the Asia Pacific, 1869–1946: Sounding Modernities*. London: Palgrave McMillan.

Yoder, Robert L. 2013. *In Performance: Walter Howard Loving and the Philippine Constabulary Band*. Manila: National Historical Commission of the Philippines.

INDEX

24th Infantry, United States Army, 53–57, 59, 63–64, 99, 180; Band of, 56, 64, 112–13, 155
48th Volunteer Infantry, United States Army, 5, 57, 59, 84

abolition, US slavery, 16–17, 19, 98
Adonay, Marcelo, 62–63
Aeta people, 92–93
African American communities: at 1904 World's Fair, 102–4; Black bandmasters, 148, 205; Black composers, 15, 54, 99–100, 105, 148, 151, 245n7, 245n9, 249n13; Black culture, 11, 14–18, 94, 99–105, 167; Black elites, 19–20, 148–49, 151–54, 214; blackface, 85, 98, 179, 247n24; Black and Filipino racialization, 70–71, 77, 78–79, 113, 120, 186; Black women, 101, 179, 181; Jim Crow, 73, 75, 80–81, 100, 178–80; Loving's identity, 5, 70, 84–85, 122–24, 148, 158, 160, 163–64, 171–72, 181, 189, 217; and migration, 11, 12; and musical traditions, 13–18, 63–66, 71, 94–96, 99–107, 139, 151–55; and PA band, 225–26; and the PC band, 19, 61, 85–86, 148, 156, 172, 204–5, 208, 236; and PPIE, 178–81, 184; and racial uplift, 19, 33, 149–52; and Scott Joplin, 101–2, 106; in the US military, 32, 53–59, 60, 63–66
Afro-American (newspaper), 139, 154, 156, 202

agency: of Filipino musicians, 32, 34, 51, 72, 121, 130, 138, 144; Loving's, 39, 241; of musicians, 42
Agoncillo, Felipe, 51–52
agricultural workers, 223–24
Aguinaldo, Emilio, 10, 51–52, 54, 61, 140, 197; Aguinaldo's March, 197, 212
Aida, 46, 129, 188
Alaska-Yukon-Pacific International Exposition (AYP), 33, 122, 160–63
Allensworth, Allen, 57
American dream, 224
American exceptionalism, 8, 16, 18, 24
American Lunetta bandstand, 140–41
Anderson, Warwick, 23
Anthony, Walter, 123–24, 165–67, 187–88
anthropology, 74–75, 92
anti-imperialism, 6, 53, 71, 76, 122, 138
Aquino, Benigno S., Jr, 31
Army, United States, 53–54, 79–82, 110, 128, 208; 6th Artillery Band in, 63; 8th Illinois regiment, 103; 8th US Volunteer Infantry of, 57, 103; 9th Cavalry, 180, 205; 24th Infantry of, 53–57, 59, 63–64, 99, 112–13, 180; 29th Volunteer Band in, 63; 48th Volunteer Infantry of, 5, 57, 59, 84; 49th Volunteer Infantry of, 57–58; Buffalo Soldiers in, 56, 180; Loving in, 56, 63, 65; Philippine Scouts in, 32, 49, 59–60, 63, 78–82, 109, 113

265

art, 12–15, 117, 191; abstract, 27; Black artistic expression, 99, 103, 149; European, 12, 15, 94, 99, 152, 225; Filipino artistic expression, 28, 46, 50, 230–31; local, 46; pure, 12; puro arte, 25; serious art music, 169, 225

Asia: anti-Asian racism, 181–82; Asian Exclusion Act, 11, 186; Asian immigrants, 11, 84, 181–82, 186, 223, 236; China, 104, 176, 181–82; colonial, 214; music traditions of, 167, 229–30; and Philippine-American War, 47, 53; Southeast, 26, 229; stereotypes of, 236, 244n14. *See also* Japan; Korea; Philippines

Asiatic Squadron, United States, 10, 51

assimilation, Filipino, 38, 42, 45; and the 1904 World's Fair, 71, 75–77, 79, 81–83, 88, 90–93; and music, 24, 26, 32, 35; and the PC band, 40, 43, 66, 69, 108, 121, 125, 139. *See also* benevolent assimilation

Atlantic City, New Jersey, PC band in, 156–58, 160, 164

Authenticity: and Black music, 17, 19, 71, 100, 151; Filipino, 20–25, 27–28, 31, 103, 120, 187

Baker, Houston A., Jr, 20
bakla, 26–27
Balance, Christine, 24, 28
Baldevarona, José, 231, 250n14
Bañas, Raymundo C., 45, 202, 207, 209–11, 229
banda tradition, 19, 21, 23–24, 32, 36; Banda Arevalo, 48; Banda Ligaya, 250n3, 251n27; Banda de Pasig, 48, 172; Banda Peñaranda, 48; history of, 38, 42, 48–49; and PC band, 51, 114, 116, 130, 218–19, 241

band music, 5; at the 1904 World's Fair, 75, 77, 91, 94–96, 108, 114; Banda Ligaya, 250n3, 251n27; bandmasters, 40, 47–48, 108, 113, 180–81, 204–6, 225–28; Euro American, 18, 41, 99, 183, 208, 212; and John Philip Sousa, 14, 84, 91, 96, 230; marching, 126; military, 4, 12–13, 32, 37–42, 51–52, 63–66; occidental bands, 111, 161; and PC band resonances, 213, 218–20, 228–29; in the Philippines, 7, 20, 23–24, 32, 41–43, 47–50, 63–66, 145; at the PPIE, 183, 189–90, 192, 194, 197–99; town bands, 8, 38, 47–50, 61; in Washington, DC, 146–47. *See also* banda tradition; bandsmen; brass bands; Philippine Constabulary (PC) Band

bandsmen, Filipino, 4–5, 19, 22–23, 29, 32–35; at the 1904 World's Fair, 83–87, 97, 117–18; and PC band tour of US, 120–21, 124, 132–33, 138–39, 142–46, 160–61, 163; and PC band legacy, 221–22, 226–27, 235–38, 240; in the Philippines, 40, 49, 64

Bascon, José, 221–22
Beasley, Delilah L., 179–80
beauty pageants, 26–27
Beethoven, Ludwig van, 8, 101, 134, 138, 164, 230
benefit concerts, 174, 192–93, 195
benevolent assimilation: at the 1904 World's Fair, 69, 70, 76, 91–92; and Filipino music, 121; and the PC band, 4–7, 18, 38–39, 144, 236–38; US project of, 9, 16
Bhabha, Homi, 8, 237, 240
Bicolano people, 133–34, 136, 144
Bizet, Georges, 142, 225
Black communities: at 1904 World's Fair, 102–4; Black bandmasters, 148, 205; Black composers, 15, 54, 99–100, 105, 148, 151, 245n7, 245n9, 249n13; Black culture, 11, 14–18, 94, 99–105, 167; Black elites, 19–20, 148–49, 151–54, 214; Black and Filipino racialization, 70–71, 77, 78–79, 113, 120, 186; Black women, 101, 179, 181; blackface, 85, 98, 179, 247n24; Jim Crow, 73, 75, 80–81, 100, 178–80; Loving's identity, 5, 70, 84–85, 122–24, 148, 158, 160, 163–64, 171–72, 181, 189, 217; and migration, 11, 12; and musical traditions, 13–18, 63–66, 71, 94–96, 99–107, 139, 151–55; and PA band, 225–26; and the PC band, 19, 61, 85–86, 148, 156, 172, 204–5, 208, 236; and PPIE, 178–81, 184; and racial uplift, 19, 33, 149–52; and Scott Joplin, 101–2, 106; in the US military, 32, 53–59, 60, 63–66

blackface minstrelsy, 85, 98, 247n24; Al Jolson and, 179
Boas, Franz, 75
Bocobo, Jorge, 224, 251n20
Bontoc groups, 88–89, 92
Boston, Massachusetts, 29–31, 34, 49, 135–38, 194; Boston Band, 183; Boston

Conservatory of Music, 4, 123; Boston Symphony Orchestra, 191; New England Conservatory of Music in, 4, 45, 57, 123, 226
Bourdieu, Pierre, 21, 159, 241
Brahms, Johannes, 190
brass bands: at the 1904 World's Fair, 83, 95–96, 107–9; all-female, 106–7; brass instruments, 37–50, 159, 239; and concert bands, 243n8; conservatives on, 13; military, 37–42, 50–51, 64–66, 208, 212; and PC band legacy, 228–29, 236, 239; in Philippines, 5, 8, 20–21, 23, 35; Philippine Scouts band, 32, 48, 77, 109, 113, 114, 246n1. *See also* banda tradition
Britain: Grenadier Guards Band of London, 4, 136, 145, 249n12; and Samuel Coleridge-Taylor, 149, 151–52; and test compositions, 136
Brown, Bill, 177
Brown, Frank L., 198–99
Buenaventura, Antonino, 221, 233
Bureau of Insular Affairs, United States, 117, 161
Bureau of Music, 94–95, 97
Burns, Lucy Mae San Pablo, 24
business interests, 39, 191, 197, 225

Cairns, Anna Sneed, 112
cakewalk, 13, 96–97, 214
Camp Crame, Philippines, 213, 233, 241
Campbell, James, 154–55
Cannell, Fenella, 24, 26
caricatures, 77, 85, 98, 100, 179
Cassasa, Charles H., 83, 190–91, 199
Catholic Church, 5, 42–45, 47
Certeau, Michel de, 42
Chi, Ch'en, 176
China, 104, 176, 181–82
Chinese communities: at 1904 World's Fair, 104; Chinese Exclusion Act (1882), 11; Chinese immigrants, 98; at PPIE, 181–82
choral societies, 148–55
Christianity: and Black spirituals, 17, 151; Catholic Church, 5, 42–45, 47; and missionaries, 43–45; in the Philippines, 42–43, 76–77, 88, 195, 246n10

citizenship, United States, 79, 88, 90–91, 182
civilian town bands, 8, 38, 47–50, 61
civilization discourse: at 1904 World's Fair, 71, 73–75, 77, 79, 82, 88–94, 108, 114; and Black musicians, 96, 99, 101; civilization work, 177; civilized music, 9, 26, 160; European, 12–13, 15, 66, 225; and Filipino musicians, 9, 16, 19–20, 120–22, 130, 145, 163, 237–38; and Filipino representations, 6–7, 10, 52; at PPIE, 174–77, 184–85, 187, 190, 196; "uncivilized" representations, 6, 68, 89, 94, 108; as US colonial project, 4, 22, 68–69, 145, 201
Civil War, United States, 11, 16, 136, 251n17
clarinets, 128, 141, 148, 187, 231, 239, 243n8
class: hierarchy, 124; high, 12, 65, 83, 95, 100, 140, 189; lower, 15, 97, 186; middle, 12, 14, 16, 19, 99, 107, 149, 152; wage-earning, 183; working, 224
classical music: and Black musicians, 63–64, 99, 147–49, 151–52; European, 12, 14, 95, 97, 103, 105, 167, 208; and the PC band, 121, 136, 138, 163–64, 194–95, 230; in the Philippines, 45
Clevenger, Martha, 77
Colegio de Niños Tiples, 45, 47
Coleridge-Taylor, Samuel, 148–53; *The Song of Hiawatha* by, 149–50, 153–54; Samuel Coleridge-Taylor Choral Society, 148–50, 152–55
collaboration: and 1904 World's Fair, 75–76; and colonial bands, 40–44, 208, 229; and the PC band, 5, 66; PC band with Black communities, 148–50, 152, 155, 171
colonialism, 23, 28; "colonial mentality" concept, 24–26; colonial military bands, 23, 32, 38–41, 109, 141; colonial subjects, 10, 21, 25, 66, 68, 76, 120, 235; colonial violence, 17–18, 121; and contact zones, 7, 32; in the Philippines, 23, 28, 32, 34, 237, 240; Spanish, 32, 43. *See also* colonization
colonization: European, 19–20; and mimicry, 25, 28; and music, 21–25, 34–35, 38–42, 46, 66, 68, 121, 212–14; US in Philippines, 4–6, 38, 74, 76, 133–34, 151, 212–13, 225
Colored American newspaper, 53, 57, 63

Columbia Park Boys' Band, 190
compositions: and Black musicians, 95–96, 104, 149–52; Filipino, 43, 47–48, 120–21, 130, 132, 194–95, 197, 214, 229–31; Loving as composer, 19, 57, 105, 188; military music, 37; Navarro as composer, 206–7; and PC Band, 64–65, 105–8, 130, 136, 138–40, 163–64, 169; Scott Joplin as composer, 101–2; Sousa as composer, 13–14, 16, 84, 95; test, 34, 49, 136, 138, 188, 250n13
concerts: at 1904 World's Fair, 106–7, 111–14, 116; American concert music, 12–14, 18–19, 208; concert bands, 14, 64, 94–96, 167, 228, 183, 243n8; concert halls, 3, 7, 29, 122; Loving farewell, 202; PA Band and, 216; PC Band and, 3, 5, 7, 29–30, 209–14, 219–20, 233–34, 239; PC Band 1909 tour, 119, 122–25, 129–30, 132–48, 161; PC Band at AYP exposition, 161, 163–70; PC Band at PPIE, 174, 183–95, 198–99; PC Band in Washington, DC, 148–59; in the Philippines, 41, 45–46, 58–59, 64–66, 206
conductors: Alfonso Fresnido as conductor, 210–11; Herbert as conductor, 195; Loving as conductor, 29–30, 64, 134–35, 139, 150, 153, 198, 218, 225–28; Navarro as conductor, 29–30, 35, 84, 189–90, 201–2, 206–7; Sousa as conductor, 27, 191
conservatories: National Conservatory of Music (New York), 15; New England Conservatory of Music (Boston), 4, 45, 57, 123, 226; in the Philippines, 45, 63
contact zones, 7, 32
Conway, Patrick, 183, 190–91
Cook, Will Marion, 148, 249n13
"coon songs," 13, 53–54, 96–102, 105–7, 113, 245n9
Corcino, Salome, 223, 250n15
cornets, 56–57, 128, 159
Court of the Universe, 189, 191, 199
Crame, Rafael, 213
creativity: creative labor, 25, 27, 121, 147; Filipino musicians and, 9–10, 23, 25–28, 44, 229; of Loving, 147, 241
Cruz, Hipolito De La, 132, 153
Cruz, Jon, 16, 19, 151
Cuba, 52, 57, 128

culture: and 1904 World's Fair, 68–69, 71–75, 82–83, 164, 167; and 1909 PC Band tour, 120–21, 130; and American popular music, 12–15, 22; Black culture, 11, 14–18, 94, 99–105, 167; cultural anxieties, 12; cultural authenticity, 19–20, 120; cultural distinctiveness, 43, 130; cultural hegemony, 10, 12, 16, 24, 26, 35, 94, 126; cultural production, 23, 103–4, 140, 234, 237; Filipino, 19, 23–29, 41–42, 44, 225–26, 234, 236–38, 240–41; Hispanicized, 44, 50, 74, 76; Japanese, 182, 230; and jazz, 214; popular, 100, 144; at PPIE, 177, 182, 184; white sense of cultural superiority, 197, 238. *See also* elite cultures; hegemony, cultural
Cunningham, Roger, 65, 208

Davis, George W., 81
de León, Felipe Padilla, 230
de León, I. T., 216
de León, Restituto, 220
del Rosario, Potenciano, 148
Densmore, Frances, 20, 92–94, 244n13, 247n19, 247n22
Detavera, T. H. Padro, 212
Dett, R. Nathaniel, 99, 151
Dewey, George, 10, 51
discipline: and Filipino musicians, 4, 6, 50, 69, 79, 135, 236; and military bands, 13, 40
"dog-eater" stereotype, 33, 79, 88, 92, 240
Donizetti, Gaetano, 124, 138, 146, 163; *Lucia di Lammermoor*, 46, 124, 138, 146, 154
Douglass, Frederick, 17, 148
Du Bois, W. E. B., 103, 179
Dulay, Sofronio, 222–23
Durand, Auguste, 188
Dvořák, Antonín, 15, 152
Dwellers in the Western World, The, 191

economic issues, 32, 47, 52, 149
Edison Concert Band, 106
education: at the 1904 World's Fair, 74–76, 95; Loving's, 4, 19, 125, 135, 160, 171, 225–26; musical, 14, 34; and PC Band, 163; in the Philippines, 45, 47, 69, 219, 240; PPIE, 178, 184, 186, 192

Edwards, Clarence R., 117
Eide, Coodalook, 176
Eilenberg, Richard, 138, 249n10; "First Heart Throbs" by, 130, 138, 154
electricity: electric sound amplification, 39; electrical outage, 116, 216; and modernity, 86–87
elite cultures: Black, 19, 33, 63, 99–100, 103, 148–49, 151–54; Filipino, 10, 22–23, 46–47, 52, 75–76, 172, 214; and PC Band, 18, 60, 124, 135, 151–54, 188; and US music, 12–15, 94–96
empire: European, 39; and military bands, 32, 38; Spanish, 51. *See also* empire, United States
empire, United States, 28; and the 1904 World's Fair, 74, 109; and band music, 32, 229; and GGIE, 218–19; and the PC Band, 5, 16, 82, 141–42, 168, 236, 241. *See also* imperialism
encores, 132, 138, 146, 153, 164, 170, 194, 238
ensembles, 40–41; as middlebrow, 96, 236; military bands as, 37–38; PC Band as, 127, 129, 144, 171, 188–89; in the Philippines, 44, 46–47, 93; and recordings, 133
entertainment industry: and 1904 World's Fair, 95, 100–102; and Black musicians, 63; and blackface minstrelsy, 85, 100; and Filipino musicians, 63–64, 69, 229
equality: and Black Americans, 19, 55, 99, 102, 148–49, 152; equal rights, 10, 149; and Filipinos, 24–25, 55, 71, 82, 139, 160, 176; inequalities, 7, 72; and PC Band, 33, 91, 118, 194, 208; and white women, 176
Escamilla, Antonio, 120, 128, 138, 140, 163
ethnologists, 20, 75, 77, 120, 140, 161, 179, 284
ethnomusicologists, 20, 29, 30–31, 244n13
ethnosympathy, 16, 71, 91, 103, 109, 151
eugenics, 77, 175, 178–79, 181, 191, 193, 249n1
Euro-American music: at 1904 World's Fair, 96, 99, 108; and Filipino musicians, 9, 42, 49, 93–95, 151, 167, 235, 240; and military bands, 63–64; and PC band, 6, 12, 17–19, 66, 83–85; and PC band 1909 tour, 119, 121, 125, 138, 208; at PPIE, 183
Europe: and 1904 World's Fair, 94–96; and colonization, 19, 40–41; European influence on Black music, 99–100, 103, 105–6, 151–52, 225; European influence on PC Band, 69, 83–84, 113, 121, 145–48, 151–52, 236–37; European travel writing, 22, 119, 177; Filipino elites in, 45–46; and Filipino music, 20–21, 32, 42–46, 48–50, 117–18, 125, 164, 167, 230; and highbrow culture, 3, 12–15, 94–96, 99, 191; and military bands, 37–39; popular music in, 96; and US immigration, 178. *See also* Euro-American music
Europe, James Reese, 15, 148, 245n9, 249n13
Europe, Mary L., 148, 153–54, 249n14
evolutionary theories, sociocultural: and Black music, 15; and Filipinos, 20, 77, 88, 92–93, 167, 195; and the PC band, 4, 6–7, 68; at PPIE, 178, 183
exceptionalism, US, 8, 16, 18, 24
exoticism, 76, 105, 134, 161, 176, 192, 240
expansion, US, 10–12, 73, 77

Fagen, David, 55
Fajardo, Daniel, 220
fiestas, 5, 48, 241
Filipino composers, 130, 132, 152, 231; Filipino musical labor, 16, 234; Filipino musicality, 6–7, 16, 19, 21–22, 33, 120, 125, 135, 203–4, 228; and Hispanicized culture, 44, 50, 74, 76; and hiya, 24, 164, 244n15; and identity, 24, 31, 120, 130, 141, 243n1; Ilocanos, 61, 82, 87, 206, 223; and imitation, 25–27; infantilization of, 22, 133, 143, 147, 158, 187, 243n4; as insurgents, 51, 53, 60, 245n11; and kundiman music, 46, 230; Lanao Maranaos, 92; Macabebes, 81–82, 87; Moros, 78–79, 87, 93, 104, 246n10, 247n25; music-making, 8, 20–22, 33, 72, 94, 120–21, 147, 151, 235; Muslim, 78, 82–83, 93, 246n10; and "Negrito" designation, 78, 93, 246n9; Pampanguenos in, 133, 136, 144; pensionados, 76, 88, 223; and Pilipino term, 28, 243n1; revolutionaries, 10, 24, 51–53, 55, 58, 60, 121, 197, 243n6; Sama Maranaos in, 92; Suyocs, 88, 92; Tagalogs, 78, 81–82, 87, 133–34, 144, 223–24; Tinguians (Itneg), 88, 92; as "uncivilized," 6, 68, 89, 94, 108; Visayans,

61, 74, 82, 87, 134, 136, 144, 223–24. *See also* bandsmen, Filipino; Igorots ("Igorrotes"); nationalism, Philippine; "tribal people," Filipinos as

Filipinos: agency of, 32, 34, 51, 72, 121, 130, 138, 144; Antonio Escamilla, 120, 128, 138, 140, 163; and artistic expression, 28, 46, 50, 230–31; autonomy of, 18–19, 24, 63, 144, 240; Black and Filipino racialization, 70–71, 77, 78–79, 113, 120, 186; in California, 34, 222–25, 251n17, 251n21; and civilization discourse, 6–7, 9–10, 16, 19–20, 120–22, 130, 145, 163, 237–38; and colonial resistance, 18, 49, 53, 60, 76, 213, 231; as "colored," 86, 127, 150; and compositions, 43, 47–48, 120–21, 130, 132, 194–95, 197, 214, 229–31; and creativity, 9–10, 23, 25–28, 44, 229; culture of, 19, 23–29, 41–42, 44, 225–26, 234, 236–38, 240–41; and discipline, 4, 6, 50, 69, 79, 135, 236; and "dog-eater" stereotype, 33, 79, 88, 92, 240; and elite culture, 10, 22–23, 46–47, 52, 75–76, 172, 214; and entertainment industry, 63–64, 69, 229; and equality, 24–25, 55, 71, 82, 139, 160, 176; and Euro-American music, 9, 42, 49, 93–95, 151, 167, 235, 240; evolutionary about, 20, 77, 88, 92–93, 167, 195; Felipe Padilla de León, 230; Filipino Agricultural Laborer's Association, 224

Fischer, Eugene P., 109
Fisk, Asa F., 143
Fisk Jubilee Singers, 151
Flandrau, Charles E., 56–57
Flores, Maidan, 128–29, 189, 209
folk music: Black, 15; and European music, 69, 95; Jewish, 247n27; in the Philippines, 214, 248n5
Forbes, Cameron, 172
Foucault, Michel, 235
France, 15, 145, 213, 245n9; Garde Républicaine Band of Paris, 4, 136, 145, 183, 213, 216, 218, 249n12
Fresnido, Alfonso J., 201–2, 209–11, 213, 220, 228–29, 232–33
Fresnido, Virgilio Ruiz, 218, 228–29, 232, 251n25

Galloway, John W., 54
Gamalinda, Emilio N., 218, 245n15, 248n43, 249n3
Gamalinda, Irene Navarro, 29, 245n15
Garde Républicaine Band of Paris, 4, 136, 145, 183, 213, 216, 218, 249n12
gender, 175–76, 187, 243n1; masculinity, 25, 48, 175. *See also* women
genre: band music as, 7, 12–13, 23, 235; Black music, 17, 96–99, 104, 151; Filipino genres, 43, 45–46, 230, 247n24
Genroku Hanami Odori, 229
Germany, 45, 108
Gilbert, Newton W., 203
Go, Julian, 23
Golden Gate International Exposition (GGIE), 1939, 34–35, 129, 201–2, 215, 220–29, 246n6
Goldman, Edwin Franco, 220–21; Goldman Band, 220
Gonzalves, Theodore, 24
Goodrich, J. Wallace, 57
Gottschild, Brenda Dixon, 95
Gould, Helen, 112
government, Philippine: civil government in, 60, 63; commonwealth, 215, 226–27; and PC Band, 219; insular, 5, 60, 81, 123, 184–85, 215; self-government, 10, 22, 52, 184, 188, 201, 209; Spanish colonial in, 51; US colonial in, 5, 58, 71, 76, 79–82, 88, 110, 114, 173–74, 204
government, United States, 69, 71; and Filipino immigration, 223; Government Indian Band, United States, 108–9; House of Representatives, 107; and PC Band, 155, 158, 208; and Philippine colonization, 5, 58, 71, 76, 79–82, 88, 110, 114, 173–74, 204
Grenadier Guards Band, 4, 136, 145, 249n12
Gruet Orchestra, 46
Guam, 10–11, 107
Guerrero, Leon Ma., 75, 184–85, 195–96

habitus, 21, 159
Hall, Stuart, 120, 235
Hammond, Wade H., 205–6
Handel, George Frederic, 140, 220

Harrison, Francis Burton, 196
Hawaii, 11, 77, 83–84, 143, 168–71, 199, 250n5; *Hawaiian Gazette*, 122, 128; Honolulu in, 83, 169–71, 227
hegemony, cultural, 10, 24; at 1904 World's Fair, 72, 77, 94; and 1909 PC Band tour, 119, 126; white musical, 12, 16, 26, 38, 126, 234
Herbert, Victor, 95, 188, 195
Hersey, Mark, 123
"Hiawatha" (Moret), 78, 97, 104, 247n23, 247n24, 247n25
high class, 12, 65, 83, 95, 100, 140, 189; "highbrow," 3, 11, 14, 96, 124
Hila, Antonio C., 204
hiya, 24, 164, 244n15
"Home Sweet Home," 227
Houston, Whitney, 27
Howard University, 129, 203, 216
Hudson, Lynn M., 178–79, 181
hybridity, 20, 44, 142, 230, 244n2

identity: cultural, 27; Filipino, 24, 31, 120, 130, 141, 243n1; indigenous Philippine, 82; Loving's racial, 5, 70, 84–85, 122–24, 148, 158, 160, 163–64, 171–72, 181, 189, 217; self, 26
Igorots ("Igorrotes"), 33, 115, 161, 171, 246n9; at 1904 World's Fair, 71, 77–79, 82, 89, 92, 114
Ileto, Reynaldo, 24, 218–19
Ilocanos, 61, 82, 87, 206, 223
imitation, 25–27
immigration: 1917 Immigration Acts, 11, 186; 1924 Immigration Act, 11, 186, 223; Asian, 11, 84, 181–82, 186, 223, 236; Chinese, 98, 259n28; Filipino to US, 25, 30–31, 86, 224–25; Irish, 11, 98; and US racism, 98, 175, 178, 244n1
"imperial ear," 6–10, 16–19, 21, 27, 120, 234, 240–41; at 1904 World's Fair, 33, 74, 82, 103, 117–18; and PC Band 1909 tour, 125, 133, 136, 141, 167; and Philippine colonialism, 42, 60, 66, 68–69
imperialism, United States, 4, 11, 15–16, 20, 22–24, 31–32, 99; and 1904 World's Fair, 74–77, 92, 110, 114; and 1909 PC Band tour, 133, 138; anti-imperialism, 6, 53, 71, 76, 122, 138; and Black soldiers, 53–54; imperial hearing, 70, 92, 94, 121; imperial pop, 214; and jazz, 214; and military bands, 38, 40; and PC Band resonances, 237–38; and PPIE, 175, 182, 187. *See also* "imperial ear"
independence, Philippine: and colonial bands, 40–41; Filipino assertion of, 34, 71, 91, 184–87, 195–96, 238; from Spain, 10, 51, 197; from US, 174, 186, 189, 204, 209, 211–12, 218, 225, 233
India, 38–39
indigenous people: at 1904 World's Fair, 74, 76–78; Alaskan, 176; Haskell Indian Band, 108; Hawaiian, 84–85; indios in Philippines, 38, 47; Native Americans, 71, 92, 108; in Philippines, 38–50, 74, 82–83, 92, 115, 230, 245n11, 246n5; US Government Indian Band, 108–9. *See also* natives, Filipinos as
infantilization, Filipino, 22, 133, 143, 147, 158, 187, 243n4
instruments: at AYP exhibition, 161, 164–65; brass, 37–50, 159, 239; of empire, 5, 32, 38–39, 113, 141, 213, 229–30, 241; indigenous Filipino, 78; and military bands, 38–40, 50, 109, 136; and PC Band reviews, 132–33, 142, 153, 159, 237; reed, 14, 187–88, 239, 243n8; string, 45, 96, 113, 159, 167, 228, 239; trombones, 188, 228; violins, 45, 62, 159, 166, 187–88, 228, 239
insular government, Philippine, 5, 60, 81, 123, 184–85, 215
insurgents, Filipino revolutionaries as, 51, 53, 60, 245n11
insurrection, Filipino resistance as, 10, 28, 53–54, 60, 197
invisibility: of Filipino culture, 15, 22, 24, 42, 60, 240; of Loving's race, 171
Irish immigrants, 11, 98
Irving, D. R. M., 43, 46

Jackson, Ida Joyce, 101
Jacobe, Gayetano, 159
Japan: and PC Band, 57, 122, 143, 183; and Philippine occupation, 201, 205, 227–33; and PPIE, 181–82; and US racism, 11, 79

jazz, 100, 183, 213–14, 224, 245n5
Jefferson Guards, 110–12
Jim Crow, 73, 75, 80–81, 100, 178–80
Johnson, James Weldon, 105, 249n13
Johnston, William H., 79, 110–11
Jones Bill, 174
Joplin, Scott, 101–2, 106, 247n21; "The Entertainer" by, 101, 106
Jordan, David Starr, 179
Juan, Baldermero Ian, 141

Kalaw, Teodoro M., 172, 249n16
Kasman, Aida G., 30, 241
Kasman, Edward S., 30, 241
Kellogg, John H., 179
Korean War, 234
Kramer, Paul, 22, 32, 53, 60; on 1904 World's Fair, 71, 74, 88; on PPIE, 185, 195
Kroeger, Ernest, 94
kulintang ensembles, 93–94
kundiman music, 46, 230
Kunkel, Charles, 104

labor: and Asian immigration to US, 11, 98; Filipino, 21, 25, 89, 145, 234, 237, 241; military, 60; musical, 7, 16, 21, 27–28, 121, 147, 189, 193, 199, 222; racialized, 177–78, 199
Lacuna, Urbano, 55
Lamar, William Bailey, 185
La Traviata, 124, 189
Layton, John T., 148, 153
legend of PC Band, 34, 48–49, 215–19; lights-out legend, 29, 49, 114, 116, 145, 213, 216–19
Levine, Lawrence, 11
Liliuokalani, Queen, 168
Liongson, Francisco, 184–85
Lippay, Alexander, 228, 251n24
Liszt, Franz, 95, 163, 189, 250n8
little brown men trope: and 1904 World's Fair, 71, 75, 91, 109; and 1909 PC Band tour, 119–20, 129–30, 142–47, 158–59, 170–71; and Filipino music, 19, 240; little brown brothers, 9, 18, 22, 91, 109, 122, 135, 166, 226; "Little Brown Brother" song, 98; little brown stepbrothers, 143–45; and PC Band, 16, 26, 33, 235–36; and PPIE, 187;

Sousa and, 190, 249n3; Taft and, 33, 109, 134–36, 156, 243n4
Lohengrin, 164
loób, 142, 219; utang na loób, 24, 203, 244n15
Lott, Eric, 85
Louisiana Purchase Exposition (LPE), 1904, 7; comparison to AYP exposition, 151, 161, 187, 189–90, 192, 195, 197; Filipinos and race in, 20, 73–82, 88–89, 92–94, 134; musical genres at, 94–109; PC band in, 3–5, 32–34, 67–73, 83–91, 96–102, 105–9, 112–18, 129–30; and PC band legacy, 49, 145, 213, 215, 219–20, 222–23; Philippine Exposition Board at, 73–75, 82, 88, 92, 110, 216, 222; the Pike in, 74, 101–2, 110
Loving, Edith McCary, 190, 201, 206–7
Loving, Walter H., 3–5, 16, 19, 29–30, 32–35, 55–56, 231–42; and 1904 World's Fair, 84–85, 102, 105, 107–8, 112–13; and 1909 PC Band tour, 132–36, 143–48; and AYP Exposition, 163–67, 169–71; career in Philippines, 201–28; and "debt of gratitude," 203; and early PC Band, 64–66; and grandchild Edith Loving Lucas, 129, 157, 234, 242, 250n12; and grandchild Walter Loving III, 129, 205–6, 242, 250n12; in Oakland, California, 34, 123, 178–79, 193, 207, 212, 222; and Pedro Navarro, 35, 62–64, 128–30, 189–90, 204–11, 214, 217, 227; and PPIE, 174, 180–81, 183, 187–90, 193, 198–200; racial identity of, 5, 70, 84–85, 122–24, 148, 158, 160, 163–64, 170–72, 181, 189, 217; and Taft inauguration, 122–30; in US military, 39, 56–59, 61; and US racial atmosphere, 70, 96–97, 99–100, 139; and Washington, DC Black community, 151–60
Loving, Walter, III, 129, 205–6, 242, 250n12
Lowe, Lisa, 236
Lucas, Edith Loving, 129, 157, 234, 242, 250n12
Lucia di Lammermoor, 46, 124, 138, 146, 154
Luneta Park concerts, PC Band, 30, 64–65, 140–41, 197, 206, 209, 211–13
lynching, 54, 103, 111, 224

Mabalon, Dawn Bohulano, 224
Macabebes, 81–82, 87

MacArthur, Douglas, 228–29
Magellan, Ferdinand, 30, 73, 145
Magsaysay, Ramon, 233
Manalansan, Martin F., 24, 26
manifest destiny, 8, 70, 74
Manila, Philippines, 31–32; and 1904 World's Fair, 73–74, 82–83; Ermita district in, 231; gay beauty pageants in, 26; Intramuros in, 51, 65, 232; Manila Bay, 10, 51, 82–83; Manila Carnival, 171; music scene in, 43–46, 97; PC Band in, 99, 117, 139–40, 171–72, 199–200, 202–7, 214–15, 226–28, 231–33; and PC Band formation, 61–66; US military in, 51–52, 57–58
Marasigan, Cynthia, 54, 205
marching bands, 3, 44, 113, 126, 236, 243n8
Marcos, Ferdinand, 31, 234
Marcos, Imelda, 234, 254n31
Marikina Orchestra, 46
Marine Band, United States, 4, 27, 37, 107, 127, 149–50, 189–90, 226; PC Band comparison to, 129–30, 139, 239
Marine Corps, United States, 13, 110–11, 180. *See also* Marine Band, United States
Markwyn, Abigail, 174, 175, 177
martial music, 161, 165
Martine, Lomberne, 135
masculinity, 25, 48, 175
Maya, Rouva Mayi, 176
McCary, Edith, 190
McCary, Michael, 190
McGee, William J., 74–75
McKinley, William, 4, 10, 16, 52, 60
media: Filipino racialization in, 6, 33, 76–77, 90, 234; mainstream, 6, 26; mass, 121; PC Band in, 121, 158, 234. *See also* newspapers
Mediavello, José, 135
mehter bands, Ottoman, 38, 42
melody: and European music, 43, 49; and Filipino musicians, 93, 231; and PC Band, 4, 85, 133, 145, 165, 231
Mendelssohn, Felix, 46, 95, 170
Mercado, Pedro, 48
Mexican bands, 108, 145, 249n12
middle class, 12, 14, 16, 18–19, 99, 107, 149, 151; middlebrow music, 13, 65, 96, 236

military: Asiatic Squadron, United States, 10, 51; independent military organizations, 126–27; Japanese in Philippines, 228–34; Loving and, 32–34, 55–56, 63–65, 84, 108, 135–36, 187, 190, 202, 208; Marine Corps, United States, 13, 110–11, 180; Philippine, 65, 71–72, 75–78, 82, 88, 109, 111; Philippine Army (PA) Band, 34, 201, 215–16, 220–21, 223–29, 233; at PPIE, 180, 183, 186, 192; US in Philippines, 54–56, 60, 63–64, 90–91, 203. *See also* Army, United States; Marine Band, United States; military band music
military band music, 4–6, 12–13, 37–39, 43, 65, 91, 144; at 1904 World's Fair, 108; and colonialism, 32, 39–42; Filipino, 19, 23; Loving's study of, 136; US, 49–52
mimicry: Black musicians and, 100; colonization and, 9; Filipino musicians and, 6, 15, 24–28, 50, 240; PC Band and, 34, 49, 130, 136, 144, 188, 190, 221
Mindt, Charles, 63
minstrelsy, 13–14, 63–64, 85, 97–100, 102, 151, 247n24
Minuet No. 1, 138, 146
missionaries, Christian, 43–45
model minority stereotype, 236, 244n14
modernity, 40–41, 50–51, 87; and 1904 World's Fair, 87; and Black soldiers, 99; and PC Band, 69, 136; in the Philippines, 43, 49–51
Moonlight Sonata, 138, 164
Moore, Charles, 180, 182, 185, 195–96
Moore, Sarah, 175
Morales, Charles, 185
Moros, 78–79, 87, 93, 104, 246n10, 247n25; and kulintang ensembles, 93–94
music: African American traditions, 13–18, 63–66, 71, 94–96, 99–107, 139, 151–55; Asian traditions, 167, 229–30; and colonization, 21–25, 34–35, 38–42, 46, 66, 68, 121, 212–14; ethnomusicologists, 20, 29, 30–31, 244n13; Filipino musicality, 6–7, 16, 19, 21–22, 33, 120, 125, 135, 203–4, 228; jazz, 100, 183, 213–14, 224, 245n5; kundiman, 46, 230; martial music, 161, 165; middlebrow, 13, 65, 96, 236; musical

aesthetics, 188; musical ensembles, 37, 93, 129, 171; musical hegemony, 12, 64; musical labor, 7, 16, 21, 27–28, 121, 147, 189, 193, 199; musicianship, 7, 16, 21, 83, 113, 124, 142, 153, 220–21, 236; musicking, 40, 42, 66; musicologists, 20, 29, 31, 57, 94, 244n13; "musicopoetic" genres, 43–44; popular, 12–15, 94–96, 99, 103–5, 183, 190, 214; "primitive," 4, 13, 20, 69, 92–94, 109, 224; ragtime, 11, 13–16, 83, 94–107, 139, 151, 183, 245n9, 247n21; reading, 34, 194, 221, 245n5; recordings of, 104, 132–33, 166; sarsuela (zarzuela), 46, 230; spirituals, 15, 17, 19, 71, 151; two-step, 96–97, 99, 105–6; waltzes, 25, 64, 106, 138, 145, 188, 194. *See also* band music; banda tradition; brass bands; classical music; compositions; concerts; Euro-American music; folk music; genre; instruments; military band music; music-making; musical performance; natural, Filipino music talent as; performance, musical; repertoire; songs; symphonies

musical performance, 21, 31, 40, 167, 191; at the 1904 World's Fair, 104; and PC Band, 66, 84, 124, 132, 144, 150–51, 153, 208, 235, 237–38

music-making: Black, 16; Filipino, 8, 20–22, 33, 72, 94, 120–21, 147, 151, 235; indigenous, 43; PC Band, 10, 18, 26, 28, 82, 127, 144, 187

musicologists, 20, 29, 31, 57, 94, 244n13

Muslim Filipinos, 78, 82–83, 93, 246n10

Musurgia Glee Club, 129

Myddleton, W. H., 139

Nagai, Matsuzo, 182
national anthems: Japanese, 229; Philippine, 61, 197, 215, 230–31; US, 65, 69, 169, 212, 215. *See also* Star-Spangled Banner
National Association for the Advancement of Colored People (NAACP), 178
National Association of Colored Women, 101
nationalism, Philippine, 24–25, 65, 211–12, 237; at 1904 World's Fair, 76; and Japanese occupation, 229, 234; and PC Band, 34, 65, 172, 187; at PPIE, 187, 189; and US independence, 225

Native Americans, 77, 92, 108–9, 246n4; Haskell Indian Band, 108; US Government Indian Band, 108–9. *See also* Indigenous people
natives, Filipinos as, 243n6, 245n11; at 1904 World's Fair, 67, 74, 76, 79–81, 93, 112; and 1909 PC Band tour, 122, 127, 133, 135–36, 142–43, 148, 157, 163; and Black soldiers in US, 52, 54–55, 61; and Filipino music, 24, 38, 40–50, 120; and PC Band in the Philippines, 214–15, 218; at PPIE, 184, 192, 196–97; and US colonization, 6, 16, 22. *See also* "tribal people," Filipinos as
nativism, 11, 179, 186, 224–25
natural, Filipino music talent as, 6–9, 18–19, 21–22, 33–34, 221, 235, 240; at 1904 World's Fair, 68, 92, 100–101, 103, 109, 118; and 1909 PC Band tour, 119–21, 133, 136, 145, 156, 159–61, 170–71; at PPIE, 177
Navarrete, Rex, 28
Navarro, Bartola, 62
Navarro, Bienvenido, 128, 245n15
Navarro, Emilio, 241, 249n3, 250n2, 251n25
Navarro, Irene Gamalinda, 29, 206, 245n14, 245n15
Navarro, Leonora, 232, 250n14
Navarro, Pedro B., 29, 35, 125, 241; and 1904 World's Fair, 117; and 1909 PC Band tour, 125, 128–31, 159; and all-female brass band, 107; "Enharmonica-Cromatica March" by, 206; and PC Band founding, 60, 62–63; and PC Band leadership, 201–2, 204–7, 210–11, 213, 217, 227, 232–33; and PPIE, 188–90, 199
New England Conservatory of Music, 4, 45, 57, 123, 226
Newman, Louise, 177
newspapers, 4, 6–7, 16, 32–34, 42, 234–35, 237–38; and 1904 World's Fair, 68, 70–72, 77–78, 87–88, 91, 102, 213; and 1909 PC Band tour, 119–22, 125–27, 133–35, 144, 147–48, 154–56, 160, 171; *Afro-American*, 139, 154, 156, 202; Black, 53, 135, 156–58, 180, 215, 249n7; *New York Age*, 135, 158; *New York Times*, 8, 134, 196; and PC Band in the Philippines, 217, 220, 223, 226–27; *Philippines Free Press*, 209, 216, 218, 226,

250n12; and PPIE, 173–74, 179–81, 187–88, 199; *San Francisco Call*, 123, 161, 163, 165, 200; *San Francisco Chronicle*, 164, 177, 181, 183, 191; and US military in Philippines, 48–49, 53, 63; *Washington Post*, 126, 129, 153

Ng, Stephanie, 24, 27

Niederlein, Gustavo, 75

Oakland, California, 34, 123, 178–79, 193, 207, 212, 222

opera: light, 147, 167, 230; overtures, 3, 16; and PC Band, 3, 46, 95–96, 124, 147, 167, 236; in the Philippines, 45–46, 65; and popular music, 13, 15

orchestras: at 1904 World's Fair, 94, 96; and Loving, 65; PC Band as, 113, 127–28, 135, 147, 159, 161, 164–67, 169–70, 226; in the Philippines, 44, 46–47; at PPIE, 187–91, 194–95; Sousa and, 14, 65

orientalism, 86, 126, 129, 134, 143–44, 147, 153, 161

Orquestra Femenina de Pandacan, 46

Ortiz, Father Mariano, 62

overtures: opera, 3, 16, 45–46, 96; and PC Band, 65, 116, 138, 188, 216, 220; and US military bands, 64–65; *William Tell Overture*, 29, 116, 124, 138, 154

Paderewski, Ignacy Jan, 138, 146, 163, 194; Minuet No. 1 by, 138, 146

Pampangueno people, 133, 136, 144

Panama Canal, 175, 177, 179

Panama-Pacific International Exposition (PPIE), 34, 173–74; and Asian immigrants, 181–82; and Black Americans, 178–81; eugenics at, 178–79; Guatemalan marimba band at, 194; Joy Zone at, 174, 176, 179, 181–82, 192, 195; masculinity at, 175–77; official exposition band at, 183, 189, 192–93, 195; Palace of Education at, 175, 179, 184; and Panama-California Exposition, 175; and Panama Canal, 175, 177, 179; PC Band after, 199–200, 201–2, 217; PC Band at, 183–95, 198–99; Philippine Board at, 184–85, 195–96; Philippine Day at, 195–97; technology at, 177–78; "Underground Slumming" concession in, 182

parades, 3, 41, 56, 81, 113, 180, 192, 222; Taft inauguration, 126–30, 145–46

Paris, France: Garde Républicaine Band of Paris, 4, 136, 145, 183, 213, 216, 218, 249n12; Treaty of Paris, 10, 52, 107

Pasig Band, 48, 172, 213

pasyon plays, 24, 43, 218–19

Paterno, Pedro A., 75

patriotism: and Black soldiers, 53, 56; and Filipinos, 7, 39, 91, 103; patriotic marches, 4, 12, 16–17, 37, 96, 163, 188, 236; and PC Band, 68–69, 71, 109, 120, 141, 163, 236; at PPIE, 174, 181, 183; US, 35, 212, 220, 230

Pedro, Artemio, 227

Pedro, Honorado S., 227

pensionados, 76, 88, 223

performance, musical, 18–22, 31, 33–34, 167, 208, 234–40; at 1904 World's Fair, 68, 82, 84, 100, 104–5, 108–9, 219; and 1909 PC Band tour, 121–22, 132, 144; and Blackface, 85; and Black musicians, 100–103, 151; and colonization, 9, 42; Filipino and Filipino American, 28–29; as mimicry, 25; and PC Band in Philippines, 213; in the Philippines, 38–39, 42–44, 49–50, 63; at PPIE, 184, 192; Sousa and, 191

Philippine-American War, 10, 23, 174, 186; as "insurrection," 10, 28, 53–54, 60, 197; and race, 51, 148, 172

Philippine Army (PA) Band, 34, 201, 215–16, 220–21, 223–29, 233

Philippine Board, PPIE, 184–85, 195–96

Philippine Commission, United States, 34, 60, 69, 168, 196, 212

Philippine Constabulary, 5, 32, 49, 60–61, 63, 205; at 1904 World's Fair, 74, 76–77, 79, 81, 88, 112–13; and 1909 PC Band tour, 134–35, 157; and Philippine Army, 215. *See also* Philippine Constabulary (PC) band

Philippine Constabulary (PC) band: at 1904 World's Fair, 3–5, 32–34, 67–73, 83–91, 96–102, 105–9, 112–18, 129–30; 1909 tour of, 119–25, 134–48; at the Academy of Music in Brooklyn, 134; in Atlantic City, New Jersey, 156–58, 160, 164; at the AYP

Exposition, 160–68; beginning of, 61, 63–66; at the Belasco Theater, 142, 147; and benefit concerts, 174, 192–93, 195; at concert halls, 3, 7, 29, 122, 161; and encores, 132, 138, 146, 153, 164, 170, 194, 238; at Festival Hall, 116; and "Hail to the Chief," 126, 168; in Hawaii, 168–71; and independent military organizations, 126–27; legend of, 29, 34, 48–49, 114, 116, 145, 213, 215–19; and Loving's identity, 5, 70, 84–85, 122–24, 148, 158, 160, 163–64, 171–72, 181, 189, 217; Luneta Park concerts, 30, 64–65, 140–41, 197, 206, 209, 211–13; as "Malay musicians," 135, 156; and Marine Band comparisons, 129–30, 139, 239; and Navarro leadership, 201–2, 204–7, 210–11, 213, 217, 227, 232–33; in the Philippines, 172, 201–28, 234–38; Philippine Scouts band comparisons, 32, 48, 77, 109, 113, 114, 246n1; and PPIE, 183–95, 198–202, 217; at Taft Inaugural Ball, 123, 127–30, 154–55; at US Capitol, 126, 250; and Washington, DC Black community, 148–56

Philippines, the: Aetas (Negritos) in, 78, 92–93, 246n9; Army of, 55, 215, 228, 233; Baguio in, 207, 233; Bataan province in, 207, 228–29; beauty pageants in, 26–27; Bicolano people in, 133–34, 136, 144; Bontoc groups in, 88–89, 92; Camp Crame in, 213, 233, 241; Cavite province in, 51, 207, 213; civil government in, 60, 63; as commonwealth, 215, 220, 227; Cordillera region in, 33, 88, 245n11, 246n5; Constables in, 71, 81–82, 85–87; Constitution of, 52; diversity of, 41, 73–75, 78, 81, 87, 122, 134, 237; fiestas in, 5, 48, 241; Igorots ("Igorrotes"), 33, 115, 161, 171, 246n9; Ilocanos in, 61, 82, 87, 206, 223; Ilocos Sur in, 61–62; Intramuros in, 51, 65, 232; Japanese occupation of, 201, 205, 227–33; and kundiman music, 46, 230; La Union province in, 59, 61, 223; Lanao Maranaos in, 92; Luzon in, 43, 80, 142; Macabebes in, 81–82, 87; military of, 34, 65, 71–72, 75–78, 82, 88, 109, 111, 228; Moros in, 78–79, 87, 93, 104, 246n10, 247n25; multicultural society in, 206, 220; Muslim Filipinos, 78, 82–83, 93, 246n10; National Anthem of, 61, 197, 215, 230–31; Pampanguenos in, 133, 136, 144; PC Band in, 172, 201–28, 234–38; Philippine Band of Manila, 63; Philippine Commission, United States, 34, 60, 69, 168, 196, 212; Philippine Exposition board, 1904 World's Fair, 73–75, 82, 88, 92, 110, 216, 222; revolutionaries in, 10, 24, 51–53, 55, 58, 60, 121, 197, 243n6; Sama Maranaos in, 92; and sarsuela, 46, 230; sovereignty of, 10, 51–52, 141, 186, 212, 225; Suyocs in, 88, 92; Tagalogs in, 78, 81–82, 87, 133–34, 144, 223–24; tambakan tradition in, 48–49, 51, 114; Tinguians (Itneg) in, 88, 92; and Tydings-McDuffie Act, 224–25; University of Santo Tomas in, 30, 45, 231–32; Visayans, 61, 74, 82, 87, 134, 136, 144, 223–24. *See also* government, Philippine; independence, Philippine; Manila, Philippines; nationalism, Philippine; Philippine-American War; "tribal people," Filipinos as

Philippine Scouts, 32, 49, 59–60, 63, 71–72, 74, 76–82, 88–90, 109–14; Philippine Scouts band, 32, 48, 77, 109, 113, 114, 246n1

Philippines Free Press, 209, 216, 218, 226, 250n12

phonographs, 93, 104
pianos, 45, 102, 104, 106, 133, 138, 247n21
plantations: in Hawaii, 11, 223; and US racism, 102, 179
Poet and Peasant overture, 138
policing, 78, 111, 126; Philippine Constabulary and, 5, 60–61, 123, 157
popular, 12–15, 94–96, 99, 103–5, 183, 190, 214
Portola, Don Gaspar de, 192–93
power, 21–22; colonial, 23, 40, 50, 72, 87, 109, 119, 222, 237; dynamics, 239; imperial, 10, 40; white, 61, 191
Pratt, Mary Louise, 7, 119, 177, 237
"primitive" music, 4, 13, 20, 69, 92–94, 109, 224
Principe, Rafael, 117
propaganda, 7, 208
Pu Lun, 104

Puccini, Giacomo, 230
Puerto Rico, 10–11, 77, 107, 250n5

Quezon, Aurora, 220
Quezon, Manuel L., 34, 186, 195–96, 206–8, 215, 217, 219–20, 226

race: and Filipinos at World's Fair, 20, 73–82, 88–89, 92–94, 134; and Loving's identity, 5, 70, 84–85, 122–24, 148, 158, 160, 163–64, 171–72, 181, 189, 217; multiracial collaboration, 149; Race Betterment Foundation, 175, 179; racial anxieties, 10–12, 18, 149; racial-colonial ideology, 190, 235; racial difference, 70, 104, 150, 159; racial domination, 21, 49, 84, 236; racial hierarchy, 16, 22, 33–34, 67–68, 124, 127, 240; racial imagination, 18–19, 24; racial others, 12, 15, 18, 20–21, 70, 77, 96, 166, 171, 235, 238; racial uplift, 19, 33, 99, 103, 148–50, 152, 177, 208, 225; racialization of music, 20–21, 66, 91, 124, 166. *See also* Black communities; Filipino communities; racism; white Americans
racism: anti-Asian, 181–82; anti-Black, 5, 22, 32, 39, 53–55, 103, 128–29; anti-Filipino, 16, 22, 53–55, 86, 123, 176, 224; anti-Japanese, 11, 79; blackface, 85, 98, 179, 247n24; derogatory stereotypes, 68, 97, 106–7, 151, 238, 246n10; discriminatory practices, 8, 24, 101–2, 172, 180, 223; eugenics, 77, 175, 178–79, 181, 191, 193, 249n1; and PC Band, 8, 85–86; at PPIE, 175, 178–79; of Sousa, 14; and white supremacy, 18, 21–22, 72, 159, 179, 189, 239; xenophobia, 11, 186; yellowface, 98; "yellow peril," 236. *See also* "savage" racial designation; segregation; stereotypes; white superiority
Rafael, Vicente, 9, 22–23, 25, 90–91
ragtime, 11, 13–16, 83, 94–107, 139, 151, 183, 245n9, 247n21
Ramos, Gilbert, 241
recordings, musical, 104, 132–33, 166
reed instruments, 14, 187–88, 239, 243n8
regimental bands, 15, 38, 47, 49, 57, 63, 205
Reily, Suzel Ana, 42

religion, 17, 24, 38, 43–44, 103. *See also* Christianity
repertoire: at 1904 World's Fair, 94–97, 108; and Black musicians, 153–54; Euro-American band, 6, 12, 21, 24, 27, 235; and Filipino music, 20, 45–46; of military bands, 38, 40; and PC Band, 17, 33, 66, 83, 99–100, 105–6, 121, 132–33, 136; and PC Band legacy, 208, 238; Sousa's, 13–14
Requiem, 190
revolutionaries, Filipino, 10, 24, 51–53, 55, 58, 60, 121, 197, 243n6
rhythm: and PC Band, 133, 139, 144; racialized understandings of, 11, 27, 93–96, 104, 247n22; and ragtime, 13, 96–98, 249n13; rhythmic patterns, 93–94
Richardson, Claiborne T., 202, 221, 227, 231, 244n22, 246n6, 250n14
Richardson, John, 72
Rigoletto, 164
rituals, 77, 92, 212
Rivera, Leonora, 223
Rizal Orchestra, 46
Rolph, James, 180, 195
Romano, Alejandro T., 228, 233
Roosevelt, Alice, 103
Roosevelt, Theodore, 10, 52, 56, 59, 122–23, 175; at 1904 World's Fair, 92, 114; and Booker T. Washington, 122, 149; PC Band escort of, 126; and Quezon, 215
Rosa, Fabian de la, 184
Ross, Burton R., 145–46
Rossini, Gioachino, 65, 116, 124, 138, 220
Rubio, Hilarion F., 49–50
Rydell, Robert, 32, 182

Samson, Helen F., 231
Samuel Coleridge-Taylor Choral Society, 148–50, 152–55
Sandugong Panaginip, 65
San Francisco: AYP in, 160–61, 163–66; GGIE in, 1939, 34–35, 129, 201–2, 215, 220–29, 246n6; PC Band in, 83, 85, 117, 122–23, 168; PPIE in, 174–75, 178–95, 200; San Francisco Bay, 57, 168, 192; *San Francisco Call*, 123, 161, 163, 165, 200; *San Francisco Chronicle*, 164, 177, 181, 183, 191

Santiago, Francisco, 214; University of Santo Tomas in, 30, 45, 231–32
Santos, Ramón P., 230
sarsuela, 46, 230
"savage" racial designation, 6–8, 16, 59; at 1904 World's Fair, 32–33, 67–68, 71, 76–78, 82, 88–90, 92, 109; and 1909 PC Band tour, 121–22, 134, 161; and Black Americans, 13–14; and PC Band, 26, 69; at PPIE, 184, 186, 195–96
Schenbeck, Lawrence, 99, 103
Schenker, Frederick, 214
Schudson, Michael, 119
Scott, Emmett J., 204, 207
Scott, James C., 42, 49
Scott, William Henry, 35, 72
See, Sarita, 27–28
segregation: of Asian immigrants, 11; and Black Americans, 32, 39, 56, 103, 150, 208; and PC Band, 40, 239; in the Philippines, 41, 44
self-government, Philippine, 10, 22, 52, 184, 188, 201, 209
Sellner, George, 158, 169
Selmes, Tilden, 56, 59
Senate, United States, 52, 59, 186
sensationalism, 68, 88, 100, 119, 122, 134–35, 159, 161
sexualized stereotypes, 25, 144, 186–87; of Filipina women, 186–87
Silos, José, 207, 233
singing, 27, 93, 142, 148; of national anthems, 54, 231
slavery, 55, 85, 89, 102, 109; abolition of, 16–17, 19, 98; and spirituals, 15, 17, 71
Small, Christopher, 42
Smith, James, 172
social mobility, 47, 61, 171
social norms, 41, 73, 110, 124
Sociedad Musical Filipina Santa Cecilia, 46
sociocultural evolutionary theory, 4, 16, 68, 167
soldiers, United States, 60, 212, 229; Black, 5, 32, 53–56, 63–64, 98–99, 113, 180; Filipino, 111–14; PC Band as, 135, 157; Philippine Scouts, 79–80, 87, 90
soloists, 29, 40, 130, 132, 141, 148, 153, 237

songs: "Aires Filipinas," 65; "All Coons Look Alike to Me," 54, 100, 245n7; "Aloha Oe," 169–70; "Amoureuse," 138, 249n10; "Auld Lang Syne," 30, 64, 198, 202; "Awit sa Paglikha ng Bagong Filipinas," 230–31; "Bedelia," 78, 97–98, 113; "Beelzebub," 153, 164; "The Belle of the Philippines," 106; "The Black Man," 191; "coon songs," 13, 53–54, 96–102, 105–7, 113, 245n9; "Cosmopolitan America, March," 106; "The Cotton Pickers," 104; "Dance of the Hours," 138; "Dixie," 116; "The Entertainer," 101, 106; "First Heart Throbs," 130, 138, 154; "Germinal, Two-Step," 106; "Hail to the Chief," 126, 168; "Hail to the Spirit of Liberty," 164, 167; "Hiawatha," 78, 97, 104, 247n23, 247n24, 247n25; "Janice Meredith, Waltzes," 106; "Jolliar, Two-Step," 105–6; "La Bella Filipina," 132; "La Gioconda," 130, 138; "La Paloma," 170; "La Sampaguita," 132; "Liga Ilocana," 206; "Los Banderilleros," 220; "Lupang Hinirang," 197, 231; "Ma Ragtime Baby," 106; "Marcha de los Colectivistas," 219; "Monkeys Have No Tails in Zamboanga," 98; "My Country, 'Tis of Thee," 37, 92, 191; "Navajo," 113; "Popular Songs of Ilocanos," 206; "Potpourri of Filipino Airs," 138, 163; "The Red Man," 191; "Rose Mousse," 139, 251; "The Sleeping Beauty and the Beast," 195; *The Song of Hiawatha*, 149–50, 153–54; "Songs of the Philippines," 120, 140; "Spring Song," 170; "Stars and Stripes Forever," 3, 27, 37, 65, 146, 190; "Suite de Valses 'España,'" 138; "Tindig, Aking Inang-Bayan," 230; "Tipperary," 191, 249n4; "Turkey in the Straw," 13–14; "Under the Rose, Waltzes," 106; "The White Man," 191. *See also* national anthems; Star-Spangled Banner
sound, 14, 18, 142, 214; and military band music, 37, 39–42; recorded, 104–5, 133
Sousa, John Philip, 13–15, 65, 95–96, 106–8, 146, 187–92; *At the King's Court* suite, 189; "The Black Man," 191; "Hail to the Spirit of Liberty," 164, 167; and PC Band, 27, 29–30, 84, 91, 125; "The Red Man," 191; Sousa

marches, 3, 83, 120, 124, 163–64, 167, 189, 214; Sousa's band, 183, 216, 236; "Stars and Stripes Forever," 3, 27, 37, 65, 146, 190; "Tipperary," 191, 249n4; "The White Man," 191
South, US, 11–12, 73, 80, 104, 123, 164
sovereignty, Philippine, 10, 51–52, 141, 186, 212, 225
Spain: Army of, 38, 47; in California, 192–93; missionaries from, 45; and music in Philippines, 5, 23, 38, 43–51, 56, 61–63, 145; and Philippine independence, 4, 10, 52, 197, 243n6; Spanish-American War, 10, 51–52, 63, 78, 98, 126, 180
Spanish-American War, 10, 51–52, 63, 78, 98, 126, 180
spectacles, 18, 25–26, 32, 125, 143, 147, 153, 240
spirituals, 15, 17, 19, 71, 151
"Spring Song," 170
Stabat Mater, 220
Stalsquez, Rosendo, 135
"Stars and Stripes Forever" (John Philip Sousa), 3, 27, 37, 65, 146, 190
Star-Spangled Banner, 20, 37, 64–65, 192, 197–98, 212–13, 239; at 1904 World's Fair, 7, 67, 90–91, 108, 116; and 1909 PC Band tour, 141, 144, 154, 169; as US national anthem, 65, 69, 169, 212, 215
Stephens, Virginia, 181
stereotypes: about Black Americans, 85, 100, 105, 150, 186, 226, 238; about Chinese immigrants, 98, 182; about Filipinos, 7–9, 21–23, 33, 68, 91, 121–22, 132–33, 236, 238; Orientalist, 144
St. Louis, Missouri, 73, 76, 80, 109, 116. *See also* World's Fair, 1904 St. Louis
Stockton, California, 223–25
string instruments, 45, 96, 113, 159, 167, 228, 239
suffragists, 176–77
Suppé, Franz von, 64, 138, 167
Suyocs, 88, 92
symphonies, 13, 101, 103; as high class, 95–96; and PA Band, 220, 223, 225; and PC Band, 16, 159, 164, 166–67, 169–70, 228, 236, 240; and Sousa, 191, 216; symphony halls, 12, 15, 33, 49, 135; symphony orchestras, 141, 144, 161, 164, 166–67, 169–70
syncopation, 13, 96–98, 102, 104–6, 139

Taft, Helen, 138–39, 156, 245n12
Taft, William Howard, 76, 81–82, 98, 134–36, 138–41, 146, 148, 208; and AYP Exposition, 160–64, 167–68; inauguration of, 33, 121–23, 126; and "little brown brother" trope, 109, 243n4; and PC Band formation, 5, 59–61; and Philippine independence, 186; Taft Glee Club, 129; as Tio Guillermo, 161
Tagalogs, 78, 81–82, 87, 133–34, 144, 223–24; Tagalog language, 48, 218, 221, 227
Tagook, Neah, 176
tambakan, 48–49, 51, 114
Tannhäuser overture, 14, 191
Taussig, R. J., 180
taxi dance halls, 25, 224, 240, 245n5, 251n21
technological progress, 175, 177–78
test compositions, 34, 49, 136, 138, 188, 250n13
Thaviu, Samuel, 183, 194, 199
Thomas, Grant, 117
timbre, 19, 27, 188, 243n8
Tin Pan Alley songs, 13, 69, 95–98, 183, 245n9
Tinguians (Itneg), 88, 92
Tobani, Theodore Moses, 95, 247n20
Tolentino, Guillermo, 226, 251n22
town bands, 8, 38, 47–50, 61
Treaty of Paris, 10, 52, 107
"tribal people," Filipinos as, 41, 134, 144, 170, 186, 226, 237; in 1904 World's Fair, 4, 73, 76–79, 82, 87–88, 92, 108–10; at AYP Exposition, 122, 160–61; as "wild," 59, 245n11
trombones, 188, 228
two-steps, 96–97, 99, 105–6
Tydings-McDuffie Act, 224–25

"uncivilized," Filipinos as, 6, 68, 89, 94, 108
unions, labor, 222, 224
University of Santo Tomas, 30, 45, 231–32
utang na loób, 24, 203, 244n15

Valderon, Russ, 222, 250n14
vaudeville, 64, 192–93, 229
Velarde, Murillo, 44
Verdi, Giuseppe, 46, 95, 124, 129, 140, 164, 189, 230; *Aida*, 46, 129, 188
Victorian era, 13, 175

violence: symbolic, 171, 243; US colonial, 10, 18, 23, 91, 121; and US racism, 11, 17, 81, 110–12, 149, 181, 224
"Violets," 107
violins, 45, 62, 159, 166, 187–88, 228, 239
Visayans, 61, 74, 82, 87, 134, 136, 144, 223–24
voting rights, 175–76

Wagner, Richard, 8, 14, 95, 104, 108, 163–64, 166–69, 189, 191
waltzes, 25, 64, 106, 138, 145, 188, 194
Wang, Grace, 167
War Department, United States, 161, 219
Washington, Booker T., 101, 122–23, 179–80
Washington, DC, 6, 33, 51–52, 186, 219; African American community in, 33, 148–56; Hippodrome in, 134, 143; Loving in, 56–57, 59, 226; M Street High School in, 56, 155; PC Band in, 126–27, 130, 132–56; *Washington Post*, 126, 129, 153
Washington Post, 126, 129, 153
Weil, William, 101, 106
"West Door, H.R.," 107
western musical traditions: and Filipinos, 7, 10, 19–20, 26–27, 44, 120, 167, 230–31; Frances Densmore on, 92–94; and military music, 37; and PC Band, 69, 119, 142, 152, 188, 190–92, 238
White, Richard Grant, 15
white Americans: and PC Band representations, 84–87, 109–11, 149–54, 171–72, 235–36, 238–40; at PPIE, 175–78, 182, 189, 199; and racialization of music, 15–28, 91, 93, 100; and US military, 53–55, 60; white audiences, 6, 16–19, 100, 149, 151–52, 239; white cultural hegemony, 12, 16, 26, 119, 126, 138, 197, 235; white gaze, 90, 240; whiteness, 22, 86, 147, 176; white supremacy, 18, 21–22, 72, 159, 179, 189, 239; white women, 22, 109–11, 176–77, 224. *See also* white superiority
White House, 122–23, 126–28, 138–40, 154, 168, 245n12
white superiority, 8, 15–16, 23–25, 133, 136, 159, 171, 235; at 1904 World's Fair, 70, 74–75, 93; at PPIE, 191, 194, 197; white supremacy, 18, 21–22, 72, 159, 179, 189, 239

Wiley, Lem H., 107
Williams, Bert, 100
William Tell overture, 29, 116, 124, 138, 154, 172
Wilson, Woodrow, 176, 186, 199
Wilson, W. P., 75
Wolff, Walter, 188
women: Black, 101, 179, 181; Irish, 11, 98; femininity, 26, 175–76; Filipino scouts and, 80; in Filipino society, 88–89, 186–87, 249n16; musicians, 46, 106–7; and PPIE, 174, 175–77, 181; sexualization of Filipino/a, 186–87; white, 22, 109–11, 175–77, 224; women composers, 106–7; working-class, 225
Wong, Deborah, 28
World's Fair, 1904 St. Louis, 7; comparison to AYP exposition, 151, 161, 187, 189–90, 192, 195, 197; Filipinos and race in, 20, 73–82, 88–89, 92–94, 134; musical genres at, 94–109; PC band in, 3–5, 32–34, 67–73, 83–91, 96–102, 105–9, 112–18, 129–30; and PC band legacy, 49, 145, 213, 215, 219–20, 222–23; Philippine Exposition Board at, 73–75, 82, 88, 92, 110, 216, 222; the Pike in, 74, 101–2, 110
World's Fairs, 3, 7, 32, 158, 183, 219, 235, 240; Alaska-Yukon-Pacific International Exposition (AYP), 33, 122, 160–63; Golden Gate International Exposition (GGIE), 34–35, 129, 201–2, 215, 220–29, 246n6; Panama-California Exposition, 175. *See also* Panama-Pacific International Exposition (PPIE); World's Fair, 1904, St. Louis
World War I, 15, 175, 191, 201, 208, 245n9
World War II, 201, 205, 227, 228–34
Wright, Ellen, 106

xenophobia, 11, 186

Yamada, Kōsaku, 230
Yamashita, Tomoyuki, 233
Yoder, Robert, 57

Zamora, Miss, 114–15
Zampa (Ferdinand Hérold), 130
zarzuela, 46

ABOUT THE AUTHOR

Mary Talusan (Mary Talusan Lacanlale) is assistant professor of Asian-Pacific Studies at California State University, Dominguez Hills. She has a PhD from the Department of Ethnomusicology at the University of California, Los Angeles, and performs Philippine gong music with the Pakaraguian Kulintang Ensemble.